PLAYS BY RENAISSAN
RESTORATION DRAMA
General Editor: Graham Store

JONSON
VOLUME 1

VOLUMES IN THIS SERIES

The plays of Cyril Tourneur, edited by George Parfitt: *The Revenger's Tragedy*; *The Atheist's Tragedy*

The selected plays of Philip Massinger, edited by Colin Gibson: *The Duke of Milan*; *The Roman Actor*; *A New Way to Pay Old Debts*; *The City Madam*

The selected plays of Thomas Middleton, edited by David L. Frost: *A Mad World, My Masters*; *A Chaste Maid in Cheapside*; *Women Beware Women*; *The Changeling* (with William Rowley)

The plays of William Wycherley, edited by Peter Holland: *Love in a Wood*; *The Gentleman Dancing Master*; *The Country Wife*; *The Plain Dealer*

The comedies of William Congreve, edited by Anthony Henderson: *The Old Batchelor*; *The Double-Dealer*; *Love for Love*; *The Way of the World*

The plays of Sir George Etherege, edited by Michael Cordner; *The Comical Revenge; or Love in a Tub*; *She Would If She Could*; *The Man of Mode; or Sir Fopling Flutter*

The selected plays of John Webster, edited by Jonathan Dollimore and Alan Sinfield: *The White Devil*; *The Devil's Law Case*; *The Duchess of Malfi*

The selected plays of John Ford, edited by Colin Gibson: *'Tis Pity She's a Whore*; *The Broken Heart*; *Perkin Warbeck*

The selected plays of John Marston, edited by MacDonald P. Jackson and Michael Neill: *Antonio and Mellida*; *Antonio's Revenge*; *The Malcontent*; *The Dutch Courtesan*; *Sophonisba*

The selected plays of Ben Jonson, volume 1, edited by Johanna Procter: *Volpone*; *Sejanus*; *Epicoene, or The Silent Woman*

The selected plays of Ben Jonson, volume 2, edited by Martin Butler: *The Alchemist*; *Bartholomew Fair*; *The New Inn*; *A Tale of a Tub*

THE SELECTED PLAYS OF BEN JONSON VOLUME 1

Sejanus

Volpone

Epicoene, or The Silent Woman

EDITED BY
JOHANNA PROCTER
Lecturer in English, University College of Swansea

WITH AN INTRODUCTION BY
MARTIN BUTLER
Lecturer in English, University of Leeds

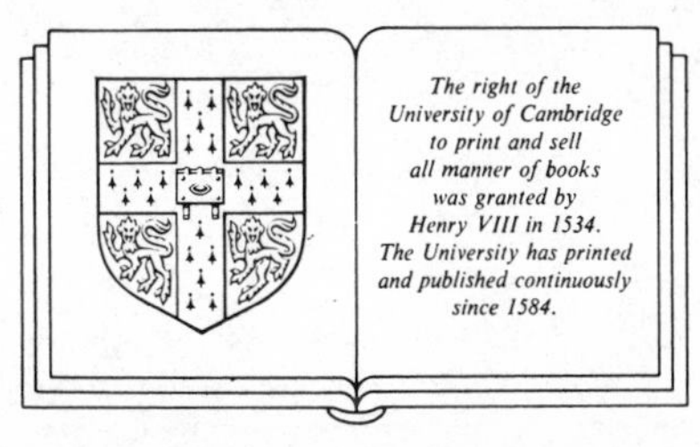
The right of the
University of Cambridge
to print and sell
all manner of books
was granted by
Henry VIII in 1534.
The University has printed
and published continuously
since 1584.

CAMBRIDGE UNIVERSITY PRESS
CAMBRIDGE
NEW YORK NEW ROCHELLE
MELBOURNE SYDNEY

Published by the Press Syndicate of the University of Cambridge
The Pitt Building, Trumpington Street, Cambridge CB2 1RP
40 West 20th Street, New York, NY 10011, USA
10 Stamford Road, Oakleigh, Melbourne 3166, Australia

First published 1989

Printed in Great Britain at the University Press, Cambridge

British Library cataloguing in publication data

Jonson, Ben, *1573–1637*
The selected plays of Ben Jonson. – (Plays
by Renaissance and Restoration dramatists).
Vol. 1
I. Title II. Procter, Johanna III. Series
822′.3

Library of Congress cataloguing in publication data

Jonson, Ben, 1573?–1637
The selected plays of Ben Jonson.
(Plays by Renaissance and Restoration dramatists)
Vol. 1.edited by Johanna Procter.
Contents: Sejanus; Volpone; Epicoene, or
The Silent Woman
I. Procter, Johanna. II. Title. III. Series.
PR2602.B87 1988 822′.3 88–9568

ISBN 0 521 21747 4 hard covers
ISBN 0 521 29248 4 paperback

WD

CONTENTS

PREFACE TO THE SERIES

This series provides the best plays (in some cases, the complete plays) of the major English Renaissance and Restoration dramatists, in fully-annotated, modern-spelling texts, soundly edited by scholars in the field.

The introductory matter in each volume is factual and historical rather than critical: it includes, where appropriate, a brief biography of the playwright, a list of his works with dates of plays' first performances, the reasons for the volume editor's choice of plays, a short critical bibliography and a note on the texts used. An introductory note to each play then gives the source material, a short stage-history, and details of the individual editions of that play.

Short notes at the foot of the page are designed to gloss the text or enlarge on its literary, historical or social allusions. Editors have added explanatory notes and have commented on textual variants.

The volumes are intended for anyone interested in English drama in two of its richest periods, but they will prove especially useful to students at all levels who want to enjoy and explore the best work of these dramatists.

Graham Storey

INTRODUCTION

Life

Ben Jonson was born between October 1572 and May 1573, the posthumous son of an impoverished gentleman who had 'turned Minister' of religion. His mother's remarriage to a master bricklayer of Westminster and the temporary apprenticeship to his stepfather's craft which the young man would later undergo left him especially sensitive to imputations of meanness of birth, but despite being 'brought up poorly' he was educated (through the good offices of an unknown benefactor) at Westminster School under the great schoolmaster William Camden; with this man, and with other scholars of his circle, such as John Selden and Robert Cotton, Jonson maintained an enduring friendship. Before appearing in the books of the theatre financier Philip Henslowe in 1597, Jonson had served as a soldier in Flanders (during which service, he later claimed, he had killed an enemy in single combat), and spent some time as a strolling player. He had also married; his wife, 'a shrew yet honest', was to bear him at least two children, both of whom died in infancy.

The first title connected with his name was the 'sedytious' comedy *The Isle of Dogs*, part authorship of which earned him two months' imprisonment in 1597. In the next two years he saw prison twice more: once for debt, once for the manslaughter of a fellow actor, Gabriel Spencer, killed in a duel after a quarrel. During this third imprisonment he became a Catholic, though he returned to the Church of England around 1610. By 1599 he was already being listed as among 'our best for Tragedie', but his earliest surviving successes were comedies performed by the Lord Chamberlain's Men, *Every Man in his Humour* (1598) and *Every Man out of his Humour* (1599); the latter was the first of three 'comical satires' that broke away from the norms of Elizabethan romantic writing represented by his own *The Case is Altered* (1598), a play he chose not to include among his collected works. In the other comical satires, *Cynthia's Revels* and *The Poetaster*, both staged in 1601 by the Children of the Chapel, Jonson attempted to work out his highly individual and experimental ideas of comic form, but found himself embroiled with John Marston and Thomas Dekker in the so-called 'War of the Theatres'. Hostilities were not so acrimonious that Jonson was unwilling to collaborate with Marston in *Eastward Ho!* (1605), but he did retire temporarily from the stage after *Poetaster* to live on the patronage of Sir Robert Townshend and Lord Aubigny.

The product of retirement was the massive, scholarly and almost equally experimental tragedy *Sejanus* (1603), written in collaboration, probably with George Chapman, and published in revised form as Jonson's own in 1605. This play was cried down by the popular audience at the Globe, but seems to have been a personal catalyst for the establishment of the mature Jonsonian comic form two years later in *Volpone* (1605), written for the King's Men. The following ten years saw a succession of major comedies: *Epicoene*, written for the Children of Her Majesty's Revels (1609–10), *The Alchemist*, performed by the King's Men (1610), and *Bartholomew Fair*, written for the Lady Elizabeth's Men at the Hope (1614). This decade deservedly established Jonson in the eyes of contemporaries as the foremost literary figure of the age; his only theatrical failure was his other demanding classical tragedy *Catiline* (1611), for which the King's Men failed to find an 'understanding auditory'.

These years also saw Jonson fulfilling the role of the leading court poet. One of the contributors to the coronation pageantry in 1604, he was invited to write the queen's entertainment for Twelfth Night, 1605, and *The Masque of Blackness*, staged in collaboration with the architect and scene designer Inigo Jones, initiated what would become a twenty-year career as foremost writer of court masques. However, Jonson's relationship with the court remained ambivalent: his conservative predilection for a stable, responsible monarchy was compromised by his moral idealism and his realism about the nature of the Jacobean dispensation. Unfriendly interpretation of suspect passages in *Sejanus* led to his being accused of 'popery and treason' at the council table in 1604, and jokes about the new king's Scottish favourites in *Eastward Ho!* left him in prison and in danger of losing his ears. Nonetheless in 1605 Jonson was making up for his indiscretions by assisting in the investigations consequent on the discovery of the Gunpowder Plot, while dedications and poems from this period attest to friendships with powerful aristocratic families such as the Sidneys, the Herberts and the Cecils, some of whom may have been instrumental in obtaining his release from his latest imprisonment. The award of a small royal pension in 1616 made Jonson poet laureate in all but name, while the folio volume of his *Works*, meticulously edited and published the same year, marked a moment of personal culmination.

And yet, after *Bartholomew Fair*, *The Devil is an Ass* (1616) seems a curiously impoverished comedy, and there are hints in both plays of Jonson's dissatisfaction with his public audiences and with the forms within which he was working. Capitalising on his court success, Jonson ceased temporarily to write for the professional stage altogether; his literary output for ten years was confined to masques for Whitehall and projects other than plays, while at the Apollo Room of the Devil Tavern he presided over an informal literary club, the 'Tribe of Ben'.

However, though honours continued to come in the 1620s, Jonson began to find that his position was being undermined from within, as his relations with Whitehall were made difficult by his personal and intellectual disagreements with his masque designer, Inigo Jones, and by his own ambivalent attitude to the new order arising under Prince Charles and the Duke of Buckingham. After the death of James, Jonson found himself rather out of place in the polite, elegant and attenuated atmosphere of the Caroline court. His slender royal pension fell increasingly into arrears, and only once, in 1631, did Charles invite him to provide a masque; on this occasion his poor artistic relationship with Jones came to a head in a major public row from which Jonson emerged the loser. In 1628 he was among those questioned about the authorship of verses in praise of the assassin of the Duke of Buckingham. A series of begging letters from this time testifies to his reduced circumstances, and though he was appointed Chronologer of the City of London in 1628, his salary was withheld from 1631 to 1634 owing to non-performance of his duties. By this stage he had suffered a stroke and was confined to his bedchamber; a project for a second volume of his works collapsed in 1631. A combination of circumstances was conspiring to force him back to the professional stage again. Jonson's late plays (*The Staple of News*, 1626; *The New Inn*, 1629; *The Magnetic Lady*, 1632; *A Tale of a Tub*, 1633; and the unfinished *Sad Shepherd*) have been overshadowed by the catastrophic failure of *The New Inn*, which was hissed from the Blackfriars stage, but the other plays, if not equalling Jonson's best work, do not deserve the label 'dotages' which Dryden stuck on them. They are, rather, an astonishing period of renewed productivity in a career already remarkable for its length, and mark a courageous and hard-won return to a changed theatre by a master playwright reassessing both his own theatrical preferences and his relationship to the dominant cultural modes of an unsympathetic age.

Though in the 1630s Jonson was shamefully neglected by the court (one courtier in 1632 expressed surprise to hear that he was still alive), his last years were not devoid of friends and supporters. His last patron, the Earl of Newcastle, provided financial help and commissioned two entertainments for presentation to the king when he visited the earl's Nottinghamshire estates; and Jonson's friendship with Edward Hyde put him in touch with a circle that included the Earl of Falkland, William Chillingworth, John Earle, Tom May and Thomas Carew. It seems to have been largely from this group that the initiative came for the volume of posthumous elegies, *Jonsonus Virbius*. Jonson died on 6 August 1637. 'All or the greatest part of nobility and gentry then in the town' attended his funeral at Westminster Abbey. His goods were valued at £8 8*s* 10*d*.

The text of this edition

Jonson was unique in his own time for closely supervising the publication of his plays in person. Consequently, the early published texts of the plays in this volume carry an unusually high degree of authorial intention in the matter of accidentals, even taking into account the unreliability of seventeenth-century typesetting. The copy-text for all three plays is the great folio volume of *Works* (1616), over which Jonson seems to have exercised considerable editorial control, though reference has also to be made to two earlier quartos. *Sejanus* had already been printed in a scrupulously exact quarto in 1605, replete with commendatory verses and substantial annotation in the margins concerning Jonson's Latin sources (mostly removed in the folio text). *Volpone* appeared in quarto in 1607, again in a text unusually reliable by Jacobean standards. Both plays were revised for their appearances in the folio, *Sejanus* more heavily than *Volpone* (though significant alterations were made to the punctuation of *Volpone*). *Epicoene* remained unpublished until the folio. Gifford mentioned a 1612 quarto, but this seems to have been a ghost (and the 1620 quarto carries no independent authority, being a careless reprint of the folio text).

In the preparation of this volume, an attempt has been

made to conserve as much as is appropriate in a modernised edition of Jonson's intentions as manifested in these early editions. The main differences from other modernised texts are:

(1) This edition preserves some of Jonson's contracted verbal forms, particularly observing *yo'are* and *yo'were* which distinguish tenses obscured by the modernised *you're*, and for which Jonson exhibits a marked preference.

(2) Some of Jonson's preferred spellings have been tentatively retained, where there would seem to be grounds for doing so. For example, Jonson preferred the form *porcpisce* to *porpoise*, as it preserved the word's etymology (*Sejanus*, V.[vii].638, *Volpone*, II.i.40); he used *moile* for *mule* at *Volpone*, I.ii.39–41, where it would seem to be in keeping with the joky tone of Mosca's show; so too *kastril* for *kestrel* at *Epicoene*, IV.iv.210 preserves the pun on *cast* in the same line.

(3) In punctuating, respect has been given to Jonson's indications of dramatic emphasis as far as it is consistent with modernisation. A very strong case can be made out for the practical value of Jonson's punctuation. Jonson had sophisticated notions of the function of punctuation (for which see his *English Grammar*), and evolved his own highly developed system of pointing which, though it seems heavy to modern readers and has been dismissed as merely rhetorical or grammatical, can repeatedly be shown to carry real theatrical force. The outstanding instance is *Volpone*, I.v.78 ('Am not I here? whom you have made? your creature?'), in which the syntactically disruptive question marks can only be explained in terms of their significance for the actor's delivery, but there are many comparable examples. In the same play, the darting, fly-like movement of Mosca's mind is underlined by the commas and semicolons that break his soliloquy into short, swooping phrases (III.i). Similarly, in *Epicoene* the capacious emptiness of La Foole's mentality is wonderfully signalled in the punctuation of his first extended speech (I.iv.41–75), held together as it is by only commas and dashes, while Truewit tortures Morose with a seemingly inexhaustible battery of clauses, linked paratactically by semicolons and subdivided by commas into part upon endless part (II.ii.21–35). So too in *Sejanus*, Silius's impotent rage at Sejanus is signalled dramatically by an explosion of clotted punctuation that obstructs the free movement of his speech (I.[i].201–12) and which contrasts

with the impression of absolute control conveyed by the heavier, exact pointing of his death speech (III.[i].319–39). In Tiberius's mouth, such weighty pointing is ominous, his laboured colons and semicolons hinting tacitly at more meaning than he intends publicly to acknowledge (III.[ii].675–89).

Inevitably, there has to be some lightening and regularising of Jonson's pointing for the convenience of the modern reader, but simply to repunctuate from scratch, following modern principles, is to forfeit an important dimension of the Jonsonian text: a comparison between the contemporary editions and any of the more radically repointed modern versions reveals starkly the loss of dramatic immediacy and even clarity which is involved. As far as possible punctuation has been respected which could be held to have potential as theatrical signals, and Jonson's punctuation has been revised only where it threatens to obscure the sense. Jonson's distinctive use of parentheses to mark asides or interruptions to otherwise continuous dialogue has been allowed to stand, as it offers no great difficulty to the modern reader.

The text of *Sejanus* follows other editions in giving continuous line numbering for each act. In references to the play in the commentary, scene numbers are placed within square brackets, as for example V.[vii].638.

The standard edition of Jonson, to which all subsequent editors are indebted, not least for its substantial introductions and notes, is the monumental 11-volume Clarendon text, *The Works of Ben Jonson* (ed. C. H. Herford, and Percy and Evelyn Simpson, Oxford, 1925–52), hereafter referred to as Herford and Simpson or H&S. A remarkable achievement for its time, this edition is not likely to be superseded in the foreseeable future. The principal editions before Herford and Simpson were those of Peter Whalley (7 vols., 1756), William Gifford (9 vols., 1816), and Francis Cunningham's revision of Gifford (3 vols., 1871). A modernised version of Herford and Simpson in four volumes with inadequate commentary has been prepared by G. A. Wilkes (1981–2). The many single-volume editions of individual plays are listed in the introductions to each play. The editor of this volume most gratefully acknowledges her indebtedness to all those preceding editors whose work has revealed the richness and vitality of Jonson's drama.

Select bibliography

Biography

It is remarkable that the life of this many-sided figure has attracted so little serious attention. At the moment, the choice of biographies is between Marchette Chute's *Ben Jonson of Westminster* (London: Robert Hale, 1954) and Rosalind Miles's *Ben Jonson, His Life and Work* (London: Routledge and Kegan Paul, 1986); the former inclines to the leisurely and sentimental, the latter to the workmanlike and breezy. Richard Helgerson has studied Jonson's processes of self-definition as a writer in *Self-Crowned Laureate* (Berkeley: University of California Press, 1983), and Jonathan Goldberg, in his dense and provocative book *James I and the Politics of Literature* (Baltimore: Johns Hopkins University Press, 1983), has investigated Jonson's contribution to the language and iconography of Stuart kingship. The shape of Jonson's career has been examined in relation to the cultural and political pressures of the day by Philip Edwards in *Threshold of a Nation* (Cambridge: Cambridge University Press, 1979) and by David Norbrook in *Poetry and Politics in the English Renaissance* (London: Routledge and Kegan Paul, 1984), but there is still plenty of room for a full-scale literary and intellectual biography, if a scholar can be found brave enough to attempt it. Much the best direct approaches to Jonson the man are through the comments of contemporaries collected in Herford and Simpson (XI, pp. 305–494) and in *The Jonson Allusion-Book* (ed. J. F. Bradley and J. Q. Adams (New Haven: Yale University Press, 1922)), and through Jonson's *Conversations with William Drummond* (Herford and Simpson, I, pp. 128–78), his own informal, unreliable but utterly fascinating self-assessment.

Criticism

Jonson has always received sympathetic commentary from practising poets. Detailed criticism begins with Dryden's account of *Epicoene* in *An Essay of Dramatic Poesy* (1668). To Coleridge, Jonson seemed a 'Mammoth or Megatherion', but he praised his 'sterling English diction', and accounted *The Alchemist* one of 'the three most perfect plots ever planned' (R. F. Brinkley (ed.), *Coleridge on the Seventeenth Century* (Durham, North Carolina: Duke University Press, 1955), pp. 637–49). T. S. Eliot's ambivalent praise in his famous essay of 1919 (collected in *Selected Essays* (London: Faber and Faber, 1932)) has had an ambivalent effect on succeeding criticism; but A. C. Swinburne's *A Study of Ben Jonson* (1888–9), though ridiculed by Eliot, deserves to be much better known, not least for its enthusiasm and its endearingly eccentric preference for *The Staple of News*.

The seminal work for modern scholarship has been L. C. Knights's *Drama and Society in the Age of Jonson* (London: Chatto and Windus, 1937), which made the first serious attempt to assess Jonson's plays in the light of their socio-economic context. Knights's approach has been refined by Brian Gibbons in *Jacobean City Comedy* (London: Rupert Hart-Davis, 1968), and criticised by Don E. Wayne, 'Drama and society in the age of Jonson: an alternative view' (*Renaissance Drama*, n.s. 13 (1982), pp. 103–29). Nicholas Grene examines the implications of Knights's failure to take *Bartholomew Fair* seriously in 'L. C. Knights's *Drama and Society in the Age of Jonson*' (*Themes in Drama*, I (1979), pp. 291–8).

Dryden's neo-classical account of the principles of Jonsonian comic form was attacked by Freda L. Townsend in *Apologie for Bartholomew Fayre: The Art of Jonson's Comedies* (New York: The Modern Language Association of America, 1947), but Townsend's structural formula of 'unity in variety' has itself been modified by Wallace A. Bacon in 'The magnetic field: the structure of Jonson's comedies' (*Huntington Library Quarterly*, 19 (1955–6), pp. 121–53). Gabriele Bernhardt Jackson's wide-ranging *Vision and Judgment in Ben Jonson's Drama* (New Haven: Yale University Press, 1968) includes a brilliant analysis of the structural mechanics of Jonsonian comedy; some of her analyses have been built upon by Gail Kern Paster in 'Ben Jonson's comedy of limitation' (*Studies in Philology*, 72 (1975), pp. 51–71). Jonson's formal debt to the Tudor morality play is investigated by A. C. Dessen in *Jonson's Moral Comedy* (Evanston: Northwestern University Press, 1971), while Leo Salingar has examined the influence of Aristophanes in 'Comic form in Ben Jonson' (reprinted in his *Dramatic Form in Shakespeare and the Jacobeans* (Cambridge: Cambridge University Press, 1986), pp. 153–74). Thomas M. Greene traces one structural pattern in 'Ben Jonson and the centred self' (*Studies in English Literature*, 10 (1970), pp. 325–48).

Amongst recent book-length studies, the most important has been Anne Barton's *Ben Jonson, Dramatist*

(Cambridge: Cambridge University Press, 1984), which traces throughout Jonson's career his twin rages for order and for chaos, radically revising the traditional stereotype of an aloof, Horatian dramatist. A similarly complex Jonson emerges from Richard Dutton's rather uneven book, *Ben Jonson: To the First Folio* (Cambridge: Cambridge University Press, 1983), while he is altogether less genial a figure in Douglas Duncan's *Ben Jonson and the Lucianic Tradition* (Cambridge: Cambridge University Press, 1979) which tellingly investigates the humanist roots of Jonson's strategies for teasing his audience towards judgement. Katharine Eisaman Maus's *Ben Jonson and the Roman Frame of Mind* (Princeton: Princeton University Press, 1984) is an important study of Jonson's personal investment in classical Latin literature, while the most recent study, Peter Womack's *Ben Jonson* (Oxford: Basil Blackwell, 1986), attempts to approach Jonson from within a Bakhtinian perspective. A range of Jonsonian topics is treated by Alexander Leggatt in *Ben Jonson: His Vision and His Art* (London: Methuen, 1981), by L. A. Beaurline in *Jonson and Elizabethan Comedy: Essays in Dramatic Rhetoric* (San Marino: The Huntington Library, 1978), and by George Parfitt in his brief but suggestive collection of essays, *Ben Jonson: Public Poet and Private Man* (London: Dent, 1976). Amongst the older studies, Edward B. Partridge's *The Broken Compass* (London: Chatto and Windus, 1958) continues to be an influential account of Jonson's imagery; Robert E. Knoll's *Ben Jonson's Plays: An Introduction* (Lincoln, Nebraska: University of Nebraska Press, 1965) remains a useful introductory work, if rather earnest in its emphasis on the morality of Jonson's writing. Most of these books give space to the three plays contained in this volume.

Sejanus has proved to be oddly resistant to criticism, and there is still no entirely satisfactory full-scale treatment of the play. Two significant early essays are J. A. Bryant's defence, 'The nature of the conflict in Jonson's *Sejanus*' (*Vanderbilt Studies in the Humanities*, ed. Richard Beatty *et al.* (1951), pp. 197–219), which tends to blunt the play's pessimism, and K. M. Burton's comparative study, 'The political tragedies of Chapman and Ben Jonson' (*Essays in Criticism*, 2 (1952), pp. 397–412), which emphasises the social dimensions of the tragedy. In a later and more substantial comparative essay, G. R. Hibbard examines Jonson's and Chapman's contrasting responses to the legacy of the immoral Marlovian hero ('Goodness and greatness: an essay on the tragedies of Ben Jonson and George Chapman', *Renaissance and Modern Studies*, 11 (1967), pp. 5–54).

By far the best work on *Sejanus* has been done on its politics, the classic statement here being Geoffrey Hill's fastidious and moralistic essay, ' "The world's proportion": Jonson's dramatic poetry in *Sejanus* and *Catiline*' (in J. R. Brown and B. Harris (eds.), *Jacobean Theatre* (Stratford-upon-Avon Studies 1, London, 1960), pp. 112–31; reprinted in G. Hill, *The Lords of Limit* (London: Deutsch, 1984)). J. W. Lever's *The Tragedy of State* (London: Methuen, 1971) takes an urgent, contemporary line on the play, and there is a brief, suggestive treatment in Jonathan Dollimore's *Radical Tragedy* (Brighton: Harvester Press, 1984). By contrast, K. W. Evans's argument that the play's politics are formulaic and anachronistic is perverse and unconvincing ('*Sejanus* and the ideal prince tradition', *Studies in English Literature*, 11 (1971), pp. 249–64). The difficulties of relating *Sejanus* to its political setting are approached by M. H. Wikander in ' "Queasy to be touched": the world of Ben Jonson's *Sejanus*' (*Journal of English and Germanic Philology*, 78 (1979), pp. 345–77), and by Philip J. Ayres in 'Jonson, Northampton and the "treason" in *Sejanus*' (*Modern Philology*, 80 (1982–3), pp. 356–63), while the implications of Jonson's choice of a Roman subject are pursued by Annabel Patterson in ' "Roman-cast similitude": Ben Jonson and the English use of Roman history' (in P. A. Ramsey (ed.), *Rome in the Renaissance* (Binghamton, New York: The State University of New York, 1982), pp. 381–94). Jonson's manipulation of his sources in order to address political issues is explored in two essays, D. C. Boughner's '*Sejanus* and Machiavelli' (*Studies in English Literature*, 1 (1961), pp. 81–100) and Richard Dutton's 'The sources, text and readers of *Sejanus*' (*Studies in Philology*, 75 (1978), pp. 181–98; partially reprinted in Dutton's *Ben Jonson: To the First Folio*).

On more purely literary matters, Christopher Ricks describes one dimension of the play's language in '*Sejanus* and dismemberment' (*Modern Language Notes*, 76 (1961), pp. 301–8), and Arthur F. Marotti discusses the play's fascination with its own theatricality in 'The self-reflexive art of Jonson's *Sejanus*' (*Texas Studies in Literature and Language*, 12 (1970), pp. 345–77). In his introduction to the Yale edition (New Haven: Yale University Press, 1965), Jonas A. Barish reflects thoughtfully on ways in which the play mediates between poetry and history. John G. Sweeney's '*Sejanus* and the people's beastly rage' (*ELH*, 48 (1981), pp. 61–82) is a psycho-sexual study which reads the conflict between Tiberius and Sejanus as a projection of Jonson's own anxieties about authorial control.

Much of the literature on *Volpone* has revolved around the related issues of the difficulty of judging the play's central figure and the question of how seriously to take Celia and Bonario. The older ironic reading of Volpone as a character who unconsciously exposes his own inadequate values is best represented by A. B. Kernan's *The Plot of Satire* (New Haven: Yale University Press, 1959), and by S. L. Goldberg's 'Folly into crime: the catastrophe of *Volpone*' (*Modern Language Quarterly*, 20 (1959), pp. 233–42). Both of these essays have their ambivalences, but the now widespread view which presents Volpone as appealing positively to our unacknowledged sympathies or to our delight in theatricality, and which sometimes involves debunking Celia and Bonario, came fully to the fore with William Empson's provocative but untrustworthy essay '*Volpone*' in *The Hudson Review* (21 (1968–9), pp. 650–66), and with Alexander Leggatt's 'The suicide of Volpone' (*University of Toronto Quarterly*, 39 (1969–70), pp. 19–32). Much the most eloquent and sympathetic account of Volpone comes from John Creaser in '*Volpone*: the mortifying of the fox' (*Essays in Criticism*, 25 (1975), pp. 329–56), while the play acquires almost tragic dimensions in Robert Westcott's '*Volpone*? – or *The Fox*?' (*The Critical Review* (Melbourne), 17 (1974), pp. 82–96). Despite its title, Stephen Greenblatt's 'The false ending in *Volpone*' (*Journal of English and Germanic Philology*, 77 (1976), pp. 90–104) is concerned with the theatricality of the title character.

The other major debate has been over the subplot, the seminal essay here being Jonas A. Barish's 'The double plot in *Volpone*' (reprinted, with a selection of other helpful criticism, in Barish's anthology *Volpone: A Casebook* (London: Macmillan, 1972)). This essay has now been superseded by John Creaser's spirited revaluation, 'A vindication of Sir Politic Would-be' (*English Studies*, 17 (1976), pp. 502–14). Also worth consulting is Judd Arnold's 'The double plot in *Volpone*' (*Seventeenth-Century News*, 23 (1965), pp. 47–52). The play's concern with sickness is examined by Harriet Hawkins in 'Folly, incurable disease, and *Volpone*' (*Studies in English Literature*, 8 (1968), pp. 335–48), and more urgently by Ian

Donaldson in 'Volpone: quick and dead' (*Essays in Criticism*, 21 (1971), pp. 121–34). Two vigorous and informative essays by R. B. Parker concern the play's sources and stage history: '*Volpone* and *Reynard the Fox*' (*Renaissance Drama*, n.s. 7 (1976), pp. 3–42) and '*Volpone* in performance: 1921–1972' (*Renaissance Drama*, n.s. 9 (1978), pp. 147–73).

Essential reading on *Epicoene* is a remarkable chapter in Jonas A. Barish's *Ben Jonson and the Language of Prose Comedy* (Cambridge, Mass.: Harvard University Press, 1960), which goes well beyond its initial concern with style. An earlier essay by Barish, 'Ovid, Juvenal and *The Silent Woman*' (*PMLA*, 71 (1956), pp. 213–24), sparked off an arid little debate on the play's supposed uncertainties of attitude; the last word on this is probably John Ferns's 'Ovid, Juvenal and *The Silent Woman*: a reconsideration' (*Modern Language Review*, 65 (1970), pp. 248–53). Much more central has been the growing realisation that the comedy is nowhere near as pleasant as it pretends to be: this has been strongly argued in relation to the play's festive background by Ian Donaldson (in *The World Upside Down* (Oxford: Clarendon Press, 1970)) and in relation to the three wits by Alexander Leggatt in 'Morose and his tormentors' (*University of Toronto Quarterly*, 45 (1975–6), pp. 221–35). W. D. Kay attempts a determined but finally unsuccessful defence of the wits in 'Jonson's urbane gallants: humanistic contexts for *Epicoene*' (*Huntington Library Quarterly*, 39 (1975–6), pp. 251–66). The first person to ask why the play was so noisy was Ray L. Heffner Jnr, in 'Unifying symbols in the comedy of Ben Jonson' (reprinted in R. J. Kaufmann (ed.), *Elizabethan Drama: Modern Essays in Criticism* (London: Oxford University Press, 1961), pp. 170–86), and the links between the noise and the city setting are brilliantly pursued by Leo Salingar in 'Farce and fashion in *The Silent Woman*' (reprinted in his *Dramatic Form in Shakespeare and the Jacobeans*, pp. 175–88); a similar tack is taken by Emrys Jones in 'The first West End comedy' (*Proceedings of the British Academy*, 68 (1982), pp. 215–58). Terence Hawkes relates the play's noise to Jonson's ideas about the social functions of language in *Shakespeare's Talking Animals* (London: Edward Arnold, 1973). There is a recent feminist reading by Barbara C. Millard, ' "An acceptable violence": sexual contest in Jonson's *Epicoene*' (*Medieval and Renaissance Drama in England*, 1 (1984), pp. 143–58).

Finally, mention should be made of an important study

of the theatre history of Jonson's plays, R. G. Noyes's *Ben Jonson on the English Stage 1660–1776* (Cambridge, Mass.: Harvard University Press, 1935). There is a fairly recent consolidated bibliography of Jonson by William L. Godshalk in T. P. Logan and Denzell S. Smith (eds.), *The New Intellectuals* (Lincoln, Nebraska: University of Nebraska Press, 1977), pp. 3–116.

SEIANVS

HIS FALL.

Written
by
BEN: IONSON.

MART. Non hîc *Centauros*, non *Gorgonas*, *Harpyasq;*
Inuenies: Hominem pagina nostra sapit.

AT LONDON
Printed by *G. Elld*, for *Thomas Thorpe*. 1605.

The Testimony of my affection, & Observance to my noble Frend Sr Robert Townseshend wch I desire may remayne wth him, & last beyond Marble.

Title-page from the 1605 quarto, with Jonson's autograph inscription to Sir Robert Townshend, reproduced by permission of the British Library.

Motto

'Not here will you find centaurs, or gorgons or harpies; my page smacks of man' (Martial, *Epigrams*, X.iv.9–10)

INTRODUCTORY NOTE

Sources

Sejanus presents a rare triumph in the use of sources: a faithful adherence to the contents, and frequently the letter, of the originals, in an imaginative recreation of history intended to convey moral truth and its lessons to the contemporary audience; as the subsequent accusation of Jonson showed, not without danger to the dramatist. The play is a tissue of classical writings on the reign of Tiberius and of material from ancient and Renaissance authorities which Jonson applied to the Rome of that date. The notes to W. D. Briggs's edition and the commentary and notes of Herford and Simpson, vol. IX, give full details of Jonson's sources; the section on *Sejanus* in the Select Bibliography (p. xvi above) refers to the main articles on his use of sources. This account outlines the main features.

The prime source for *Sejanus* is the *Annals* of Tacitus, books I–VI, but especially books IV and V which recount the events that form the action of the play: Sejanus's bid for power, and Tiberius's defeat of his former favourite. Whilst Jonson favours the interpretation which saw a determined calculation in Sejanus's ambition, and presents only the cruel and ruthless side of Tiberius, he follows Tacitus closely, sometimes translating passages of the *Annals*; most notably, Tiberius's speech, I.[i].454–502, and Cremutius Cordus's defence before the Senate in III.[i].407–60. On occasions he alters the time-sequence, as in III.[i], where Silius's suicide unhistorically becomes the climax of his trial; the other show trial of the scene, the accusation of Cordus, took place a year or so after Silius's. Arruntius, the play's most outspoken critic of Sejanus and Tiberius, does not figure in Tacitus's historical narrative until after the fall of Sejanus, but his reputation for independence and integrity makes him, like Lepidus, suitable for the roles of commentator and chorus. Tacitus is augmented by other writings; Suetonius's gossipy *Life of Tiberius* provides details such as Tiberius's hatred of flattery, fear of thunder, and ability to see in the dark; and the fall of Sejanus, lost from the defective book V of the *Annals*, is supplied from Dio Cassius's *History of the Roman People*, books LVII and LVIII, supplemented by Juvenal's account of the popular reaction to Sejanus's downfall in his Tenth Satire. The account of the dismemberment comes from Claudian's description of the fate of Rufinus (in *Against Rufinus*) some three centuries after Sejanus's death; but its tone is in keeping with Jonson's play. Such synthesis of diverse classical literature in *Sejanus* is typical. Juvenal's *Satires* are used to point the baseness and servility of spies and flatterers encouraged by the regime; and the lofty sentiments with which the Germanican patricians face adversity and suffering, their refusal to change with changing circumstances, owe much to the Stoicism of Seneca's *Moral Essays*, even if Jonson's admiration for the Germanicans is not wholehearted.[1] Senecan tragedy, especially *Thyestes*, and Lucan's epic narrative, *Pharsalia*, contribute to the more monstrous aspects of Sejanus's calculating villainy and blind hubris, as in II.[ii].150–6 and V.[i].7 ff.; and to the chilling precepts of tyranny expressed particularly in the conversation between Tiberius and Sejanus in II.[ii]. Their political philosophy is also analogous to the doctrines of Machiavelli's *The Prince*, and his *Discourses on Livy*.

Senecan tragedy has an influence on the structure of *Sejanus*, although, as Jonson points out in 'To the Readers', the play is not cast throughout in the classical mould. The emphasis on speeches rather than on stage action, the frequent choric role played by Arruntius and Lepidus, and the narration at the end of the play of the violence carried out against Sejanus and his children, all reflect Senecan practice. Nearer home, the influence of the English history play can be seen in the dramatic realisation of plot and character, and the interaction of character with character. Jonson took up the challenge offered by Shakespeare's first major Roman play, *Julius Caesar* (1599), by writing about a darker period of Roman history, and in a manner that owes nothing to that of his fellow dramatist.

Jonson's practice and attitude to his authorities are aptly summed up in his *Timber, or Discoveries*: 'to all the observations of the ancients, we have our own experience: which, if we will use, and apply, we have better means to pronounce. It is true they opened the gates, and made the way that went before us; but as guides, not commanders.'[2] The result is a play which brings to life a period of ancient history, and demonstrates how little tyranny and its attendant evils have changed down the centuries.

---

1 See Marvin Vawter, 'The seeds of virtue: political imperatives in Jonson's *Sejanus*', *Studies in the Literary Imagination*, 6 (1973), pp. 41–60; A. Richard Dutton, 'The sources, text, and readers of *Sejanus*: Jonson's "integrity in the story" ', *Studies in Philology*, 85 (1978), pp. 181–98.

2 H&S, VIII, p. 567.

Stage history

The original version of *Sejanus* was a collaboration, almost certainly with George Chapman.[3] It was first performed at court in the autumn or winter of 1603[4] by the King's Men. The list of players appended to the folio text is headed by Richard Burbage and William Shakespeare, who probably played Sejanus and Tiberius respectively. The play aroused political displeasure, and Jonson later told Drummond of Hawthornden that 'he was called before the Council for his *Sejanus*, and accused both of popery and treason' by 'his mortal enemy', the Earl of Northampton.[5] The grounds and substance of these charges are still a matter of debate,[6] but nothing came of them. *Sejanus* was given a public performance at the Globe in 1604, probably soon after the theatres reopened in April,[7] and was hissed off the stage. Jonson's revisions for the 1605 quarto publication, however, were not made because of the failure in the public playhouse.[8] There appear not to have been any further Jacobean performances. At the Restoration, *Sejanus* was amongst the plays listed as performed by Killigrew's company, but not amongst their principal old stock plays. In 1752 Francis Gentleman made a destructive adaptation of *Sejanus*, which Garrick, to his credit, rejected. William Poel revived Jonson's play at the Holborn Empire, London, in 1928, where he attempted to reproduce the Elizabethan apron stage, and to add to the period atmosphere of the production the actors who took the parts of Arruntius and Cordus were made up to resemble Jonson and Shakespeare. In recent years, there have been two university productions, both with heavy cuts: one by a University of Sussex *ad hoc* company in 1973, and one by the Cambridge Amateur Dramatic Club in 1979. The impression made by *Sejanus* in performance on both

---

3 See R. P. Corballis, 'The "second pen" in the stage version of *Sejanus*', *Modern Philology*, 76 (1978–9), pp. 273–7.
4 E. K. Chambers, *The Elizabethan Stage* (Oxford: Clarendon Press, 1923), III, p. 367.
5 H&S, I, p. 141.
6 See, for example, Dutton, 'Sources'; Philip J. Ayres, 'Jonson, Northampton, and the "treason" in *Sejanus*', *Modern Philology*, 80 (1982–3), pp. 356–63.
7 Chambers, *Elizabethan Stage*, II, p. 210.
8 See note on 1605 quarto, p. 431 below.

occasions can be summed up by Peter Holland's verdict: 'it is a superbly theatrical drama'.[9]

Definitive and individual editions

The definitive edition of *Sejanus* is in Herford and Simpson (introduction, vol. II; text, vol. IV; stage history, commentary and notes, vol. IX). Herford and Simpson reprint the folio text of 1616; and the folio is the base text for three of the four twentieth-century individual editions of the play: the earliest, that of W. D. Briggs in the Heath Belles Lettres series (Boston, Mass.: Heath, 1911), a wise and still useful edition; that of Jonas A. Barish for the Yale Ben Jonson (New Haven and London: Yale University Press, 1965), a modernised text, with excellent introduction and the usual full and careful annotation of that series; and that by W. F. Bolton in the New Mermaid series (London: Ernest Benn, 1966), with pithy annotation, modernised spelling, but the folio punctuation. Henry de Vocht, *Materials for the Study of Old English Drama*, vol. XI (Louvain: C. Uystpruyst, 1935), printed the quarto text of 1605, which is reproduced in facsimile by The English Experience (Amsterdam and New York: Da Capo Press and Theatrum Orbis Terrarum, 1970).

---

9 Reviewing the Cambridge production for 'A census of Renaissance drama productions', *Research Opportunities in Renaissance Drama*, 22 (1979), p. 77; see also vol. 17 of the same journal (1974), p. 70.

[DEDICATORY EPISTLE]

TO THE NO LESS
NOBLE, BY VIRTUE,
THAN BLOOD:
Esmé,
Lord Aubigné

My lord,
If ever any ruin were so great, as to survive; I think this be one I send you: *The Fall of Sejanus*. It is a poem, that (if I well remember) in your lordship's sight, suffered no less violence from our people here, than the subject of it did from the rage of the people of Rome; but with a different fate, as (I hope) merit: for this hath outlived their malice, and begot itself a greater favour than he lost, the love of good men. Amongst whom, if I make your lordship the first it thanks, it is not without a just confession of the bond your benefits have, and ever shall hold upon me.

Your lordship's most faithful honourer,
BEN. JONSON.

Esmé, Lord Aubigné: Esmé Stuart, Seigneur d'Aubigné (1574–1624), Jonson's friend, patron, and host for five years, celebrated in *Epigrams*, 127.

3 *poem*: play; that which has a 'fable' (plot) and 'fiction', and contains 'things like the truth' (*Discoveries*, H&S, VIII, p. 635).

TO THE READERS

The following, and voluntary labours of my friends, prefixed to my book, have relieved me in much, whereat (without them) I should necessarily have touched: now, I will only use three or four short, and needful notes, and so rest.

First, if it be objected, that what I publish is no true poem, in the strict laws of time, I confess it: as also in the want of a proper chorus, whose habit, and moods are such, and so difficult, as not any, whom I have seen since the ancients (no, not they who have most presently affected laws), have yet come in the way of. Nor is it needful, or almost possible, in these our times, and to such auditors as commonly things are presented, to observe the old state, and splendour of dramatic poems, with preservation of any popular delight. But of this I shall take more seasonable cause to speak in my *Observations upon Horace his Art of Poetry*, which (with the text translated) I intend shortly to publish. In the meantime, if in truth of argument, dignity of persons, gravity and height of elocution, fulness and frequency of sentence, I have discharged the other offices of a tragic writer, let not the absence of these forms be imputed to me, wherein I shall give you occasion hereafter (and without my boast) to think I could better prescribe, than omit the due use, for want of a convenient knowledge.

TO THE READERS: see Textual Note, p. 431 below.

1 *following . . . labours*: commendatory verses; see Textual Note, p. 431 below.

7 *strict laws of time*: one of the neo-classical 'unities' which held that the action of a play should take place within twenty-four hours. *Sejanus* covers the period AD 23–31. On the unities see also the Additional Note to *Volpone*, Prologue 31, p. 439 below.

8 *habit*: behaviour.
moods: manner.

11 *presently affected laws*: at this time adopted the rules (of classical drama).

17–18 *Observations . . . Art of Poetry*: Jonson's commentary was burnt in the fire which destroyed his library in 1623; his verse translation was published in 1640.

19–20 *truth of argument*: historical accuracy.

20 *dignity of persons*: nobility of characters.

20–1 *height of elocution*: the 'high' style proper to noble subjects.

21 *sentence*: maxims.

26 *convenient*: proper.

The next is, lest in some nice nostril the quotations might savour affected, I do let you know that I abhor nothing more; and have only done it to show my integrity in the story, and save myself in those common torturers, that bring all wit to the rack: whose noses are ever like swine spoiling, and rooting up the Muses' gardens, and their whole bodies, like moles, as blindly working under earth to cast any, the least, hills upon virtue.

Whereas they are in Latin and the work in English, it was presupposed none but the learned would take the pains to confer them, the authors themselves being all in the learned tongues, save one, with whose English side I have had little to do: to which it may be required, since I have quoted the page, to name what edition I followed. Tacitus, *Works*, ed. Justus Lipsius, in quarto, Antwerp, 1600. Dio Cassius, *History of the Romans*, ed. Henri Etienne, folio, 1592. For the rest, as Suetonius, Seneca, etc. the chapter doth sufficiently direct, or the edition is not varied.

Lastly I would inform you, that this book, in all numbers, is not the same with that which was acted on the public stage, wherein a second pen had a good share: in place of which I have rather chosen to put weaker (and no doubt less pleasing) of mine own, than to defraud so happy a genius of his right, by my loathed usurpation.

Fare you well. And if you read farther of me, and like, I shall not be afraid of it though you praise me out.

Neque enim mihi cornea fibra est.

---

27 *nice*: over-refined.
quotations: Jonson's references to classical and Renaissance authorities; see Textual Note, p. 431 below.
30 *in those*: amongst those.
36 *they*: the quotations.
38 *confer*: compare.
39 *one*: Richard Greenway's translation of Tacitus's *Annals* (1598), apparently followed by Jonson in IV.[iv].399.
42–5 *Tacitus . . . 1592*: see Textual Note, p. 431 below.
49 *numbers*: verses.
50 *second pen*: that of George Chapman.
56–7 *praise me out*: thoroughly appraise me; also, 'heartily commend me'.
58 *Neque . . . est*: 'For my heart is not made of horn' (Persius, *Satires*, I.47): I am not unmoved by praise.

But that I should plant my felicity in your general saying 'good', or 'well', etc. were a weakness which the better sort of you might worthily contemn, if not absolutely hate me for.

BEN. JONSON, and no such,

Quem palma negata macrum, donata reducit opimum.

---

64 *Quem . . . opimum*: 'Whom the palm denied sends back lean; the palm bestowed, sends back plump' (Horace, *Epistles*, II.i.181); expressing Jonson's independent attitude to popularity; also, a joking reference to his portly figure.

THE ARGUMENT

Aelius Sejanus, son to Sejus Strabo, a gentleman of Rome, and born at Vulsinium, after his long service in court; first, under Augustus, afterward, Tiberius: grew into that favour with the latter, and won him by those arts, as there wanted nothing, but the name, to make him a co-partner of the Empire. Which greatness of his, Drusus, the emperor's son not brooking, after many smothered dislikes (it one day breaking out) the prince struck him publicly on the face. To revenge which disgrace, Livia, the wife of Drusus (being before corrupted by him to her dishonour, and the discovery of her husband's counsels) Sejanus practiseth with, together with her physician, called Eudemus, and one Lygdus, an eunuch, to poison Drusus. This their inhuman act having successful, and unsuspected passage, it emboldeneth Sejanus to farther, and more insolent projects, even the ambition of the Empire: where finding the lets he must encounter to be many, and hard, in respect of the issue of Germanicus (who were next in hope for the succession) he deviseth to make Tiberius' self his means: and instils into his ears many doubts, and suspicions, both against the princes, and their mother Agrippina: which Caesar jealously hearkening to, as covetously consenteth to their ruin, and their friends'. In this time, the better to mature and strengthen his design, Sejanus labours to marry Livia, and worketh (with all his engine) to remove Tiberius from the knowledge of public business, with allurements of a quiet and retired life: the latter of which, Tiberius (out of a proneness to lust, and a desire to hide those unnatural pleasures, which he could not so publicly practise) embraceth: the former enkindleth his fears, and there gives him first cause of doubt, or suspect toward Sejanus. Against whom, he

---

11 *being before corrupted*: historically accurate; Jonson reverses the order of these events in the play.
12 *discovery*: revealing.
13 *practiseth*: plots.
17 *insolent*: arrogant.
18 *lets*: hindrances.
24 *jealously*: suspiciously, apprehensively.
25 *covetously*: eagerly.
28 *engine*: ingenuity; also, 'stratagem'.
35 *suspect*: suspicion.

raiseth (in private) a new instrument, one Sertorius Macro, and by him underworketh, discovers the other's counsels, his means, his ends, sounds the affections of the senators, divides, distracts them: at last, when Sejanus least looketh, and is most secure (with pretext of doing him an unwonted honour in the Senate) he trains him from his guards, and with a long doubtful letter, in one day, hath him suspected, accused, condemned, and torn in pieces, by the rage of the people.

This do we advance as a mark of terror to all traitors, and treasons; to show how just the heavens are in pouring and thundering down a weighty vengeance on their unnatural intents, even to the worst princes; much more to those, for guard of whose piety and virtue, the angels are in continual watch, and God himself miraculously working.

---

36 *instrument*: agent, tool.
37 *underworketh*: works covertly.
42 *trains*: lures.
42–3 *and with a long . . . in one day*: see Textual Note, p. 431 below.
43 *doubtful*: ambiguous.
46–52 *This do we . . . miraculously working*: a politic and political disclaimer on Jonson's part; see Textual Note, p. 431 below.

THE PERSONS OF THE PLAY

TIBERIUS

DRUSUS SENIOR	SEJANUS
NERO	LATIARIS
DRUSUS JUNIOR	VARRO
CALIGULA	MACRO
ARRUNTIUS	COTTA
SILIUS	AFER
SABINUS	HATERIUS
LEPIDUS	SANQUINIUS
CORDUS	POMPONIUS
GALLUS	POSTHUMUS
REGULUS	TRIO
TERENTIUS	MINUTIUS
LACO	SATRIUS
EUDEMUS	NATTA
RUFUS	OPSIUS

TRIBUNI

AGRIPPINA } LIVIA, SOSIA

PRAECONES	LICTORES
FLAMEN	MINISTRI
TUBICINES	TIBICINES
NUNTIUS	SERVUS
	[SERVI]

THE SCENE
ROME

THE PERSONS: see Additional Note, p. 435 below.

17 TRIBUNI: tribunes.

21 PRAECONES: heralds.
LICTORES: lictors, attendants on the chief magistrate, who carried the symbols of his office, the axes and rods.

22 FLAMEN: priest.
MINISTRI: his attendants.

23 TUBICINES: trumpeters.
TIBICINES: flautists.

24 NUNTIUS: messenger.
SERVUS: servant.

25 [SERVI]: servants.

SEJANUS HIS FALL: A TRAGEDY

ACT I

[SCENE I]

[*Enter*] SABINUS, SILIUS.

SABINUS. Hail, Caius Silius.
SILIUS. Titius Sabinus, hail.
Yo'are rarely met in court!
SABINUS. Therefore, well met.
SILIUS. 'Tis true: indeed, this place is not our sphere.
SABINUS. No, Silius, we are no good enginers;
We want the fine arts, and their thriving use,
Should make us graced, or favoured of the times:
We have no shift of faces, no cleft tongues,
No soft, and glutinous bodies, that can stick,
Like snails, on painted walls; or, on our breasts,
Creep up, to fall, from that proud height, to which
We did by slavery, not by service, climb.
We are no guilty men, and then no great;
We have nor place in court, office in state,
That we can say, we owe unto our crimes:
We burn with no black secrets, which can make
Us dear to the pale authors; or live feared
Of their still waking jealousies, to raise
Ourselves a fortune, by subverting theirs.
We stand not in the lines that do advance
To that so courted point.

[*Enter* SATRIUS, NATTA.]

SILIUS. But yonder lean
A pair that do.

---

4 *enginers*: plotters, schemers.
5 *want*: lack.
7 *shift of faces*: changes of expression (to fit the occasion).
cleft tongues: indicative of flattery (see V.[i].38–9).
15 *burn*: i.e. with the knowledge of guilty secrets.
16 *dear to*: treated with favour by; also, 'costly to'.
authors: evil-doers.
17 *Of*: by.
still: ever.
jealousies: suspicions.
19 *lines*: way.
20 *lean*: incline.

[*Enter* LATIARIS.]

SABINUS. [*greets him*] (Good cousin Latiaris.)
SILIUS. Satrius Secundus, and Pinnarius Natta,
The great Sejanus' clients: there be two,
Know more than honest counsels; whose close breasts
Were they ripped up to light, it would be found
A poor, and idle sin, to which their trunks
Had not been made fit organs. These can lie,
Flatter, and swear, forswear, deprave, inform,
Smile, and betray; make guilty men; then beg
The forfeit lives, to get the livings; cut
Men's throats with whisperings; sell to gaping suitors
The empty smoke that flies about the palace;
Laugh, when their patron laughs; sweat, when he sweats;
Be hot, and cold with him; change every mood,
Habit, and garb, as often as he varies;
Observe him, as his watch observes his clock;
And true, as turquoise in the dear lord's ring,
Look well, or ill with him: ready to praise
His lordship, if he spit, or but piss fair,
Have an indifferent stool, or break wind well,
Nothing can 'scape their catch.
SABINUS. Alas! these things
Deserve no note, conferred with other vile,
And filthier flatteries, that corrupt the times:
When, not alone our gentry's chief are fain
To make their safety from such sordid acts,
But all our consuls, and no little part

---

23 *clients*: servile dependants.
24 *close*: secretive.
26 *idle*: negligible.
27 *organs*: instruments.
29–30 *beg . . . livings*: plead for the condemned, to gain complete control over them and their revenues. See Additional Note, p. 436 below.
31–2 *sell . . . palace*: make baseless promises of the emperor's favour to greedy, gullible suitors who then give rewards (proverbial, from Martial, *Epigrams*, IV.v.7).
36 *Observe . . . clock*: see Additional Note, p. 436 below.
37 *turquoise*: supposed to change colour according to the state of the wearer's health.
42 *conferred*: compared.
46 *consuls*: the two chief magistrates of the Roman state.

Of such as have been praetors, yea, the most
Of senators (that else not use their voices)
Start up in public Senate, and there strive
Who shall propound most abject things, and base,
So much, as oft Tiberius hath been heard,
Leaving the court, to cry, 'O race of men
Prepared for servitude!' which showed that he
Who least the public liberty could like,
As loathly brooked their flat servility.

SILIUS. Well, all is worthy of us, were it more,
Who with our riots, pride, and civil hate,
Have so provoked the justice of the gods.
We, that (within these fourscore years) were born
Free, equal lords of the triumphèd world,
And knew no masters, but affections,
To which betraying first our liberties,
We since became the slaves to one man's lusts;
And now to many: every ministering spy
That will accuse, and swear, is lord of you,
Of me, of all, our fortunes, and our lives.
Our looks are called to question and our words,
How innocent soever, are made crimes;
We shall not shortly dare to tell our dreams,
Or think, but 'twill be treason.

SABINUS. Tyrants' arts
Are to give flatterers, grace; accusers, power;
That those may seem to kill whom they devour.

[*Enter* CORDUS, ARRUNTIUS.]

Now good Cremutius Cordus.

CORDUS. Hail, to your lordship.
They whisper.

NATTA. Who's that salutes your cousin?

LATIARIS. 'Tis one Cordus,

---

47 *praetors*: officials below consular rank.
48 *senators . . . voices)*: *Pediarii* (Jonson's marginal note); a lower order of senators who gave a silent vote unless called upon to speak.
55 *flat*: downright.
57 *riots*: riotous living, excesses.
civil hate: hatred and faction between Roman families.
60 *triumphèd*: conquered.
61 *affections*: passions.
64 *ministering spy*: professional informer.
72 *those*: flatterers and accusers.
they: tyrants.

A gentleman of Rome: one, that has writ
Annals of late, they say, and very well.
NATTA. Annals? of what times?
LATIARIS. I think of Pompey's,
And Caius Caesar's; and so down to these.
NATTA. How stands h'affected to the present state?
Is he or Drusian? or Germanican?
Or ours? or neutral?
LATIARIS. I know him not so far.
NATTA. Those times are somewhat queasy to be touched.
Have you or seen, or heard part of his work?
LATIARIS. Not I, he means they shall be public shortly.
NATTA. Oh. Cordus do you call him?
LATIARIS. Ay.
[*Exeunt* NATTA, SATRIUS.]
SABINUS. But these our times
Are not the same, Arruntius.
ARRUNTIUS. Times? the men,
The men are not the same: 'tis we are base,
Poor, and degenerate from th'exalted strain
Of our great fathers. Where is now the soul
Of god-like Cato? he, that durst be good,
When Caesar durst be evil; and had power,
As not to live his slave, to die his master.
Or where the constant Brutus, that (being proof
Against all charm of benefits) did strike
So brave a blow into the monster's heart
That sought unkindly to captìve his country?

---

77 *Pompey*: 106–48 BC; triumvir and general, defeated by Julius Caesar at Pharsalia attempting to curb Caesar's growing power; later killed in Egypt.
78 *Caius Caesar*: 20 BC–AD 4; grandson of Augustus.
82 *queasy*: sensitive.
88 *degenerate*: fallen away from ancestral virtue.
90 *Cato*: 95–46 BC; opponent of Julius Caesar and supporter of Pompey, whom he followed into exile after Pharsalia; committed suicide at Utica after the final defeat of his party.
92 *his master*: his own master.
93 *Brutus*: 85–42 BC; friend, and, with Cassius, leading assassin of Caesar in the conspiracy which attempted to restore the Republic; committed suicide at Philippi after he and Cassius were defeated by Mark Antony and Octavius.
94 *charm*: bewitching power.
96 *unkindly*: unnaturally.
captive: enthral.

Oh, they are fled the light. Those mighty spirits
Lie raked up, with their ashes in their urns,
And not a spark of their eternal fire
Glows in a present bosom. All's but blaze,
Flashes, and smoke, wherewith we labour so,
There's nothing Roman in us; nothing good,
Gallant, or great: 'tis true, that Cordus says,
'Brave Cassius was the last of all that race.'

DRUSUS *passeth by* [*with* HATERIUS *and attendants*].

SABINUS. Stand by, Lord Drusus.
HATERIUS. Th'emperor's son, give place.
SILIUS. I like the prince well.
ARRUNTIUS. A riotous youth,
There's little hope of him.
SABINUS. That fault his age
Will, as it grows, correct. Methinks, he bears
Himself, each day, more nobly than other:
And wins no less on men's affections,
Than doth his father lose. Believe me, I love him;
And chiefly for opposing to Sejanus.
SILIUS. And I, for gracing his young kinsmen so,
The sons of Prince Germanicus: it shows
A gallant clearness in him, a straight mind,
That envies not, in them, their father's name.
ARRUNTIUS. His name was, while he lived, above all envy;
And being dead, without it. Oh, that man!
If there were seeds of the old virtue left,
They lived in him.
SILIUS. He had the fruits, Arruntius,
More than the seeds: Sabinus, and myself
Had means to know him, within; and can report him.

---

104 *Brave . . . race*: attributed by Plutarch (*Life of Brutus*, xliv) to Brutus after Cassius's suicide at Philippi, and used by Shakespeare in *Julius Caesar* (1599), V.iii.99.
105 *by*: aside.
114 *Germanicus*: 15 BC–AD 19; nephew of Tiberius, who was suspicious and jealous of his popularity and military success; believed to have been poisoned at the instigation of Tiberius or his mother Livia.
115 *clearness*: nobility.
118 *without*: beyond.
122 *within*: in his true nature.

We were his followers (he would call us friends).
He was a man most like to virtue'; in all,
And every action, nearer to the gods,
Than men, in nature: of a body'as fair
As was his mind; and no less reverend
In face, than fame: he could so use his state,
Tempering his greatness with his gravity,
As it avoided all self-love in him,
And spite in others. What his funerals lacked
In images, and pomp, they had supplied
With honourable sorrow, soldiers' sadness,
A kind of silent mourning, such, as men
(Who know no tears, but from their captives) use
To show in so great losses.

CORDUS. I thought once,
Considering their forms, age, manner of deaths,
The nearness of the places where they fell,
T'have paralleled him with great Alexander:
For both were of best feature, of high race,
Yeared but to thirty, and, in foreign lands,
By their own people, àlike made away.

SABINUS. I know not, for his death, how you might wrest it:
But for his life, it did as much disdain
Comparison with that voluptuous, rash,
Giddy, and drunken Macedon's, as mine
Doth with my bondman's. All the good in him
(His valour, and his fortune) he made his;
But he had other touches of late Romans,
That more did speak him: Pompey's dignity,
The innocence of Cato, Caesar's spirit,
Wise Brutus' temperance, and every virtue,
Which, parted unto others, gave them name,
Flowed mixed in him. He was the soul of goodness:

---

124 *virtue'*: the apostrophe indicates that the second syllable is elided to fit the verse line, as also in *body'* at 126.
128 *state*: high rank.
129 *gravity*: dignity.
130 *avoided*: cast out.
132 *images*: painted masks of the dead man and his ancestors worn by relatives in the funeral procession.
135 *use*: are accustomed.
138 *The nearness . . . fell*: Alexander the Great died at Babylon, Germanicus near Antioch.
150 *speak*: describe.
153 *parted unto*: divided amongst.

And all our praises of him are like streams
Drawn from a spring, that still rise full, and leave
The part remaining greatest.

ARRUNTIUS. I am sure
He was too great for us, and that they knew
Who did remove him hence.

SABINUS. When men grow fast
Honoured, and loved, there is a trick in state
(Which jealous princes never fail to use)
How to decline that growth, with fair pretèxt,
And honourable colours of employment,
Either by embassy, the war, or such,
To shift them forth into another air,
Where they may purge, and lessen; so was he:
And had his seconds there, sent by Tiberius,
And his more subtle dam, to discontent him;
To breed, and cherish mutinies; detract
His greatest actions; give audacious check
To his commands; and work to put him out
In open act of treason. All which snares
When his wise cares prevented, a fine poison
Was thought on, to mature their practices.

CORDUS. Here comes Sejanus.

SILIUS. Now observe the stoops,
The bendings, and the falls.

ARRUNTIUS. Most creeping base!

[*Enter*] SEJANUS, SATRIUS, TERENTIUS, *etc. They pass over the stage.*

SEJANUS. I note 'em well: no more. Say you.

SATRIUS. My lord,
There is a gentleman of Rome would buy –

SEJANUS. How call you him you talked with?

SATRIUS. Please your lordship,
It is Eudemus, the physician
To Livia, Drusus' wife.

---

160 *state*: statecraft.
161 *jealous*: suspicious.
163 *colours*: appearances.
166 *purge*: be relieved of their influence.
167 *seconds*: supporters.
168 *dam*: mother; Livia, widow of Augustus.
173 *fine*: subtle.
174 *practices*: plots.
175–6 *stoops . . . falls*: obsequious bowing and scraping.
180 *physician*: four syllables.

SEJANUS. On with your suit.
Would buy, you said –
SATRIUS. A tribune's place, my lord.
SEJANUS. What will he give?
SATRIUS. Fifty sestertia.
SEJANUS. Livia's physician, say you, is that fellow?
SATRIUS. It is, my lord; your lordship's answer?
SEJANUS. To what?
SATRIUS. The place, my lord. 'Tis for a gentleman
Your lordship will well like of, when you see him;
And one, you may make yours, by the grant.
SEJANUS. Well, let him bring his money, and his name.
SATRIUS. Thank your lordship. He shall, my lord.
SEJANUS. Come hither.
Know you this same Eudemus? Is he learned?
SATRIUS. Reputed so, my lord: and of deep practice.
SEJANUS. Bring him in, to me, in the gallery;
And take you cause to leave us there, together:
I would confer with him, about a grief. – On.
[*Exeunt* SEJANUS, SATRIUS, TERENTIUS, *etc.*]
ARRUNTIUS. So, yet! another? yet? O desperate state
Of grovelling honour! See'st thou this, O sun,
And do we see thee after? Methinks, day
Should lose his light, when men do lose their shames,
And for the empty circumstance of life,
Betray their cause of living.
SILIUS. Nothing so.
Sejanus can repair, if Jove should ruin.
He is the now court-god; and well applied
With sacrifice of knees, of crooks, and cringe,
He will do more than all the house of heaven
Can, for a thousand hecatombs. 'Tis he
Makes us our day, or night; Hell, and Elysium
Are in his look: we talk of Rhadamanth,

---

182 *tribune*: high-ranking official; here, probably a paymaster or judge.
183 *Fifty sestertia*: '£375 of our money' (Jonson's marginal note).
195 *grief*: ailment.
207 *Elysium*: the Happy Fields to which the spirits of dead heroes went.
208 *Rhadamanth*: Rhadamanthus, judge of the dead.

Furies, and fire-brands; but 'tis his frown
That is all these, where, on the adverse part,
His smile is more, than ere (yet) poets feigned
Of bliss, and shades, nectar –

ARRUNTIUS. A serving boy?
I knew him, at Caius' trencher, when for hire,
He prostituted his abusèd body
To that great gourmand, fat Apicius;
And was the noted pathic of the time.

SABINUS. And now, the second face of the whole world.
The partner of the Empire, hath his image
Reared equal with Tiberius', borne in ensigns,
Commands, disposes every dignity,
Centurions, tribunes, heads of provinces,
Praetors, and consuls, all that heretofore
Rome's general suffrage gave, is now his sale.
The gain, or rather spoil, of all the earth,
One, and his house, receives.

SILIUS. He hath of late
Made him a strength too, strangely, by reducing
All the praetorian bands into one camp,
Which he commands: pretending, that the soldier
By living loose, and scattered, fell to riot;
And that if any sudden enterprise
Should be attempted, their united strength
Would be far more, than severed; and their life
More strict, if from the city more removed.

SABINUS. Where, now, he builds what kind of forts he please,
Is hard to court the soldier, by his name,
Woos, feasts the chiefest men of action,
Whose wants, not loves, compel them to be his.
And though he ne'er were liberal by kind,
Yet, to his own dark ends, he's most profuse,

---

209 *Furies*: avenging deities.
213 *Caius'*: Caius Caesar's.
215 *Apicius*: a notorious epicure.
216 *pathic*: boy kept for immoral purposes.
226 *strangely*: in an unusual manner.
reducing: bringing together.
227 *praetorian bands*: imperial bodyguard and Rome's garrison.
229 *loose*: free of military discipline.
235 *hard*: tenacious; but see Textual Note, p. 431 below.
238 *kind*: nature.

Lavish, and letting fly, he cares not what
To his ambition.
ARRUNTIUS. Yet, hath he ambition?
Is there that step in state can make him higher?
Or more? or anything he is, but less?
SILIUS. Nothing, but emperor.
ARRUNTIUS. The name Tiberius
I hope, will keep; how e'er he hath foregone
The dignity, and power.
SILIUS. Sure, while he lives.
ARRUNTIUS. And dead, it comes to Drusus. Should he fail,
To the brave issue of Germanicus;
And they are three: too many (ha?) for him
To have a plot upon?
SABINUS. I do not know
The heart of his designs; but, sure, their face
Looks farther than the present.
ARRUNTIUS. By the gods,
If I could guess he had but such a thought,
My sword should cleave him down from head to heart,
But I would find it out: and with my hand
I'd hurl his panting brain about the air,
In mites, as small as *atomi*, to'undo
The knotted bed –
SABINUS. You are observed, Arruntius.
ARRUNTIUS. Death! I dare tell him so; and all his spies:

He turns to SEJANUS' *clients.*

You, sir, I would, do you look? and you.
SABINUS. Forbear.

[*Enter*] SATRIUS, EUDEMUS.

SATRIUS. Here he will instant be; let's walk a turn.
Yo'are in a muse, Eudemus?
EUDEMUS. Not I, sir.
I wonder he should mark me out so! Well,
Jove, and Apollo form it for the best.
SATRIUS. Your fortune's made unto you now, Eudemus,

---

247 *fail*: die.
257 *atomi*: atoms.
258 *knotted bed*: tangled nest (as of snakes or toads).
261 *Here*: see Additional Note, p. 436 below.

If you can but lay hold upon the means;
Do but observe his humour, and – believe it –
He's the noblest Roman, where he takes –
Here comes his lordship.

[*Enter* SEJANUS.]

SEJANUS. Now, good Satrius.
SATRIUS. This is the gentleman, my lord.
SEJANUS. Is this?
Give me your hand, we must be more acquainted.
Report, sir, hath spoke out your art, and learning:
And I am glad I have so needful cause
(How ever in itself painful, and hard)
To make me known to so great virtue. Look,
Who's that? Satrius –

[*Exit* SATRIUS.]

I have a grief, sir,
That will desire your help. Your name's Eudemus?
EUDEMUS. Yes.
SEJANUS. Sir?
EUDEMUS. It is, my lord.
SEJANUS. I hear, you are
Physician to Livia, the princess?
EUDEMUS. I minister unto her, my good lord.
SEJANUS. You minister to a royal lady, then.
EUDEMUS. She is, my lord, and fair.
SEJANUS. That's understood
Of all their sex, who are, or would be so;
And those that would be, physic soon can make 'em:
For those that are, their beauties fear no colours.
EUDEMUS. Your lordship is conceited.
SEJANUS. Sir, you know it.
And can (if need be) read a learnèd lecture,
On this, and other secrets. Pray you tell me,
What more of ladies, besides Livia,
Have you your patients?
EUDEMUS. Many, my good lord.

---

267 *humour*: mood.
275 *virtue*: (man of) ability; but irony is unavoidable.
284 *physic*: course of medical treatment.
285 *colours*: cosmetics (i.e. they are not afraid their complexions will wash off); also, 'military colours', 'ensigns' (i.e. they are not afraid of any painted rival).
286 *conceited*: witty.

The great Augusta, Urgulania,
Mutilia Prisca, and Plancina, divers –
SEJANUS. And all these tell you the particulars
Of every several grief? how first it grew,
And then increased, what action causèd that;
What passion that: and answer to each point
That you will put 'em.
EUDEMUS. Else, my lord, we know not
How to prescribe the remedies.
SEJANUS. Go to,
Yo'are a subtle nation, you physicians!
And grown the only cabinets, in court,
To ladies' privacies. Faith, which of these
Is the most pleasant lady, in her physic?
Come, you are modest now.
EUDEMUS. 'Tis fit, my lord.
SEJANUS. Why, sir, I do not ask you of their urines,
Whose smells most violet? or whose siege is best?
Or who makes hardest faces on her stool?
Which lady sleeps with her own face, a'nights?
Which puts her teeth off, with her clothes, in court?
Or which her hair? which her complexion?
And in which box she puts it? These were questions
That might, perhaps, have put your gravity
To some defence of blush. But I enquired,
Which was the wittiest? merriest? wantonest?
Harmless intergatories, but conceits.
Methinks, Augusta should be most perverse,
And froward in her fit?
EUDEMUS. She's so, my lord.
SEJANUS. I knew it. And Mutilia the most jocund?

291 *Augusta*: Livia, widow of Augustus, mother of Tiberius.
291–2 *Urgulania, Mutilia Prisca, and Plancina*: friends of Livia. Plancina was suspected, with her husband Piso, of being an accessory to the poisoning of Germanicus.
294 *several*: individual, particular.
296 *passion*: painful disorder; but also the modern sense.
299 *nation*: group of people.
300 *cabinets*: repositories.
301 *privacies*: secrets.
302 *physic*: medical treatment involving purgation.
305 *siege*: stool.
313 *wantonest*: most sportive; but also the modern sense.
314 *intergatories, but conceits*: questions, only fanciful notions.
316 *froward*: difficult.
fit: indisposition.

EUDEMUS. 'Tis very true, my lord.
SEJANUS. And why would you
Conceal this from me, now? Come, what's Livia?
I know she's quick, and quaintly spirited,
And will have strange thoughts, when she's at leisure;
She tells 'em all to you?
EUDEMUS. My noblest lord,
He breathes not in the Empire, or on earth,
Whom I would be ambitious to serve
(In any act, that may preserve mine honour)
Before your lordship.
SEJANUS. Sir, you can lose no honour,
By trusting aught to me. The coarsest act
Done to my service, I can so requite,
As all the world shall style it honourable:
Your idle, virtuous definitions
Keep honour poor, and are as scorned, as vain:
Those deeds breathe honour, that do suck in gain.
EUDEMUS. But, good my lord, if I should thus betray
The counsels of my patient, and a lady's
Of her high place, and worth; what might your lordship
(Who presently are to trust me with your own)
Judge of my faith?
SEJANUS. Only the best, I swear.
Say now, that I should utter you my grief;
And with it, the true cause; that it were love;
And love to Livia: you should tell her this?
Should she suspect your faith? I would you could
Tell me as much, from her; see, if my brain
Could be turned jealous.
EUDEMUS. Happily, my lord,
I could, in time, tell you as much, and more;
So I might safely promise but the first,
To her, from you.
SEJANUS. As safely, my Eudemus
(I now dare call thee so), as I have put
The secret into thee.
EUDEMUS. My lord –

---

320 *quick, and quaintly spirited*: lively, and of an ingenious turn of mind.
324 *ambitious*: four syllables.
330 *idle*: foolish.
343 *Happily*: perhaps.

SEJANUS. Protest not.
Thy looks are vows to me, use only speed,
And but affect her with Sejanus' love,
Thou art a man, made, to make consuls. Go.
EUDEMUS. My lord, I'll promise you a private meeting
This day, together.
SEJANUS. Canst thou?
EUDEMUS. Yes.
SEJANUS. The place?
EUDEMUS. My gardens, whither I shall fetch your lordship.
SEJANUS. Let me adore my Aesculapius.
Why, this indeed is physic! and outspeaks
The knowledge of cheap drugs, or any use
Can be made out of it! more comforting
Than all your opiates, juleps, apozemes,
Magistral syrups, or – Begone, my friend,
Not barely stylèd, but created so;
Expect things, greater than thy largest hopes,
To overtake thee: Fortune shall be taught
To know how ill she hath deserved thus long,
To come behind thy wishes. Go, and speed.
[*Exit* EUDEMUS.]
Ambition makes more trusty slaves, than need.
These fellows, by the favour of their art,
Have, still, the means to tempt, ofttimes, the power.
If Livia will be now corrupted, then
Thou hast the way, Sejanus, to work out
His secrets, who (thou knowest) endures thee not,
Her husband Drusus: and to work against them.
Prosper it, Pallas, thou that betterest wit;
For Venus hath the smallest share in it.

---

350 *affect*: move.
351 *Thou . . . consuls*: you are a made man, who will have the power to exercise patronage even over the highest office.
355 *Aesculapius*: god of medicine.
356 *outspeaks*: goes beyond.
359 *juleps*: soothing sweet syrups.
apozemes: medicinal liquor made by boiling down or steeping a vegetable or animal substance.
360 *Magistral*: sovereign, supremely effective.
365 *speed*: be successful.
373 *Pallas*: Pallas Athene, goddess of wisdom.

[*Enter*] TIBERIUS, DRUSUS [*and attendants*]. *One kneels to him.*

TIBERIUS. We not endure these flatteries, let him stand;
Our empire, ensigns, axes, rods, and state
Take not away our human nature from us:
Look up, on us, and fall before the gods.
SEJANUS. How like a god, speaks Caesar!
ARRUNTIUS. There, observe!
He can endure that second, that's no flattery.
Oh, what is it, proud slime will not believe
Of his own worth, to hear it equal praised
Thus with the gods?
CORDUS. He did not hear it, sir.
ARRUNTIUS. He did not? Tut, he must not, we think meanly.
'Tis your most courtly, known confederacy,
To have your private parasite redeem
What he, in public subtlety, will lose
To making him a name.
HATERIUS. Right mighty lord –
TIBERIUS. We must make up our ears, 'gainst these assaults
Of charming tongues; we pray you use, no more,
These contumelies to us: style not us
Or lord, or mighty, who profess ourself
The servant of the Senate, and are proud
T'enjoy them our good, just, and favouring lords.
CORDUS. Rarely dissembled.
ARRUNTIUS. Prince-like, to the life.
SABINUS. When power, that may command, so much descends,
Their bondage, whom it stoops to, it intends.
TIBERIUS. Whence are these letters?

---

374 s.d. [*Enter*] TIBERIUS: see Additional Note, p. 436 below.
376 *empire*: imperial dignity.
axes, rods: the *fasces*, bundles of rods bound round axes, symbols of authority carried before the chief magistrate.
383 CORDUS: see Textual Note, p. 431 below.
384 *meanly*: putting a moderate construction on it.
385, 386 *your*: used contemptuously.
385 *courtly, known confederacy*: court-like, recognised conspiracy.
386–8 *To have your . . . him a name*: where the prince's personal flatterer recovers for him the name the prince wants to establish for himself, but cunningly disclaims in public.
389 *make up*: close (military metaphor).

HATERIUS. From the Senate.
TIBERIUS. So.
Whence these?
LATIARIS. From thence too.
TIBERIUS. Are they sitting, now?
LATIARIS. They stay thy answer, Caesar.
SILIUS. If this man
Had but a mind allied unto his words,
How blest a fate were it to us, and Rome?
We could not think that state, for which to change,
Although the aim were our old liberty:
The ghosts of those that fell for that, would grieve
Their bodies lived not, now, again to serve.
Men are deceived, who think there can be thrall
Beneath a virtuous prince. Wished liberty
Ne'er lovelier looks, than under such a crown.
But when his grace is merely but lip-good,
And that no longer, than he airs himself
Abroad in public, there, to seem to shun
The strokes, and stripes of flatterers, which within
Are lechery unto him, and so feed
His brutish sense with their afflicting sound,
As (dead to virtue) he permits himself
Be carried like a pitcher, by the ears,
To every act of vice: this is a case
Deserves our fear, and doth presage the nigh,
And close approach of blood and tyranny.
Flattery is midwife unto princes' rage:
And nothing sooner doth help forth a tyrant,
Than that, and whisperers' grace, who have the time,
The place, the power, to make all men offenders.
ARRUNTIUS. He should be told this; and be bid dissemble
With fools, and blind men: we that know the evil,
Should hunt the palace rats, or give them bane;

---

403 *think*: imagine.
change: exchange.
404 *old liberty*: i.e. of the Republic.
413 *strokes*: caresses (proverbially contrasted with stripes); also, 'blows'; i.e. the soothing flatteries, which Tiberius publicly protests against, secretly delight him (as blows stimulate perverse sexual pleasure).
423 *whisperers' grace*: favour given to informers.
427 *bane*: poison.

Fright hence these worse than ravens, that devour
The quick, where they but prey upon the dead:
He shall be told it.
SABINUS. Stay, Arruntius,
We must abide our opportunity:
And practise what is fit, as what is needful.
It is not safe t'enforce a sovereign's ear:
Princes hear well, if they at all will hear.
ARRUNTIUS. Ha? Say you so? well. In the meantime, Jove
(Say not, but I do call upon thee now),
Of all wild beasts, preserve me from a tyrant;
And of all tame, a flatterer.
SILIUS. 'Tis well prayed.
TIBERIUS. Return the lords this voice, we are their creature:
And it is fit, a good, and honest prince,
Whom they, out of their bounty, have instructed
With so dilate, and absolute a power,
Should owe the office of it to their service;
And good of all, and every citizen.
Nor shall it e'er repent us, to have wished
The Senate just, and favouring lords unto us,
Since their free loves do yield no less defence
T'a prince's state, than his own innocence.
Say then, there can be nothing in their thought
Shall want to please us, that hath pleasèd them;
Our suffrage rather shall prevent, than stay
Behind their wills: 'tis empire, to obey
Where such, so great, so grave, so good determine.
Yet, for the suit of Spain, t'erect a temple
In honour of our mother, and ourself,
We must (with pardon of the Senate) not
Assent thereto. Their lordships may object
Our not denying the same late request
Unto the Asian cities: we desire
That our defence, for suffering that, be known
In these brief reasons, with our after purpose.

---

429 *quick*: living.
439 *creature*: servant.
441 *instructed*: furnished.
442 *dilate*: extended.
450 *want*: fail.
451 *prevent*: anticipate.
461 *after purpose*: subsequent determination.

Since deified Augustus hindered not
A temple to be built, at Pergamum,
In honour of himself, and sacred Rome,
We, that have all his deeds, and words observed
Ever, in place of laws, the rather followed
That pleasing precedent, because, with ours,
The Senate's reverence also, there, was joined.
But as t'have once received it, may deserve
The gain of pardon, so, to be adored
With the continued style, and note of gods,
Through all the provinces, were wild ambition,
And no less pride: yea, ev'n Augustus' name
Would early vanish, should it be profaned
With such promiscuous flatteries. For our part,
We here protest it, and are covetous
Posterity should know it, we are mortal;
And can but deeds of men: 'twere glory'enough,
Could we be truly a prince. And they shall add
Abounding grace unto our memory,
That shall report us worthy our forefathers,
Careful of your affairs, constant in dangers,
And not afraid of any private frown
For public good. These things shall be to us
Temples, and statues, rearèd in your minds,
The fairest, and most during imagery:
For those of stone, or brass, if they become
Odious in judgement of posterity,
Are more contemned, as dying sepulchres,
Than ta'en for living monuments. We then
Make here our suit, alike to gods, and men,
The one, until the period of our race,
T'inspire us with a free, and quiet mind,
Discerning both divine, and human laws;
The other, to vouchsafe us after death,
An honourable mention, and fair praise,
T'accompany our actions, and our name:
The rest of greatness princes may command,
And (therefore) may neglect; only a long,
A lasting, high, and happy memory
They should, without being satisfied, pursue.
Contempt of fame begets contempt of virtue.

---

471 *note*: ceremony.
475 *promiscuous*: indiscriminate.
478 *can*: are able to do.
492 *period of our race*: end of my life.

NATTA. Rare!
SATRIUS. Most divine!
SEJANUS. The oracles are ceased,
That only Caesar, with their tongue, might speak.
ARRUNTIUS. Let me be gone, most felt, and open this!
CORDUS. Stay.
ARRUNTIUS. What? to hear more cunning, and fine words,
With their sound flattered, ere their sense be meant?
TIBERIUS. Their choice of Antium, there to place the gift
Vowed to the goddess, for our mother's health,
We will the Senate know, we fairly like;
As also, of their grant to Lepidus,
For his repairing the Aemilian place,
And restoration of those monuments:
Their grace too in confining of Silanus
To t'other isle Cithera, at the suit
Of his religious sister, much commends
Their policy, so tempered with their mercy.
But for the honours, which they have decreed
To our Sejanus, to advance his statue
In Pompey's theatre (whose ruining fire
His vigilance, and labour kept restrained
In that one loss) they have, therein, outgone
Their own great wisdoms, by their skilful choice,
And placing of their bounties, on a man,
Whose merit more adorns the dignity,
Than that can him: and gives a benefit,
In taking, greater, than it can receive.
Blush not, Sejanus, thou great aid of Rome,

---

503 *The oracles are ceased*: see Additional Note, p. 436 below.
505 *felt*: palpable.
508–9 *gift . . . goddess*: *Fortuna equestris* (Jonson's marginal note): the statue of Fortune presented by the knights of Rome.
510 *fairly like*: fully approve.
512 *Aemilian place*: court built by the family Aemilii, to which Lepidus belonged.
514 *Silanus*: a governor of Asia, convicted of extortion and exiled to the Cyclades.
515 *t'other isle*: Cythnum, less forbidding than Gyaros.
516 *religious sister*: a vestal priestess.
517 *policy*: wisdom.
519 *advance*: raise.

Associate of our labours, our chief helper,
Let us not force thy simple modesty
With offering at thy praise, for more we cannot,
Since there's no voice can take it. No man, here,
Receive our speeches, as hyperboles;
For we are far from flattering our friend
(Let envy know) as from the need to flatter.
Nor let them ask the causes of our praise;
Princes have still their grounds reared with themselves,
Above the poor low flats of common men,
And who will search the reasons of their acts,
Must stand on equal bases. Lead, away.
Our loves unto the Senate.

[*Exeunt* TIBERIUS, SEJANUS, *attendants.*]

ARRUNTIUS. Caesar.

SABINUS. Peace.

CORDUS. Great Pompey's theatre was never ruined
Till now, that proud Sejanus hath a statue
Reared on his ashes.

ARRUNTIUS. Place the shame of soldiers,
Above the best of generals? crack the world!
And bruise the name of Romans into dust,
Ere we behold it!

SILIUS. Check your passion;
Lord Drusus tarries.

DRUSUS. Is my father mad?
Weary of life, and rule, lords? thus to heave
An idol up with praise! make him his mate!
His rival in the Empire!

ARRUNTIUS. O, good prince!

DRUSUS. Allow him statues? titles? honours? such
As he himself refuseth?

ARRUNTIUS. Brave, brave Drusus!

DRUSUS. The first ascents to sovereignty are hard,
But, entered once, there never wants or means,
Or ministers, to help th'aspirer on.

---

530 *force*: do violence to.
simple: unaffected.
531 *offering at*: attempting.
532 *take*: perform.
537–8 *Princes . . . flats*: princes by virtue of their position are always on an elevated plane, above the lowly levels.
540 *equal bases*: equal footing.
545 *crack the world*: let the world split asunder.
551 *rival*: partner.

ARRUNTIUS. True, gallant Drusus.
DRUSUS. We must shortly pray
To modesty, that he will rest contented –
ARRUNTIUS. Ay, where he is, and not write emperor.

SEJANUS, [LATIARIS,] *etc. He enters, followed with clients.*

SEJANUS. There is your bill, and yours; bring you your man:
I have moved for you too, Latiaris.
DRUSUS. What?
Is your vast greatness grown so blindly bold,
That you will over us?
SEJANUS. Why, then give way.
DRUSUS. Give way, Colossus? Do you lift? Advance you?
Take that.

DRUSUS *strikes him.*

ARRUNTIUS. Good! brave! excellent brave prince!
DRUSUS. Nay, come, approach. What? stand you off? at gaze?
It looks too full of death, for thy cold spirits.
Avoid mine eye, dull camel, or my sword
Shall make thy bravery fitter for a grave,
Than for a triumph. I'll advance a statue,
O'your own bulk; but't shall be on the cross:
Where I will nail your pride, at breadth, and length,
And crack those sinews, which are yet but stretched
With your swoll'n fortune's rage.
ARRUNTIUS. A noble prince!

---

558 *modesty*: moderation.
559 *write*: style himself.
563 *over*: master (Scots); also, 'raise yourself above'.
564 *Colossus*: gigantic statue, the most famous being that of Helios at Rhodes.
lift: rear (like a horse).
566 *at gaze*: bewildered (used of deer).
568 *camel*: great hulking fellow.
569 *bravery*: fine clothes.
570 *triumph*: entrance into Rome in a grand procession, granted as an honour to a conquering general; at this period, reserved for members of the royal family.
571 *bulk*: body.
cross: the most ignominious death, reserved for slaves.

ALL. A Castor, a Castor, a Castor, a Castor!
[*Exeunt all but*] SEJANUS.
SEJANUS. He that, with such wrong moved, can bear it through
With patience, and an even mind, knows how
To turn it back. Wrath, covered, carries fate:
Revenge is lost, if I profess my hate.
What was my practice late, I'll now pursue
As my fell justice. This hath styled it new. [*Exit.*]

Chorus – of musicians.

ACT II

[SCENE I]

[*Enter*] SEJANUS, LIVIA, EUDEMUS.

SEJANUS. Physician, thou art worthy of a province,
For the great favours done unto our loves;
And but that greatest Livia bears a part
In the requital of thy services,
I should alone despair of aught, like means,
To give them worthy satisfaction.
LIVIA. Eudemus (I will see it) shall receive
A fit, and full reward, for his large merit.
But for this potion we intend to Drusus
(No more our husband, now), whom shall we choose
As the most apt, and abled instrument,
To minister it to him?
EUDEMUS. I say, Lygdus.
SEJANUS. Lygdus? what's he?
LIVIA. An eunuch Drusus loves.
EUDEMUS. Ay, and his cup-bearer.
SEJANUS. Name not a second.

---

575 *Castor*: famous gladiator; Drusus's nickname, on account of his belligerent and violent temper.
578 *fate*: death.
581 *fell*: merciless.
581 s.d. *Chorus – of musicians*: see Additional Note, p. 436 below.
5 *like*: adequate.

If Drusus love him, and he have that place,
We cannot think a fitter.
EUDEMUS. True, my lord,
For free access, and trust, are two main aids.
SEJANUS. Skilful physician!
LIVIA. But he must be wrought
To th'undertaking, with some laboured art.
SEJANUS. Is he ambitious?
LIVIA. No.
SEJANUS. Or covetous?
LIVIA. Neither.
EUDEMUS. Yet, gold is a good general charm.
SEJANUS. What is he then?
LIVIA. Faith, only wanton, light.
SEJANUS. How! Is he young? and fair?
EUDEMUS. A delicate youth.
SEJANUS. Send him to me, I'll work him. Royal lady,
Though I have loved you long, and with that height
Of zeal, and duty (like the fire, which more
It mounts, it trembles) thinking nought could add
Unto the fervour, which your eye had kindled;
Yet now I see your wisdom, judgement, strength,
Quickness, and will, to apprehend the means
To your own good, and greatness, I protest
Myself through rarefied, and turned all flame
In your affection: such a spirit as yours,
Was not created for the idle second
To a poor flash, as Drusus; but to shine
Bright, as the moon, among the lesser lights,
And share the sovereignty of all the world.
Then Livia triumphs in her proper sphere,
When she, and her Sejanus shall divide
The name of Caesar; and Augusta's star
Be dimmed with glory of a brighter beam:
When Agrippina's fires are quite extinct,
And the scarce-seen Tiberius borrows all
His little light from us, whose folded arms

---

32 *through rarefied*: thoroughly refined.
turned all flame: i.e. purged of all grosser elements (fire was the purest of the four elements – the others being earth, water, and air – believed to constitute all matter).
35 *flash*: thing of momentary brightness.
44 *folded*: embracing.

Shall make one perfect orb.
[*Knocking within.*]
Who's that? Eudemus,
Look, 'tis not Drusus?
[*Exit* EUDEMUS.]
Lady, do not fear.
LIVIA. Not I, my lord. My fear, and love of him
Left me at once.
SEJANUS. Illustrous lady! stay –

[*Enter* EUDEMUS.]

EUDEMUS. I'll tell his lordship.
SEJANUS. Who is't, Eudemus?
EUDEMUS. One of your lordship's servants, brings you word
The emperor hath sent for you.
SEJANUS. Oh! where is he?
With your fair leave, dear princess. I'll but ask
A question, and return. *He goes out.*
EUDEMUS. Fortunate princess!
How are you blest in the fruition
Of this unequalled man, this soul of Rome,
The Empire's life, and voice of Caesar's world!
LIVIA. So blessèd, my Eudemus, as to know
The bliss I have, with what I ought to owe
The means that wrought it. How do'I look today?
EUDEMUS. Excellent clear, believe it. This same fucus
Was well laid on.
LIVIA. Methinks, 'tis here not white.
EUDEMUS. Lend me your scarlet, lady. 'Tis the sun
Hath given some little taint unto the ceruse,
You should have used of the white oil I gave you.
Sejanus, for your love! his very name
Commandeth above Cupid, or his shafts –
LIVIA. (Nay, now yo'have made it worse.
EUDEMUS. I'll help it straight.)
And but pronounced, is a sufficient charm

---

45 *perfect*: because the circle is a symbol of perfection and completeness.
48 *Illustrous*: illustrious; also, 'lustrous'.
54 *fruition*: enjoyment.
60 *clear*: beautiful.
fucus: cosmetic colour wash.
63 *ceruse*: cosmetic of white lead.

Against all rumour; and of absolute power
To satisfy for any lady's honour.
LIVIA. (What do you now, Eudemus?
EUDEMUS. Make a light fucus,
To touch you o'er withal.) Honoured Sejanus!
What act (though ne'er so strange, and insolent)
But that addition will at least bear out,
If't do not expiate?
LIVIA. Here, good physician.
EUDEMUS. I like this study to preserve the love
Of such a man, that comes not every hour
To greet the world. ('Tis now well, lady, you should
Use of the dentifrice I prescribed you, too,
To clear your teeth, and the prepared pomatum,
To smooth the skin.) A lady cannot be
Too curious of her form, that still would hold
The heart of such a person, made her captive,
As you have his: who, to endear him more
In your clear eye, hath put away his wife,
The trouble of his bed, and your delights,
Fair Apicata, and made spacious room
To your new pleasures.
LIVIA. Have not we returned
That, with our hate of Drusus, and discovery
Of all his counsels?
EUDEMUS. Yes, and wisely, lady,
The ages that succeed, and stand far off
To gaze at your high prudence, shall admire
And reckon it an act, without your sex:
It hath that rare appearance. Some will think
Your fortune could not yield a deeper sound,
Than mixed with Drusus'; but, when they shall hear
That, and the thunder of Sejanus meet,
Sejanus, whose high name doth strike the stars,

73 *insolent*: unaccustomed; also, 'improper'.
74 *addition*: title.
bear out: lend support to.
76 *study*: employment.
80 *pomatum*: scented ointment.
82 *curious*: careful.
85 *clear*: lustrous, bright.
89 *discovery*: revealing.
93 *without*: beyond.

And rings about the concave, great Sejanus,
Whose glories, style, and titles are himself,
The often iterating of Sejanus:
They then will lose their thoughts, and be ashamed
To take acquaintance of them.

[*Enter* SEJANUS.]

SEJANUS. I must make
A rude departure, lady. Caesar sends
With all his haste both of command, and prayer.
Be resolute in our plot; you have my soul,
As certain yours, as it is my body's.
And, wise physician, so prepare the poison
As you may lay the subtle operation
Upon some natural disease of his.
Your eunuch send to me. I kiss your hands,
Glory of ladies, and commend my love
To your best faith, and memory.

LIVIA. My lord,
I shall but change your words. Farewell. Yet this
Remember for your heed, he loves you not;
You know what I have told you: his designs
Are full of grudge, and danger: we must use
More than a common speed.

SEJANUS. Excellent lady,
How you do fire my blood!

LIVIA. Well, you must go?
The thoughts be best, are least set forth to show.

[*Exit* SEJANUS.]

EUDEMUS. When will you take some physic, lady?

LIVIA. When
I shall, Eudemus: but let Drusus' drug
Be first prepared.

EUDEMUS. Were Lygdus made, that's done;
I have it ready. And tomorrow morning,
I'll send you a perfume, first to resolve,
And procure sweat, and then prepare a bath

---

99 *concave*: vault of heaven.
100 *style*: distinguishing title.
104 *rude*: abrupt: see Additional Note, p. 437 below.
114 *change*: exchange.
121 *physic*: purgative.
123 *made*: prepared.
125 *resolve*: dissolve.

To cleanse, and clear the cutis; against when,
I'll have an excellent new fucus made,
Resistive 'gainst the sun, the rain, or wind,
Which you shall lay on with a breath, or oil,
As you best like, and last some fourteen hours.
This change came timely, lady, for your health;
And the restoring your complexion,
Which Drusus' choler had almost burnt up:
Wherein your fortune hath prescribed you better
Than art could do.

LIVIA. Thanks, good physician,
I'll use my fortune (you shall see) with reverence.
Is my coach ready?

EUDEMUS. It attends your highness.

[*Exeunt.*]

[SCENE II]

[*Enter*] SEJANUS.

SEJANUS. If this be not revenge, when I have done
And made it perfect, let Egyptian slaves,
Parthians, and bare-foot Hebrews brand my face,
And print my body full of injuries.
Thou lost thyself, child Drusus, when thou thought'st
Thou could'st outskip my vengeance: or outstand
The power I had to crush thee into air.
Thy follies now shall taste what kind of man
They have provoked, and this thy father's house
Crack in the flame of my incensèd rage,
Whose fury shall admit no shame, or mean.
Adultery? it is the lightest ill
I will commit. A race of wicked acts
Shall flow out of my anger, and o'erspread
The world's wide face, which no posterity
Shall e'er approve, nor yet keep silent: things,

---

127 *cutis*: the true skin, underlying the epidermis or cuticle.

140–1 *Egyptian slaves, Parthians . . . Hebrews*: races owing homage to Rome, by whom it would therefore be most demeaning to be punished.

143 *child*: prince; or possibly, contemptuous: 'boy'.

144 *outstand*: withstand.

149 *mean*: moderation.

That for their cunning, close, and cruel mark,
Thy father would wish his; and shall (perhaps)
Carry the empty name, but we the prize.
On then, my soul, and start not in thy course;
Though heaven drop sulphur, and Hell belch out fire,
Laugh at the idle terrors: tell proud Jove,
Between his power, and thine, there is no odds.
'Twas only fear, first, in the world made gods.

[*Enter*] TIBERIUS [*and attendants*].

TIBERIUS. Is yet Sejanus come?
SEJANUS. He's here, dread Caesar.
TIBERIUS. Let all depart that chamber, and the next:
[*Exeunt attendants.*]
Sit down, my comfort. When the master-prince
Of all the world, Sejanus, saith, he fears;
Is it not fatal?
SEJANUS. Yes, to those are feared.
TIBERIUS. And not to him?
SEJANUS. Not, if he wisely turn
That part of fate he holdeth, first on them.
TIBERIUS. That nature, blood, and laws of kind forbid.
SEJANUS. Do policy, and state forbid it?
TIBERIUS. No.
SEJANUS. The rest of poor respects, then, let go by:
State is enough to make th'act just, them guilty.
TIBERIUS. Long hate pursues such acts.
SEJANUS. Whom hatred frights,
Let him not dream on sovereignty.
TIBERIUS. Are rites
Of faith, love, piety, to be trod down?
Forgotten? and made vain?
SEJANUS. All for a crown.
The prince, who shames a tyrant's name to bear,
Shall never dare do anything, but fear;
All the command of sceptres quite doth perish
If it begin religious thoughts to cherish:

---

158 *start*: flinch.
170 *kind*: kindred.
171 *state*: statecraft.
172 *respects*: scruples.
172–209 for the use of rhyme here, and in 238–77, see Additional Note, p. 437 below.

Whole empires fall, swayed by those nice respects.
It is the licence of dark deeds protects
Ev'n states most hated: when no laws resist
The sword, but that it acteth what it list.

TIBERIUS. Yet so, we may do all things cruelly,
Not safely.

SEJANUS. Yes, and do them thoroughly.

TIBERIUS. Knows yet, Sejanus, whom we point at?

SEJANUS. Ay,
Or else my thought, my sense, or both do err:
'Tis Agrippina?

TIBERIUS. She; and her proud race.

SEJANUS. Proud? dangerous, Caesar. For in them apace
The father's spirit shoots up. Germanicus
Lives in their looks, their gait, their form, t'upbraid us
With his close death, if not revenge the same.

TIBERIUS. The act's not known.

SEJANUS. Not proved. But whispering fame
Knowledge, and proof doth to the jealous give,
Who, than to fail, would their own thought believe.
It is not safe, the children draw long breath,
That are provokèd by a parent's death.

TIBERIUS. It is as dangerous, to make them hence,
If nothing but their birth be their offence.

SEJANUS. Stay, till they strike at Caesar: then their crime
Will be enough, but late, and out of time
For him to punish.

TIBERIUS. Do they purpose it?

SEJANUS. You know, sir, thunder speaks not till it hit.
Be not secure: none swiftlier are oppressed,
Than they, whom confidence betrays to rest.
Let not your daring make your danger such:

---

182 *nice*: over-scrupulous.
188 *Ay*: see Textual Note, p. 431 below.
193 *gait*: bearing.
194 *close death*: secret murder.
195 *fame*: rumour.
196 *jealous*: suspicious.
197 *fail*: lack proof.
198 *draw . . . breath*: should be allowed to live long.
206 *secure*: over-confident.

All power's to be feared, where 'tis too much.
The youths are (of themselves) hot, violent,
Full of great thought; and that male-spirited dame,
Their mother, slacks no means to put them on,
By large allowance, popular presentings,
Increase of train, and state, suing for titles,
Hath them commended with like prayers, like vows,
To the same gods, with Caesar: days and nights
She spends in banquets, and ambitious feasts
For the nobility; where Caius Silius,
Titius Sabinus, old Arruntius,
Asinius Gallus, Furnius, Regulus,
And others of that discontented list,
Are the prime guests. There, and to these, she tells
Whose niece she was, whose daughter, and whose wife,
And then must they compare her with Augusta,
Ay, and prefer her too, commend her form,
Extol her fruitfulness; at which a shower
Falls for the memory of Germanicus,
Which they blow over straight, with windy praise,
And puffing hopes of her aspiring sons:
Who, with these hourly ticklings, grow so pleased,
And wantonly conceited of themselves,
As now, they stick not to believe they're such
As these do give 'em out: and would be thought
(More than competitors) immediate heirs.
Whilst to their thirst of rule they win the rout
(That's still the friend of novelty) with hope
Of future freedom, which on every change,
That greedily, though emptily, expects.
Caesar, 'tis age in all things breeds neglects,
And princes that will keep old dignity,

---

210 *hot*: headstrong.
212 *slacks*: neglects.
put them on: encourage them.
213 *large . . . presentings*: indulgent approval, presenting them to the people.
220 *Furnius*: put to death AD 26 for committing adultery with Agrippina's niece, Claudia Pulchra.
Regulus: unlikely to be the Regulus of Act V.
223 *niece*: granddaughter (Latin *neptis*).
230 *ticklings*: gratifications.
234 *competitors*: claimants.
238 *expects*: awaits.

Must not admit too youthful heirs stand by;
Not their own issue: but so darkly set
As shadows are in picture, to give height,
And lustre to themselves.

TIBERIUS. We will command
Their rank thoughts down, and with a stricter hand
Than we have yet put forth, their trains must bate,
Their titles, feasts and factions.

SEJANUS. Or your state.
But how sir, will you work?

TIBERIUS. Confine 'em.

SEJANUS. No.
They are too great, and that too faint a blow,
To give them now: it would have served at first,
When, with the weakest touch, their knot had burst.
But, now, your care must be, not to detect
The smallest cord, or line of your suspect,
For such, who know the weight of princes' fear,
Will, when they find themselves discovered, rear
Their forces, like seen snakes, that else would lie
Rolled in their circles, close: nought is more high,
Daring, or desperate, than offenders found;
Where guilt is, rage and courage both abound.
The course must be, to let 'em still swell up,
Riot, and surfeit on blind Fortune's cup;
Give 'em more place, more dignities, more style,
Call 'em to court, to Senate: in the while,
Take from their strength some one or twain, or more
Of the main fautors (it will fright the store);

242–4 *Not their . . . themselves*: i.e. even their own sons should be kept in the background, to set off the princes' own stature and glory, as shadows set off the subjects of a portrait.
245 *rank*: over-weening, haughty.
246 *trains must bate*: retinues must be diminished.
251 *knot*: band of associates; perhaps also a reference to the intricate Gordian knot, which Alexander the Great burst by cutting it through with his sword.
252 *detect*: reveal.
253 *suspect*: suspicion.
257 *high*: arrogant.
259 *both*: see Textual Note, p. 431 below.
264 *strength*: followers.
265 *fautors*: supporters.
store: group, crowd of them.

And by some by-occasion. Thus, with slight
You shall disarm them first, and they (in night
Of their ambition) not perceive the train,
Till, in the engine, they are caught, and slain.
TIBERIUS. We would not kill, if we knew how to save;
Yet, than a throne, 'tis cheaper give a grave.
Is there no way to bind them by deserts?
SEJANUS. Sir, wolves do change their hair, but not
their hearts.
While thus your thought unto a mean is tied,
You neither dare enough, nor do provide.
All modesty is fond; and chiefly where
The subject is no less compelled to bear,
Than praise his sovereign's acts.
TIBERIUS. We can no longer
Keep on our mask to thee, our dear Sejanus;
Thy thoughts are ours, in all, and we but proved
Their voice, in our designs, which by assenting
Hath more confirmed us, than if heartening Jove
Had, from his hundred statues, bid us strike,
And at the stroke clicked all his marble thumbs.
But who shall first be struck?
SEJANUS. First, Caius Silius;
He is the most of mark, and most of danger:
In power, and reputation equal strong,
Having commanded an imperial army
Seven years together, vanquished Sacrovir
In Germany, and thence obtained to wear
The ornaments triumphal. His steep fall,
By how much it doth give the weightier crack,

---

266 *by-occasion*: incidental opportunity.
slight: small trifles; or perhaps 'sleight', deception.
267 *them*: see Textual Note, p. 431 below.
268 *train*: plot.
269 *engine*: trap.
273 *wolves do change their hair*: proverbial.
275 *provide*: use foresight.
276 *modesty*: moderation.
fond: foolish.
280 *proved*: tested.
281 *voice*: support.
284 *clicked . . . thumbs*: gave the thumbs up sign, which meant death for a defeated gladiator.
286 *of mark*: important.
289 *Sacrovir*: led a revolt in Gaul in AD 21.
291 *ornaments triumphal*: robes and insignia accorded to a victorious general in place of the triumph.

Will send more wounding terror to the rest,
Command them stand aloof, and give more way
To our surprising of the principal.
TIBERIUS. But what, Sabinus?
SEJANUS. Let him grow awhile,
His fate is not yet ripe: we must not pluck
At all together, lest we catch ourselves.
And there's Arruntius too, he only talks.
But Sosia, Silius' wife, would be wound in
Now, for she hath a Fury in her breast
More, than Hell ever knew; and would be sent
Thither in time. Then is there one Cremutius
Cordus, a writing fellow, they have got
To gather notes of the precedent times,
And make them into annals; a most tart
And bitter spirit (I hear) who, under colour
Of praising those, doth tax the present state,
Censures the men, the actions, leaves no trick,
No practice unexamined, parallels
The times, the governments, a professed champion
For the old liberty –
TIBERIUS. A perishing wretch.
As if there were that chaos bred in things,
That laws, and liberty would not rather choose
To be quite broken, and ta'en hence by us,
Than have the stain to be preserved by such.
Have we the means to make these guilty, first?
SEJANUS. Trust that to me: let Caesar, by his power,
But cause a formal meeting of the Senate,
I will have matter, and accusers ready.
TIBERIUS. But how? let us consult.
SEJANUS. We shall misspend
The time of action. Counsels are unfit
In business, where all rest is more pernicious
Than rashness can be. Acts of this close kind
Thrive more by execution, than advice.
There is no lingering in that work begun,
Which cannot praisèd be, until through done.

---

300 *wound in*: ensnared.
302 *More*: greater.
303 *in time*: sooner or later.
312 *perishing*: destructive; perhaps also, 'his fate is sealed'.
325 *advice*: consultation.
327 *through*: thoroughly.

TIBERIUS. Our edict shall, forthwith, command a
court.
While I can live, I will prevent earth's fury:
ἐμοῦ θανόντος γαῖα μιχθήτω πυρί. [*Exit.*]

[*Enter*] POSTHUMUS.

POSTHUMUS. My lord Sejanus –
SEJANUS. Julius Posthumus,
Come with my wish! what news from Agrippina's?
POSTHUMUS. Faith none. They all lock up
themselves a'late;
Or talk in character: I have not seen
A company so changed. Except they had
Intelligence by augury'of our practice.
SEJANUS. When were you there?
POSTHUMUS. Last night.
SEJANUS. And what guests found you?
POSTHUMUS. Sabinus, Silius (the old list), Arruntius,
Furnius, and Gallus.
SEJANUS. Would not these talk?
POSTHUMUS. Little.
And yet we offered choice of argument.
Satrius was with me.
SEJANUS. Well: 'tis guilt enough
Their often meeting. You forgot t'extol
The hospitable lady?
POSTHUMUS. No, that trick
Was well put home, and had succeeded too,
But that Sabinus coughed a caution out;
For she began to swell:
SEJANUS. And may she burst.
Julius, I would have you go instantly
Unto the palace of the great Augusta,
And (by your kindest friend) get swift access;
Acquaint her, with these meetings: tell the words
You brought me (t'other day) of Silius,
Add somewhat to 'em. Make her understand
The danger of Sabinus, and the times,

---

330 a favourite Greek saying of Tiberius's: 'When I am dead, let fire consume the earth.'
334 *character*: code.
340 *argument*: subject.
343 *hospitable*: accented on the first and third syllables.
349 *kindest friend*: *Mutilia Prisca* (Jonson's marginal note).

Out of his closeness. Give Arruntius words
Of malice against Caesar; so, to Gallus:
But (above all) to Agrippina. Say
(As you may truly) that her infinite pride,
Propped with the hopes of her too fruitful womb,
With popular studies gapes for sovereignty;
And threatens Caesar. Pray Augusta then,
That for her own, great Caesar's, and the pub-
Lic safety, she be pleased to urge these dangers.
Caesar is too secure (he must be told,
And best he'll take it from a mother's tongue).
Alas! what is't for us to sound, t'explore,
To watch, oppose, plot, practise, or prevent,
If he, for whom it is so strongly laboured,
Shall, out of greatness, and free spirit, be
Supinely negligent? Our city's now
Divided as in time o'th'civil war,
And men forbear not to declare themselves
Of Agrippina's party. Every day,
The faction multiplies; and will do more
If not resisted: you can best enlarge it
As you find audience. Noble Posthumus,
Commend me to your Prisca: and pray her,
She will solicit this great business
To earnest, and most present execution,
With all her utmost credit with Augusta.

POSTHUMUS. I shall not fail in my instructions.
[*Exit.*]

SEJANUS. This second (from his mother) will well urge
Our late design, and spur on Caesar's rage:
Which else might grow remiss. The way, to put
A prince in blood, is to present the shapes
Of dangers, greater than they are (like late,
Or early shadows) and, sometimes, to feign
Where there are none, only to make him fear;
His fear will make him cruel: and once entered,
He doth not easily learn to stop, or spare

---

354 *Out of his closeness*: arising from his secret plots.
359 *popular studies*: support, devotion (Latin *studium*) of the people.
gapes for: covets.
361–2 *pub-Lic*: a classicism, *synapheia*, found in Horace and Catullus, and, among seventeenth-century poets, Donne and Herrick.
368 *free*: noble.

Where he may doubt. This have I made my rule,
To thrust Tiberius into tyranny,
And make him toil, to turn aside those blocks,
Which I alone, could not remove with safety.
Drusus once gone, Germanicus' three sons
Would clog my way; whose guards have too much faith
To be corrupted: and their mother known
Of too too unreproved a chastity,
To be attempted, as light Livia was.
Work then, my art, on Caesar's fears, as they
On those they fear, till all my lets be cleared:
And he in ruins of his house, and hate
Of all his subjects, bury his own state:
When, with my peace, and safety, I will rise,
By making him the public sacrifice. [*Exit.*]

[SCENE III]

[*Enter*] SATRIUS, NATTA.

SATRIUS. They're grown exceeding circumspect, and wary.
NATTA. They have us in the wind: and yet Arruntius
Cannot contain himself.
SATRIUS. Tut, he's not yet
Looked after, there are others more desired,
That are more silent.
NATTA. Here he comes. Away.
[*Exeunt* SATRIUS, NATTA.]

[*Enter*] SABINUS, ARRUNTIUS, CORDUS.

SABINUS. How is it, that these beagles haunt the house
Of Agrippina?
ARRUNTIUS. Oh, they hunt, they hunt.
There is some game here lodged, which they must rouse,

---

390 *doubt*: suspect.
398 *attempted*: tempted.
400 *lets*: see Textual Note, p. 431 below.
406 *have us in the wind*: have scent of us.
412 *lodged*: gone to its lair (hunting term).

To make the great one's sport.
CORDUS. Did you observe
How they inveighed 'gainst Caesar?
ARRUNTIUS. Ay, baits, baits,
For us to bite at: would I have my flesh
Torn by the public hook, these qualified hangmen
Should be my company.
CORDUS. Here comes another.

[AFER *passeth by*.]

ARRUNTIUS. Ay, there's a man, Afer the orator!
One that hath phrases, figures, and fine flowers,
To strew his rhetoric with, and doth make haste
To get him note, or name, by any offer
Where blood, or gain be objects; steeps his words,
When he would kill, in artificial tears:
The crocodile of Tiber! him I love,
That man is mine. He hath my heart, and voice,
When I would curse, he, he.
SABINUS. Contemn the slaves,
Their present lives will be their future graves.
[*Exeunt* SABINUS, ARRUNTIUS, CORDUS.]

[*Enter*] SILIUS, AGRIPPINA, NERO, SOSIA.

SILIUS. May't please your highness not forget yourself,
I dare not, with my manners, to attempt
Your trouble farther.
AGRIPPINA. Farewell, noble Silius.
SILIUS. Most royal princess.
AGRIPPINA. Sosia stays with us?
SILIUS. She is your servant, and doth owe your grace
An honest, but unprofitable love.
AGRIPPINA. How can that be, when there's no gain, but virtue's?
SILIUS. You take the moral, not the politic sense.
I meant, as she is bold, and free of speech,

---

416 *public hook*: executioner's hook, by which executed criminals were dragged to the Gemonian steps and, three days later, to the Tiber.
qualified: fit (to be).
417 s.d. AFER *passeth by*: see Textual Note, p. 431 below.
419 *phrases, figures, and fine flowers*: rhetorical devices and ornaments.
434 *virtue's*: see Textual Note, p. 431 below.

Earnest to utter what her zealous thought
Travails withal, in honour of your house;
Which act, as it is simply born in her,
Partakes of love, and honesty, but may,
By th'over-often, and unseasoned use,
Turn to your loss, and danger: for your state
Is waited on by envies, as by eyes;
And every second guest your tables take
Is a fee'd spy, t'observe who goes, who comes,
What conference you have, with whom, where,
when,
What the discourse is, what the looks, the thoughts
Of every person there, they do extract,
And make into a substance.
AGRIPPINA. Hear me, Silius,
Were all Tiberius' body stuck with eyes,
And every wall, and hanging in my house
Transparent, as this lawn I wear, or air;
Yea, had Sejanus both his ears as long
As to my inmost closet: I would hate
To whisper any thought, or change an act,
To be made Juno's rival. Virtue's forces
Show ever noblest in conspicuous courses.
SILIUS. 'Tis great, and bravely spoken, like the spirit
Of Agrippina: yet your highness knows,
There is nor loss, nor shame in providence:
Few can, what all should do, beware enough.
You may perceive with what officious face,
Satrius, and Natta, Afer, and the rest
Visit your house, of late, t'enquire the secrets;
And with what bold, and privileged art, they rail
Against Augusta: yea, and at Tiberius,
Tell tricks of Livia and Sejanus, all
T'excite, and call your indignation on,
That they might hear it at more liberty.
AGRIPPINA. Yo'are too suspicious, Silius.

---

439 *simply*: sincerely.
441 *unseasoned*: untimely.
443 *envies*: malignant enmities, but see 450.
448–9 *do extract . . . substance*: take parts of, and make these into a summary of the whole proceedings.
449 AGRIPPINA: see Textual Note, p. 431 below.
450 *stuck with eyes*: as allegorical figures of envy, rumour and ill-report were commonly represented.
460 *providence*: foresight.

SILIUS. Pray the gods,
I be so Agrippina: but I fear
Some subtle practice. They, that durst to strike
At so exampless, and unblamed a life,
As that of the renowned Germanicus,
Will not sit down with that exploit alone:
He threatens many, that hath injured one.
NERO. 'Twere best rip forth their tongues, sear out their eyes,
When next they come.
SOSIA. A fit reward for spies.

[*Enter*] DRUSUS JUNIOR.

DRUSUS JUNIOR. Hear you the rumour?
AGRIPPINA. What?
DRUSUS JUNIOR. Drusus is dying.
AGRIPPINA. Dying?
NERO. That's strange!
AGRIPPINA. Yo'were with him, yesternight.
DRUSUS JUNIOR. One met Eudemus, the physician,
Sent for but now: who thinks he cannot live.
SILIUS. Thinks? if't be arrived at that, he knows,
Or none.
AGRIPPINA. This's quick! what should be his disease?
SILIUS. Poison. Poison –
AGRIPPINA. How, Silius!
NERO. What's that?
SILIUS. Nay, nothing. There was (late) a certain blow
Given o'the face.
NERO. Ay, to Sejanus?
SILIUS. True.
DRUSUS JUNIOR. And what of that?
SILIUS. I'm glad I gave it not.
NERO. But there is somewhat else?
SILIUS. Yes, private meetings,
With a great lady, at a physician's,
And a wife turned away –
NERO. Ha!
SILIUS. Toys, mere toys:
What wisdom's now i'th'streets? i'th'common mouth?
DRUSUS JUNIOR. Fears, whisperings, tumults, noise,

---

473 *exampless*: i.e. 'example-less', unexampled.
491 *Toys*: trifles.

I know not what:
They say, the Senate sit.
SILIUS. I'll thither, straight;
And see what's in the forge.
AGRIPPINA. Good Silius, do.
Sosia and I will in.
SILIUS. Haste you, my lords,
To visit the sick prince: tender your loves,
And sorrows to the people. This Sejanus
(Trust my divining soul) hath plots on all:
No tree, that stops his prospect, but must fall.
[*Exeunt.*]

Chorus – of musicians.

ACT III

[SCENE I:] *The Senate.*

[*Enter*] SEJANUS, VARRO, LATIARIS, COTTA, AFER: PRAECONES, LICTORES.

SEJANUS. 'Tis only you must urge against him, Varro,
Nor I, nor Caesar may appear therein,
Except in your defence, who are the consul:
And, under colour of late enmity
Between your father and his, may better do it,
As free from all suspicion of a practice.
Here be your notes, what points to touch at; read:
Be cunning in them. Afer has them too.
VARRO. But is he summoned?
SEJANUS. No. It was debated
By Caesar, and concluded as most fit
To take him unprepared.
AFER. And prosecute
All under name of treason.

---

500 *prospect*: view; also, 'expectations'.
1 *urge*: bring forward (an accusation).
5 *his*: should read 'him'. See Additional Note, p. 437 below.
8 *cunning*: knowledgeable, well versed.
11 *take him*: see Textual Note, p. 431 below.

VARRO. I conceive.

[*Enter* SABINUS,] GALLUS, LEPIDUS, ARRUNTIUS.

SABINUS. Drusus being dead, Caesar will not be here.
GALLUS. What should the business of this Senate be?
ARRUNTIUS. That can my subtle whisperers tell you: we,
That are the good-dull-noble lookers-on,
Are only called to keep the marble warm.
What should we do with those deep mysteries,
Proper to these fine heads? let them alone.
Our ignorance may, perchance, help us be saved
From whips, and Furies.
GALLUS. See, see, see, their action!
ARRUNTIUS. Ay, now their heads do travail, now they work;
Their faces run like shuttles, they are weaving
Some curious cobweb to catch flies.
SABINUS. Observe,
They take their places.
ARRUNTIUS. What, so low?
GALLUS. Oh yes,
They must be seen to flatter Caesar's grief
Though but in sitting.
VARRO. Bid us silence.
PRAECO. Silence.
VARRO. 'Fathers conscript, may this our present meeting
Turn fair, and fortunate to the Commonwealth.'

[*Enter*] SILIUS.

SEJANUS. See, Silius enters.
SILIUS. Hail, grave fathers.
LICTOR. Stand.
Silius, forbear thy place.
SENATORS. How!

---

12 *conceive*: understand.
21 *whips, and Furies*: torments of the wicked in Hades.
action: activity; also, 'gestures' (theatrical term).
24 *curious*: intricate.
28 *conscript*: enrolled members added to the Senate on the establishment of the Republic.
30 SEJANUS: see Textual Note, p. 431 below.

PRAECO. Silius, stand forth,
The consul hath to charge thee.
LICTOR. Room for Caesar.
ARRUNTIUS. Is he come too? Nay then expect a trick.
SABINUS. Silius accused? Sure he will answer nobly.

[*Enter*] TIBERIUS [*and attendants*].

TIBERIUS. We stand amazed, fathers, to behold
This general dejection. Wherefore sit
Rome's consuls thus dissolved, as they had lost
All the remembrance both of style, and place?
It not becomes. No woes are of fit weight
To make the honour of the Empire stoop:
Though I, in my peculiar self, may meet
Just reprehension, that so suddenly,
And in so fresh a grief, would greet the Senate,
When private tongues, of kinsmen, and allies
(Inspired with comforts), loathly are endured,
The face of men not seen, and scarce the day,
To thousands, that communicate our loss.
Nor can I argue these of weakness; since
They take but natural ways: yet I must seek
For stronger aids, and those fair helps draw out
From warm embraces of the Commonwealth.
Our mother, great Augusta, 's struck with time,
Ourself impressed with agèd characters,
Drusus is gone, his children young, and babes,
Our aims must now reflect on those, that may
Give timely succour to these present ills,
And are our only glad-surviving hopes,
The noble issue of Germanicus,
Nero, and Drusus: might it please the consul
Honour them in (they both attend without).
I would present them to the Senate's care,
And raise those suns of joy, that should drink up
These floods of sorrow, in your drownèd eyes.
ARRUNTIUS. By Jove, I am not Oedipus enough,

---

37 *dissolved*: negligent (Latin *dissolutus*).
38 *style*: title.
41 *peculiar self*: own person.
44 *allies*: relatives.
47 *communicate*: share (Latin *communico*).
48 *argue*: convict.
53 *impressed with agèd characters*: scored with marks of age.
64 *Oedipus*: who freed Thebes from the tyranny of the Sphinx by answering its riddle.

To understand this Sphinx.
SABINUS. The princes come.

[*Enter*] NERO, DRUSUS JUNIOR.

TIBERIUS. Approach you, noble Nero, noble Drusus,
These princes, fathers, when their parent died,
I gave unto their uncle, with this prayer,
That, though he'd proper issue of his own,
He would no less bring up, and foster these,
Than that self blood; and by that act confirm
Their worths to him, and to posterity:
Drusus ta'en hence, I turn my prayers to you,
And 'fore our country, and our gods, beseech
You take, and rule Augustus' nephew's sons,
Sprung of the noblest ancestors; and so
Accomplish both my duty, and your own.
Nero, and Drusus, these shall be to you
In place of parents, these your fathers, these,
And not unfitly: for you are so born,
As all your good, or ill's the Commonwealth's.
Receive them, you strong guardians; and blest gods,
Make all their actions answer to their bloods:
Let their great titles find increase by them,
Not they by titles. Set them, as in place,
So in example, above all the Romans:
And may they know no rivals, but themselves.
Let Fortune give them nothing; but attend
Upon their virtue; and that still come forth
Greater than hope, and better than their fame.
Relieve me, fathers, with your general voice.
SENATORS. 'May all the gods consent to Caesar's wish,
And add to any honours, that may crown
The hopeful issue of Germanicus.'
TIBERIUS. We thank you, reverend fathers, in their right.
ARRUNTIUS. If this were true now! But the space, the space
Between the breast, and lips – Tiberius' heart
Lies a thought farther, than another man's.

---

65 *Sphinx*: a monster with the face and bust of a woman, the wings of an eagle, and the body of a lion.
68 *uncle*: Drusus.
92 'A form of speaking they had' (Jonson's marginal note).

TIBERIUS. My comforts are so flowing in my joys,
As, in them, all my streams of grief are lost,
No less than are land-waters in the sea,
Or showers in rivers; though their cause was such,
As might have sprinkled ev'n the gods with tears:
Yet since the greater doth embrace the less,
We covetously obey.
ARRUNTIUS. [*aside*] (Well acted, Caesar.)
TIBERIUS. And now I am the happy witness made
Of your so much desired affections,
To this great issue, I could wish the Fates
Would here set peaceful period to my days;
However, to my labours, I entreat
(And beg it of this Senate) some fit ease.
ARRUNTIUS. [*aside*] (Laugh, fathers, laugh: ha'you no spleens about you?)
TIBERIUS. The burden is too heavy I sustain
On my unwilling shoulders; and I pray
It may be taken off, and reconferred
Upon the consuls, or some other Roman,
More able, and more worthy.
ARRUNTIUS. [*aside*] (Laugh on, still.)
SABINUS. Why, this doth render all the rest suspected!
GALLUS. It poisons all.
ARRUNTIUS. Oh, do you taste it then?
SABINUS. It takes away my faith to anything
He shall hereafter speak.
ARRUNTIUS. Ay, to pray that,
Which would be to his head as hot as thunder
('Gainst which he wears that charm), should but the court
Receive him at his word.
GALLUS. Hear.
TIBERIUS. For myself,
I know my weakness, and so little covet

---

105 *covetously*: eagerly.
108 *Fates*: in classical mythology, the three sisters who apportioned to man his share of good and evil, and finally cut his thread of life.
112 *spleens*: the spleen was believed to be the seat of laughter.
119 *taste*: perceive.
123 *charm*: 'A wreath of laurel' (Jonson's marginal note), a preservative against the thunderbolt.

(Like some gone past) the weight that will oppress me,
As my ambition is the counter-point.
ARRUNTIUS. [*aside*] (Finely maintained; good still.)
SEJANUS. But Rome, whose blood,
Whose nerves, whose life, whose very frame relies
On Caesar's strength, no less than Heav'n on Atlas,
Cannot admit it but with general ruin.
ARRUNTIUS. [*aside*] (Ah! are you there, to bring him off?)
SEJANUS. Let Caesar
No more then urge a point so contrary
To Caesar's greatness, the grieved Senate's vows,
Or Rome's necessity.
GALLUS. [*aside to* ARRUNTIUS] (He comes about.
ARRUNTIUS. [*aside to* GALLUS] More nimbly than Vertumnus.)
TIBERIUS. For the public,
I may be drawn, to show, I can neglect
All private aims; though I affect my rest:
But if the Senate still command me serve,
I must be glad to practise my obedience.
ARRUNTIUS. [*aside*] (You must, and will, sir. We do know it.)
SENATORS. 'Caesar,
Live long, and happy, great, and royal Caesar,
The gods preserve thee, and thy modesty,
Thy wisdom, and thy innocence.'
ARRUNTIUS. [*aside*] (Where is't?
The prayer's made before the subject.)
SENATORS. 'Guard
His meekness, Jove, his piety, his care,
His bounty – '
ARRUNTIUS. [*aside*] And his subtlety, I'll put in:

---

127 *counter-point*: exact opposite.
129 *nerves*: sinews.
130 *Atlas*: Titan condemned to bear the vault of Heaven on his shoulders.
131 *admit*: permit.
132 *bring him off*: help him.
135 *comes about*: veers round.
136 *Vertumnus*: god of the changing year.
138 *affect*: desire.
142 'Another form' (i.e. of speech – Jonson's marginal note).

Yet he'll keep that himself, without the gods.
All prayers are vain for him.

TIBERIUS. We will not hold
Your patience, fathers, with long answer; but
Shall still contend to be what you desire,
And work to satisfy so great a hope:
Proceed to your affairs.

ARRUNTIUS. Now, Silius, guard thee;
The curtain's drawing. Afer advanceth.

PRAECO. Silence.

AFER. Cite Caius Silius.

PRAECO. Caius Silius.

SILIUS. Here.

AFER. The triumph that thou hadst in Germany
For thy late victory on Sacrovir,
Thou hast enjoyed so freely, Caius Silius,
As no man it envied thee; nor would Caesar,
Or Rome admit, that thou wert then defrauded
Of any honours thy deserts could claim,
In the fair service of the Commonwealth:
But now, if, after all their loves, and graces
(Thy actions, and their courses being discovered),
It shall appear to Caesar, and this Senate,
Thou hast defiled those glories, with thy crimes –

SILIUS. Crimes?

AFER. Patience, Silius.

SILIUS. Tell thy moile of patience,
I am a Roman. What are my crimes? Proclaim
them.
Am I too rich? too honest for the times?
Have I or treasure, jewels, land, or houses
That some informer gapes for? Is my strength
Too much to be admitted? Or my knowledge?
These now are crimes.

AFER. Nay, Silius, if the name
Of crime so touch thee, with what impotence
Wilt thou endure the matter to be searched?

SILIUS. I tell thee, Afer, with more scorn, than fear:
Employ your mercenary tongue, and art.
Where's my accuser?

---

154 *The curtain's drawing*: the plot is about to be revealed. See Additional Note, p. 437 below.

167 *moile*: mule; the lawyer's mount (see *Volpone*, I.ii.107).

174 *impotence*: lack of self-restraint (Latin *impotentia*).

VARRO. Here.
ARRUNTIUS. Varro? The consul?
Is he thrust in?
VARRO. 'Tis I accuse thee, Silius.
Against the majesty of Rome, and Caesar,
I do pronounce thee here a guilty cause,
First, of beginning, and occasioning,
Next, drawing out the war in Gallia,
For which thou late triumph'st; dissembling long
That Sacrovir to be an enemy,
Only to make thy entertainment more,
Whilst thou, and thy wife Sosia polled the
province;
Wherein, with sordid-base desire of gain,
Thou hast discredited thy action's worth
And been a traitor to the state.
SILIUS. Thou liest.
ARRUNTIUS. I thank thee, Silius, speak so still, and
often.
VARRO. If I not prove it, Caesar, but injustly
Have called him into trial, here I bind
Myself to suffer, what I claim 'gainst him;
And yield, to have what I have spoke, confirmed
By judgement of the court, and all good men.
SILIUS. Caesar, I crave to have my cause deferred,
Till this man's consulship be out.
TIBERIUS. We cannot,
Nor may we grant it.
SILIUS. Why? shall he design
My day of trial? Is he my accuser,
And must he be my judge?
TIBERIUS. It hath been usual,
And is a right, that custom hath allowed
The magistrate, to call forth private men;
And to appoint their day: which privilege
We may not in the consul see infringed,
By whose deep watches, and industrious care

---

181 *cause*: agent.
184–7 *dissembling long . . . polled the province*: see Additional Note, p. 437 below.
186 *entertainment*: employment.
187 *polled*: fleeced.
199–200 *design . . . trial*: bring a prosecution (Latin *diem dicere*); identical in meaning with *appoint their day* at 204.
206 *deep watches*: careful, thorough watchfulness.

It is so laboured, as the Commonwealth
Receive no loss, by any oblique course.
SILIUS. Caesar, thy fraud is worse than violence.
TIBERIUS. Silius, mistake us not, we dare not use
The credit of the consul, to thy wrong,
But only do preserve his place, and power,
So far as it concerns the dignity,
And honour of the state.
ARRUNTIUS. Believe him, Silius.
COTTA. Why, so he may, Arruntius.
ARRUNTIUS. I say so.
And he may choose to.
TIBERIUS. By the Capitol,
And all our gods, but that the dear Republic,
Our sacred laws, and just authority
Are interessed therein, I should be silent.
AFER. Please Caesar to give way unto his trial.
He shall have justice.
SILIUS. Nay, I shall have law;
Shall I not Afer? speak.
AFER. Would you have more?
SILIUS. No, my well-spoken man, I would no more;
Nor less; might I enjoy it natural,
Not taught to speak unto your present ends,
Free from thine, his, and all your unkind handling,
Furious enforcing, most unjust presuming,
Malicious, and manifold applying,
Foul wresting, and impossible construction.
AFER. He raves, he raves.
SILIUS. Thou durst not tell me so,
Hadst thou not Caesar's warrant. I can see
Whose power condemns me.
VARRO. This betrays his spirit.
This doth enough declare him what he is.
SILIUS. What am I? speak.
VARRO. An enemy to the state.

---

207 *as*: so that.
216 *to*: see Textual Note, p. 431 below.
Capitol: Rome's national temple, dedicated to Jupiter.
217 *Republic*: state (Latin *res publica*).
219 *interessed*: concerned.
224 *natural*: instinctively felt to be right and fair.
226 *unkind*: unnatural; also, 'cruel'.
227 *Furious enforcing*: fierce pressing home.
229 *construction*: interpretation.

SILIUS. Because I am an enemy to thee,
And such corrupted ministers o'the state,
That here art made a present instrument
To gratify it with thine own disgrace.
SEJANUS. This, to the consul, is most insolent!
And impious!
SILIUS. Ay, take part. Reveal yourselves.
Alas, I scent not your confederacies?
Your plots, and combinations? I not know
Minion Sejanus hates me; and that all
This boast of law, and law, is but a form,
A net of Vulcan's filing, a mere engine,
To take that life by a pretext of justice,
Which you pursue in malice? I want brain,
Or nostril to persuade me, that your ends,
And purposes are made to what they are,
Before my answer? O, you equal gods,
Whose justice not a world of wolf-turned men
Shall make me to accuse (how e'er provoke)
Have I for this so oft engaged myself?
Stood in the heat, and fervour of a fight,
When Phoebus sooner hath forsook the day
Than I the field? Against the blue-eyed Gauls?
And crispèd Germans? when our Roman eagles
Have fanned the fire, with their labouring wings,
And no blow dealt, that left not death behind it?
When I have charged, alone, into the troops
Of curled Sicambrians, routed them, and came
Not off, with backward ensigns of a slave,
But forward marks, wounds on my breast, and
face,

---

237 *present instrument*: tool for the occasion.
242 *combinations*: conspiracies.
245 *filing*: fine workmanship; also, 'artful trap' (like the net in which Vulcan caught his wife Venus and her lover Mars).
248 *nostril*: perception (the Latin usage implies scorn).
250 *equal*: impartial, just.
252 *provoke*: provoked.
253 *engaged*: exposed to risk.
257 *crispèd*: curly-haired.
Roman eagles: the eagle images of the legionary standards.
261 *curled*: curly-haired.
Sicambrians: Sugambrians, a Germanic tribe.
262 *backward ensigns*: marks on the back (such as a coward or a slave would bear).
263 *forward*: on the front; perhaps also, 'zealous' – 'wounds which declared my zeal'.

Were meant to thee, O Caesar, and thy Rome?
And have I this return? Did I, for this,
Perform so noble, and so brave defeat,
On Sacrovir? (O Jove, let it become me
To boast my deeds, when he, whom they concern,
Shall thus forget them.)

AFER. Silius, Silius,
These are the common customs of thy blood,
When it is high with wine, as now with rage:
This well agrees with that intemperate vaunt,
Thou lately mad'st at Agrippina's table,
That when all other of the troops were prone
To fall into rebellion, only yours
Remained in their obedience. You were he,
That saved the Empire; which had then been lost,
Had but your legions, there, rebelled, or mutined.
Your virtue met, and fronted every peril.
You gave to Caesar, and to Rome their surety.
Their name, their strength, their spirit, and their state,
Their being was a donative from you.

ARRUNTIUS. Well worded, and most like an orator.

TIBERIUS. Is this true, Silius?

SILIUS. Save thy question, Caesar.
Thy spy, of famous credit, hath affirmed it.

ARRUNTIUS. Excellent Roman!

SABINUS. He doth answer stoutly.

SEJANUS. If this be so, there needs no farther cause
Of crime against him.

VARRO. What can more impeach
The royal dignity, and state of Caesar,
Than to be urgèd with a benefit
He cannot pay?

COTTA. In this, all Caesar's fortune
Is made unequal to the courtesy.

---

270 *blood*: disposition, temperament.
278 *mutined*: mutinied.
279 *fronted*: confronted.
280 *surety*: security, safety.
282 *donative*: bountiful gift.
285 *famous credit*: ironically ambiguous – 'famous for truth', and 'of infamous reputation'.
288 *crime*: accusation.
290 *urgèd*: strongly charged.

LATIARIS. His means are clean destroyed, that
should requite.
GALLUS. Nothing is great enough for Silius' merit.
ARRUNTIUS. [*aside*] Gallus on that side too?
SILIUS. Come, do not hunt,
And labour so about for circumstance,
To make him guilty, whom you have foredoomed:
Take shorter ways, I'll meet your purposes.
The words were mine, and more I now will say:
Since I have done thee that great service, Caesar,
Thou still hast feared me; and in place of grace,
Returned me hatred: so soon, all best turns,
With doubtful princes, turn deep injuries
In estimation, when they greater rise,
Than can be answered. Benefits, with you,
Are of no longer pleasure, than you can
With ease restore them; that transcended once,
Your studies are not how to thank, but kill.
It is your nature, to have all men slaves
To you, but you acknowledging to none.
The means that makes your greatness, must not
come
In mention of it; if it do, it takes
So much away, you think: and that, which helped,
Shall soonest perish, if it stand in eye,
Where it may front, or but upbraid the high.
COTTA. Suffer him speak no more.
VARRO. Note but his spirit.
AFER. This shows him in the rest.
LATIARIS. Let him be censured.
SEJANUS. He hath spoke enough to prove him
Caesar's foe.
COTTA. His thoughts look through his words.
SEJANUS. A censure.
SILIUS. Stay,
Stay, most officious Senate, I shall straight
Delude thy fury. Silius hath not placed
His guards within him, against Fortune's spite,

---

296 *circumstance*: compare 'circumstantial evidence'.
303 *With doubtful princes, turn deep*: see Textual Note, p. 431 below.
314 *eye*: sight, view.
315 *front*: affront.
317 *censured*: judged.
319 *censure*: judgement.

So weakly, but he can escape your gripe
That are but hands of Fortune: she herself
When virtue doth oppose, must lose her threats.
All that can happen in humanity,
The frown of Caesar, proud Sejanus' hatred,
Base Varro's spleen, and Afer's bloodying tongue,
The Senate's servile flattery, and these
Mustered to kill, I am fortified against;
And can look down upon: they are beneath me.
It is not life whereof I stand enamoured:
Nor shall my end make me accuse my fate.
The coward, and the valiant man must fall,
Only the cause, and manner how, discerns them:
Which then are gladdest, when they cost us
dearest.
Romans, if any here be in this Senate,
Would know to mock Tiberius' tyranny,
Look upon Silius, and so learn to die.
[*Stabs himself.*]

VARRO. O, desperate act!
ARRUNTIUS. An honourable hand!
TIBERIUS. Look, is he dead?
SABINUS. 'Twas nobly struck, and home.
ARRUNTIUS. My thought did prompt him to it.
Farewell, Silius.
Be famous ever for thy great example.
TIBERIUS. We are not pleased in this sad accident,
That thus hath stallèd, and abused our mercy,
Intended to preserve thee, noble Roman:
And to prevent thy hopes.
ARRUNTIUS. [*aside*] Excellent wolf!
Now he is full, he howls.
SEJANUS. Caesar doth wrong
His dignity, and safety, thus to mourn
The deserved end of so professed a traitor,
And doth, by this his lenity, instruct
Others as factious, to the like offence.
TIBERIUS. The confiscation merely of his state
Had been enough.
ARRUNTIUS. [*aside*] Oh, that was gaped for then?

---

335 *discerns*: distinguishes.
336 *gladdest*: most welcome.
345 *stallèd*: forestalled.
347 *prevent*: anticipate.
353 *state*: estate.

VARRO. Remove the body.
SEJANUS. Let citation
Go out for Sosia.
GALLUS. Let her be proscribed.
And for the goods, I think it fit that half
Go to the treasure, half unto the children.
LEPIDUS. With leave of Caesar, I would think that fourth
Part, which the law doth cast on the informers,
Should be enough; the rest go to the children:
Wherein the prince shall show humanity,
And bounty, not to force them by their want
(Which in their parents' trespass they deserved)
To take ill courses.
TIBERIUS. It shall please us.
ARRUNTIUS. [*aside to* SABINUS] Ay,
Out of necessity. This Lepidus
Is grave and honest, and I have observed
A moderation still in all his censures.
SABINUS. And bending to the better – Stay, who's this?

[*Enter* CORDUS, *guarded;* SATRIUS, NATTA.]

Cremutius Cordus? What? is he brought in?
ARRUNTIUS. More blood unto the banquet? Noble Cordus,
I wish thee good: be as thy writings, free,
And honest.
TIBERIUS. [*aside to* SEJANUS] What is he?
SEJANUS. [*aside to* TIBERIUS] For th'annals, Caesar.
PRAECO. Cremutius Cordus.
CORDUS. Here.
PRAECO. Satrius Secundus,
Pinnarius Natta, you are his accusers.
ARRUNTIUS. Two of Sejanus' bloodhounds, whom he breeds
With human flesh, to bay at citizens.
AFER. Stand forth before the Senate, and confront him.
SATRIUS. I do accuse thee here, Cremutius Cordus,

---

355 *citation*: summoning to the court of justice.
356 *proscribed*: condemned (to exile).
358 *treasure*: treasury.
372 *free*: noble.

To be a man factious, and dangerous,
A sower of sedition in the state,
A turbulent, and discontented spirit,
Which I will prove from thine own writings, here,
The annals thou hast published; where thou bit'st
The present age, and with a viper's tooth,
Being a member of it, dar'st that ill
Which never yet degenerous bastard did
Upon his parent.

NATTA. To this, I subscribe;
And forth a world of more particulars,
Instance in only one: comparing men
And times, thou praisest Brutus, and affirm'st
That Cassius was the last of all the Romans.

COTTA. How! what are we then?

VARRO. What is Caesar? nothing?

AFER. My lords, this strikes at every Roman's private,
In whom reigns gentry, and estate of spirit,
To have a Brutus brought in parallel,
A parricide, an enemy of his country,
Ranked, and preferred to any real worth
That Rome now holds. This is most strangely invective.
Most full of spite, and insolent upbraiding.
Nor is't the time alone is here disprized,
But the whole man of time, yea Caesar's self
Brought in disvalue; and he aimed at most
By òblique glance of his licentious pen.
Caesar, if Cassius were the last of Romans,
Thou hast no name.

TIBERIUS. Let's hear him answer. Silence.

CORDUS. So innocent I am of fact, my lords,
As but my words are argued; yet those words
Not reaching either prince, or prince's parent:

---

385 *viper's tooth*: symbolic of ingratitude (vipers were believed to eat their way out of their mother's body).
387 *degenerous*: unworthy of family.
390 *Instance in*: cite an instance in proof.
394 *private*: personal honour.
395 *estate*: nobility.
397 *parricide*: traitor (Latin *parricida*).
399 *invective*: abusive.
402 *whole*: greatest.
407 *fact*: deed.
408 *argued*: called in question.
409 *parent*: kinsman.

The which your law of treason comprehends.
Brutus, and Cassius, I am charged t'have praised:
Whose deeds, when many more, besides myself,
Have writ, not one hath mentioned without honour.
Great Titus Livius, great for eloquence,
And faith, amongst us, in his history,
With so great praises Pompey did extol,
As oft Augustus called him a Pompeian:
Yet this not hurt their friendship. In his book
He often names Scipio, Afranius,
Yea, the same Cassius, and this Brutus too,
As worthi'st men; not thieves, and parricides,
Which notes, upon their fames, are now imposed.
Asinius Pollio's writings quite throughout
Give them a noble memory; so Messalla
Renowned his general Cassius: yet both these
Lived with Augustus, full of wealth, and honours.
To Cicero's book, where Cato was heaved up
Equal with Heav'n, what else did Caesar answer,
Being then dictator, but with a penned oration,
As if before the judges? Do but see
Antonius' letters; read but Brutus' pleadings:
What vile reproach they hold against Augustus,
False I confess, but with much bitterness.
The epigrams of Bibaculus, and Catullus,
Are read, full stuffed with spite of both the Caesars;
Yet deified Julius, and no less Augustus!
Both bore them, and contemned them (I not know

---

414 *Titus Livius*: Livy, the Roman historian.
415 *faith*: truth.
419 *Scipio*: Metullus Scipio, Pompey's father-in-law.
Afranius: Lucius Afranius, consul and follower of Pompey.
422 *notes*: blots (from Latin *nota censoria*, a mark put against the name of those censured).
423 *Asinius Pollio*: Augustan poet and historian.
424 *Messalla*: Marcus Corvinus, second-in-command to Brutus and Cassius at Philippi; later wrote a history of the civil war.
427 *Cicero's book*: the *Cato* (now lost) of Cicero, Roman statesman and orator.
431 *Antonius' letters*: Mark Antony's, quoted by the historian Suetonius in his *Augustus*.
Brutus' pleadings: now lost.
434 *Bibaculus*: Roman poet, whose *Epigrams* are now lost.
Catullus: Roman lyric poet, whose abuse of Julius Caesar is in *Poems*, 11, 29, 54, 57, 93.

Promptly to speak it, whether done with more
Temper, or wisdom): for such obloquies
If they despisèd be, they die suppressed,
But if with rage acknowledged, they are confessed.
The Greeks I slip, whose licence not alone,
But also lust did 'scape unpunishèd:
Or where someone (by chance) exception took,
He words with words revenged. But, in my work,
What could be aimed more free, or farther off
From the time's scandal, than to write of those,
Whom death from grace, or hatred had exempted?
Did I, with Brutus, and with Cassius,
Armed, and possessed of the Philippi fields,
Incense the people in the civil cause,
With dangerous speeches? or do they, being slain
Seventy years since, as by their images
(Which not the conqueror hath defaced) appears,
Retain that guilty memory with writers?
Posterity pays every man his honour.
Nor shall there want, though I condemnèd am,
That will not only Cassius well approve,
And of great Brutus' honour mindful be,
But that will, also, mention make of me.

ARRUNTIUS. Freely, and nobly spoken.

SABINUS. With good temper.
I like him, that he is not moved with passion.

ARRUNTIUS. He puts 'em to their whisper.

TIBERIUS. Take him hence,
We shall determine of him at next sitting.

[*Exit* CORDUS, *guarded.*]

COTTA. Meantime, give order that his books be burnt,
To the aediles.

SEJANUS. You have well advised.

AFER. It fits not such licentious things should live
T'upbraid the age.

ARRUNTIUS. If th'age were good, they might.

LATIARIS. Let 'em be burnt.

---

438 *Promptly to speak*: readily how to describe.
439 *Temper*: moderation.
442 *licence*: flouting of decorum (in attacking prominent Athenians in the Old Comedy).
446 *aimed more free*: intended more innocently.
453 *images*: statues.
455 *Retain that*: i.e. retain only that.
466 *aediles*: officers responsible for public order.

GALLUS. All sought, and burnt, today.
PRAECO. The Court is up, lictors, resume the fasces.
[*Exeunt all but*] ARRUNTIUS,
SABINUS, LEPIDUS.
ARRUNTIUS. Let 'em be burnt! Oh, how ridiculous
Appears the Senate's brainless diligence,
Who think they can, with present power, extinguish
The memory of all succeeding times!
SABINUS. 'Tis true, when (contrary) the punishment
Of wit doth make th'authority increase.
Nor do they aught, that use this cruelty
Of interdiction, and this rage of burning;
But purchase to themselves rebuke, and shame,
And to the writers an eternal name.
LEPIDUS. It is an argument the times are sore,
When virtue cannot safely be advanced;
Nor vice reproved.
ARRUNTIUS. Ay, noble Lepidus,
Augustus well foresaw what we should suffer,
Under Tiberius, when he did pronounce
The Roman race most wretched, that should live
Between so slow jaws, and so long a-bruising.
[*Exeunt.*]

[SCENE II]

[*Enter*] TIBERIUS, SEJANUS.

TIBERIUS. This business hath succeeded well, Sejanus:
And quite removed all jealousy of practice
'Gainst Agrippina, and our nephews. Now,
We must bethink us how to plant our engines
For t'other pair, Sabinus, and Arruntius,
And Gallus too (howe'er he flatter us),
His heart we know.
SEJANUS. Give it some respite, Caesar.
Time shall mature, and bring to perfect crown,

---

476 *wit*: learning.
481 *sore*: sick.
495 *crown*: fulfilment.

What we, with so good vultures, have begun:
Sabinus shall be next.
TIBERIUS. Rather Arruntius.
SEJANUS. By any means, preserve him. His frank tongue
Being lent the reins, will take away all thought
Of malice, in your course against the rest.
We must keep him to stalk with.
TIBERIUS. Dearest head,
To thy most fortunate design I yield it.
SEJANUS. Sir – I have been so long trained up in grace,
First, with your father, great Augustus, since,
With your most happy bounties so familiar,
As I not sooner would commit my hopes
Or wishes to the gods, than to your ears.
Nor have I ever, yet, been covetous
Of overbright, and dazzling honours: rather
To watch, and travail in great Caesar's safety,
With the most common soldier.
TIBERIUS. 'Tis confessed.
SEJANUS. The only gain, and which I count most fair
Of all my fortunes, is that mighty Caesar
Hath thought me worthy his alliance. Hence
Begin my hopes.
TIBERIUS. H'mh?
SEJANUS. I have heard, Augustus
In the bestowing of his daughter, thought
But even of gentlemen of Rome: if so,
(I know not how to hope so great a favour)
But if a husband should be sought for Livia,
And I be had in mind, as Caesar's friend,
I would but use the glory of the kindred.
It should not make me slothful, or less caring
For Caesar's state; it were enough to me
It did confirm, and strengthen my weak house,
Against the now unequal opposition
Of Agrippina; and for dear regard

---

496 *so good vultures*: identifying Afer and Varro with the propitious birds of augury: omens of success.

502 *fortunate*: prosperous.

514 *his alliance*: 'His daughter was betrothed to Claudius his son' (Jonson's marginal note): Sejanus's infant daughter had been betrothed to the baby son of Claudius, Tiberius's nephew.

517 *But even of gentlemen*: gentlemen equal (to noblemen).

Unto my children, this I wish: myself
Have no ambition farther, than to end
My days in service of so dear a master.
TIBERIUS. We cannot but commend thy piety,
Most loved Sejanus, in acknowledging
Those, bounties; which we, faintly, such
remember.
But to thy suit. The rest of mortal men,
In all their drifts, and counsels, pùrsue profit:
Princes, alone, are of a different sort,
Directing their main actions still to fame.
We therefore will take time to think, and answer.
For Livia, she can best, herself, resolve
If she will marry, after Drusus, or
Continue in the family; besides
She hath a mother, and a granddam yet,
Whose nearer counsels she may guide her by:
But I will simply deal. That enmity
Thou fear'st in Agrippina, would burn more,
If Livia's marriage should (as 'twere in parts)
Divide th'imperial house; an emulation
Between the women might break forth: and
discord
Ruin the sons, and nephews, on both hands.
What if it cause some present difference?
Thou art not safe, Sejanus, if thou prove it.
Canst thou believe, that Livia, first the wife
To Caius Caesar, then my Drusus, now
Will be contented to grow old with thee,
Born but a private gentleman of Rome?
And raise thee with her loss, if not her shame?
Or say, that I should wish it, canst thou think
The Senate, or the people (who have seen
Her brother, father, and our ancestors,
In highest place of Empire) will endure it?

---

530 *piety*: dutifulness.
532 *Those, bounties*: see Textual Note, p. 432 below.
534 *drifts*: designs.
541 *mother . . . granddam*: Antonia; Livia, Tiberius's mother.
543 *simply*: honestly.
549 *present difference*: immediate dissension.
550 *prove*: put to the test.
551 *first*: see Textual Note, p. 432 below.
552 *Caius Caesar*: grandson of Augustus.
my: see Textual Note, p. 432 below.
558 *brother, father*: Germanicus; Nero Drusus, Tiberius's brother.

The state thou hold'st already, is in talk;
Men murmur at thy greatness; and the nobles
Stick not, in public, to upbraid thy climbing
Above our father's favours, or thy scale:
And dare accuse me, from their hate to thee.
Be wise, dear friend. We would not hide these things
For friendship's dear respect. Nor will we stand
Adverse to thine, or Livia's designments.
What we had purposed to thee, in our thought,
And with what near degrees of love to bind thee,
And make thee equal to us; for the present,
We will forbear to speak. Only, thus much
Believe, our loved Sejanus, we not know
That height in blood, or honour, which thy virtue,
And mind to us, may not aspire with merit.
And this we'll publish, on all watched occasion
The Senate, or the people shall present.

SEJANUS. I am restored, and to my sense again,
Which I had lost in this so blinding suit.
Caesar hath taught me better to refuse,
Than I knew how to ask. How pleaseth Caesar
T'embrace my late advice, for leaving Rome?

TIBERIUS. We are resolved.

SEJANUS. [*gives him a paper*] Here are some motives more
Which I have thought on since, may more confirm.

TIBERIUS. Careful Sejanus! We will straight peruse them:
Go forward in our main design, and prosper.

[*Exit.*]

SEJANUS. If those but take, I shall. Dull, heavy Caesar!
Would'st thou tell me, thy favours were made crimes?
And that my fortunes were esteemed thy faults?
That thou, for me, wert hated? and not think
I would with wingèd haste prevent that change,
When thou might'st win all to thyself again,
By forfeiture of me? Did those fond words
Fly swifter from thy lips, than this my brain,

---

562 *Stick*: scruple.
563 *scale*: degree, station in life.
575 *watched*: public.
592 *fond*: foolish.

This sparkling forge, created me an armour
T'encounter chance, and thee? Well, read my charms,
And may they lay that hold upon thy senses,
As thou hadst snuffed up hemlock, or ta'en down
The juice of poppy, and of mandrakes. Sleep,
Voluptuous Caesar, and security
Seize on thy stupid powers, and leave them dead
To public cares, awake but to thy lusts.
The strength of which makes thy libidinous soul
Itch to leave Rome; and I have thrust it on:
With blaming of the city business,
The multitude of suits, the confluence
Of suitors, then their importunacies,
The manifold distractions he must suffer,
Besides ill rumours, envies, and reproaches,
All which, a quiet and retirèd life
(Larded with ease, and pleasure) did avoid;
And yet, for any weighty, 'nd great affair,
The fittest place to give the soundest counsels.
By this, shall I remove him both from thought,
And knowledge of his own most dear affairs;
Draw all dispatches through my private hands;
Know his designments, and pursue mine own;
Make mine own strengths, by giving suits, and places;
Conferring dignities, and offices:
And these, that hate me now, wanting access
To him, will make their envy none, or less.
For when they see me arbiter of all,
They must observe: or else, with Caesar fall.
[*Exit.*]

[*Enter*] TIBERIUS.

TIBERIUS. To marry Livia? will no less, Sejanus,
Content thy aims? no lower object? well!
Thou know'st how thou art wrought into our trust;
Woven in our design; and think'st, we must

597–8 *hemlock . . . poppy . . . mandrakes*: opiates.
600 *stupid*: stupefied.
610 *Larded*: garnished.
did: would.
614 *dear*: important.
617 *strengths*: companies of supporters.

Now use thee, whatsoe'er thy projects are:
'Tis true. But yet with caution, and fit care.
And now we better think – who's there, within?

[*Enter*] SERVUS.

SERVUS. Caesar?
TIBERIUS. To leave our journey off, were sin
'Gainst our decreed delights; and would appear
Doubt: or (what less becomes a prince) low fear.
Yet doubt hath law, and fears have their excuse,
Where princes' states plead necessary use;
As ours doth now: more in Sejanus' pride,
Than all fell Agrippina's hates beside.
Those are the dreadful enemies, we raise
With favours, and make dangerous, with praise;
The injured by us may have will alike,
But 'tis the favourite hath the power, to strike:
And fury ever boils more high, and strong,
Heat' with ambition, than revenge of wrong.
'Tis then a part of supreme skill, to grace
No man too much; but hold a certain space
Between th'ascender's rise, and thine own flat,
Lest, when all rounds be reached, his aim be that.
'Tis thought – [*To* SERVUS] Is Macro in the palace? See:
If not, go, seek him, to come to us –
[*Exit* SERVUS.]
He
Must be the organ, we must work by now;
Though none less apt for trust: need doth allow
What choice would not. I have heard that aconite,
Being timely taken, hath a healing might
Against the scorpion's stroke; the proof we'll give:
That, while two poisons wrestle, we may live.
He hath a spirit too working, to be used
But to th'encounter of his like; excused
Are wiser sovereigns then, that raise one ill

633 *law*: right.
636 *fell*: ruthless.
637 *dreadful*: to be feared.
642 *Heat'*: heated.
645 *flat*: level.
646 *rounds*: rungs of a ladder.
651 *aconite*: poisonous plant.
655 *working*: active.

Against another, and both safely kill:
The prince, that feeds great natures, they will sway him;
Who nourisheth a lion, must obey him.

[Enter] MACRO, SERVUS.

Macro, we sent for you.
MACRO. I heard so, Caesar.
TIBERIUS. *[to* SERVUS*]* (Leave us a while.)
[Exit SERVUS.*]*
When you shall know, good Macro,
The causes of our sending, and the ends;
You then will hearken nearer: and be pleased
You stand so high, both in our choice, and trust.
MACRO. The humblest place in Caesar's choice or trust,
May make glad Macro proud; without ambition,
Save to do Caesar service.
TIBERIUS. Leave our courtings.
We are in purpose, Macro, to depart
The city for a time, and see Campania;
Not for our pleasures, but to dedicate
A pair of temples, one, to Jupiter
At Capua; t'other at Nola, to Augustus:
In which great work, perhaps, our stay will be
Beyond our will produced. Now, since we are
Not ignorant what danger may be born
Out of our shortest absence, in a state
So subject unto envy, and embroiled
With hate, and faction; we have thought on thee
(Amongst a field of Romans), worthiest Macro,
To be our eye, and ear; to keep strict watch
On Agrippina, Nero, Drusus; ay,
And on Sejanus: not, that we distrust
His loyalty, or do repent one grace,
Of all that heap, we have conferred on him
(For that were to disparage our election,
And call that judgement now in doubt, which then
Seemed as unquestioned as an oracle),
But greatness hath his cankers. Worms, and moths

663 *our*: see Textual Note, p. 432 below.
668 *our courtings*: courtly addresses of us.
675 *produced*: extended.
686 *election*: choice.
689 *cankers*: ulcerous diseases.

Breed out of too fit matter, in the things
Which after they consume, transferring quite
The substance of their makers, int'themselves.
Macro is sharp, and apprehends. Besides,
I know him subtle, close, wise, and well read
In man, and his large nature: he hath studied
Affections, passions, knows their springs, their
ends,
Which way, and whether they will work: 'tis proof
Enough of his great merit, that we trust him.
Then, to a point (because our conference
Cannot be long without suspicion),
Here, Macro, we assign thee, both to spy,
Inform, and chastise; think, and use thy means,
Thy ministers, what, where, on whom thou wilt;
Explore, plot, practise: all thou dost in this
Shall be as if the Senate, or the laws
Had giv'n it privilege, and thou thence styled
The saviour both of Caesar, and of Rome.
We will not take thy answer, but in act:
Whereto, as thou proceed'st, we hope to hear
By trusted messengers. If't be enquired
Wherefore we called you, say, you have in charge
To see our chariots ready, and our horse:
Be still our loved, and (shortly) honoured Macro.
[*Exit.*]

MACRO. I will not ask, why Caesar bids do this:
But joy, that he bids me. It is the bliss
Of courts, to be employed; no matter, how:
A prince's power makes all his actions virtue.
We, whom he works by, are dumb instruments,
To do, but not enquire: his great intents
Are to be served, not searched. Yet, as that bow
Is most in hand, whose owner best doth know
T'effect his aims, so let that statesman hope
Most use, most price, can hit his prince's scope.

---

690 *too fit matter*: i.e. matter so constituted that it engenders worms and moths out of itself. See Textual Note, p. 432 below.
691 *transferring*: converting.
696 *Affections*: desires.
707 *saviour*: see Textual Note, p. 432 below.
721 *most in hand*: most effectively managed.
721–2 *know T'effect*: know how to accomplish.
723 *price*: value.
scope: target.

Nor must he look at what, or whom to strike,
But loose at all; each mark must be alike.
Were it to plot against the fame, the life
Of one, with whom I twinned; remove a wife
From my warm side, as loved as is the air;
Practise away each parent; draw mine heir
In compass, though but one; work all my kin
To swift perdition: leave no untrainèd engine,
For friendship, or for innocence; nay, make
The gods all guilty: I would undertake
This, being imposed me, both with gain, and ease.
The way to rise, is to obey, and please.
He that will thrive in state, he must neglect
The trodden paths, that truth and right respect;
And prove new, wilder ways: for virtue, there,
Is not that narrow thing, she is elsewhere.
Men's fortune there is virtue; reason, their will:
Their licence, law; and their observance, skill.
Occasion is their foil; conscience, their stain;
Profit, their lustre: and what else is, vain.
If then it be the lust of Caesar's power,
T'have raised Sejanus up, and in an hour
O'erturn him, tumbling, down, from height of all;
We are his ready engine: and his fall
May be our rise. It is no uncouth thing
To see fresh buildings from old ruins spring.
[*Exit.*]

Chorus – of musicians.

---

725 *loose*: shoot (arrow).
mark: target, aim.
729 *Practise away*: plot the death of.
729–30 *draw . . . compass*: inveigle my heir by a stratagem.
742 *Occasion is their foil*: opportunity sets them off (to advantage); *foil*: thin leaf of metal placed behind a jewel to set off its brilliancy.
744 *lust*: inclination.
748 *uncouth*: unknown.

ACT IV

[SCENE I]

[*Enter*] GALLUS, AGRIPPINA.

GALLUS. You must have patience, royal Agrippina.
AGRIPPINA. I must have vengeance, first: and that were nectar
Unto my famished spirits. O, my Fortune,
Let it be sudden thou prepar'st against me;
Strike all my powers of understanding blind,
And ignorant of destiny to come:
Let me not fear, that cannot hope.
GALLUS. Dear princess,
These tyrannies, on yourself, are worse than Caesar's.
AGRIPPINA. Is this the happiness of being born great?
Still to be aimed at? still to be suspected?
To live the subject of all jealousies?
At least the colour made, if not the ground
To every painted danger? Who would not
Choose once to fall, than thus to hang forever?
GALLUS. You might be safe, if you would –
AGRIPPINA. What, my Gallus?
Be lewd Sejanus' strumpet? Or the bawd
To Caesar's lusts, he now is gone to practise?
Not these are safe, where nothing is. Yourself,
While thus you stand but by me, are not safe.
Was Silius safe? or the good Sosia safe?
Or was my niece, dear Claudia Pulchra safe?
Or innocent Furnius? They, that latest have
(By being made guilty) added reputation
To Afer's eloquence? Oh, foolish friends,
Could not so fresh example warn your loves,
But you must buy my favours, with that loss
Unto yourselves: and when you might perceive

12–13 *the colour . . . danger*: made the pretext, if not the basis, of every feigned danger (from painting: *colour*: hue; *ground*: background colour).

21 *Claudia Pulchra*: Agrippina's cousin; prosecuted for adultery with Furnius, and for plotting to poison Caesar.

That Caesar's cause of raging must forsake him,
Before his will? Away, good Gallus, leave me.
Here to be seen, is danger; to speak, treason:
To do me least observance, is called faction.
You are unhappy in me, and I in all.
Where are my sons? Nero? and Drusus? We
Are they be shot at; let us fall apart:
Not, in our ruins, sepulchre our friends.
Or shall we do some action, like offence,
To mock their studies, that would make us faulty?
And frustrate practice, by preventing it?
The danger's like: for what they can contrive,
They will make good. No innocence is safe,
When power contests. Nor can they trespass more,
Whose only being was all crime, before.

[*Enter*] NERO, DRUSUS JUNIOR, CALIGULA.

NERO. You hear, Sejanus is come back from Caesar?
GALLUS. No. How? Disgraced?
DRUSUS JUNIOR. More graced now, than ever.
GALLUS. By what mischance?
CALIGULA. A fortune, like enough
Once to be bad.
DRUSUS JUNIOR. But turned too good, to both.
GALLUS. What was't?
NERO. Tiberius sitting at his meat,
In a farmhouse they call Spelunca, sited
By the seaside, among the Fundane hills,
Within a natural cave, part of the grot
(About the entry) fell, and overwhelmed
Some of the waiters; others ran away:
Only Sejanus, with his knees, hands, face,
O'erhanging Caesar, did oppose himself
To the remaining ruins, and was found
In that so labouring posture, by the soldiers
That came to succour him. With which adventure,
He hath so fixed himself in Caesar's trust,
As thunder cannot move him, and is come

---

32 *unhappy*: unfortunate.
37 *studies*: contrivings.
38 *preventing*: anticipating.
42 *only being*: mere existence.
49 *Fundane hills*: near Fondi, between Rome and Naples.
52 *waiters*: attendants.

With all the height of Caesar's praise, to Rome.
AGRIPPINA. And power, to turn those ruins all on us;
And bury whole posterities beneath them.
Nero, and Drusus, and Caligula,
Your places are the next, and therefore most
In their offence. Think on your birth, and blood,
Awake your spirits, meet their violence,
'Tis princely, when a tyrant doth oppose;
And is a fortune sent to exercise
Your virtue, as the wind doth try strong trees:
Who by vexation grow more sound, and firm.
After your father's fall, and uncle's fate,
What can you hope, but all the change of stroke
That force, or sleight can give? Then stand upright;
And though you do not act, yet suffer nobly:
Be worthy of my womb, and take strong cheer;
What we do know will come, we should not fear.
[*Exeunt.*]

[SCENE II]

[*Enter*] MACRO.

MACRO. Returned so soon? renewed in trust, and grace?
Is Caesar then so weak? or hath the place
But wrought this alteration, with the air;
And he, on next remove, will all repair?
Macro, thou art engaged: and what before
Was public; now, must be thy private, more.
The weal of Caesar, fitness did imply;
But thine own fate confers necessity
On thy employment: and the thoughts born nearest
Unto ourselves, move swiftest still, and dearest.
If he recover, thou art lost: yea, all

---

64 *next*: nearest to the throne.
65 *their offence*: displeasure of Tiberius and Sejanus.
70 *vexation*: tossing.
72 *change of stroke*: variety of blows.
80 *remove*: stage of his journey.
82 *public*: public duty.
private: personal concern.
83 *weal*: well-being.

The weight of preparation to his fall
Will turn on thee, and crush thee. Therefore, strike
Before he settle, to prevent the like
Upon thyself. He doth his vantage know,
That makes it home, and gives the foremost blow.
[*Exit.*]

[SCENE III]

[*Enter*] LATIARIS, RUFUS, OPSIUS.

LATIARIS. It is a service great Sejanus will
See well requited, and accept of nobly.
Here place yourselves, between the roof, and
ceiling,
And when I bring him to his words of danger,
Reveal yourselves, and take him.
RUFUS. Is he come?
LATIARIS. I'll now go fetch him. [*Exit.*]
OPSIUS. With good speed. I long
To merit from the state, in such an action.
RUFUS. I hope it will obtain the consulship
For one of us.
OPSIUS. We cannot think of less,
To bring in one, so dangerous as Sabinus.
RUFUS. He was a follower of Germanicus,
And still is an observer of his wife,
And children, though they be declined in grace;
A daily visitant, keeps them company
In private, and in public; and is noted
To be the only client of the house:
Pray Jove, he will be free to Latiaris.
OPSIUS. H'is allied to him, and doth trust him well.
RUFUS. And he'll requite his trust?
OPSIUS. To do an office
So grateful to the state, I know no man

---

92 *makes it home*: takes full advantage.
95 *between the roof, and ceiling*: see Additional Note, p. 437 below.
ceiling: curtain, hanging.
104 *observer*: follower.
108 *client*: adherent.
110 *allied*: related.
112 *grateful*: pleasing.

But would strain nearer bands, than kindred –
RUFUS. List,
I hear them come.
OPSIUS. Shift to our holes, with silence.
[*They withdraw.*]

[*Enter*] LATIARIS, SABINUS.

LATIARIS. It is a noble constancy you show
To this afflicted house: that not like others,
(The friends of season) you do follow Fortune,
And in the winter of their fate, forsake
The place, whose glories warmed you. You are just,
And worthy such a princely patron's love,
As was the world's renowned Germanicus:
Whose ample merit when I call to thought,
And see his wife and issue, objects made
To so much envy, jealousy, and hate,
It makes me ready to accuse the gods
Of negligence, as men of tyranny.
SABINUS. They must be patient, so must we.
LATIARIS. O Jove.
What will become of us, or of the times,
When, to be high, or noble, are made crimes?
When land, and treasure are most dangerous faults?
SABINUS. Nay, when our table, yea our bed assaults
Our peace, and safety? when our writings are
By any envious instruments (that dare
Apply them to the guilty) made to speak
What they will have, to fit their tyrannous wreak?
When ignorance is scarcely innocence:
And knowledge made a capital offence?
When not so much, but the bare empty shade
Of liberty, is reft us? and we made
The prey to greedy vultures, and vile spies,
That first transfix us with their murdering eyes?
LATIARIS. Methinks, the genius of the Roman race
Should not be so extinct, but that bright flame
Of liberty might be revived again
(Which no good man but with his life, should lose),

---

114 *Shift*: remove.
117 *friends of season*: fair-weather friends.
135 *wreak*: vengeance.

And we not sit like spent, and patient fools
Still puffing in the dark at one poor coal,
Held on by hope, till the last spark is out.
The cause is public, and the honour, name,
The immortality of every soul
That is not bastard, or a slave in Rome,
Therein concerned: whereto, if men would change
The wearied arm, and for the weighty shield
So long sustained, employ the ready sword,
We might have some assurance of our vows.
This ass's fortitude doth tire us all.
It must be active valour must redeem
Our loss, or none. The rock, and our hard steel
Should meet, t'enforce those glorious fires again,
Whose splendour cheered the world, and heat
gave life
No less than doth the sun's.

SABINUS. 'Twere better stay
In lasting darkness, and despair of day.
No ill should force the subject undertake
Against the sovereign, more than hell should make
The gods do wrong. A good man should, and must
Sit rather down with loss, than rise unjust.
Though, when the Romans first did yield
themselves
To one man's power, they did not mean their lives,
Their fortunes, and their liberties, should be
His absolute spoil, as purchased by the sword.

LATIARIS. Why we are worse, if to be slaves, and
bond
To Caesar's slave, be such, the proud Sejanus!
He that is all, does all, gives Caesar leave
To hide his ulcerous, and anointed face,
With his bald crown at Rhodes, while he here stalks

---

146 *spent*: exhausted.
152–4 *if men . . . sword*: i.e. instead of merely parrying the blows of tyranny, take up arms for liberty.
154 *ready*: see Textual Note, p. 432 below.
163 *undertake*: commit himself to an enterprise.
166 *Sit . . . down with*: submit to.
174 *anointed*: smeared with ointment.
174, 175 The ulcers and the baldness indicate the physical effects of Caesar's lusts.
175 *Rhodes*: see Additional Note, p. 437 below.

Upon the heads of Romans, and their princes,
Familiarly to empire.

SABINUS. Now you touch
A point indeed, wherein he shows his art,
As well as power.

LATIARIS. And villainy in both.
Do you observe where Livia lodges? How
Drusus came dead? What men have been cut off?

SABINUS. Yes, those are things removed: I nearer looked,
Into his later practice, where he stands
Declared a master in his mystery.
First, ere Tiberius went, he wrought his fear
To think that Agrippina sought his death.
Then put those doubts in her; sent her oft word,
Under the show of friendship, to beware
Of Caesar, for he laid to poison her:
Drove them to frowns, to mutual jealousies,
Which, now, in visible hatred are burst out.
Since, he hath had his hired instruments
To work on Nero, and to heave him up;
To tell him Caesar's old; that all the people,
Yea, all the army have their eyes on him;
That both do long to have him undertake
Something of worth, to give the world a hope;
Bids him to court their grace: the easy youth,
Perhaps, gives ear, which straight he writes to Caesar;
And with this comment: 'See yond dangerous boy;
Note but the practice of the mother, there;
She's tying him, for purposes at hand,
With men of sword.' Here's Caesar put in fright
'Gainst son, and mother. Yet, he leaves not thus.
The second brother Drusus (a fierce nature,
And fitter for his snares, because ambitious,
And full of envy) him he clasps, and hugs,
Poisons with praise, tells him what hearts he wears,

---

177 *Familiarly*: without ceremony.
empire: either a noun, 'imperial rule'; or a verb, 'to rule'.
182 *removed*: remote, of the past.
184 *mystery*: trade, craft.
193 *heave him up*: raise his ambition.
198 *easy*: credulous.
202 *tying*: bringing into association.

How bright he stands in popular expectance;
That Rome doth suffer with him, in the wrong
His mother does him, by preferring Nero:
Thus sets he them asunder, each 'gainst other,
Projects the course that serves him to condemn,
Keeps in opinion of a friend to all,
And all drives on to ruin.

LATIARIS. Caesar sleeps,
And nods at this?

SABINUS. Would he might ever sleep,
Bogged in his filthy lusts.

[*Enter*] OPSIUS, RUFUS.

OPSIUS. Treason to Caesar.

RUFUS. Lay hands upon the traitor, Latiaris,
Or take the name thyself.

LATIARIS. I am for Caesar.

SABINUS. Am I then catched?

RUFUS. How think you, sir? you are.

SABINUS. Spies of this head! so white! so full of years!
Well, my most reverend monsters, you may live
To see yourselves thus snared.

OPSIUS. Away with him.

LATIARIS. Hale him away.

RUFUS. To be a spy for traitors,
Is honourable vigilance.

SABINUS. You do well,
My most officious instruments of state;
Men of all uses: drag me hence, away.
The year is well begun, and I fall fit,
To be an offering to Sejanus. Go.

OPSIUS. Cover him with his garments, hide his face.

SABINUS. It shall not need. Forbear your rude assault,
The fault's not shameful villainy makes a fault.

[*Exeunt.*]

---

209 *popular expectance*: expectation of the people.
220 *catched*: detected.
221 *head*: age (from hunting: 'of the first head' describes deer at the age when their antlers begin to sprout).
228–9 *The year . . . Sejanus*: i.e. Sabinus is a New Year's gift and sacrificial victim to god Sejanus; ironic, as no executions took place during this sacred season.
230 *Cover him*: i.e. like a criminal condemned to death.

[SCENE IV]

[*Enter*] MACRO, CALIGULA.

MACRO. Sir, but observe how thick your dangers meet
In his clear drifts! Your mother, and your brothers,
Now cited to the Senate! Their friend, Gallus,
Feasted today by Caesar, since committed!
Sabinus, here we met, hurried to fetters!
The senators all struck with fear, and silence,
Save those, whose hopes depend not on good means,
But force their private prey, from public spoil!
And you must know, if here you stay, your state
Is sure to be the subject of his hate,
As now the object.

CALIGULA. What would you advise me?

MACRO. To go for Capreae presently: and there
Give up yourself, entirely, to your uncle.
Tell Caesar (since your mother is accused
To fly for succours to Augustus' statue,
And to the army, with your brethren) you
Have rather chose to place your aids in him,
Than live suspected; or in hourly fear
To be thrust out, by bold Sejanus' plots:
Which, you shall confidently urge, to be
Most full of peril to the state, and Caesar,
As being laid to his peculiar ends,
And not to be let run, with common safety.
All which (upon the second) I'll make plain,
So both shall love, and trust with Caesar gain.

CALIGULA. Away then, let's prepare us for our journey.

[*Exeunt.*]

[*Enter*] ARRUNTIUS.

---

234 *drifts*: intentions.
237 *here . . . met*: whom we met here.
241–3 *if here . . . object*: your princely rank already draws Sejanus's hatred, but if you stay in Rome, you will undoubtedly become the victim of his hate.
247 *To fly*: of flying.
254 *his peculiar*: Sejanus's own.
255 *common*: general.
256 *upon the second*: in support.

ARRUNTIUS. Still, dost thou suffer, Heav'n? Will no flame,
No heat of sin make thy just wrath to boil
In thy distempered bosom, and o'erflow
The pitchy blazes of impiety,
Kindled beneath thy throne? Still canst thou sleep,
Patient, while vice doth make an antic face
At thy dread power, and blow dust, and smoke
Into thy nostrils? Jove, will nothing wake thee?
Must vile Sejanus pull thee by the beard,
Ere thou wilt open thy black-lidded eye,
And look him dead? Well! Snore, on dreaming gods:
And let this last of that proud giant race
Heave mountain upon mountain, 'gainst your state –
Be good unto me, Fortune, and you powers,
Whom I, expostulating, have profaned;
I see (what's equal with a prodigy)
A great, a noble Roman, and an honest,

[*Enter*] LEPIDUS.

Live an old man! O, Marcus Lepidus,
When is our turn to bleed? Thyself, and I
(Without our boast) are a'most all the few
Left, to be honest, in these impious times.
LEPIDUS. What we are left to be, we will be, Lucius,
Though tyranny did stare as wide as death,
To fright us from it.
ARRUNTIUS. 'T hath so, on Sabinus.
LEPIDUS. I saw him now drawn from the Gemonies,
And (what increased the direness of the fact)
His faithful dog (upbraiding all us Romans)
Never forsook the corpse, but seeing it thrown
Into the stream, leaped in, and drowned with it.
ARRUNTIUS. O act! to be envied him, of us men.
We are the next the hook lays hold on, Marcus:
What are thy arts (good patriot, teach them me)

---

259 *suffer*: wait patiently.
264 *antic face*: grimace.
270–1 *giant race . . . state*: the Giants, sons of Uranus, who, by piling Mt Ossa on Mt Pelion, tried unsuccessfully to scale Olympus and unseat Jupiter.
274 *prodigy*: wonder.
283 *Gemonies*: Gemonian steps; see II.[iii].416 n.

That have preserved thy hairs, to this white dye,
And kept so reverend, and so dear a head,
Safe, on his comely shoulders?

LEPIDUS. Arts, Arruntius?
None, but the plain, and passive fortitude,
To suffer, and be silent; never stretch
These arms, against the torrent; live at home,
With my own thoughts, and innocence about me,
Not tempting the wolves' jaws: these are my arts.

ARRUNTIUS. I would begin to study 'em, if I thought
They would secure me. May I pray to Jove,
In secret, and be safe? ay, or aloud?
With open wishes? so I do not mention
Tiberius, or Sejanus? Yes, I must,
If I speak out. 'Tis hard, that. May I think,
And not be racked? What danger is't to dream?
Talk in one's sleep? or cough? who knows the law?
May I shake my head, without a comment? say
It rains, or it holds up, and not be thrown
Upon the Gemonies? These now are things,
Whereon men's fortune, yea their fate depends.
Nothing hath privilege 'gainst the violent ear.
No place, no day, no hour (we see) is free
(Not our religious, and most sacred times)
From some one kind of cruelty: all matter,
Nay all occasion pleaseth. Madmen's rage,
The idleness of drunkards, women's nothing,
Jesters' simplicity, all, all is good
That can be catched at. Nor is now th'event
Of any person, or for any crime,
To be expected; for 'tis always one:
Death, with some little difference of place,
Or time – what's this? Prince Nero? guarded?

[*Enter*] LACO, NERO [*and* LICTORES].

---

311 *violent ear*: informer out to destroy.
315 *occasion*: pretext.
316 *idleness*: empty talk.
nothing: idle chatter.
317 *simplicity*: artless, simple-minded speech; see Additional Note, p. 437 below.
318 *catched at*: seized on.
event: outcome.
319 *Of*: for.
320 *expected*: awaited.

LACO. On, lictors, keep your way: my lords, forbear.
On pain of Caesar's wrath, no man attempt
Speech with the prisoner.
NERO. Noble friends, be safe:
To lose yourselves for words, were as vain hazard,
As unto me small comfort: fare you well.
Would all Rome's sufferings in my fate did dwell.
LACO. Lictors, away.
LEPIDUS. Where goes he, Laco?
LACO. Sir,
H'is banished into Pontia, by the Senate.
ARRUNTIUS. Do' I see? and hear? and feel? May I trust sense?
Or doth my fant'sy form it?
LEPIDUS. Where's his brother?
LACO. Drusus is prisoner in the palace.
ARRUNTIUS. Ha?
I smell it now: 'tis rank. Where's Agrippina?
LACO. The princess is confined, to Pandataria.
ARRUNTIUS. Bolts, Vulcan; bolts for Jove! Phoebus, thy bow;
Stern Mars, thy sword; and blue-eyed maid, thy spear;
Thy club, Alcides: all the armoury
Of Heaven is too little! – Ha? to guard
The gods, I meant. Fine, rare dispatch! This same
Was swiftly born! confined? imprisoned? banished?
Most tripartite! The cause, sir?
LACO. Treason.
ARRUNTIUS. Oh?
The complement of all accusing? that
Will hit, when all else fails.
LEPIDUS. [*aside to* ARRUNTIUS] This turn is strange!
But yesterday, the people would not hear

---

330 *Pontia*: an island near Naples, where, like his mother and brother, Nero starved to death.
332 *fant'sy*: imagination.
334 *'tis rank*: it stinks.
335 *Pandataria*: in the Pontia group of islands.
336 *Bolts*: thunderbolts, manufactured for Jupiter by the black-smith god, Vulcan.
337 *blue-eyed maid*: Pallas Athene, the warrior-maiden goddess.
338 *Alcides*: Hercules, iconographically depicted with a mighty club.

Far less objected, but cried Caesar's letters
Were false, and forged; that all these plots were malice:
And that the ruin of the prince's house
Was practised 'gainst his knowledge. Where are now
Their voices? now, that they behold his heirs
Locked up, disgraced, led into exile?
ARRUNTIUS. [*aside to* LEPIDUS]. Hushed.
Drowned in their bellies. Wild Sejanus' breath
Hath, like a whirlwind, scattered that poor dust,
With this rude blast.
He turns to LACO, *and the rest.*
We'll talk no treason, sir,
If that be it you stand for? Fare you well.
We have no need of horse-leeches. Good spy,
Now you are spied, begone.
[*Exeunt* LACO, NERO, LICTORES.]
LEPIDUS. I fear, you wrong him.
He has the voice to be an honest Roman.
ARRUNTIUS. And trusted to this office? Lepidus,
I'd sooner trust Greek Sinon, than a man
Our state employs. He's gone: and being gone,
I dare tell you (whom I dare better trust)
That our night-eyed Tiberius doth not see
His minion's drifts; or if he do, h'is not
So arrant subtle, as we fools do take him:
To breed a mongrel up, in his own house,
With his own blood, and (if the good gods please)
At his own throat, flesh him, to take a leap.
I do not beg it, Heav'n: but if the Fates
Grant it these eyes, they must not wink.
LEPIDUS. They must
Not see it, Lucius.
ARRUNTIUS. Who should let 'em?

---

346 *objected*: put forward as a crime.
356 *horse-leeches*: very large leeches; 'bloodsuckers'.
360 *Greek Sinon*: who deceived the Trojans into taking the wooden horse into Troy.
363 *night-eyed*: sharp-sighted (Tiberius was said to be able to see in the dark).
365 *arrant*: absolutely.
368 *flesh him, to take a leap*: make him eager for prey by tasting blood.

LEPIDUS. Zeal,
And duty; with the thought, he is our prince.
ARRUNTIUS. He is our monster: forfeited to vice
So far, as no racked virtue can redeem him.
His loathèd person fouler than all crimes:
An emperor, only in his lusts. Retired
(From all regard of his own fame, or Rome's)
Into an obscure island; where he lives
(Acting his tragedies with a comic face)
Amidst his rout of Chaldees: spending hours,
Days, weeks, and months, in the unkind abuse
Of grave astrology, to the bane of men,
Casting the scope of men's nativities,
And having found aught worthy in their fortune,
Kill, or precipitate them in the sea,
And boast, he can mock fate. Nay, muse not: these
Are far from ends of evil, scarce degrees.
He hath his slaughterhouse, at Capreae;
Where he doth study murder, as an art:
And they are dearest in his grace, that can
Devise the deepest tortures. Thither, too,
He hath his boys, and beauteous girls ta'en up,
Out of our noblest houses, the best formed,
Best nurtured, and most modest: what's their good
Serves to provoke his bad. Some are allured,
Some threatened; others (by their friends detained)
Are ravished hence, like captives, and in sight
Of their most grievèd parents, dealt away
Unto his spintries, sellaries, and slaves,
Masters of strange, and new-commènted lusts,
For which wise nature hath not left a name.
To this (what most strikes us, and bleeding Rome)
He is, with all his craft, become the ward
To his own vassal, a stale catamite:
Whom he (upon our low, and suffering necks)

---

374 *racked*: constrained, drawn from him by constraint.
379 *comic face*: mask proper to the performance of classical comedy. The grotesque theatrical indecorum emphasises Tiberius's perverse enjoyment of what should arouse pity and fear.
380 *Chaldees*: astrologers (astrology was an art cultivated by the Chaldeans).
383 *scope*: horoscope.
387 *degrees*: steps.
399 *spintries, sellaries*: male prostitutes for unnatural vice.
400 *new-commènted*: newly invented.

Hath raised, from excrement, to side the gods,
And have his proper sacrifice in Rome:
Which Jove beholds, and yet will sooner rive
A senseless oak with thunder, than his trunk.

[Enter] *to them,* LACO, POMPONIUS, MINUTIUS.

LACO. These letters make men doubtful what t'expect,
Whether his coming, or his death.
POMPONIUS. Troth, both:
And which comes soonest, thank the gods for.
ARRUNTIUS. [*aside to* LEPIDUS] (List,
Their talk is Caesar, I would hear all voices.)
MINUTIUS. One day, he's well; and will return to Rome:
The next day, sick; and knows not when to hope it.
LACO. True, and today, one of Sejanus' friends
Honoured by special writ; and on the morrow
Another punished –
POMPONIUS. By more special writ.
MINUTIUS. This man receives his praises of Sejanus,
A second, but slight mention: a third, none:
A fourth, rebukes. And thus he leaves the Senate
Divided, and suspended, all uncertain.
LACO. These forkèd tricks, I understand 'em not,
Would he would tell us whom he loves, or hates,
That we might follow, without fear, or doubt.
ARRUNTIUS. [*aside to* LEPIDUS] (Good heliotrope!
Is this your honest man?
Let him be yours so still. He is my knave.)
POMPONIUS. I cannot tell, Sejanus still goes on,
And mounts, we see: new statues are advanced,
Fresh leaves of titles, large inscriptions read,
His fortune sworn by, himself new gone out
Caesar's colleague, in the fifth consulship,
More altars smoke to him, than all the gods:
What would we more?

---

406 *side*: be beside.
407 *proper*: own.
414 MINUTIUS: see Textual Note, p. 432 below.
423 *forkèd*: ambiguous.
426 *heliotrope*: plant that turns towards the sun. Laco is attracted to follow the powerful.
431 *gone out*: completed a term as.

ARRUNTIUS. [*aside*] (That the dear smoke would choke him,
That would I more.
LEPIDUS. [*aside to* ARRUNTIUS] Peace, good Arruntius.)
LACO. But there are letters come (they say) ev'n now,
Which do forbid that last.
MINUTIUS. Do you hear so?
LACO. Yes.
POMPONIUS. By Pollux, that's the worst.
ARRUNTIUS. [*aside*] (By Hercules, best.)
MINUTIUS. I did not like the sign, when Regulus
(Whom all we know no friend unto Sejanus)
Did, by Tiberius' so precise command,
Succeed a fellow in the consulship:
It boded somewhat.
POMPONIUS. Not a mote. His partner,
Fulcinius Trio, is his own; and sure.
Here comes Terentius. He can give us more.

[*Enter*] TERENTIUS.

They whisper with TERENTIUS.

LEPIDUS. I'll ne'er believe, but Caesar hath some scent
Of bold Sejanus' footing. These cross points
Of varying letters, and opposing consuls,
Mingling his honours, and his punishments,
Feigning now ill, now well, raising Sejanus,
And then depressing him (as now of late
In all reports we have it), cannot be
Empty of practice: 'tis Tiberius' art.
For (having found his favourite grown too great,
And, with his greatness, strong; that all the soldiers
Are, with their leaders, made at his devotion;
That almost all the Senate are his creatures,
Or hold on him their main dependences,

---

435 *That*... *Arruntius*: see Textual Note, p. 432 below.
438 *Pollux*... *Hercules*: see Textual Note, p. 432 below.
443 *mote*: jot.
445 s.d. *They* ... TERENTIUS: see Textual Note, p. 432 below.
447 *footing*: track.
cross: conflicting.
449 *Mingling*: see Textual Note, p. 432 below.
451 *depressing*: putting down.
456 *made at his devotion*: mustered at his command.

Either for benefit, or hope, or fear;
And that himself hath lost much of his own,
By parting unto him; and by th'increase
Of his rank lusts, and rages, quite disarmed
Himself of love, or other public means,
To dare an open contestation)
His subtlety hath chose this doubling line,
To hold him even in: not so to fear him,
As wholly put him out, and yet give check
Unto his farther boldness. In meantime,
By his employments, makes him odious
Unto the staggering rout, whose aid (in fine)
He hopes to use, as sure, who (when they sway)
Bear down, o'erturn all objects in their way.
ARRUNTIUS. You may be a Linceus, Lepidus: yet I
See no such cause, but that a politic tyrant
(Who can so well disguise it) should have ta'en
A nearer way: feigned honest, and come home
To cut his throat, by law.
LEPIDUS. Ay, but his fear
Would ne'er be masked, albe his vices were.
POMPONIUS. His lordship then is still in grace?
TERENTIUS. Assure you,
Never in more, either of grace, or power.
POMPONIUS. The gods are wise, and just.
ARRUNTIUS. [*aside*] (The fiends they are.
To suffer thee belie 'em?)
TERENTIUS. I have here
His last, and present letters, where he writes him
The 'partner of his cares', and 'his Sejanus' –
LACO. But is that true, it is prohibited,
To sacrifice unto him?
TERENTIUS. Some such thing
Caesar makes scruple of, but forbids it not;
No more than to himself: says, he could wish
It were forborne to all.

---

461 *parting unto*: sharing with.
462 *rank*: gross.
465 *doubling*: ambiguous.
466 *even in*: in check.
470 *staggering rout*: unstable mob.
in fine: at last.
473 *Linceus*: Argonaut famed for keen sight.
474 *cause*: reason.
478 *albe*: albeit.

LACO. Is it no other?
TERENTIUS. No other, on my trust. For your more surety,
Here is that letter too.
ARRUNTIUS. [*aside to* LEPIDUS] (How easily,
Do wretched men believe what they would have!
Looks this like plot?
LEPIDUS. [*aside to* ARRUNTIUS] Noble Arruntius, stay.)
LACO. He names him here without his titles.
LEPIDUS. [*aside to* ARRUNTIUS] (Note.
ARRUNTIUS. [*aside to* LEPIDUS] Yes, and come off your notable fool. I will.)
LACO. No other, than 'Sejanus'.
POMPONIUS. That's but haste
In him that writes. Here he gives large amends.
MINUTIUS. And with his own hand written?
POMPONIUS. Yes.
LACO. Indeed?
TERENTIUS. Believe it, gentlemen, Sejanus' breast
Never received more full contentments in,
Than at this present.
POMPONIUS. Takes he well th'escape
Of young Caligula, with Macro?
TERENTIUS. Faith,
At the first air, it somewhat troubled him.
LEPIDUS. [*aside to* ARRUNTIUS] (Observe you?
ARRUNTIUS. [*aside to* LEPIDUS] Nothing. Riddles. Till I see
Sejanus struck, no sound thereof strikes me.)
[*Exeunt* ARRUNTIUS, LEPIDUS.]
POMPONIUS. I like it not. I muse h'would not attempt
Somewhat against him in the consulship,
Seeing the people 'gin to favour him.
TERENTIUS. He doth repent it, now; but h'has employed
Pagonianus after him: and he holds
That correspondence, there, with all that are
Near about Caesar, as no thought can pass
Without his knowledge, thence, in act to front him.

---

490 *more surety*: greater assurance.
498 MINUTIUS: see Textual Note, p. 432 below.
503 *air*: announcement.
507 *him*: Caligula.
513 *front*: confront.

POMPONIUS. I gratulate the news.
LACO. But how comes Macro
So in trust, and favour, with Caligula?
POMPONIUS. O sir, he has a wife; and the young prince
An appetite: he can look up, and spy
Flies in the roof, when there are fleas i'bed;
And hath a learnèd nose t'assure his sleeps.
Who, to be favoured of the rising sun,
Would not lend little of his waning moon?
'Tis the saf'st ambition. Noble Terentius.
TERENTIUS. The night grows fast upon us. At your service.

[*Exeunt.*]

Chorus – of musicians.

ACT V

[SCENE I]

[*Enter*] SEJANUS.

SEJANUS. Swell, swell, my joys: and faint not to declare
Yourselves, as ample, as your causes are.
I did not live, till now; this my first hour:
Wherein I see my thoughts reached by my power.
But this, and gripe my wishes. Great, and high,
The world knows only two, that's Rome, and I.
My roof receives me not; 'tis air I tread:
And, at each step, I feel m'advancèd head
Knock out a star in heaven! Reared to this height,
All my desires seem modest, poor and slight,

514 *gratulate*: welcome.
LACO: see Textual Note, p. 432 below.

516–17 *the young . . . appetite*: Caligula's affair with Macro's wife in fact took place later, in AD 37.

519 *hath . . . sleeps*: has well schooled his senses to give him unbroken rest.

5 *But this*: i.e. I have only to exert my power; perhaps accompanied by the gesture of reaching out his hand and closing his fist tightly, as if seizing an object greedily desired.

That did before sound impudent: 'tis place,
Not blood, discerns the noble, and the base.
Is there not something more, than to be Caesar?
Must we rest there? It irks, t'have come so far,
To be so near a stay. Caligula,
Would thou stood'st stiff, and many, in our way.
Winds lose their strength, when they do empty fly,
Unmet of woods or buildings; great fires die
That want their matter to withstand them: so,
It is our grief, and will be'our loss, to know
Our power shall want opposites; unless
The gods, by mixing in the cause, would bless
Our fortune with their conquest. That were worth
Sejanus' strife, durst Fates but bring it forth.

[*Enter*] TERENTIUS [*and* SERVUS].

TERENTIUS. Safety, to great Sejanus.
SEJANUS. Now, Terentius?
TERENTIUS. Hears not my lord the wonder?
SEJANUS. Speak it, no.
TERENTIUS. I meet it violent in the people's mouths,
Who run, in routs, to Pompey's theatre,
To view your statue: which, they say, sends forth
A smoke, as from a furnace, black, and dreadful.
SEJANUS. Some traitor hath put fire in: [*To* SERVUS] you, go see.
And let the head be taken off, to look
What 'tis –

[*Exit* SERVUS.]

Some slave hath practised an imposture
To stir the people. How now? why return you?

[*Enter*] *to them* SATRIUS, NATTA, [SERVUS].

SATRIUS. The head, my lord, already is ta'en off,
I saw it: and, at opening, there leapt out
A great, and monstrous serpent!
SEJANUS. Monstrous! why?
Had it a beard? and horns? no heart? a tongue
Forkèd as flattery? looked it of the hue,

---

19 *withstand*: oppose.
21 *opposites*: antagonists.
22 *mixing in the cause*: engaging in the conflict.
27 *violent*: loud.
39 *hue*: appearance.

To such as live in great men's bosoms? was
The spirit of it Macro's?

NATTA. May it please
The most divine Sejanus, in my days
(And by his sacred fortune, I affirm it)
I have not seen a more extended, grown,
Foul, spotted, venomous, ugly –

SEJANUS. O, the Fates!
What a wild muster's here of attributes,
T'express a worm, a snake?

TERENTIUS. But how that should
Come there, my lord?

SEJANUS. What! and you too, Terentius?
I think you mean to make't a prodigy
In your reporting?

TERENTIUS. Can the wise Sejanus
Think Heaven hath meant it less?

SEJANUS. O, superstition!
Why, then the falling of our bed, that broke
This morning, burdened with the populous weight
Of our expecting clients, to salute us,
Or running of the cat, betwixt our legs,
As we set forth unto the Capitol,
Were prodigies.

TERENTIUS. I think them ominous!
And would they had not happened. As, today,
The fate of some your servants! who, declining
Their way, not able, for the throng, to follow,
Slipped down the Gemonies, and broke their
necks!
Besides, in taking your last augury,
No prosperous bird appeared, but croaking ravens
Flagged up and down: and from the sacrifice
Flew to the prison, where they sat, all night,
Beating the air with their obstreperous beaks!
I dare not counsel, but I could entreat
That great Sejanus would attempt the gods,
Once more, with sacrifice.

---

52 *bed*: couch.
59 *declining*: turning out of.
62 *augury*: divination by interpreting the flight of birds.
63 *prosperous*: auspicious.
64 *Flagged*: flew unsteadily.
66 *Beating . . . beaks*: making a clamorous and empty outcry.
68 *attempt*: urgently address, try to move.

SEJANUS. What excellent fools
Religion makes of men! Believes Terentius
(If these were dangers, as I shame to think them)
The gods could change the certain course of fate?
Or if they could, they would (now, in a moment)
For a beef's fat, or less, be bribed t'invert
Those long decrees? Then think the gods, like flies,
Are to be taken with the steam of flesh,
Or blood, diffused about their altars: think
Their power as cheap, as I esteem it small.
Of all the throng, that fill th'Olympian hall,
And (without pity) lade poor Atlas' back,
I know not that one deity, but Fortune,
To whom I would throw up, in begging smoke,
One grain of incense: or whose ear I'd buy
With thus much oil. Her, I, indeed, adore;
And keep her grateful image in my house,
Sometimes belonging to a Roman king,
But now called mine, as by the better style:
To her, I care not, if (for satisfying
Your scrupulous fant'sies) I go offer. Bid
Our priest prepare us honey, milk, and poppy,
His masculine odours, and night vestments: say,
Our rites are instant, which performed, you'll see
How vain, and worthy laughter, your fears be.
[*Exeunt.*]

[*Enter*] COTTA, POMPONIUS.

COTTA. Pomponius! whither in such speed?
POMPONIUS. I go
To give my lord Sejanus notice –
COTTA. What?
POMPONIUS. Of Macro.
COTTA. Is he come?
POMPONIUS. Entered but now
The house of Regulus.
COTTA. The opposite consul?
POMPONIUS. Some half hour since.

---

75 *long*: longstanding.
80 *lade*: burden.
86 *Sometimes*: formerly.
91 *masculine odours*: finest frankincense (called in Latin *mascula tura*).

COTTA. And by night too! stay, sir;
I'll bear you company.
POMPONIUS. Along, then –
[*Exeunt.*]

[SCENE II]

[*Enter*] MACRO, REGULUS [*and* SERVUS].

MACRO. 'Tis Caesar's will, to have a frequent Senate.
And therefore must your edict lay deep mulct
On such as shall be absent.
REGULUS. So it doth.
[*To* SERVUS] Bear it my fellow consul to adscribe.
MACRO. And tell him it must early be proclaimed;
The place, Apollo's temple.
[*Exit* SERVUS.]
REGULUS. That's remembered.
MACRO. And at what hour?
REGULUS. Yes.
MACRO. You do forget
To send one for the provost of the watch?
REGULUS. I have not: here he comes.

[*Enter* LACO.]

MACRO. Gracinus Laco,
You are a friend most welcome: by and by,
I'll speak with you. [*To* REGULUS] (You must procure this list
Of the praetorian cohorts, with the names
Of the centurions, and their tribunes.
REGULUS. Ay.)
MACRO. I bring you letters, and a health from Caesar –
LACO. Sir, both come well.
MACRO. [*to* REGULUS] (And hear you, with your note,

---

100 *frequent*: full.
101 *deep mulct*: heavy fine.
103 *adscribe*: subscribe.
105 *remembered*: mentioned.
109 *by and by*: immediately.
113 *health*: salutation, greeting.

Which are the eminent men, and most of action.
REGULUS. That shall be done you too.)
MACRO. Most worthy Laco,
The consul goes out.
Caesar salutes you. (Consul! death, and furies!
Gone now?) The argument will please you, sir.
(Ho! Regulus? The anger of the gods
Follow his diligent legs, and overtake 'em,

[REGULUS] *returns.*

In likeness of the gout.) O, good my lord,
We lacked you present; I would pray you send
Another to Fulcinius Trio, straight,
To tell him, you will come, and speak with him
(The matter we'll devise), to stay him there,
While I, with Laco, do survey the watch.
What are your strengths, Gracinus?
LACO. Seven cohorts.
[REGULUS] *goes out again.*
MACRO. You see what Caesar writes: and (– gone again?
H'has sure a vein of mercury in his feet)
Knew you, what store of the praetorian soldiers
Sejanus holds about him, for his guard?
LACO. I cannot the just number: but, I think,
Three centuries.
MACRO. Three? good.
LACO. At most, not four.
MACRO. And who be those centurions?
LACO. That the consul
Can best deliver you.
MACRO. [*aside*] (When h'is away:
Spite, on his nimble industry.) Gracinus,
You find what place you hold, there, in the trust
Of royal Caesar?
LACO. Ay, and I am –
MACRO. Sir,
The honours, there proposed, are but beginnings
Of his great favours.
LACO. They are more –

---

130 *store*: number.
132 *cannot*: do not know.
just: exact.

MACRO. I heard him
When he did study, what to add –
LACO. My life,
And all I hold –
MACRO. You were his own first choice;
Which doth confirm as much as you can speak:
And will (if we succeed) make more – Your guards
Are seven cohorts you say?
LACO. Yes.
MACRO. Those we must
Hold still in readiness, and undischarged.
LACO. I understand so much. But how it can –
MACRO. Be done without suspicion, you'll object?

[REGULUS *returns*.]

REGULUS. What's that?
LACO. The keeping of the watch in arms,
When morning comes.
MACRO. The Senate shall be met, and set
So early, in the temple, as all mark
Of that will be avoided.
REGULUS. If we need,
We have commission to possess the palace;
Enlarge Prince Drusus, and make him our chief.
MACRO. [*aside*] (That secret would have burnt his reverend mouth,
Had he not spit it out, now.) [*To* REGULUS] By the gods,
You carry things too – Let me borrow a man,
Or two, to bear these – That of freeing Drusus,
Caesar projected as the last, and utmost;
Not else to be remembered.

[*Enter* SERVI.]

REGULUS. Here are servants.
MACRO. [*gives them letters*] These to Arruntius, these to Lepidus,
This bear to Cotta, this to Latiaris.
If they demand you'of me, say I have ta'en
Fresh horse, and am departed.
[*Exeunt* SERVI.]
You (my lord)
To your colleague; and be you sure to hold him
With long narration, of the new fresh favours
Meant to Sejanus, his great patron; I,
With trusted Laco here, are for the guards:

Then, to divide. For night hath many eyes,
Whereof, though most do sleep, yet some are spies.

[*Exeunt.*]

[SCENE III]

[*Enter*] PRAECONES, FLAMEN, MINISTRI, [TUBICINES, TIBICINES;] SEJANUS, TERENTIUS, SATRIUS, [NATTA,] *etc.*

PRAECONES. 'Be all profane far hence; fly, fly far off:
Be absent far; far hence be all profane.'

TUBICINES [*and*] TIBICINES *sound, while the* FLAMEN *washeth.*

FLAMEN. We have been faulty, but repent us now;
And bring pure hands, pure vestments, and pure minds.
[FIRST] MINISTER. Pure vessels.
[SECOND] MINISTER. And pure offerings.
[THIRD] MINISTER. Garlands pure.
FLAMEN. Bestow your garlands: and (with reverence) place
The vervin on the altar.
PRAECO. Favour your tongues.

While they sound again, the FLAMEN *takes of the honey with his finger, and tastes, then ministers to all the rest: so of the milk, in an earthen vessel, he deals about; which done, he sprinkleth, upon the altar, milk; then imposeth the honey, and kindleth his gums, and after censing about the altar placeth his censer thereon, into which they put several branches of poppy, and the music ceasing, proceed.*

---

169 *divide*: separate.
V.[iii].s.d. FLAMEN, MINISTRI, [TUBICINES, TIBICINES]: priest, attendants, trumpeters, flautists.
172 s.d. *sound*: play.
175 FIRST . . . SECOND . . . THIRD: see Textual Note, p. 432 below.
177 *vervin*: verbena; or bough of laurel, etc., used in sacrifices. *Favour your tongues*: be silent (Latin *favete linguis*); *Favour it with your tongues* (182) is identical in meaning.

FLAMEN. Great mother Fortune, queen of human state,
Rectress of action, arbitress of fate,
To whom all sway, all power, all empire bows,
Be present, and propitious to our vows.
PRAECO. Favour it with your tongues.
[FIRST] MINISTER. Be present, and propitious to our vows.
Accept our offering, and be pleased, great goddess.
TERENTIUS. See, see, the image stirs!
SATRIUS. And turns away!
NATTA. Fortune averts her face!
FLAMEN. Avert, you gods,
The prodigy. Still! still! Some pious rite
We have neglected. Yet! Heaven, be appeased.
And be all tokens false, or void, that speak
Thy present wrath.
SEJANUS. Be thou dumb, scrupulous priest:
And gather up thyself, with these thy wares,
Which I, in spite of thy blind mistress, or
Thy juggling mystery, religion, throw
Thus, scorned on the earth. [*Overturns the altar.*]
[*Addresses the statue*] Nay, hold thy look
Averted, till I woo thee, turn again;
And thou shalt stand, to all posterity,
Th'eternal game, and laughter, with thy neck
Writhed to thy tail, like a ridiculous cat.
Avoid these fumes, these superstitious lights,
And all these cosening ceremonies: you,
Your pure, and spicèd conscience.
[*Exeunt* FLAMEN, *attendants.*]
I, the slave,
And mock of fools (scorn on my worthy head)
That have been titled, and adored a god,
Yea, sacrificed unto, myself, in Rome,
No less than Jove: and I be brought, to do
A peevish giglot rites? Perhaps the thought,

---

179 *Rectress*: directress.
193 *juggling mystery*: cheating trade.
197 *game*: joke, laughing-stock.
198 *Writhed*: turned.
199 *Avoid*: remove.
201 *spicèd*: dainty, scrupulous.
206 *giglot*: wanton.

And shame of that made Fortune turn her face,
Knowing herself the lesser deity,
And but my servant. Bashful queen, if so,
Sejanus thanks thy modesty. Who's that?

[*Enter*] POMPONIUS, MINUTIUS.

POMPONIUS. His fortune suffers, till he hears my news:
I have waited here too long. Macro, my lord –
SEJANUS. Speak lower, and withdraw.
TERENTIUS. Are these things true?
MINUTIUS. Thousands are gazing at it, in the streets.
SEJANUS. What's that?
TERENTIUS. Minutius tells us here, my lord,
That, a new head being set upon your statue,
A rope is since found wreathed about it! and
But now, a fiery meteor, in the form
Of a great ball, was seen to roll along
The troubled air, where yet it hangs, unperfect,
The amazing wonder of the multitude!
SEJANUS. No more. That Macro's come, is more than all!
TERENTIUS. Is Macro come?
POMPONIUS. I saw him.
TERENTIUS. Where? with whom?
POMPONIUS. With Regulus.
SEJANUS. Terentius –
TERENTIUS. My lord?
SEJANUS. Send for the tribunes, we will straight have up
More of the soldiers, for our guard.
[*Exit* TERENTIUS.]
Minutius,
We pray you, go for Cotta, Latiaris,
Trio the consul, or what senators
You know are sure, and ours.
[*Exit* MINUTIUS.]
You, my good Natta,
For Laco, provost of the watch.
[*Exit* NATTA.]
Now, Satrius,

---

218 *meteor*: portentous of the death of a great person.
220 *unperfect*: halted in its progress.

The time of proof comes on. Arm all our servants,
And without tumult.
[*Exit* SATRIUS.]
You, Pomponius,
Hold some good correspondence with the consul,
Attempt him, noble friend.
[*Exit* POMPONIUS.]
These things begin
To look like dangers, now, worthy my Fates.
Fortune, I see thy worst: let doubtful states,
And things uncertain hang upon thy will:
Me surest death shall render certain still.
Yet why is, now, my thought turned toward death,
Whom Fates have let go on, so far, in breath,
Unchecked, or unreproved? I, that did help
To fell the lofty cedar of the world,
Germanicus; that, at one stroke, cut down
Drusus, that upright elm; withered his vine;
Laid Silius, and Sabinus, two strong oaks,
Flat on the earth; besides those other shrubs,
Cordus, and Sosia, Claudia Pulchra,
Furnius, and Gallus, which I have grubbed up;
And since, have set my axe so strong, and deep
Into the root of spreading Agrippine;
Lopped off, and scattered her proud branches, Nero,
Drusus, and Caius too, although replanted;
If you will, Destinies, that, after all,
I faint, now, ere I touch my period,
You are but cruel: and I already have done
Things great enough. All Rome hath been my slave;
The Senate sat an idle looker-on,
And witness of my power; when I have blushed,
More, to command, than it to suffer; all

---

231 *proof*: testing.
233 *correspondence*: conversation.
234 *Attempt*: sound out.
242 *cedar*: emblematic of royalty.
244 *vine*: Livia, Drusus's wife; elm and vine are emblems of husband and wife.
252 *Caius*: Caligula.
253 *Destinies*: the Fates, the three goddesses who governed human destiny; see III.[i].108 n., V.[v].418 n.
254 *period*: end.
259 *suffer*: submit.

The fathers have sat ready, and prepared,
To give me empire, temples, or their throats,
When I would ask 'em; and (what crowns the top)
Rome, Senate, people, all the world have seen
Jove, but my equal: Caesar, but my second.
'Tis then your malice, Fates, who (but your own)
Envy, and fear, t'have any power long known.
[*Exit.*]

[*Enter*] TERENTIUS, TRIBUNES.

TERENTIUS. Stay here: I'll give his lordship you are come.

[*Enter*] MINUTIUS, COTTA, LATIARIS.

MINUTIUS. Marcus Terentius, pray you tell my lord,
Here's Cotta, and Latiaris.
TERENTIUS. Sir, I shall. [*Exit.*]
They confer their letters.
COTTA. My letter is the very same with yours;
Only requires me to be present there,
And give my voice, to strengthen his design.
LATIARIS. Names he not what it is?
COTTA. No, nor to you.
LATIARIS. 'Tis strange, and singular doubtful!
COTTA. So it is!
It may be all is left to lord Sejanus.

[*Enter*] *to them* NATTA, LACO.

NATTA. Gentlemen, where's my lord?
TRIBUNE. We wait him here.
COTTA. The provost Laco? what's the news?
LATIARIS. My lord –

[*Enter*] *to them* SEJANUS.

SEJANUS. Now, my right dear, noble, and trusted friends;
How much I am a captive to your kindness!
Most worthy Cotta, Latiaris; Laco,
Your valiant hand; and gentlemen, your loves.
I wish I could divide myself unto you;
Or that it lay, within our narrow powers,

---

262 *crowns the top*: puts the final flourish on my achievement.
269 s.d. *confer*: compare.
272 *voice*: vote.
274 *singular*: extraordinary.

To satisfy for so enlargèd bounty.
Gracinus, we must pray you, hold your guards
Unquit, when morning comes. Saw you the consul?
MINUTIUS. Trio will presently be here, my lord.
COTTA. They are but giving order for the edict,
To warn the Senate.
SEJANUS. How! the Senate?
LATIARIS. Yes.
This morning, in Apollo's temple.
COTTA. We
Are charged, by letter, to be there, my lord.
SEJANUS. By letter? pray you let's see!
LATIARIS. Knows not his lordship!
COTTA. It seems so!
SEJANUS. A Senate warned? without my knowledge?
And on this sudden? Senators by letters
Requirèd to be there! – Who brought these?
COTTA. Macro.
SEJANUS. Mine enemy! And when?
COTTA. This midnight.
SEJANUS. Time,
With every other circumstance, doth give
It hath some strain of engine in't!

[*Enter*] SATRIUS.

How now?
SATRIUS. My lord, Sertorius Macro is without,
Alone, and prays t'have private conference
In business, of high nature, with your lordship
(He says to me), and which regards you much.
SEJANUS. Let him come here.
SATRIUS. Better, my lord, withdraw,
You will betray what store, and strength of friends
Are now about you; which he comes to spy.
SEJANUS. Is he not armed?
SATRIUS. We'll search him.
SEJANUS. No, but take,
And lead him to some room, where you, concealed,
May keep a guard upon us.
[*Exit* SATRIUS.]
Noble Laco,
You are our trust: and till our own cohorts

---

289 *warn*: summon.

Can be brought up, your strengths must be our guard.
Now, good Minutius, honoured Latiaris,
He salutes them humbly.
Most worthy, and my most unwearied friends:
I return instantly. [*Exit* SEJANUS.]
LATIARIS. Most worthy lord!
COTTA. His lordship is turned instant kind, methinks,
I'have not observed it in him, heretofore.
FIRST TRIBUNE. 'Tis true, and it becomes him nobly.
MINUTIUS. I
Am rapt withal.
SECOND TRIBUNE. By Mars, he has my lives
(Were they a million) for this only grace.
LACO. Ay, and to name a man!
LATIARIS. As he did me!
MINUTIUS. And me!
LATIARIS. Who would not spend his life and fortunes,
To purchase but the look of such a lord?
LACO. [*aside*] He, that would nor be lord's fool, nor the world's.

[SCENE IV]

[*Enter*] SEJANUS, MACRO [*and* SATRIUS].

SEJANUS. Macro! most welcome, as most coveted friend!
[*Embracing him*] Let me enjoy my longings. When arrived you?
MACRO. About the noon of night.
SEJANUS. Satrius, give leave.
[*Exit* SATRIUS.]
MACRO. I have been, since I came, with both the consuls,
On a particular design from Caesar.
SEJANUS. How fares it with our great, and royal master?
MACRO. Right plentifully well; as with a prince,
That still holds out the great proportion

---

318 *only*: one.
324 *Let me enjoy my longings*: the embrace is to ascertain that Macro is unarmed.

Of his large favours, where his judgement hath
Made once divine election: like the god,
That wants not, nor is wearied to bestow
Where merit meets his bounty, as it doth
In you, already the most happy, and ere
The sun shall climb the south, most high Sejanus.
Let not my lord be'amused. For to this end
Was I by Caesar sent for, to the isle,
With special caution to conceal my journey;
And, thence, had my dispatch as privately
Again to Rome; charged to come here by night;
And only to the consuls, make narration
Of his great purpose: that the benefit
Might come more full, and striking, by how much
It was less looked for, or aspired by you,
Or least informèd to the common thought.

SEJANUS. What may this be? part of myself, dear Macro!
If good, speak out: and share with your Sejanus.

MACRO. If bad, I should forever loathe myself,
To be the messenger to so good a lord.
I do exceed m'instructions, to acquaint
Your lordship with thus much; but 'tis my venture
On your retentive wisdom: and because
I would no jealous scruple should molest
Or rack your peace of thought. For, I assure
My noble lord, no senator yet knows
The business meant: though all, by several letters,
Are warnèd to be there, and give their voices,
Only to add unto the state, and grace
Of what is purposed.

SEJANUS. You take pleasure, Macro,
Like a coy wench, in torturing your lover.
What can be worth this suffering?

---

331 *large*: generous.
333 *wants not*: does not lack (bounty).
337 *amused*: puzzled.
347 *part of myself*: addressed ingratiatingly to Macro; a phrase modelled on the Latin partitive genitive; compare Horace, *Odes*, III.xxx.6, *multaque pars mei*, great part of myself.
353 *retentive wisdom*: sound judgement not to reveal (what I shall tell you).
354 *jealous scruple*: suspicious doubt; or, 'jot of suspicion'.
357 *several*: individual.
361 *lover*: friend.

MACRO. That which follows,
The tribunicial dignity, and power:
Both which Sejanus is to have this day
Conferred upon him, and by public Senate.
SEJANUS. Fortune, be mine again; thou hast satisfied
For thy suspected loyalty.
MACRO. My lord,
I have no longer time, the day approacheth,
And I must back to Caesar.
SEJANUS. Where's Caligula?
MACRO. That I forgot to tell your lordship. Why,
He lingers yonder, about Capreae,
Disgraced; Tiberius hath not seen him yet:
He needs would thrust himself to go with me,
Against my wish, or will, but I have quitted
His forward trouble, with as tardy note
As my neglect, or silence could afford him.
Your lordship cannot now command me aught,
Because I take no knowledge that I saw you,
But I shall boast to live to serve your lordship:
And so take leave.
SEJANUS. Honest, and worthy Macro,
Your love, and friendship. Who's there? Satrius,
Attend my honourable friend forth.
[*Exit* MACRO.]
Oh!
How vain, and vile a passion is this fear?
What base, uncomely things it makes men do?
Suspect their noblest friends (as I did this),
Flatter poor enemies, entreat their servants,
Stoop, court, and catch at the benevolence
Of creatures, unto whom (within this hour)
I would not have vouchsafed a quarter-look,
Or piece of face? By you, that fools call gods,
Hang all the sky with your prodigious signs,
Fill earth with monsters, drop the scorpion down

---

363 *tribunicial dignity, and power*: title conferring highest state powers, including the right of veto in state business, and held by the emperor.
375 *forward trouble*: troublesome presumptuousness.
note: attention.
389 *quarter-look*: averted look (in contempt).
390 *piece of face*: glance.
By: as for.

Out of the zodiac, or the fiercer lion,
Shake off the loosened globe from her long hinge,
Roll all the world in darkness, and let loose
Th'enragèd winds to turn up groves and towns;
When I do fear again, let me be struck
With forkèd fire, and unpitied die:
Who fears, is worthy of calamity. [*Exit.*]

[SCENE V]

[*Enter*] *to the rest* POMPONIUS, REGULUS, TRIO.

POMPONIUS. Is not my lord here?
TERENTIUS. Sir, he will be straight.
COTTA. What news, Fulcinius Trio?
TRIO. Good, good tidings.
(But keep it to yourself.) My lord Sejanus
Is to receive this day, in open Senate,
The tribunicial dignity.
COTTA. Is't true?
TRIO. No words; not to your thought: but, sir, believe it.
LATIARIS. What says the consul?
COTTA. (Speak it not again.)
He tells me, that today my lord Sejanus –
TRIO. (I must entreat you Cotta, on your honour
Not to reveal it.
COTTA. On my life, sir.)
LATIARIS. Say.
COTTA. Is to receive the tribunicial power.
But as you are an honourable man,
Let me conjure you, not to utter it:
For it is trusted to me, with that bond.
LATIARIS. I am Harpocrates.
TERENTIUS. Can you assure it?
POMPONIUS. The consul told it me, but keep it close.
MINUTIUS. Lord Latiaris, what's the news?
LATIARIS. I'll tell you,
But you must swear to keep it secret –

[*Enter*] *to them* SEJANUS.

---

394 *hinge*: axis.
414 *Harpocrates*: god of silence and secrecy.

SEJANUS. I knew the Fates had on their distaff left
More of our thread, than so.
REGULUS. Hail, great Sejanus.
TRIO. Hail, the most honoured.
COTTA. Happy.
LATIARIS. High Sejanus.
SEJANUS. Do you bring prodigies too?
TRIO. May all presage
Turn to those fair effects, whereof we bring
Your lordship news.
REGULUS. May't please my lord withdraw?
SEJANUS. Yes. *To some that stand by.*
(I will speak with you, anon.)
TERENTIUS. My lord,
What is your pleasure for the tribunes?
SEJANUS. Why,
Let 'em be thanked, and sent away.
MINUTIUS. My lord –
LACO. Will't please your lordship to command me –
SEJANUS. No.
You are troublesome.
MINUTIUS. The mood is changed.
[FIRST] TRIBUNE. Not speak?
[SECOND] TRIBUNE. Nor look?
LACO. Ay. He is wise, will make him friends
Of such, who never love, but for their ends.
[*Exeunt.*]

[SCENE VI]

[*Enter*] ARRUNTIUS, LEPIDUS, *divers other senators passing by them.*

ARRUNTIUS. Ay, go, make haste; take heed you be not last
To tender your 'all hail', in the wide hall
Of huge Sejanus: run, a lictor's pace;
Stay not to put your robes on; but away,
With the pale troubled ensigns of great friendship

---

418 *Fates*: the three goddesses spun, wound, and cut the thread of men's lives at their destined end.
422 *effects*: outcome.
428, 429 FIRST . . . SECOND: see Textual Note, p. 432 below.
435 *ensigns*: marks.

Stamped i'your face! Now, Marcus Lepidus,
You still believe your former augury?
Sejanus must go downward? you perceive
His wane approaching fast?

LEPIDUS. Believe me, Lucius,
I wonder at this rising!

ARRUNTIUS. Ay, and that we
Must give our suffrage to it? you will say,
It is to make his fall more steep, and grievous?
It may be so. But think it, they that can
With idle wishes 'ssay to bring back time:
In cases desperate, all hope is crime.
See, see! what troops of his officious friends
Flock to salute my lord! and start before
My great, proud lord! to get a lordlike nod!
Attend my lord, unto the Senate house!
Bring back my lord! like servile ushers, make
Way for my lord! proclaim his idol lordship,
More than ten criers, or six noise of trumpets!
Make legs, kiss hands, and take a scattered hair
From my lord's eminent shoulder! See,
Sanquinius!
With his slow belly, and his dropsy! look,
What toiling haste he makes! Yet here's another,
Retarded with the gout, will be afore him!
Get thee Liburnian porters, thou gross fool,
To bear thy obsequious fatness, like thy peers.
They are met! The gout returns, and his great
carriage.

LICTORES, *consuls*, SEJANUS, *etc., pass over the stage.*

LICTOR. Give way, make place; room for the consul.

SANQUINIUS. Hail,
Hail, great Sejanus!

HATERIUS. Hail, my honoured lord.

---

444 *'ssay*: attempt.
445 *crime*: sin.
452 *noise*: bands.
453 *Make legs*: bow.
456 *another*: Haterius.
458 *Liburnian porters*: Illyrian slaves used in Rome as sedan-chair bearers.
460 *carriage*: load (i.e. Sanquinius's great belly).

ARRUNTIUS. We shall be marked anon, for our not-hail.
LEPIDUS. That is already done.
ARRUNTIUS. It is a note
Of upstart greatness, to observe, and watch
For these poor trifles, which the noble mind
Neglects, and scorns.
LEPIDUS. Ay, and they think themselves
Deeply dishonoured, where they are omitted,
As if they were necessities, that helped
To the perfection of their dignities:
And hate the men, that but refrain 'em.
ARRUNTIUS. Oh!
There is a farther cause of hate. Their breasts
Are guilty, that we know their obscure springs,
And base beginnings: thence the anger grows. On.
Follow.
[*Exeunt.*]

[*Enter*] MACRO, LACO.

MACRO. When all are entered, shut the temple doors;
And bring your guards up to the gate.
LACO. I will.
MACRO. If you shall hear commotion in the Senate,
Present yourself: and charge on any man
Shall offer to come forth.
LACO. I am instructed.
[*Exeunt.*]

[SCENE VII]

[*Enter*] *the Senate.* HATERIUS, TRIO, SANQUINIUS, COTTA, REGULUS, SEJANUS, POMPONIUS, LATIARIS, LEPIDUS, ARRUNTIUS, [SENATORS;] PRAECONES, LICTORES [*and* PRAETORES].

HATERIUS. How well his lordship looks today!
TRIO. As if
He had been born, or made for this hour's state.
COTTA. Your fellow consul's come about, methinks?
TRIO. Ay, he is wise.

---

473 *obscure*: accented on the first syllable.

SANQUINIUS. Sejanus trusts him well.
TRIO. Sejanus is a noble, bounteous lord.
HATERIUS. He is so, and most valiant.
LATIARIS. And most wise.
[FIRST] SENATOR. He's everything.
LATIARIS. Worthy of all, and more
Than bounty can bestow.
TRIO. This dignity
Will make him worthy.
POMPONIUS. Above Caesar.
SANQUINIUS. Tut,
Caesar is but the rector of an isle,
He of the Empire.
TRIO. Now he will have power
More to reward, than ever.
COTTA. Let us look
We be not slack in giving him our voices.
LATIARIS. Not I.
SANQUINIUS. Nor I.
COTTA. The readier we seem
To propagate his honours, will more bind
His thought, to ours.
HATERIUS. I think right, with your lordship.
It is the way to have us hold our places.
SANQUINIUS. Ay, and get more.
LATIARIS. More office, and more titles.
POMPONIUS. I will not lose the part I hope to share
In these his fortunes, for my patrimony.
LATIARIS. See, how Arruntius sits, and Lepidus.
TRIO. Let 'em alone, they will be marked anon.
[FIRST] SENATOR. I'll do with others.
[SECOND] SENATOR. So will I.
[THIRD] SENATOR. And I.
Men grow not in the state, but as they are planted
Warm in his favours.
COTTA. Noble Sejanus!
HATERIUS. Honoured Sejanus!
LATIARIS. Worthy, and great Sejanus!
ARRUNTIUS. Gods! how the sponges open, and take in!
And shut again! Look, look! is not he blest

---

486 FIRST: see Textual Note, p. 432 below.
489 *rector*: ruler.
502 FIRST . . . SECOND . . . THIRD: see Textual Note, p. 432 below.

That gets a seat in eye-reach of him? more,
That comes in ear, or tongue-reach? Oh, but most,
Can claw his subtle elbow, or with a buzz
Fly-blow his ears.

PRAETOR. Proclaim the Senate's peace;
And give last summons by the edict.

PRAECO. Silence:
In name of Caesar, and the Senate. Silence.
'Memmius Regulus and Fulcinius Trio, consuls,
these present kalends of June, with the first light,
shall hold a Senate, in the temple of Apollo
Palatine, all that are fathers, and are registered
fathers, that have right of entering the Senate, we
warn, or command, you be frequently present;
take knowledge the business is the Commonwealth's; whosoever is absent, his fine, or mulct,
will be taken, his excuse will not be taken.'

TRIO. Note who are absent, and record their names.

REGULUS. 'Fathers conscript. May what I am to utter,
Turn good, and happy, for the Commonwealth.'
And thou, Apollo, in whose holy house
We here are met, inspire us all, with truth,
And liberty of censure, to our thought.
The majesty of great Tiberius Caesar
Propounds to this grave Senate, the bestowing
Upon the man he loves, honoured Sejanus,
The tribunicial dignity, and power;
Here are his letters, signed with his signet:
'What pleaseth now the fathers to be done?'

SENATORS. Read, read 'em, open, publicly, read 'em.

COTTA. Caesar hath honoured his own greatness much,
In thinking of this act.

TRIO. It was a thought
Happy, and worthy Caesar.

LATIARIS. And the lord
As worthy it, on whom it is directed!

---

510 *claw his . . . elbow*: pluck his elbow; also, 'flatter him'.
511 *Fly-blow*: corrupt.
515 *kalends*: first day of the month.
517 *registered*: conscripted.
519 *frequently*: in full numbers.
528 *censure*: judgement.

HATERIUS. Most worthy!
SANQUINIUS. Rome did never boast the virtue
That could give envy bounds, but his: Sejanus –
[FIRST] SENATOR. Honoured, and noble!
[SECOND] SENATOR. Good, and great Sejanus!
ARRUNTIUS. O most tame slavery, and fierce flattery!
PRAECO. Silence.

The Epistle is read.

'Tiberius Caesar to the Senate, greeting. If you, conscript fathers, with your children, be in health, it is abundantly well: we with our friends here, are so. The care of the Commonwealth, howsoever we are removed in person, cannot be absent to our thought; although, oftentimes, even to princes most present, the truth of their own affairs is hid: than which, nothing falls out more miserable to a state, or makes the art of governing more difficult. But since it hath been our easeful happiness to enjoy both the aids, and industry of so vigilant a Senate, we profess to have been the more indulgent to our pleasures, not as being careless of our office, but rather secure of the necessity. Neither do these common rumours of many, and infamous libels published against our retirement, at all afflict us; being born more out of men's ignorance, than their malice: and will, neglected, find their own grave quickly; whereas too sensibly acknowledged, it would make their obloquy ours. Nor do we desire their authors (though found) be censured, since in a free state (as ours) all men ought to enjoy both their minds, and tongues free.'

(ARRUNTIUS. [*aside*] The lapwing, the lapwing.)

'Yet in things which shall worthily, and more near concern the majesty of a prince, we shall fear to be so unnaturally cruel to our own fame, as to neglect them. True it is, conscript fathers, that we have

---

542 FIRST ... SECOND: see Textual Note, p. 432 below.
557–8 *secure of the necessity*: confident that the Senate will carry out the necessary duties.
563 *sensibly*: with sensitivity.
568 *lapwing*: supposed to call loudly at a distance from its nest to decoy predators: i.e. Tiberius's words are far from his real meaning.

raised Sejanus, from obscure, and almost unknown gentry,'

(SENATORS. How! How!)

'to the highest, and most conspicuous point of greatness, and (we hope) deservingly; yet not without danger: it being a most bold hazard in that sovereign, who, by his particular love to one, dares adventure the hatred of all his other subjects.'

(ARRUNTIUS. [*aside*] This touches, the blood turns.)

'But we affy in your loves, and understandings, and do no way suspect the merit of our Sejanus to make our favours offensive to any.'

(SENATORS. Oh! good, good.)

'Though we could have wished his zeal had run a calmer course against Agrippina, and our nephews, howsoever the openness of their actions declared them delinquents; and that he would have remembered, no innocence is so safe, but it rejoiceth to stand in the sight of mercy: the use of which in us, he hath so quite taken away, toward them, by his loyal fury, as now our clemency would be thought but wearied cruelty, if we should offer to exercise it.'

(ARRUNTIUS. [*aside*] I thank him, there I looked for't. A good fox!)

'Some there be, that would interpret this his public severity to be particular ambition; and that, under a pretext of service to us, he doth but remove his own lets: alleging the strengths he hath made to himself, by the praetorian soldiers, by his faction in court, and Senate, by the offices he holds himself, and confers on others, his popularity, and dependents, his urging (and almost driving) us to this our unwilling retirement, and lastly his aspiring to be our son-in-law.'

(SENATORS. This's strange!

ARRUNTIUS. [*aside to* LEPIDUS] I shall anon believe your vultures, Marcus.)

'Your wisdoms, conscript fathers, are able to examine, and censure these suggestions. But were they left to our absolving voice, we durst pro-

---

583 *affy*: trust.
599 *particular*: personal.

nounce them, as we think them, most malicious.'

(SENATORS. Oh, he has restored all, list.)

'Yet are they offered to be averred, and on the lives of the informers. What we should say, or rather what we should not say, lords of the Senate, if this be true, our gods and goddesses confound us if we know! Only, we must think, we have placed our benefits ill: and conclude, that, in our choice, either we were wanting to the gods, or the gods to us.'

The senators shift their places.

(ARRUNTIUS. [*aside*] The place grows hot, they shift.)

'We have not been covetous, honourable fathers, to change; neither is it now, any new lust that alters our affection, or old loathing: but those needful jealousies of state, that warn wiser princes, hourly, to provide their safety; and do teach them how learned a thing it is to beware of the humblest enemy; much more of those great ones, whom their own employed favours have made fit for their fears.'

([FIRST] SENATOR. Away.

[SECOND] SENATOR. Sit farther.

COTTA. Let's remove –

ARRUNTIUS. Gods! how the leaves drop off, this little wind!)

'We therefore desire, that the offices he holds, be first seized by the Senate; and himself suspended from all exercise of place, or power – '

(SENATORS. How!

SANQUINIUS. By your leave.

ARRUNTIUS. Come, porcpisce (where's Haterius?
His gout keeps him most miserably constant),
Your dancing shows a tempest.)

SEJANUS. Read no more.

REGULUS. Lords of the Senate, hold your seats: read on.

---

625 *lust*: liking.

631 *employed*: bestowed.

633 FIRST . . . SECOND: see Textual Note, p. 432 below.

638 *porcpisce*: porpoise: Jonson's seventeenth-century Latinate spelling reflects the etymology, 'pig-fish'.

640 *dancing shows a tempest*: the porpoise's activity was said to be a sign of coming storms.

SEJANUS. These letters, they are forged.
REGULUS. A guard, sit still.
LACO *enters with the guards.*
ARRUNTIUS. There's change.
REGULUS. Bid silence, and read forward.
PRAECO. Silence – 'and himself suspended from all exercise of place, or power, but till due and mature trial be made of his innocency, which yet we can faintly apprehend the necessity to doubt. If, conscript fathers, to your more searching wisdoms, there shall appear farther cause (or of farther proceeding, either to seizure of lands, goods, or more –) it is not our power that shall limit your authority, or our favour, that must corrupt your justice: either were dishonourable in you, and both uncharitable to ourself. We would willingly be present with your counsels in this business, but the danger of so potent a faction (if it should prove so) forbids our attempting it: except one of the consuls would be entreated for our safety, to undertake the guard of us home, then we should most readily adventure. In the meantime, it shall not be fit for us to importune so judicious a Senate, who know how much they hurt the innocent, that spare the guilty: and how grateful a sacrifice, to the gods, is the life of an ingrateful person. We reflect not, in this, on Sejanus (notwithstanding, if you keep an eye upon him – and there is Latiaris a senator, and Pinnarius Natta, two of his most trusted ministers, and so professed, whom we desire not to have apprehended) but as the necessity of the cause exacts it.'
REGULUS. A guard on Latiaris.
ARRUNTIUS. Oh, the spy!
The reverend spy is caught, who pities him?
Reward, sir, for your service: now you ha'done
Your property, you see what use is made?
Hang up the instrument.
SEJANUS. Give leave.
LACO. Stand, stand,

673–4 *done Your property*: been used as a tool.
675 *Hang up the instrument*: replace the musical instrument on its hook (with a more sinister meaning).

He comes upon his death, that doth advance
An inch toward my point.
SEJANUS. Have we no friends here?
ARRUNTIUS. Hushed. Where now are all the hails,
and acclamations?

[*Enter*] MACRO.

MACRO. Hail to the consuls, and this noble Senate.
SEJANUS. [*aside*] Is Macro here? O, thou art lost,
Sejanus.
MACRO. Sit still, and unaffrighted, reverend fathers.
Macro, by Caesar's grace, the new-made provost,
And now possessed of the praetorian bands,
An honour late belonged to that proud man,
Bids you, be safe: and to your constant doom
Of his deservings, offers you the surety
Of all the soldiers, tribunes, and centurions,
Received in our command.
REGULUS. Sejanus, Sejanus,
Stand forth, Sejanus.
SEJANUS. Am I called?
MACRO. Ay, thou,
Thou insolent monster, art bid stand.
SEJANUS. Why, Macro,
It hath been otherwise, between you and I!
This court, that knows us both, hath seen a
difference,
And can (if it be pleased to speak) confirm,
Whose insolence is most.
MACRO. Come down, Typhoeus,
If mine be most, lo, thus I make it more;
Kick up thy heels in air, tear off thy robe,
Play with thy beard, and nostrils. Thus 'tis fit
(And no man take compassion of thy state)
To use th'ingrateful viper, tread his brains
Into the earth.
REGULUS. Forbear.
MACRO. If I could lose
All my humanity now, 'twere well to torture
So meriting a traitor. Wherefore, fathers,

---

685 *doom*: judgement.
686 *deservings*: merits.
694 *Typhoeus*: hideous monster struck down by Jove's thunderbolt; his defeat assured Jove's final and lasting supremacy.

Sit you amazed, and silent? and not censure
This wretch, who in the hour he first rebelled
'Gainst Caesar's bounty, did condemn himself?
Phlegra, the field, where all the sons of earth
Mustered against the gods, did ne'er acknowledge
So proud, and huge a monster.
REGULUS. Take him hence.
And all the gods guard Caesar.
TRIO. Take him hence.
HATERIUS. Hence.
COTTA. To the dungeon with him.
SANQUINIUS. He deserves it.
SENATORS. Crown all our doors with bays.
SANQUINIUS. And let an ox
With gilded horns, and garlands, straight be led
Unto the Capitol.
HATERIUS. And sacrificed
To Jove, for Caesar's safety.
TRIO. All our gods
Be present still to Caesar.
COTTA. Phoebus.
SANQUINIUS. Mars.
HATERIUS. Diana.
SANQUINIUS. Pallas.
SENATORS. Juno, Mercury,
All guard him.
MACRO. Forth, thou prodigy of men.
[*Exit* SEJANUS *guarded.*]
COTTA. Let all the traitor's titles be defaced.
TRIO. His images, and statues be pulled down.
HATERIUS. His chariot wheels be broken.
ARRUNTIUS. And the legs
Of the poor horses, that deservèd naught,
Let them be broken too.
LEPIDUS. Oh, violent change,
And whirl of men's affections!
ARRUNTIUS. Like as both
Their bulks and souls were bound on Fortune's wheel,
And must act only with her motion!

---

706 *Phlegra*: where the Giants ('sons of earth') assembled to attack Jove.
717 *prodigy*: monster.
724 *bulks*: bodies.
725 *motion*: three syllables.

[*Exeunt all but*] LEPIDUS, ARRUNTIUS.

LEPIDUS. Who would depend upon the popular air,
Or voice of men, that have today beheld
(That which if all the gods had foredeclared,
Would not have been believed) Sejanus' fall?
He, that this morn rose proudly, as the sun?
And breaking through a mist of clients' breath,
Came on as gazed at, and admired, as he
When superstitious Moors salute his light!
That had our servile nobles waiting him
As common grooms; and hanging on his look,
No less than human life on destiny!
That had men's knees as frequent, as the gods;
And sacrifices, more than Rome had altars:
And this man fall! Fall? Ay, without a look,
That durst appear his friend; or lend so much
Of vain relief, to his changed state, as pity!

ARRUNTIUS. They, that before like gnats played in his beams,
And thronged to circumscribe him, now not seen!
Nor deign to hold a common seat with him!
Others, that waited him unto the Senate,
Now inhumanely ravish him to prison!
Whom (but this morn) they followed as their lord,
Guard through the streets, bound like a fugitive!
Instead of wreaths, give fetters; strokes, for stoops:
Blind shame, for honours; and black taunts, for titles!
Who would trust slippery Chance?

LEPIDUS. They, that would make
Themselves her spoil: and foolishly forget,
When she doth flatter, that she comes to prey.
Fortune, thou hadst no deity, if men
Had wisdom: we have placèd thee so high,
By fond belief in thy felicity.

Shout within.

---

726 *popular air*: breath of popular favour.
733 *superstitious Moors*: the Romans held that the Libyans worshipped the sun.
734 *waiting*: attending.
735 *grooms*: servants.
743 *circumscribe*: surround.
746 *ravish*: drag off.
748 *fugitive*: runaway slave.
756 *fond*: foolish.

SENATORS. The gods guard Caesar. All the gods
guard Caesar.

[*Enter*] MACRO, REGULUS, SENATORS.

MACRO. Now great Sejanus, you that awed the state,
And sought to bring the nobles to your whip,
That would be Caesar's tutor, and dispose
Of dignities, and offices! that had
The public head still bare to your designs,
And made the general voice to echo yours!
That looked for salutations, twelve score off,
And would have pyramids, yea, temples reared
To your huge greatness! Now, you lie as flat,
As was your pride advanced.
REGULUS. Thanks, to the gods.
SENATORS. And praise to Macro, that hath savèd
Rome.
Liberty, liberty, liberty. Lead on,
And praise to Macro, that hath savèd Rome.
[*Exeunt all but*] ARRUNTIUS, LEPIDUS.
ARRUNTIUS. I prophesy, out of this Senate's flattery,
That this new fellow, Macro, will become
A greater prodigy in Rome, than he
That now is fall'n.

[*Enter* TERENTIUS.]

TERENTIUS. O you, whose minds are good,
And have not forced all mankind from your
breasts;
That yet have so much stock of virtue left,
To pity guilty states, when they are wretched:
Lend your soft ears to hear, and eyes to weep
Deeds done by men, beyond the acts of Furies.
The eager multitude (who never yet
Knew why to love, or hate, but only pleased
T'express their rage of power) no sooner heard
The murmur of Sejanus in decline,
But with that speed, and heat of appetite,

---

760 *tutor*: guardian, custodian.
764 *twelve score*: either 240 paces, or 240 yards: the common distance for a shot in archery.
765 *pyramids*: obelisks.
775 *mankind*: humanity.
782 *rage of*: violent desire for.
784 *heat of appetite*: fervour of desire.

With which they greedily devour the way
To some great sports, or a new theatre,
They filled the Capitol, and Pompey's cirque;
Where, like so many mastiffs biting stones,
As if his statues now were sensive grown
Of their wild fury, first, they tear them down:
Then fastening ropes, drag them along the streets,
Crying in scorn, 'This, this was that rich head
Was crowned with garlands, and with odours, this
That was in Rome so reverenced! Now
The furnace, and the bellows shall to work,
The great Sejanus crack, and piece by piece,
Drop in the founder's pit.'

LEPIDUS. O popular rage!

TERENTIUS. The whilst, the Senate, at the temple of Concord,
Make haste to meet again, and thronging cry,
'Let us condemn him, tread him down in water,
While he doth lie upon the bank; away.'
Where some, more tardy, cry unto their bearers,
'He will be censured ere we come, run knaves';
And use that furious diligence, for fear
Their bondmen should inform against their slackness,
And bring their quaking flesh unto the hook:
The rout, they follow with confusèd voice,
Crying, they're glad; say they could ne'er abide him;
Enquire, what man he was? what kind of face?
What beard he had? what nose? what lips? protest,
They ever did presage h'would come to this:
They never thought him wise, nor valiant: ask
After his garments, when he dies? what death?
And not a beast of all the herd demands,
What was his crime? or, who were his accusers?
Under what proof, or testimony, he fell?
'There came' (says one) 'a huge, long, worded letter
From Capreae against him.' Did there so?
Oh, they are satisfied, no more.

LEPIDUS. Alas!

---

787 *cirque*: theatre.
789 *sensive*: capable of feeling.
797 *Drop in the founder's pit*: be melted down.

They follow Fortune, and hate men condemned,
Guilty, or not.
ARRUNTIUS. But had Sejanus thrived
In his design, and prosperously oppressed
The old Tiberius, then, in that same minute
These very rascals, that now rage like Furies,
Would have proclaimed Sejanus emperor.
LEPIDUS. But what hath followed?
TERENTIUS. Sentence, by the Senate;
To lose his head: which was no sooner off,
But that, and th'unfortunate trunk were seized
By the rude multitude; who not content
With what the forward justice of the state
Officiously had done, with violent rage
Have rent it, limb from limb. A thousand heads,
A thousand hands, ten thousand tongues, and voices,
Employed at once in several acts of malice!
Old men not staid with age, virgins with shame,
Late wives with loss of husbands, mothers of children,
Losing all grief in joy of his sad fall,
Run quite transported with their cruelty!
These mounting at his head, these at his face,
These digging out his eyes, those with his brain,
Sprinkling themselves, their houses, and their friends;
Others are met, have ravished thence an arm,
And deal small pieces of the flesh for favours;
These with a thigh; this hath cut off his hands;
And this his feet; these fingers, and these toes;
That hath his liver; he his heart: there wants
Nothing but room for wrath, and place for hatred!
What cannot oft be done, is now o'er done.
The whole, and all of what was great Sejanus,
And next to Caesar did possess the world,
Now torn, and scattered, as he needs no grave,
Each little dust covers a little part:
So lies he nowhere, and yet often buried!

[*Enter*] NUNTIUS.

---

839 *mounting*: perhaps 'clambering on each other's backs'; see Textual Note, p. 432 below; or perhaps an intended irony: the overreaching ambition of Sejanus here replaced by the mob's barbaric aspiration to tear his body after his fall.

ARRUNTIUS. More of Sejanus?
NUNTIUS. Yes.
LEPIDUS. What can be added?
We know him dead.
NUNTIUS. Then, there begin your pity.
There is enough behind, to melt ev'n Rome,
And Caesar into tears (since never slave
Could yet so highly'offend, but tyranny,
In torturing him, would make him worth lamenting):
A son, and daughter, to the dead Sejanus
(Of whom there is not now so much remaining
As would give fastening to the hangman's hook),
Have they drawn forth for farther sacrifice;
Whose tenderness of knowledge, unripe years,
And childish silly innocence was such,
As scarce would lend them feeling of their danger:
The girl so simple, as she often asked,
'Where they would lead her? for what cause they dragged her?'
Cried, 'she would do no more. That she could take
Warning with beating.' And because our laws
Admit no virgin immature to die,
The wittily, and strangely cruel Macro
Delivered her to be deflowered, and spoiled,
By the rude lust of the licentious hangman,
Then to be strangled with her harmless brother.
LEPIDUS. O, act most worthy hell, and lasting night,
To hide it from the world!
NUNTIUS. Their bodies thrown
Into the Gemonies (I know not how,
Or by what accident returned), the mother,
Th'expulsèd Apicata, finds them there;
Whom when she saw lie spread on the degrees,
After a world of fury on herself,
Tearing her hair, defacing of her face,
Beating her breasts, and womb, kneeling amazed,
Crying to Heaven, then to them; at last,
Her drownèd voice got up above her woes:

865 *silly*: simple.
866 *feeling*: perception.
871 *Admit*: permit.
872 *wittily, and strangely*: ingeniously and unusually.
881 *degrees*: steps.

And with such black, and bitter execrations
(As might affright the gods, and force the sun
Run backward to the east, nay, make the old
Deformèd Chaos rise again, t'o'erwhelm
Them, us, and all the world) she fills the air;
Upbraids the heavens with their partial dooms,
Defies their tyrannous powers, and demands
What she, and those poor innocents have transgressed,
That they must suffer such a share in vengeance,
Whilst Livia, Lygdus, and Eudemus live,
Who (as she says, and firmly vows, to prove it
To Caesar, and the Senate) poisoned Drusus?
LEPIDUS. Confederates with her husband?
NUNTIUS. Ay.
LEPIDUS. Strange act!
ARRUNTIUS. And strangely opened: what says now my monster,
The multitude? they reel now? do they not?
NUNTIUS. Their gall is gone, and now they 'gin to weep
The mischief they have done.
ARRUNTIUS. I thank 'em, rogues!
NUNTIUS. Part are so stupid, or so flexible,
As they believe him innocent; all grieve:
And some, whose hands yet reek with his warm blood,
And gripe the part which they did tear of him,
Wish him collected, and created new.
LEPIDUS. How Fortune plies her sports, when she begins
To practise 'em! pursues, continues, adds!
Confounds, with varying her impassioned moods!
ARRUNTIUS. Dost thou hope, Fortune, to redeem thy crimes?
To make amends, for thy ill-placèd favours,
With these strange punishments? Forbear, you things,
That stand upon the pinnacles of state,
To boast your slippery height; when you do fall,
You pash yourselves in pieces, ne'er to rise,
And he that lends you pity, is not wise.

---

892 *partial*: unjust.
906 *reek*: smoke.

TERENTIUS. Let this example move th'insolent man,
Not to grow proud, and careless of the gods:
It is an odious wisdom, to blaspheme,
Much more to slighten, or deny their powers.
For whom the morning saw so great, and high,
Thus low, and little, 'fore the even doth lie.
[*Exeunt.*]

THE END

This tragedy was first
acted in the year
1603
by the King's Majesty's
Servants.
The principal tragedians were

Richard Burbage	William Shakespeare
Augustine Phillips	John Heminges
William Sly	Henry Condell
John Lowin	Alexander Cooke

With the allowance of the Master of the Revels.

Endnote: *This tragedy . . . Revels*: see Textual Note, p. 432 below.

BEN: IONSON

his

VOLPONE

Or

THE FOXE.

— *Simul & iucunda, & idonea dicere vitæ.*

Printed for *Thomas Thorppe.*
1607.

Title-page from the 1607 quarto, reproduced by permission of the British Library

Motto

'Mixing sweet, and fit, to teach life the right' (Jonson's translation of Horace, *The Art of Poetry*, 334)

INTRODUCTORY NOTE

Sources

Whilst there is no direct source for *Volpone*,[1] Jonson fuses a wide range of different material, classical, humanist, medieval and contemporary; much of it satirical in origin, or used satirically in the play.

The basic motif of legacy hunting derives chiefly from three classical works – Horace's *Satires*, II, v; parts of Petronius's *Satyricon*; and Lucian's *Dialogues of the Dead*, V–IX – which variously set out the lengths to which hopeful heirs go in vice and flattery, and the satisfying comic 'biter bit' situation when their intended victim outwits them. The barest of hints for the characters of the unscrupulous lawyer, and the unnatural father and husband, are found in Horace; Lady Would-be is a brilliant creation from the insufferably garrulous wife in Libanius of Antioch's declamation, *The Loquacious Woman*, and the absurdly pretentious bluestocking of Juvenal's Sixth Satire.[2] Lucian's *Gallus* (the dialogue of the cobbler and the cock), supplemented from Diogenes Laertius's *Lives of the Eminent Philosophers*, provides Mosca's interlude in I.ii, which is also indebted to the Renaissance tradition of 'folly' literature: the fool's song derives from Erasmus's *The Praise of Folly* (1511). Elsewhere, for his line of jeering deflation, Mosca draws on Juvenal's Satire X (the description of old age in I.v.39 ff.), and on the humanist Cornelius Agrippa's *The Vanity and Uncertainty of Arts and Sciences* (transl. 1575), chapters XCIII and LXXXIII, for his account of the lawyer and doctors (I.iii.52–66; I.iv.20 ff.). Volpone's different approach to literary texts, that of witty debasement, is seen in the opening speech of I.i, with its parody of Ovid's account of the Golden Age in *Metamorphoses*, book I, and, superlatively, in the transformation of Catullus's persuasion-to-love fifth lyric, 'Vivamus, mea Lesbia', to the seduction song, 'Come, my Celia' (III.vii).[3] Beyond such examples, literary echoes, especially classical ones, are found everywhere in the text.

The predatory world of the legacy hunters is extended

---

1 The most comprehensive recent treatment of sources and analogues is found in R. B. Parker's 1983 edition of *Volpone*, pp. 11 ff.

2 Both works are important sources for *Epicoene*.

3 Reprinted, with slight alterations, in *The Forest*, v (H&S, VIII).

into the beast fable of the play; pervasively in the influence of the medieval beast epic, *The History of Reynard the Fox*, translated by Caxton (1481). Volpone is Reynard's human counterpart, and shares not only his cunning, but some of his adventures – for example, the basic device of the fox playing dead to feed off would-be scavengers; the fox as physician, false preacher, and seducer; the fox tried by a venal court.[4] Aesop, too, is recalled in Volpone's references to the tale of the fox, the crow and the cheese (I.ii.94–6; V.viii.11–14), and in Sir Pol's tortoise in V.iv. It is in keeping that the characterisation of the main figures of the plot and subplot is influenced by animal lore, derived both from tradition and from the bestiaries.

Jonson's setting embodies and endorses the popular view of Venice – associated with mercantile importance, great wealth, the allure of high sophistication, and super-subtle dealings and corruption – in a wide and exact presentation of the city, including topographical detail and Italian phrases, which reflects his dedication to technical accuracy. The information about the administration and institutions comes largely from Lewkenor's translation of Contarini, *The Commonwealth and Government of Venice* (1599); and the references to distinctive features of Venetian life and culture – the courtesans, the mountebanks, the pastimes and punishments – can in many instances be paralleled in the later account of an English traveller, *The Crudities* of Thomas Coryate (1611). Jonson had not visited Italy; such detail probably came from friends who had been there, including John Florio, whose Italian tutor, *Second Fruits* (1598), contained such useful precepts for travellers as those on which Peregrine acts, and Sir Pol does not. The inspiration for Sir Pol may have come from an English knight in Venice, Sir Anthony Shirley, who like Pol had ambitions to serve the Republic against the Turks, and who made an ignominious departure to Zante and Aleppo, recorded in *A True Account of Sir Anthony Shirley's Journey Overland to Venice* (1600).

Although in 'The Epistle' Jonson stresses his adherence to the principles of ancient comedy,[5] it is not a major influence on plot and characterisation: intrigue, and characters defined by profession, social rank, and age, had long been regular features of English comedy; and indeed Mosca the

4 See R. B. Parker's introduction, pp. 18 ff.
5 Epistle, 122 ff.

parasite points out how far he outgoes his classical originals (III.i.13 ff.). A stronger direct influence is that of one of Roman comedy's descendants, the appropriately Venetian drama of *commedia dell' arte*. Corvino refers to some of the *commedia* 'masks' in II.iii when he breaks up the mountebank scene, which itself has an analogue, *Flavio's Fortunes*, a *scenario* of Flaminio Scala, a leading Venetian actor and director.[6] The brilliant entertainment of *Volpone*, with the constant multiplication of the plays-within-the-play created by Volpone and Mosca, dependent on the predictable responses of the characters, and on skilful improvisation, reflects the repertoire and methods of *commedia*.[7] However, the overall form is a native one – a Jonsonian, blackly comic morality play, with Volpone and Mosca as the Vices tempting the gullible and greedy, and Celia and Bonario presenting the virtuous figures. Jonson's twist to the morality structure results, not in the victory of good over evil, but in the evil defeating themselves by typically Renaissance acts of overreaching, in this comic exposé of greed, deception and self-deception that Jonson sees at the heart of corruption in the individual and in society.

Stage history

Volpone was written in five weeks – an unusually short period of composition for Jonson – and performed by the King's Men at the Globe Theatre in 1606, probably before 25 March.[8] Richard Burbage played Volpone; other members of the cast included Henry Condell (probably the first Mosca), and John Lowin, who later took over the title role after Burbage's death in 1619. The King's Men performed the play at Oxford and, presumably, Cambridge, on one or both of their visits of 1606 and 1607, when the members of the two universities gave it the gracious reception Jonson refers to in 'The Epistle'; but *Volpone* was popular and successful from the first, and was frequently revived throughout the Jacobean and Caroline periods. Its popularity continued in the Restoration from its early performance by the King's Company in 1662; on 14 January 1665, Pepys declared it 'a most excellent play; the best I think I

---

6 Reprinted in Parker, Appendix B, v, p. 328.
7 See Parker, pp. 24 ff.; also Additional Notes to II.iii.3 and II.iii.8, p. 439 below.
8 See Additional Note, p. 437 below.

ever saw, and well acted', with Michael Mohun as Volpone and Charles Hart as Mosca. In the regular revivals of the eighteenth century, some of the leading actors were associated with the play, notably James Quin with the role of Volpone from 1731 to 1750, and Robert Wilks with that of Mosca (1712–26); the eighteenth-century emphasis on Corbaccio as the outstanding example of stupid greed is marked by the distinguished list of actors who took the part, including the dramatist's namesake Ben Johnson, Ned Shuter, and William Parsons. However, taste was changing; and the final performances of the century in 1783–5 were of George Colman's 1771 adaptation of *Volpone*, which removed the Elizabethan allusions, and shortened and bowdlerised Jonson's play. *Volpone* was next revived in 1921 by the Phoenix Society at the Lyric, Hammersmith, with Elizabethan staging and décor in the William Poel tradition, and in 1923 by the Marlowe Dramatic Society at Cambridge University; productions which heralded the numerous performances by professional and student companies in the twentieth century.[9]

Volpone has been performed by all the major English theatre companies, and has attracted some of the century's leading actors and directors. Birmingham Repertory's production at the 1935 Malvern Festival had a notable Volpone in Wilfrid Lawson, cruel and cunning; but the role was to be dominated by Donald Wolfit, who played the part first in 1938, and subsequently in his own productions from 1940 to 1953. Wolfit's Volpone had vigour, virility and an enormous appetite for life; his Moscas, who included Alan Wheatley (1938) and John Wynyard (1947 and 1953), were deliberately reduced in dramatic stature, and often upstaged – sometimes by noisy scene changes; and, in common with a number of productions, the Politic Would-bes were either omitted or their roles scaled down.[10] Michael MacOwan's production of 1938 starring Wolfit was among the first in which the characterisation reflected the bestiary imagery of the play; and this aspect appeared again in two Stratford productions, with the less assertive Volpone of actor–producer Robert Atkins in 1944, and Ralph Richardson's curiously languid interpret-

---

9 See R. B. Parker, '*Volpone* in performance: 1921–1972', *Renaissance Drama*, n.s. 9 (1978), pp. 147–73.

10 See R. B. Parker, 'Wolfit's Fox: an interpretation of *Volpone*', *University of Toronto Quarterly*, 45 (1976), pp. 200–20.

ation, directed by George Devine in 1952, with Anthony Quayle as an outstandingly fly-like Mosca. The Sir Pol subplot was retained despite heavy cuts elsewhere, and full use was made of the Memorial Theatre's elaborate staging: the action was dominated by a sumptuous Venetian set. In contrast, Joan Littlewood's 1955 production for Theatre Workshop, Stratford East, was in modern dress; Mosca was presented as a post-war 'spiv', and Sir Pol's tortoise shell was replaced by a diving-suit. Harry Corbett as Sir Pol and Miss Littlewood as Lady Would-be gave fine performances. The same year saw a successful production at the Bristol Old Vic; Eric Porter's Volpone was in the Wolfit tradition, and Alan Dobie's Mosca slily understated. Dobie gave this interpretation again in Frank Hauser's 1966 *Volpone* at the Oxford Playhouse. Although the Sir Pol subplot was omitted, and too much emphasis was laid on the farcical elements of the play, Hauser's attempt to bring out a psychological motivation in the characters recognisable to the twentieth-century audience resulted in a subtle yet vivid presentation of Corvino's sadism by Leonard Rossiter; and, by making Bonario foolish and Celia at least capable of being tempted by Volpone's allurements, gave some dramatic life, perhaps not wholly supported by the text, to characters colourless to a modern audience; similar interpretations were later used by Peter Hall in 1977. Tyrone Guthrie's production for the National Theatre at the Old Vic in 1968 developed the animal-imagery approach of his 1964 Minneapolis *Volpone*, with costumes, stage business and sounds reflecting the world of beasts rather than men. Richard David's Bristol Old Vic production in 1972, celebrating the four-hundredth anniversary of Jonson's birth, used the bestiary aspect less blatantly, and the intricate setting of balconies, ramps and platforms provided a visual metaphor for the complications of Jonson's play. The most recent major production was Peter Hall's for the National Theatre: Paul Scofield was a slightly weary Venetian grandee, Ben Kingsley an energetic Mosca, and Sir John Gielgud a delightful Sir Pol; the light and elegant set admirably suggested Renaissance Venice. Later *Volpone*s on the English stage include David Scase's for the Library Theatre, Manchester, 1978; an Experimental Theatre Club production at the Oxford Playhouse in 1980; and one by the Royal Shakespeare Company in 1983.

The renewed interest in Jonson in this century has led to productions of *Volpone* being staged all over the English-speaking world; the popularity of his most successful and frequently performed play shows no sign of diminishing.

Volpone has also appeared in modern media and guises unknown to Jonson. There have been radio and television versions, including a BBC television recording of Wolfit's last performance of 1959; a 1940 French film of Romains's translation of Zweig, and, more loosely related to *Volpone*, Joseph Mankiewicz's 1966 film, *The Honeypot*; the 1964 Broadway musical, *Foxy*, set in the Yukon goldrush, and Larry Gelbart's Broadway hit, *Sly Fox* (1976), are both indebted to Jonson's play. It has also been turned into a Viennese opera with music by Francis Burt (1960), and into an English one, composed by Malcolm Williamson, in 1964.

Definitive and individual editions

The definitive edition of *Volpone* is in Herford and Simpson (introduction, vol. II; text, vol. V; stage history, commentary and notes, vol. IX). Herford and Simpson print the 1616 folio text, as do all but one of the twentieth-century editors of individual editions. John D. Rea's *Volpone*, Yale Studies in English, 59 (New Haven: Yale University Press, 1919), is the first full modern critical edition. Alvin B. Kernan's Yale Ben Jonson edition (New Haven and London: Yale University Press, 1962) has a modernised text, with a good critical introduction and full annotation. Philip Brockbank's New Mermaid edition (London: Ernest Benn, 1968) modernises Jonson's punctuation to some extent; there are some good points about staging in the introduction, and the appendix contains some analogues and source material. The best recent edition is John Creaser's in the London Medieval and Renaissance Series (London: Hodder and Stoughton, 1978), modernised in spelling and punctuation, with a scholarly and critical introduction, and detailed commentary; an excellent student text. R. B. Parker's Revels Plays edition (Manchester, and Dover, New Hampshire: Manchester University Press, 1983) deals successfully and with enthusiasm with the many levels of the play in his introduction; the modernised text has erudite annotation. The appendixes give selections of the sources, and details about modern versions and productions. Other editors include Arthur Sale (London: University Tutorial Press, 1951); Jonas A. Barish (Baltimore: Croft's Classics, 1958); David Cook (London: Methuen, 1962); J. B. Bamborough

(London: Macmillan, 1963); J. L. Halio (Edinburgh: Oliver and Boyd, 1968). Henry de Vocht printed the 1607 quarto version in the *Materials for the Study of Old English Drama* series (Louvain: 1937), and the quarto was published in facsimile by the Scolar Press (Menston: 1968).

[DEDICATORY EPISTLE]

TO THE MOST NOBLE
AND MOST EQUAL
SISTERS,
THE TWO FAMOUS UNIVERSITIES,
FOR THEIR LOVE
AND
ACCEPTANCE
SHOWN TO HIS POEM
IN THE PRESENTATION,
BEN. JONSON,
THE GRATEFUL ACKNOWLEDGER,
DEDICATES
BOTH IT AND HIMSELF.

There follows an Epistle, if
you dare venture on the length.

TO . . . HIMSELF: see Textual Note, p. 432 below.
2 EQUAL: equal in merit; also, 'just'.
4 UNIVERSITIES: Oxford and Cambridge.
8 POEM: play.
9 PRESENTATION: see Additional Note, p. 437 below.
There follows . . . on the length: see Textual Note, p. 432 below.

THE EPISTLE

Never (most equal sisters) had any man a wit so presently excellent, as that it could raise itself; but there must come both matter, occasion, commenders, and favourers to it: if this be true, and that the fortune of all writers doth daily prove it, it behoves the careful to provide well toward these accidents; and having acquired them, to preserve that part of reputation most tenderly, wherein the benefit of a friend is also defended. Hence is it, that I now render myself grateful, and am studious to justify the bounty of your act: to which, though your mere authority were satisfying, yet, it being an age, wherein poetry, and the professors of it hear so ill, on all sides, there will a reason be looked for in the subject. It is certain, nor can it with any forehead be opposed, that the too-much licence of poetasters, in this time, hath much deformed their mistress; that, every day, their manifold, and manifest ignorance, doth stick unnatural reproaches upon her: but for their petulancy, it were an act of the greatest injustice, either to let the learned suffer, or so divine a skill (which indeed should not be attempted with unclean hands) to fall under the least contempt. For, if men will impartially, and not asquint, look toward the offices, and function of a poet, they will easily conclude to themselves, the impossibility of any man's being the good poet, without first being a good man. He that is said to be able

---

EPISTLE: see Additional Note, p. 438 below.

1 *wit*: mind (intellectual and imaginative qualities).

2 *raise itself*: exalt its own reputation.

4 *that*: that it is.

6 *accidents*: adjuncts (to talent; those of 3–4).

8 *benefit*: good.

11 *satisfying*: sufficient.

12–13 *professors*: practitioners.

13 *hear so ill*: are spoken of so ill (Latin *tam male audiunt*).

14 *subject*: i.e. of bounty: Jonson himself.

15 *with any forehead*: confidently.

16 *poetasters*: petty, paltry poets (Jonson's coinage).

19 *petulancy*: insolence.

24 *asquint*: without prejudice.

25–7 *the impossibility . . . a good man*: a Stoic commonplace, here from Strabo's *Geography*, I.ii.5, perhaps reinforced by Quintilian, *The Principles of Oratory*, I, Pref. 9–10.

27–35 *He that is said . . . business of mankind*: from Minturno, *Of the Poet* (1599), p. 8; but originates in Horace, *Epistles*, II.i.126–31.

to inform young men to all good disciplines, inflame grown men to all great virtues, keep old men in their best and supreme state, or as they decline to childhood, recover them to their first strength; that comes forth the interpreter, and arbiter of nature, a teacher of things divine, no less than human, a master in manners; and can alone (or with a few) effect the business of mankind: this, I take him, is no subject for pride, and ignorance to exercise their railing rhetoric upon. But it will here be hastily answered, that the writers of these days are other things; that, not only their manners, but their natures are inverted; and nothing remaining with them of the dignity of poet, but the abused name, which every scribe usurps: that now, especially in dramatic, or (as they term it) stage poetry, nothing but ribaldry, profanation, blasphemy, all licence of offence to God, and man, is practised. I dare not deny a great part of this (and am sorry, I dare not) because in some men's abortive features (and would they had never boasted the light) it is over-true: but that all are embarked in this bold adventure for Hell, is a most uncharitable thought, and, uttered, a more malicious slander. For my particular, I can (and from a most clear conscience) affirm, that I have ever trembled to think toward the least profaneness; have loathed the use of such foul, and unwashed bawdry, as is now made the food of the scene. And howsoever I cannot escape, from some, the imputation of sharpness, but that they will say, I have taken a pride, or lust, to be bitter, and not my youngest infant but hath come into the world with all his teeth; I would ask of these

---

28 *inform*: shape, mould.
30–1 *childhood*: i.e. second childhood.
31 *first strength*: innocence.
34 *manners*: behaviour.
34–5 *effect . . . mankind*: bring about the proper functioning of society.
47 *abortive features*: miscarried creations.
51 *particular*: own part.
55 *scene*: stage (Latin *scena*).
57 *lust*: delight.
58 *youngest infant*: possibly *Sejanus* (1603), or *Eastward Ho!* (1605); see Additional Note, p. 438 below.

supercilious politics, what nation, society, or general order, or state I have provoked? What public person? Whether I have not (in all these) preserved their dignity, as mine own person, safe? My works are read, allowed (I speak of those that are entirely mine) look into them: what broad reproofs have I used? Where have I been particular? Where personal? except to a mimic, cheater, bawd, or buffoon, creatures (for their insolencies) worthy to be taxed? Yet to which of these so pointingly, as he might not either ingenuously have confessed, or wisely dissembled his disease? But it is not rumour can make men guilty, much less entitle me, to other men's crimes. I know that nothing can be so innocently writ, or carried, but may be made obnoxious to construction; marry, whilst I bear mine innocence about me, I fear it not. Application is, now, grown a trade with many; and there are, that profess to have a key for the deciphering of everything: but let wise and noble persons take heed how they be too credulous, or give leave to these invading interpreters, to be over-familiar with their fames, who cunningly, and often, utter their own virulent malice, under other men's simplest meanings. As for those, that will (by faults which charity hath raked up, or common honesty concealed) make themselves a name with the multi-

---

60 *politics*: people who pose as shrewd and knowing about public affairs; compare Sir Politic Would-be in the play.

60–1 *what . . . provoked*: a somewhat disingenuous disclaimer; see Additional Note, p. 438 below.

64 *allowed*: licensed by the censor.

64–5 *entirely mine*: apart from the recent collaborations of *Sejanus* and *Eastward Ho!*, Jonson had been in trouble with the authorities and imprisoned in 1597 for his additions to Thomas Nashe's *The Isle of Dogs*.

65 *broad*: licentious.

66 *been particular*: described individuals.

67 *mimic*: actor; pretender, imitator.

71 *rumour can*: rumour that can (omitted relative, frequent in Jonson).

74–5 *obnoxious to construction*: liable to misinterpretation; or perhaps, 'harmful by misinterpretation'.

76 *Application*: interpreting literature in terms of contemporary events, or as referring to living persons.

82 *utter*: pass off (as counterfeit coin is passed for genuine).

84 *up*: over.
honesty: decency.

tude, or (to draw their rude, and beastly claps) care not whose living faces they entrench, with their petulant styles; may they do it, without a rival, for me: I choose rather to live graved in obscurity, than share with them, in so preposterous a fame. Nor can I blame the wishes of those severe, and wiser patriots, who providing the hurts these licentious spirits may do in a state, desire rather to see fools, and devils, and those antique relics of barbarism retrieved, with all other ridiculous, and exploded follies: than behold the wounds of private men, of princes, and nations. For, as Horace makes Trebatius speak, among these:

Sibi quisque timet, quamquam est intactus, et odit.

And men may justly impute such rages, if continued, to the writer, as his sports. The increase of which lust in liberty, together with the present trade of the stage, in all their misc'line interludes, what learned or liberal soul doth not already abhor? where nothing but the filth of the time is uttered, and that with such impropriety of phrase, such plenty of solecisms, such dearth of sense, so bold prolepses, so racked metaphors, with brothelry, able to violate the ear of a pagan, and blasphemy, to turn the blood of a

---

86 *rude*: ignorant.
87 *entrench*: cut, disfigure.
88 *petulant styles*: insolent pens (Latin *stylus*, a sharp, pointed instrument for incising letters on wax tablets); with a pun on 'style', manner of writing.
89 *graved*: buried; with a pun on 'engraved'.
90 *preposterous*: perverse (literally, 'back to front').
91 *patriots*: the modern sense, introduced by Jonson; the usual seventeenth-century meaning was 'fellow countrymen'.
92 *providing*: foreseeing.
93 *fools, and devils*: of the late morality plays: the triumph of good over evil was marked by the Devil carrying off the Vice, dressed in a long fool's coat, on his back to Hell.
94 *antique*: old-fashioned; perhaps with a play on 'antic' = bizarre, uncouthly ludicrous.
95 *exploded*: clapped and hissed off the stage.
98 *Sibi quisque . . . et odit*: *Satires*, II.i.23, translated by Jonson: 'In satires, each man (though untouched) complains / As he were hurt; and hates such biting strains' (*Poetaster*, III.v.41–2).
99 *rages*: anger caused by the satirist.
100 *sports*: diversions, amusements.
102 *misc'line interludes*: jumbled or hotch-potch entertainments.
103 *liberal*: educated (in the manner of a gentleman).
105 *solecisms*: grammatical errors.
106 *prolepses*: anachronisms.

Christian to water. I cannot but be serious in a cause of this nature, wherein my fame, and the reputations of divers honest, and learned are the question; when a name, so full of authority, antiquity, and all great mark, is (through their insolence) become the lowest scorn of the age: and those men subject to the petulancy of every vernaculous orator, that were wont to be the care of kings, and happiest monarchs. This it is, that hath not only rapt me to present indignation, but made me studious, heretofore; and by all my actions, to stand off, from them: which may most appear in this my latest work (which you, most learned arbitresses, have seen, judged, and to my crown, approved) wherein I have laboured, for their instruction, and amendment, to reduce, not only the ancient forms, but manners of the scene, the easiness, the propriety, the innocence, and last the doctrine, which is the principal end of poesy, to inform men, in the best reason of living. And though my catastrophe may, in the strict rigour of comic law, meet with censure, as turning back to my promise; I desire the learned, and charitable critic to have so much faith in me, to think it was done of industry: for with what ease I could have varied it nearer his scale (but that I fear to boast my own faculty) I could here insert. But my special aim being to put the snaffle in their mouths, that cry out, we never punish vice in our interludes, etc., I took the more liberty; though not

111 *question*: subject of discussion.
115 *vernaculous*: scurrilous.
117 *rapt*: carried away.
121–2 *to my crown*: as my chief ornament.
124 *ancient . . . scene*: formal features, but also the customary rules of behaviour of classical comedy.
easiness: facility; also, 'lack of harshness'.
125 *innocence*: harmlessness.
doctrine: teaching.
127 *reason*: basis.
catastrophe: dénouement.
128 *strict rigour of comic law*: neo-classical comic theory held that comedy should end in harmony and reconciliation.
129 *turning back to*: going back on.
131 *of industry*: on purpose.
133 *faculty*: ability.
136 *interludes*: plays of a popular nature (but used by Puritans in a denigratory sense of any play).

without some lines of example, drawn even in the ancients themselves, the goings-out of whose comedies are not always joyful, but ofttimes, the bawds, the servants, the rivals, yea, and the masters are mulcted: and fitly, it being the office of a comic poet, to imitate justice, and instruct to life, as well as purity of language, or stir up gentle affections. To which, I shall take the occasion elsewhere to speak. For the present (most reverenced sisters) as I have cared to be thankful for your affections past, and here made the understanding acquainted with some ground of your favours; let me not despair their continuance, to the maturing of some worthier fruits: wherein, if my muses be true to me, I shall raise the despised head of poetry again, and stripping her out of those rotten and base rags, wherewith the times have adulterated her form, restore her to her primitive habit, feature, and majesty, and render her worthy to be embraced, and kissed, of all the great and master-spirits of our world. As for the vile, and slothful, who never affected an act worthy of celebration, or are so inward with their own vicious natures, as they worthily fear her; and think it a high point of policy, to keep her in contempt with their declamatory, and windy invectives: she shall out of just rage incite her servants (who are *genus irritabile*) to spout ink in their faces, that shall eat, farther than their marrow, into their fames; and not Cinnamus the barber, with his art, shall be able to take out the

137 *lines of example*: see Additional Note, p. 438 below.
138 *goings-out*: endings.
141 *mulcted*: fined; also, 'punished'.
143 *gentle affections*: noble emotions.
144 *elsewhere*: probably in his commentary on Horace's *Art of Poetry* (referred to in the Epistle to *Sejanus*), lost in the fire that destroyed his library in 1623.
147 *understanding*: discerning readers.
153 *adulterated*: debased.
153–4 *primitive habit*: first dress.
154 *feature*: form.
156 *master-spirits*: most noble leaders.
157 *affected*: loved, desired to achieve.
162 *genus irritabile*: an irascible race, 'a touchy crowd' (Horace, *Epistles*, II.ii.102).
164 *Cinnamus*: barber-surgeon celebrated by Martial for his skill in removing brands (*Epigrams*, IV.lxiv.26).

brands, but they shall live, and be read, till the wretches die, as things worst deserving of themselves in chief, and then of all mankind.

From my house in the Blackfriars,
this 11. of February, 1607.

169–70 *From my house . . . 1607*: see Textual Note, p. 432 below.

THE PERSONS OF THE PLAY

VOLPONE, *a magnifico*
MOSCA, *his parasite*
VOLTORE, *an advocate*
CORBACCIO, *an old gentleman*
CORVINO, *a merchant*
AVOCATORI, *four magistrates*
NOTARIO, *the register*
NANO, *a dwarf*
CASTRONE, *an eunuch*
POLITIC WOULD-BE, *a knight*
PEREGRINE, *a gentleman-traveller*
BONARIO, *a young gentleman*
Fine MADAM WOULD-BE, *the knight's wife*
CELIA, *the merchant's wife*
COMMENDATORI, *officers*
MERCATORI, *three merchants*
ANDROGYNO, *a hermaphrodite*
SERVITORE, *a servant*
[*Two*] WOMEN, [*attendants on Lady Would-Be*]
GREGE

THE SCENE
VENICE

---

1 VOLPONE: 'an old fox, . . . an old, crafty, sly, subtle companion [contemptible fellow], sneaking lurking wily deceiver' (John Florio, *A World of Words*, 1598).
magnifico: honorary title of a Venetian magnate.
2 MOSCA: 'any kind of fly' (Florio, 1598).
3 VOLTORE: 'a ravenous bird called a vulture . . . Also a greedy cormorant [rapacious person]' (Florio, 1598).
4 CORBACCIO: 'a filthy [disgusting] great raven'; diminutive *corbacchione*: 'Also a filthy fellow, a gull or ninny' (Florio, 1598).
5 CORVINO: crow.
7 *register*: registrar (to the court).
11 PEREGRINE: '*Pellegrino*, a wanderer, a pilgrim . . . a stranger, . . . a foreigner . . . Also a haggard hawk' (Florio, 1598).
12 BONARIO: good man.
14 CELIA: heavenly one.
20 GREGE: crowd.

THE ARGUMENT

VOLPONE, childless, rich, feigns sick, despairs,
O ffers his state to hopes of several heirs,
L ies languishing; his parasite receives
P resents of all, assures, deludes: then weaves
O ther cross-plots, which ope themselves, are told.
N ew tricks for safety, are sought; they thrive, when, bold,
E ach tempts th'other again, and all are sold.

The acrostic form is modelled on that used in editions of Plautus (compare also *The Alchemist*'s argument).

2 *state*: estate.
5 *cross-plots*: counter-plots.
7 *sold*: tricked, bilked.

PROLOGUE

Now, luck yet send us, and a little wit
  Will serve, to make our play hit
(According to the palates of the season);
  Here is rhyme, not empty of reason:
This we were bid to credit, from our poet,
  Whose true scope, if you would know it,
In all his poems, still, hath been this measure,
  To mix profit, with your pleasure;
And not as some (whose threats their envy failing)
  Cry hoarsely, 'All he writes, is railing':
And when his plays come forth, think they can flout
    them,
  With saying, 'He was a year about them.'
To these there needs no lie, but this his creature,
  Which was, two months since, no feature;
And though he dares give them five lives to mend it,
  'Tis known, five weeks fully penned it:
From his own hand, without a coadjutor,
  Novice, journeyman, or tutor.
Yet thus much I can give you, as a token
  Of his play's worth, no eggs are broken;

The curious metre of the Prologue may be modelled on Latin comic prosody. The use of feminine rhymes from 3 on confirms the impression that Jonson is here inventing a comic metre of his own.

1 *yet*: also, in addition; see Textual Note, p. 432 below. F's awkward construction appears to petition for 'luck' as a gift additional to 'wit', which has already been bestowed on man as an intelligent creature.
and: and, as a consequence.

2 *hit*: succeed.

3 *According . . . season*: in keeping with the discerning tastes of the day.

6 *scope*: aim.

7 *poems*: plays.
measure: balance.

8 *To mix . . . pleasure*: see Additional Note, p. 438 below.

9 *some*: Marston in particular (see Additional Note, p. 438 below).

10, 12 These charges are also recorded in the 'Apologetical Dialogue' of *Poetaster* (1601), 185 ff.

13 *creature*: creation.

14 *no feature*: lacking form, shape; not in existence.

17–18 See Additional Note, p. 438 below.

17 *coadjutor*: collaborator who wrote particular parts of the play.

18 *Novice*: apprentice.
journeyman: hack-writer and adaptor of old plays.
tutor: supervisor and corrector of the novice's and journeyman's work.

Nor quaking custards with fierce teeth affrighted,
  Wherewith your rout are so delighted;
Nor hales he in a gull, old ends reciting,
  To stop gaps in his loose writing;
With such a deal of monstrous, and forced action,
  As might make Bedlam a faction:
Nor made he his play, for jests, stolen from each
        table,
  But makes jests, to fit his fable.
And so presents quick comedy, refined,
  As best critics have designed,
The laws of time, place, persons he observeth,
  From no needful rule he swerveth.
All gall, and copperas, from his ink he draineth,
  Only, a little salt remaineth;
Wherewith he'll rub your cheeks, till (red with
        laughter)
  They shall look fresh, a week after.

---

21 *quaking custards*: 'cowardy custards', cowards (a hit at Marston; see Additional Note, p. 438 below); also, a reference to the huge custard at the lord mayor's feasts into which fools jumped for the guests' entertainment. Jonson's point is that *he* avoids slapstick.

23 *gull*: dupe.
old ends: tags, proverbs.

25 *forced action*: exaggerated gestures.

26 *make Bedlam a faction*: win the support of madmen (whose unnatural and eccentric movements the actor's posturing would resemble).
Bedlam: the hospital of St Mary of Bethlehem for the insane.

28 *fable*: plot.

29 *quick*: lively.

31 *The laws . . . persons*: see Additional Note, p. 439 below.

33 *gall, and copperas*: ingredients of ink: oak galls (with a play on 'bitterness', supposed to be produced by the gall bladder), and a ferrous sulphate.

34 *salt*: wit. Salt was not used in ink, though ferrous sulphate was also called 'iron salt'.

ACT I

SCENE I

[*Enter*] VOLPONE, MOSCA.

VOLPONE. Good morning to the day; and next, my gold:
Open the shrine, that I may see my saint.
[MOSCA *reveals the treasure*.]
Hail the world's soul, and mine. More glad than is
The teeming earth, to see the longed-for sun
Peep through the horns of the celestial Ram,
Am I, to view thy splendour, darkening his:
That lying here, amongst my other hoards,
Show'st like a flame, by night; or like the day
Struck out of chaos, when all darkness fled
Unto the centre. O, thou son of Sol
(But brighter than thy father), let me kiss,
With adoration, thee, and every relic
Of sacred treasure, in this blessèd room.
Well did wise poets, by thy glorious name,
Title that age, which they would have the best;
Thou being the best of things: and far transcending
All style of joy, in children, parents, friends,
Or any other waking dream on earth.
Thy looks, when they to Venus did ascribe,

---

2 *Open the shrine*: see Additional Note, p. 439 below.
3–27 Volpone's blasphemous morning hymn to his gold signals the perversion of traditional values which he and Mosca act on and perpetrate in the play.
3 *world's soul*: divine power that gives and sustains life.
4 *teeming*: fertile and ready to bring forth life.
5 *celestial Ram*: the astrological sign Aries, which the sun enters at the spring equinox.
8 *Show'st like a flame, by night*: possibly a blasphemous parody of the pillar of flame by which God guided the Israelites (Exodus 14.21).
day: of creation.
10 *centre*: of the earth.
son of Sol: son of the sun, the alchemical description of gold.
15 *that age*: golden age, the first age of the world, distinguished by harmony between man and man, and man and nature.
17 *All style*: every title.
19 *Venus*: called 'golden' in classical poetry.

They should have given her twenty thousand
Cupids;
Such are thy beauties, and our loves! Dear saint,
Riches, the dumb god, that giv'st all men tongues:
That canst do nought, and yet mak'st men do all
things;
The price of souls; even Hell, with thee to boot,
Is made worth Heaven! Thou art virtue, fame,
Honour, and all things else! Who can get thee,
He shall be noble, valiant, honest, wise –

MOSCA. And what he will, sir. Riches are in fortune
A greater good, than wisdom is in nature.

VOLPONE. True, my beloved Mosca. Yet, I glory
More in the cunning purchase of my wealth,
Than in the glad possession; since I gain
No common way: I use no trade, no venture;
I wound no earth with ploughshares, fat no beasts
To feed the shambles; have no mills for iron,
Oil, corn, or men, to grind 'em into powder;
I blow no subtle glass; expose no ships
To threatenings of the furrow-facèd sea;
I turn no moneys in the public bank;
Nor usure private.

MOSCA. No, sir, nor devour
Soft prodigals. You shall ha'some will swallow

---

23 *That . . . things*: parodying God as the Unmoved Mover.
24 *The price of souls*: for Volpone, gold replaces Christ's redeeming blood.
to boot: into the bargain.
28–9 *Riches . . . wisdom in nature*: i.e. wealth, the gift of fortune, is a greater good than wisdom, the gift of nature.
31 *cunning*: both 'clever' and 'sly'.
purchase: acquisition: at this time, frequently in the sense of 'dishonest gain' (see I.v.90).
33 *venture*: commercial speculation.
34–40 see Additional Note, p. 439 below.
35 *shambles*: slaughter-house.
37 *subtle*: delicate. Venice is still a centre for the manufacture of fine glass.
39 *turn*: circulate (alluding to the practice of transferring to a creditor debts owed to his debtor by a third party; an abuse of the monetary system of the Banco della Piazza di Rialto, the 'public bank').
40 *usure private*: engage in usury privately.
41 *Soft*: compliant; foolish; also, 'pleasing to the taste'.
some will: some who will: omitted relative, frequent in Jonson.

A melting heir, as glibly as your Dutch
Will pills of butter, and ne'er purge for't;
Tear forth the fathers of poor families
Out of their beds, and coffin them, alive,
In some kind, clasping prison, where their bones
May be forthcoming, when the flesh is rotten:
But your sweet nature doth abhor these courses;
You loathe the widow's, or the orphan's tears
Should wash your pavements; or their piteous cries
Ring in your roofs; and beat the air, for vengeance.
VOLPONE. Right, Mosca, I do loathe it.
MOSCA. And besides, sir,
You are not like the thresher, that doth stand
With a huge flail, watching a heap of corn,
And, hungry, dares not taste the smallest grain,
But feeds on mallows, and such bitter herbs;
Nor like the merchant, who hath filled his vaults
With Romagnìa and rich Candian wines,
Yet drinks the lees of Lombard's vinegar:
You will not lie in straw, whilst moths, and worms
Feed on your sumptuous hangings, and soft beds.
You know the use of riches, and dare give, now,
From that bright heap, to me, your poor observer,
Or to your dwarf, or your hermaphrodite,
Your eunuch, or what other household trifle
Your pleasure allows maintenance –
VOLPONE. Hold thee, Mosca,
[*Gives him money.*]
Take, of my hand; thou strik'st on truth, in all;
And they are envious, term thee parasite.
Call forth my dwarf, my eunuch, and my fool,

---

42 *melting*: spendthrift.
your: used indefinitely, like the ethic dative 'you', often contemptuous.
Dutch: noted for their fondness for butter.
43 *ne'er purge*: not need a laxative (so completely 'digested' is their victim); i.e. not be punished; or perhaps, 'not suffer a qualm'.
46 *clasping*: close, confining; also, 'embracing' (carrying on the irony of 'kind').
51 *beat the air*: clamour.
56 *mallows*: common field plant.
58 *Romagnìa*: rumney, a popular sweet Greek wine.
Candian wines: malmsey, which came from Crete (Candy).
63 *observer*: obsequious servant.
64–5 *your dwarf* . . . *hermaphrodite* . . . *eunuch*: see Additional Note, p. 439 below.
66 *Hold thee*: have for yourself.

And let 'em make me sport.
[*Exit* MOSCA.]
What should I do,
But cocker up my genius, and live free
To all delights my fortune calls me to?
I have no wife, no parent, child, ally,
To give my substance to; but whom I make,
Must be my heir: and this makes men observe me.
This draws new clients, daily, to my house,
Women, and men, of every sex, and age,
That bring me presents, send me plate, coin, jewels,
With hope, that when I die (which they expect
Each greedy minute) it shall then return,
Tenfold, upon them; whilst some, covetous
Above the rest, seek to engross me whole,
And counter-work, the one unto the other,
Contend in gifts, as they would seem, in love:
All which I suffer, playing with their hopes,
And am content to coin 'em into profit,
And look upon their kindness, and take more,
And look on that; still bearing them in hand,
Letting the cherry knock against their lips,
And draw it by their mouths, and back again. How now!

SCENE II

[*Enter*] MOSCA, NANO, ANDROGYNO, CASTRONE.

NANO. Now, room, for fresh gamesters, who do will you to know,

---

71 *cocker up my genius*: indulge my natural inclinations.
73 *ally*: relative.
77 *every*: each.
83 *unto*: in opposition to.
85 *suffer*: allow.
88 *bearing them in hand*: deluding them.
89 *cherry*: in the game of bob-cherry, the player attempted to bite at and catch a cherry dangling from a string.
1 *gamesters*: entertainers.

They do bring you neither play, nor university show;
And therefore do entreat you, that whatsoever they rehearse,
May not fare a whit the worse, for the false pace of the verse.
If you wonder at this, you will wonder more, ere we pass,
For know, here is enclosed the soul of Pythagoras,
That juggler divine, as hereafter shall follow;
Which soul (fast and loose, sir) came first from Apollo,
And was breathed into Aethalides, Mercurius his son,
Where it had the gift to remember all that ever was done.
From thence it fled forth, and made quick transmigration
To goldy-locked Euphorbus, who was killed, in good fashion,
At the siege of old Troy, by the cuckold of Sparta.
Hermotimus was next (I find it, in my charta)
To whom it did pass, where no sooner it was missing,

---

2 *university show*: neo-classical academic drama, usually in Latin.

3 *rehearse*: recite.

4 *false pace of the verse*: old-fashioned, loose four-stressed verse, irregular in rhythm, used in the morality plays.

6 *here*: in Androgyno.
Pythagoras: sixth-century BC Greek philosopher, whose teaching included the theory of transmigration of souls to other bodies after death.

7 *juggler*: sorcerer; conjurer; also, 'buffoon'.

8 *fast and loose*: slippery, inconstant (from a game in which one player had to guess whether or not a stick was held fast in the intricate folds of a leather belt).

9 *Aethalides*: herald of the Argonauts, whose prodigious memory was a gift of his father Mercury.

12 *Euphorbus*: Trojan who wounded Patroclus and was later killed by Menelaus, king of Sparta, whose wife Helen had been carried off to Troy by Paris.

14 *Hermotimus*: fifth-century BC Greek philosopher.
charta: either the script, or the source of the entertainment (see Introductory Note, p. 135 above).

But with one Pyrrhus of Delos, it learned to go a-fishing:
And thence, did it enter the sophist of Greece.
From Pythagore, she went into a beautiful piece,
Hight Aspasia, the meretrix; and the next toss of her
Was, again, of a whore, she became a philosopher,
Crates the Cynic (as itself doth relate it).
Since, kings, knights, and beggars, knaves, lords and fools gat it,
Besides ox, and ass, camel, mule, goat, and brock,
In all which it hath spoke, as in the cobbler's cock.
But I come not here, to discourse of that matter,
Or his one, two, or three, or his great oath, 'By Quater',
His musics, his trigon, his golden thigh,
Or his telling how elements shift: but I
Would ask, how of late, thou hast suffered translation,
And shifted thy coat, in these days of reformation?

---

16 *Pyrrhus*: ancient philosopher, who, Diogenes tells us, was a fisherman.
17 *sophist*: Pythagoras, who was 'a teacher of wisdom', and, in the reductive treatment of the entertainment, 'a specious reasoner'.
19 *Hight*: called.
Aspasia: cultured and faithful mistress of Pericles.
meretrix: Latin 'prostitute' (with a play on 'merry tricks').
20 *of*: just like.
21 *Crates*: fourth-century BC, pupil of Diogenes the Cynic.
22 *gat*: begat.
23 *brock*: badger.
24 *cobbler's cock*: of Lucian's dialogue.
26 *Quater*: the tetractys or trigon, the triangle of four of Pythagorean arithmetic (1 + 2 + 3 + 4): .·:·:·., considered sacred by the followers of Pythagoras because symbolic of the principles of harmony in the universe and in human morality.
27 *His musics*: Pythagoras developed the theory of the music of the spheres, on which harmony depended the order of the cosmos.
golden thigh: attributed to Pythagoras; possibly of alchemical significance (see *The Alchemist*, II.i.92).
28 *shift*: are transmuted.
29 *translation*: transformation.
30 *shifted thy coat*: compare 'turncoat': changed to suit the times, adapted to the Protestant 'reformation'.

ANDROGYNO. Like one of the reformed, a fool, as you see,
Counting all old doctrine heresy.
NANO. But not on thine own forbid meats hast thou ventured?
ANDROGYNO. On fish, when first a Carthusian I entered.
NANO. Why, then, thy dogmatical silence hath left thee?
ANDROGYNO. Of that an obstreperous lawyer bereft me.
NANO. O wonderful change! when Sir Lawyer forsook thee,
For Pythagore's sake, what body then took thee?
ANDROGYNO. A good dull moile.
NANO. And how! by that means,
Thou wert brought to allow of the eating of beans?
ANDROGYNO. Yes.
NANO. But, from the moile, into whom didst thou pass?
ANDROGYNO. Into a very strange beast, by some writers called an ass;
By others, a precise, pure, illuminate brother,
Of those devour flesh, and sometimes one another;
And will drop you forth a libel, or a sanctified lie,
Betwixt every spoonful of a nativity-pie.
NANO. Now quit thee, for Heaven, of that profane nation;
And gently report thy next transmigration.
ANDROGYNO. To the same that I am.

---

31 *reformed*: Puritans.

34 *Carthusian*: Pythagoreans did not eat fish, but the Carthusian monks' strict diet allowed it.

35 *dogmatical silence*: on first joining the sect, Pythagoreans kept a strict five-year silence.

39 *moile*: mule.

40 *eating of beans*: forbidden by Pythagoras because, according to Plutarch and Cicero, they provoked lust (see Erasmus, *Proverbs or Adagies*, transl. R. Tavener, 1539, Gvii).

43 *precise*: Puritanical.
illuminate: divinely inspired, possessing the 'inner light'.

46 *nativity-pie*: Christmas pie (mocking the Puritans' avoidance of words containing the popish syllable 'mas(s)'.

47 *nation*: sect.

NANO. A creature of delight?
And (what is more than a fool) an hermaphrodite?
Now pray thee, sweet soul, in all thy variation,
Which body would'st thou choose, to take up thy station?
ANDROGYNO. Troth, this I am in, even here would I tarry.
NANO. 'Cause here, the delight of each sex thou canst vary?
ANDROGYNO. Alas, those pleasures be stale, and forsaken;
No, 'tis your fool, wherewith I am so taken,
The only one creature that I can call blessèd:
For all other forms I have proved most distressèd.
NANO. Spoke true, as thou wert in Pythagoras still.
This learnèd opinion we celebrate will,
Fellow eunuch (as behoves us) with all our wit, and art,
To dignify that, whereof ourselves are so great, and special a part.
VOLPONE. Now very, very pretty: Mosca, this
Was thy invention?
MOSCA. If it please my patron,
Not else.
VOLPONE. It doth, good Mosca.
MOSCA. Then it was, sir.

Song

Fools, they are the only nation
Worth men's envy, or admiration;
Free from care, or sorrow-taking,
Selves, and others merry making:
All they speak, or do, is sterling.
Your fool, he is your great man's dearling,
And your lady's sport, and pleasure;
Tongue and bable are his treasure.
E'en his face beggeth laughter,

---

62 *that*: i.e. folly.
65 s.d. *Song*: sung by Nano and Castrone.
70 *sterling*: of outstanding quality; perhaps also, 'has currency'.
73 *bable*: 'babble', and 'bauble': the stick with a jester's head carried by a fool; also, slang term for phallus.

And he speaks truth, free from slaughter;
He's the grace of every feast,
And, sometimes, the chiefest guest;
Hath his trencher, and his stool,
When wit waits upon the fool.
Oh, who would not be
He, he, he?

One knocks without.

VOLPONE. Who's that? Away, look Mosca.

[*Exeunt* NANO, CASTRONE.]

MOSCA. Fool, begone.

[*Exit* ANDROGYNO.]

'Tis Signior Voltore, the advocate,
I know him by his knock.

VOLPONE. Fetch me my gown,
My furs, and nightcaps; say my couch is changing:
And let him entertain himself awhile,
Without i'th'gallery.

[*Exit* MOSCA.]

Now, now, my clients
Begin their visitation! Vulture, kite,
Raven, and gorcrow, all my birds of prey,
That think me turning carcass, now they come:
I am not for 'em yet.

[*Enter* MOSCA.]

How now? the news?

MOSCA. A piece of plate, sir.

VOLPONE. Of what bigness?

MOSCA. Huge,
Massy, and antique, with your name inscribed,
And arms engraven.

VOLPONE. Good! and not a fox
Stretched on the earth, with fine delusive sleights,
Mocking a gaping crow? ha, Mosca?

MOSCA. Sharp, sir.

---

75 *free from slaughter*: with impunity (alluding to the licence allowed to the fool).

81 *He, he, he*: the song probably ends in a giggle.

81 s.d. *without*: outside, off stage.

88 *visitation*: sick visit; also, 'formal visit'.

89 *gorcrow*: carrion crow.

94–6 *a fox . . . a gaping crow*: alluding to the trick, in fox lore and literature (and confirmed by observation), by which a fox pretends to be dead, and snaps up one of the carrion birds when it comes to devour the carcass.

VOLPONE. Give me my furs. Why dost thou laugh so, man?
MOSCA. I cannot choose, sir, when I apprehend
What thoughts he has (without) now, as he walks:
That this might be the last gift he should give;
That this would fetch you; if you died today,
And gave him all, what he should be tomorrow;
What large return would come of all his ventures;
How he should worshipped be, and reverenced;
Ride, with his furs, and foot-cloths; waited on
By herds of fools, and clients; have clear way
Made for his moile, as lettered as himself;
Be called the great, and learned advocate;
And then concludes, there's nought impossible.
VOLPONE. Yes, to be learned, Mosca.
MOSCA. O, no: rich
Implies it. Hood an ass with reverend purple,
So you can hide his two ambitious ears,
And he shall pass for a cathedral doctor.
VOLPONE. My caps, my caps, good Mosca, fetch him in.
[VOLPONE *gets into bed.*]
MOSCA. Stay, sir, your ointment for your eyes.
VOLPONE. That's true;
Dispatch, dispatch: I long to have possession
Of my new present.
MOSCA. That, and thousands more,
I hope to see you lord of.
VOLPONE. Thanks, kind Mosca.
MOSCA. And that, when I am lost in blended dust,
And hundred such as I am, in succession –
VOLPONE. Nay, that were too much, Mosca.
MOSCA. You shall live,
Still, to delude these harpies.
VOLPONE. Loving Mosca,
'Tis well, my pillow now, and let him enter.
[*Exit* MOSCA.]

---

105 *foot-cloths*: embroidered ceremonial cloths spread on a horse's back, and, like the furs, a sign of rank.
107 *moile*: mule, the lawyer's mount.
111 *reverend purple*: purple was the colour of the hood of Doctors of Divinity.
112 *ambitious*: aspiring to high position; also 'towering'.
122 *harpies*: rapacious folk (from the creatures of Greek myth, with women's faces and the body and wings of a bird).

Now, my feigned cough, my phthisic, and my gout,
My apoplexy, palsy, and catarrhs,
Help, with your forcèd functions, this my posture,
Wherein, this three year, I have milked their
hopes.
He comes, I hear him (uh, uh, uh, uh) Oh!

SCENE III

[*Enter*] MOSCA, VOLTORE.

MOSCA. You still are, what you were, sir. Only you
(Of all the rest) are he, commands his love:
And you do wisely, to preserve it, thus,
With early visitation, and kind notes
Of your good meaning to him, which, I know,
Cannot but come most grateful. Patron, sir.
Here's Signior Voltore is come –
VOLPONE. What say you?
MOSCA. Sir, Signior Voltore is come, this morning,
To visit you.
VOLPONE. I thank him.
MOSCA. And hath brought
A piece of antique plate, bought of St Mark,
With which he here presents you.
VOLPONE. He is welcome.
Pray him to come more often.
MOSCA. Yes.
VOLTORE. What says he?
MOSCA. He thanks you, and desires you see him
often.
VOLPONE. Mosca.
MOSCA. My patron?
VOLPONE. Bring him near, where is he?
I long to feel his hand.
MOSCA. The plate is here, sir.
VOLTORE. How fare you, sir?

---

124 *phthisic*: consumption or asthma.
126 *posture*: imposture.
4 *notes*: tokens.
6 *grateful*: welcome, pleasing.
10 *bought of St Mark*: bought in St Mark's Square, famous for goldsmiths' shops.

VOLPONE. I thank you, Signior Voltore.
Where is the plate? mine eyes are bad.
VOLTORE. I'm sorry
To see you still thus weak.
MOSCA. [*aside*] That he is not weaker.
VOLPONE. You are too munificent.
VOLTORE. No, sir, would to Heaven
I could as well give health to you, as that plate.
VOLPONE. You give, sir, what you can. I thank you. Your love
Hath taste in this, and shall not be unanswered.
I pray you see me often.
VOLTORE. Yes, I shall, sir.
VOLPONE. Be not far from me.
MOSCA. [*to* VOLTORE] Do you observe that, sir?
VOLPONE. Hearken unto me, still: it will concern you.
MOSCA. You are a happy man, sir, know your good.
VOLPONE. I cannot now last long –
MOSCA. [*to* VOLTORE] (You are his heir, sir.
VOLTORE. Am I?)
VOLPONE. I feel me going (uh, uh, uh, uh!),
I am sailing to my port (uh, uh, uh, uh!),
And I am glad, I am so near my haven.
MOSCA. Alas, kind gentleman, well, we must all go –
VOLTORE. But Mosca –
MOSCA. Age will conquer.
VOLTORE. Pray thee, hear me.
Am I inscribed his heir, for certain?
MOSCA. Are you?
I do beseech you, sir, you will vouchsafe
To write me i'your family. All my hopes
Depend upon your worship. I am lost,
Except the rising sun do shine on me.
VOLTORE. It shall both shine, and warm thee, Mosca.
MOSCA. Sir,
I am a man that have not done your love
All the worst offices: here I wear your keys,
See all your coffers and your caskets locked,
Keep the poor inventory of your jewels,
Your plate, and moneys, am your steward, sir,
Husband your goods here.

---

22 *Hath taste*: is felt.
26 *happy*: fortunate.
35 *write me i'your family*: put my name down amongst those of your servants in your household book.

VOLTORE. But am I sole heir?
MOSCA. Without a partner, sir, confirmed this morning;
The wax is warm yet, and the ink scarce dry
Upon the parchment.
VOLTORE. Happy, happy me!
By what good chance, sweet Mosca?
MOSCA. Your desert, sir;
I know no second cause.
VOLTORE. Thy modesty
Is loath to know it; well, we shall requite it.
MOSCA. He ever liked your course, sir; that first took him.
I, oft, have heard him say how he admired
Men of your large profession, that could speak
To every cause, and things mere contraries,
Till they were hoarse again, yet all be law;
That, with most quick agility, could turn,
And re-turn; make knots, and undo them;
Give forkèd counsel; take provoking gold
On either hand, and put it up: these men,
He knew, would thrive, with their humility.
And (for his part) he thought he should be blessed
To have his heir of such a suffering spirit,
So wise, so grave, of so perplexed a tongue,
And loud withal, that would not wag, nor scarce
Lie still, without a fee; when every word
Your worship but lets fall, is a chequeen!
Another knocks.
Who's that? One knocks, I would not have you seen, sir.
And yet – pretend you came, and went in haste;
I'll fashion an excuse. And, gentle sir,
When you do come to swim, in golden lard,

---

53 *large*: prolix.
54 *mere contraries*: absolute opposites.
57 *knots*: difficulties, complications.
58 *forkèd*: equivocal.
provoking: inviting; also, 'appealing' (with a play on the legal meaning of 'provoke' = to appeal to a judge or court to take up one's cause).
59 *put it up*: pocket it.
62 *suffering*: meek.
63 *perplexed*: intricate.
66 *chequeen*: Italian coin worth between 7 shillings and 9 shillings and sixpence.

Up to the arms, in honey, that your chin
Is borne up stiff, with fatness of the flood,
Think on your vassal; but remember me:
I ha'not been your worst of clients.

VOLTORE. Mosca –

MOSCA. When will you have your inventory brought, sir?
Or see a copy of the will?
[*Knocking again.*]
(Anon!)
I'll bring 'em to you, sir. Away, be gone,
Put business i'your face.
[*Exit* VOLTORE.]

VOLPONE. Excellent, Mosca!
Come hither, let me kiss thee.

MOSCA. Keep you still, sir.
Here is Corbaccio.

VOLPONE. Set the plate away.
The vulture's gone, and the old raven's come.

SCENE IV

MOSCA. Betake you to your silence, and your sleep.
[*He sets the plate with the treasure.*]
Stand there, and multiply. Now shall we see
A wretch, who is (indeed) more impotent,
Than this can feign to be; yet hopes to hop
Over his grave.

[*Enter* CORBACCIO.]

Signior Corbaccio!
Yo'are very welcome, sir.

CORBACCIO. How does your patron?

MOSCA. Troth, as he did, sir, no amends.

CORBACCIO. What? mends he?

MOSCA. No, sir: he is rather worse.

CORBACCIO. That's well. Where is he?

MOSCA. Upon his couch, sir, newly fallen asleep.

CORBACCIO. Does he sleep well?

---

72 *fatness*: richness.
73 *but*: only.
4 *this*: i.e. Volpone.

MOSCA. No wink, sir, all this night,
Nor yesterday, but slumbers.
CORBACCIO. Good! He should take
Some counsel of physicians: I have brought him
An opiate here, from mine own doctor –
MOSCA. He will not hear of drugs.
CORBACCIO. Why? I myself
Stood by while't was made; saw all th'ingredients:
And know it cannot but most gently work.
My life for his, 'tis but to make him sleep.
VOLPONE.[*aside*] Ay, his last sleep, if he would take it.
MOSCA. Sir,
He has no faith in physic.
CORBACCIO. Say you? say you?
MOSCA. He has no faith in physic: he does think
Most of your doctors are the greater danger,
And worse disease, t'escape. I often have
Heard him protest, that your physician
Should never be his heir.
CORBACCIO. Not I his heir?
MOSCA. Not your physician, sir.
CORBACCIO. Oh, no, no, no,
I do not mean it.
MOSCA. No, sir, nor their fees
He cannot brook: he says they flay a man,
Before they kill him.
CORBACCIO. Right, I do conceive you.
MOSCA. And then, they do it by experiment;
For which the law not only doth absolve 'em,
But gives them great reward: and he is loath
To hire his death so.
CORBACCIO. It is true, they kill,
With as much licence as a judge.
MOSCA. Nay, more;
For he but kills, sir, where the law condemns,
And these can kill him, too.
CORBACCIO. Ay, or me:

---

11 *but slumbers*: merely dozes.
23 *your physician*: i.e. doctors in general; but Corbaccio obtusely takes it as referring to his personal doctor.
27 *flay*: skin alive; also, 'fleece'.
28 *conceive*: understand.

Or any man. How does his apoplex?
Is that strong on him, still?
MOSCA. Most violent.
His speech is broken, and his eyes are set,
His face drawn longer, than 'twas wont –
CORBACCIO. How? how?
Stronger, than he was wont?
MOSCA. No, sir: his face
Drawn longer, than 'twas wont.
CORBACCIO. Oh, good.
MOSCA. His mouth
Is ever gaping, and his eyelids hang.
CORBACCIO. Good.
MOSCA. A freezing numbness stiffens all his joints,
And makes the colour of his flesh like lead.
CORBACCIO. 'Tis good.
MOSCA. His pulse beats slow, and dull.
CORBACCIO. Good symptoms, still.
MOSCA. And from his brain –
CORBACCIO. Ha? how? not from his brain?
MOSCA. Yes, sir, and from his brain –
CORBACCIO. (I conceive you, good.)
MOSCA. Flows a cold sweat, with a continual rheum,
Forth the resolvèd corners of his eyes.
CORBACCIO. Is't possible? yet I am better, ha!
How does he, with the swimming of his head?
MOSCA. Oh, sir, 'tis past the scotomy; he, now,
Hath lost his feeling, and hath left to snort:
You hardly can perceive him, that he breathes.
CORBACCIO. Excellent, excellent, sure I shall outlast him:
This makes me young again, a score of years.
MOSCA. I was a-coming for you, sir.
CORBACCIO. Has he made his will?
What has he given me?
MOSCA. No, sir.
CORBACCIO. Nothing? ha?
MOSCA. He has not made his will, sir.

---

36 *apoplex*: apoplexy. Mosca goes on to describe the symptoms of a fatal illness, the strong apoplexy.
48 *rheum*: watery discharge (believed to be the last stage of the strong apoplexy, hence Corbaccio's excitement).
49 *resolvèd*: slackened; watery.
52 *scotomy*: dizziness and dimness of sight.

CORBACCIO. Oh, oh, oh.
What then did Voltore, the lawyer, here?
MOSCA. He smelt a carcass, sir, when he but heard
My master was about his testament
(As I did urge him to it, for your good –)
CORBACCIO. He came unto him, did he? I thought so.
MOSCA. Yes, and presented him this piece of plate.
CORBACCIO. To be his heir?
MOSCA. I do not know, sir.
CORBACCIO. True,
I know it too.
MOSCA. By your own scale, sir.
CORBACCIO. Well,
I shall prevent him, yet. See, Mosca, look,
Here, I have brought a bag of bright chequeens,
Will quite weigh down his plate.
MOSCA. Yea, marry, sir!
This is true physic, this your sacred medicine,
No talk of opiates, to this great elixir.
CORBACCIO. 'Tis *aurum palpabile*, if not *potabile*.
MOSCA. It shall be ministered to him, in his bowl?
CORBACCIO. Ay, do, do, do.
MOSCA. Most blessèd cordial!
This will recover him.
CORBACCIO. Yes, do, do, do.
MOSCA. I think it were not best, sir.
CORBACCIO. What?
MOSCA. To recover him.
CORBACCIO. Oh, no, no, no; by no means.
MOSCA. Why, sir, this
Will work some strange effect, if he but feel it.
CORBACCIO. 'Tis true, therefore, forbear, I'll take my venture:
Give me't again.
MOSCA. At no hand, pardon me;

---

67 *By your own scale*: i.e. 'measuring his motives by your own'; but if Corbaccio overhears, Mosca could seem to say 'you've made your own (correct) judgement'.

68 *prevent*: be ahead of.

72 *elixir*: drug which would prolong life indefinitely; alchemically identified with the essence or 'stone' which was to turn base metal into gold.

73 *aurum palpabile, if not potabile*: palpable, if not potable gold: the latter = a cordial medicine of drinkable gold (as in 75).

75 *cordial*: medicine invigorating for the heart.

You shall not do yourself that wrong, sir. I
Will so advise you, you shall have it all.
CORBACCIO. How?
MOSCA. All, sir, 'tis your right, your own; no man
Can claim a part: 'tis yours, without a rival,
Decreed by destiny.
CORBACCIO. How? how, good Mosca?
MOSCA. I'll tell you, sir. This fit he shall recover –
CORBACCIO. I do conceive you.
MOSCA. And, on first advantage
Of his gained sense, will I re-importune him
Unto the making of his testament:
And show him this.
CORBACCIO. Good, good.
MOSCA. 'Tis better yet,
If you will hear, sir.
CORBACCIO. Yes, with all my heart.
MOSCA. Now would I counsel you, make home with speed;
There, frame a will: whereto you shall inscribe
My master your sole heir.
CORBACCIO. And disinherit
My son?
MOSCA. Oh, sir, the better: for that colour
Shall make it much more taking.
CORBACCIO. O, but colour?
MOSCA. This will, sir, you shall send it unto me.
Now, when I come to enforce (as I will do)
Your cares, your watchings, and your many prayers,
Your more than many gifts, your this day's present,
And, last, produce your will; where (without thought,
Or least regard, unto your proper issue,
A son so brave, and highly meriting)
The stream of your diverted love hath thrown you
Upon my master, and made him your heir:

---

89 *gained*: regained.
96 *colour*: semblance, false appearance.
97 *but*: merely.
100 *watchings*: religious devotions carried out at night.
103 *proper*: own.

He cannot be so stupid, or stone dead,
But, out of conscience, and mere gratitude –
CORBACCIO. He must pronounce me, his?
MOSCA. 'Tis true.
CORBACCIO. This plot
Did I think on before.
MOSCA. I do believe it.
CORBACCIO. Do you not believe it?
MOSCA. Yes, sir.
CORBACCIO. Mine own project.
MOSCA. Which when he hath done, sir –
CORBACCIO. Published me his heir?
MOSCA. And you so certain, to survive him –
CORBACCIO. Ay.
MOSCA. Being so lusty a man –
CORBACCIO. 'Tis true.
MOSCA. Yes, sir –
CORBACCIO. I thought on that too. See, how he should be
The very organ, to express my thoughts!
MOSCA. You have not only done yourself a good –
CORBACCIO. But multiplied it on my son?
MOSCA. 'Tis right, sir.
CORBACCIO. Still, my invention.
MOSCA. 'Las, sir, Heaven knows,
It hath been all my study, all my care
(I e'en grow grey withal), how to work things –
CORBACCIO. I do conceive, sweet Mosca.
MOSCA. You are he,
For whom I labour here.
CORBACCIO. Ay, do, do, do:
I'll straight about it.
MOSCA. Rook go with you, raven.
CORBACCIO. I know thee honest.
MOSCA. You do lie, sir –
CORBACCIO. And –
MOSCA. Your knowledge is no better than your ears, sir.
CORBACCIO. I do not doubt, to be a father to thee.
MOSCA. Nor I, to gull my brother of his blessing.

---

107 *stupid*: insensible.
124 *Rook go with you*: may you be cheated.
128 *gull . . . blessing*: dupe Bonario, as Jacob did Esau (Genesis 27).

CORBACCIO. I may ha'my youth restored to me, why
not?
MOSCA. Your worship is a precious ass –
CORBACCIO. What say'st thou?
MOSCA. I do desire your worship, to make haste, sir.
CORBACCIO. 'Tis done, 'tis done, I go. [*Exit.*]
VOLPONE. Oh, I shall burst;
Let out my sides, let out my sides –
MOSCA. Contain
Your flux of laughter, sir: you know this hope
Is such a bait, it covers any hook.
VOLPONE. Oh, but thy working, and thy placing it!
I cannot hold; good rascal, let me kiss thee:
I never knew thee in so rare a humour.
MOSCA. Alas, sir, I but do as I am taught;
Follow your grave instructions; give 'em words;
Pour oil into their ears: and send them hence.
VOLPONE. 'Tis true, 'tis true. What a rare punishment
Is avarice, to itself!
MOSCA. Ay, with our help, sir.
VOLPONE. So many cares, so many maladies,
So many fears attending on old age,
Yea, death so often called on, as no wish
Can be more frequent with 'em, their limbs faint,
Their senses dull, their seeing, hearing, going,
All dead before them; yea, their very teeth,
Their instruments of eating, failing them:
Yet this is reckoned life! Nay, here was one,
Is now gone home, that wishes to live longer!
Feels not his gout, nor palsy, feigns himself
Younger, by scores of years, flatters his age,
With confident belying it, hopes he may
With charms, like Aeson, have his youth restored:
And with these thoughts so battens, as if fate
Would be as easily cheated on, as he,

---

134 *flux*: flow, 'discharge' (still playing on the medical terms of the last encounter).

138 *rare a humour*: fanciful a mood.

140 *give 'em words*: deceive them, giving them nothing but empty promises.

141 *Pour . . . ears*: speak soothing flatteries to them.

148 *going*: ability to walk.

156 *Aeson*: Jason's father, whose youth was restored to him by the sorceress Medea.

157 *battens*: thrives.

And all turns air!

Another knocks.

Who's that, there, now? a third?
MOSCA. Close, to your couch again; I hear his voice.
It is Corvino, our spruce merchant.
VOLPONE. Dead.
MOSCA. Another bout, sir, with your eyes. Who's there?

SCENE V

[*Enter*] CORVINO.

Signior Corvino! come most wished for! Oh,
How happy were you, if you knew it, now!
CORVINO. Why? what? wherein?
MOSCA. The tardy hour is come, sir.
CORVINO. He is not dead?
MOSCA. Not dead, sir, but as good;
He knows no man.
CORVINO. How shall I do, then?
MOSCA. Why, sir?
CORVINO. I have brought him, here, a pearl.
MOSCA. Perhaps, he has
So much remembrance left, as to know you, sir;
He still calls on you, nothing but your name
Is in his mouth: is your pearl orient, sir?
CORVINO. Venice was never owner of the like.
VOLPONE. [*faintly*] Signior Corvino.
MOSCA. Hark.
VOLPONE. Signior Corvino.
MOSCA. He calls you, step and give it him. H'is here, sir,
And he has brought you a rich pearl.
CORVINO. How do you, sir?
Tell him, it doubles the twelfth caract.
MOSCA. Sir,

---

160 *Close*: be hidden.
161 *spruce*: dapper, modish.
162 *bout*: application of ointment.
9 *orient*: lustrous, of fine quality (pearls from the East were finer than European ones).
14 *caract*: measure of weight for precious stones (then 3½ grams).

He cannot understand, his hearing's gone;
And yet it comforts him, to see you –
CORVINO. Say,
I have a diamond for him, too.
MOSCA. Best show't, sir,
Put it into his hand; 'tis only there
He apprehends: he has his feeling, yet.
See, how he grasps it!
CORVINO. 'Las, good gentleman!
How pitiful the sight is!
MOSCA. Tut, forget, sir.
The weeping of an heir should still be laughter
Under a visor.
CORVINO. Why? am I his heir?
MOSCA. Sir, I am sworn, I may not show the will,
Till he be dead: but here has been Corbaccio,
Here has been Voltore, here were others too,
I cannot number 'em, they were so many,
All gaping here for legacies; but I,
Taking the vantage of his naming you,
'Signior Corvino, Signior Corvino', took
Paper, and pen, and ink, and there I asked him,
Whom he would have his heir? 'Corvino'. Who
Should be executor? 'Corvino'. And
To any question he was silent to,
I still interpreted the nods he made
(Through weakness) for consent: and sent home th'others,
Nothing bequeathed them, but to cry, and curse.
They embrace.
CORVINO. Oh, my dear Mosca. Does he not perceive us?
MOSCA. No more than a blind harper. He knows no man,
No face of friend, nor name of any servant,
Who 'twas that fed him last, or gave him drink:
Not those he hath begotten, or brought up
Can he remember.
CORVINO. Has he children?
MOSCA. Bastards,

---

22 *still*: always.
23 *visor*: mask.
28 *gaping*: covetous, awaiting greedily.
39 *blind harper*: proverbial figure (from a traditional way in which a blind man could earn a living).

Some dozen, or more, that he begot on beggars,
Gypsies, and Jews, and black-moors, when he was drunk.
Knew you not that, sir? 'Tis the common fable.
The dwarf, the fool, the eunuch are all his;
H'is the true father of his family,
In all, save me: but he has given 'em nothing.

CORVINO. That's well, that's well. Art sure he does not hear us?

MOSCA. Sure, sir? Why, look you, credit your own sense.
[*Shouts in* VOLPONE*'s ear.*]
The pox approach, and add to your diseases,
If it would send you hence the sooner, sir.
For your incontinence, it hath deserved it
Throughly and throughly, and the plague to boot.
(You may come near, sir.) – Would you once close
Those filthy eyes of yours, that flow with slime,
Like two frog-pits; and those same hanging cheeks,
Covered with hide, instead of skin (Nay, help, sir),
That look like frozen dish-clouts, set on end.

CORVINO. Or like an old smoked wall, on which the rain
Ran down in streaks.

MOSCA. Excellent, sir, speak out;
You may be louder yet: a culverin,
Dischargèd in his ear, would hardly bore it.

CORVINO. His nose is like a common sewer, still running.

MOSCA. 'Tis good! and what his mouth?

CORVINO. A very draught.

MOSCA. Oh, stop it up –

CORVINO. By no means.

MOSCA. Pray you, let me.
Faith, I could stifle him, rarely, with a pillow,
As well as any woman, that should keep him.

---

46 *fable*: report.
48 *family*: household.
52 *pox*: syphilis.
55 *Throughly and throughly*: to the full.
56 *once*: once for all.
60 *dish-clouts*: dish-cloths.
63 *culverin*: a type of musket.
66 *draught*: cesspool.
69 *keep*: look after.

CORVINO. Do as you will, but I'll be gone.
MOSCA. Be so;
It is your presence makes him last so long.
CORVINO. I pray you, use no violence.
MOSCA. No, sir? why?
Why should you be thus scrupulous? pray you, sir?
CORVINO. Nay, at your discretion.
MOSCA. Well, good sir, be gone.
CORVINO. I will not trouble him now, to take my pearl?
MOSCA. Puh, nor your diamond. What a needless care
Is this afflicts you? Is not all, here, yours?
Am not I here? whom you have made? your creature?
That owe my being to you?
CORVINO. Grateful Mosca!
Thou art my friend, my fellow, my companion,
My partner, and shalt share in all my fortunes.
MOSCA. Excepting one.
CORVINO. What's that?
MOSCA. Your gallant wife, sir.
[*Exit* CORVINO.]
Now is he gone: we had no other means
To shoot him hence, but this.
VOLPONE. My divine Mosca!
Thou hast today outgone thyself.
Another knocks.
Who's there?
I will be troubled with no more. Prepare
Me music, dances, banquets, all delights;
The Turk is not more sensual, in his pleasures,
Than will Volpone.
[*Exit* MOSCA.]
Let me see, a pearl?
A diamond? plate? chequeens? good morning's purchase;
Why, this is better than rob churches, yet:

---

75 *take*: take back.
78 Jonson's punctuation indicates the delivery of the line.
made: set up financially.
creature: servant.
82 *gallant*: finely dressed.
84 *shoot him*: dispatch him quickly.
90 *purchase*: booty (thieves' cant).

Or fat, by eating (once a month) a man.
[*Enter* MOSCA.]
Who is't?
MOSCA. The beauteous Lady Would-be, sir,
Wife to the English knight, Sir Politic Would-be
(This is the style, sir, is directed me),
Hath sent to know, how you have slept tonight,
And if you would be visited.
VOLPONE. Not now.
Some three hours hence –
MOSCA. I told the squire so much.
VOLPONE. When I am high with mirth, and wine:
then, then.
'Fore Heaven, I wonder at the desperate valour
Of the bold English, that they dare let loose
Their wives, to all encounters!
MOSCA. Sir, this knight
Had not his name for nothing, he is politic,
And knows, howe'er his wife affect strange airs,
She hath not yet the face, to be dishonest.
But, had she Signior Corvino's wife's face –
VOLPONE. Has she so rare a face?
MOSCA. Oh, sir, the wonder,
The blazing star of Italy! a wench
O'the first year! a beauty, ripe, as harvest!
Whose skin is whiter than a swan, all over!
Than silver, snow, or lilies! a soft lip,
Would tempt you to eternity of kissing!
And flesh, that melteth, in the touch, to blood!

---

92 *fat, by eating*: grow fat by financially ruining.
95 *style*: title, formal description.
is directed me: that I am directed to use.
96 *tonight*: last night.
98 *squire*: attendant; perhaps also, 'apple squire' = pimp.
101 *let loose*: allow to go unrestricted. (The English were the amused wonder of Europe for the freedom they allowed their wives.)
102 *encounters*: amatory meetings.
104 *strange*: foreign; odd; also, of a harlot ('strange woman').
105 *face*: looks.
dishonest: unchaste.
109 *O'the first year*: pure, unblemished (applied to the sacrificial lamb in Leviticus 9.13); young and delicate (colloquially, of a woman).
113 *blood*: blushes; also 'passion', which she arouses (and, Mosca implies, responds to).

Bright as your gold! and lovely, as your gold!
VOLPONE. Why had not I known this before?
MOSCA. Alas, sir,
Myself but yesterday discovered it.
VOLPONE. How might I see her?
MOSCA. Oh, not possible;
She's kept as warily, as is your gold:
Never does come abroad, never takes air,
But at a window. All her looks are sweet,
As the first grapes, or cherries: and are watched
As near as they are.
VOLPONE. I must see her –
MOSCA. Sir,
There is a guard, of ten spies thick, upon her;
All his whole household: each of which is set
Upon his fellow, and have all their charge,
When he goes out, when he comes in, examined.
VOLPONE. I will go see her, though but at her window.
MOSCA. In some disguise, then.
VOLPONE. That is true, I must
Maintain mine own shape, still, the same: we'll think.
[*Exeunt.*]

ACT II

SCENE I

[*Enter*] POLITIC WOULD-BE, PEREGRINE.

SIR POLITIC. Sir, to a wise man, all the world's his soil.
It is not Italy, nor France, nor Europe,
That must bound me, if my fates call me forth.
Yet, I protest, it is no salt desire

---

125 *charge*: duty, responsibility.
129 *shape*: appearance; disguise; also, 'theatrical part', impersonation, with make-up and costume.
4 *protest*: declare (a foppish affectation of speech).
salt: wanton.

Of seeing countries, shifting a religion,
Nor any disaffection to the state
Where I was bred (and unto which I owe
My dearest plots) hath brought me out; much less,
That idle, antique, stale, grey-headed project
Of knowing men's minds, and manners, with
Ulysses:
But a peculiar humour of my wife's,
Laid for this height of Venice, to observe,
To quote, to learn the language, and so forth –
I hope you travel, sir, with licence?
PEREGRINE. Yes.
SIR POLITIC. I dare the safelier converse – How long,
sir,
Since you left England?
PEREGRINE. Seven weeks.
SIR POLITIC. So lately!
You ha'not been with my lord ambassador?
PEREGRINE. Not yet, sir.
SIR POLITIC. Pray you, what news, sir,
vents our climate?
I heard, last night, a most strange thing reported
By some of my lord's followers, and I long
To hear how 'twill be seconded!
PEREGRINE. What was't, sir?
SIR POLITIC. Marry, sir, of a raven, that should build
In a ship royal of the king's.
PEREGRINE. [*aside*] This fellow

---

7 *owe*: either 'am indebted for' (the Gunpowder Plot was topical), or 'am under an obligation to render'.

10 *Ulysses*: 'who after Troy was sacked/ Saw many towns, and men, and could their manners tract' (i.e. treat) (Jonson's translation of Horace's rendering of the *Odyssey*, I.3, in *The Art of Poetry*, 201–2, H&S, VIII, p. 343).

11 *peculiar humour*: particular whim, fancy.

12 *Laid for this height*: directed to this latitude.

13 *quote*: mark, take note.

14 *licence*: passport issued by the king's council.

17 *lord ambassador*: Sir Henry Wotton, a friend of Jonson's. Sometimes thought to be a model for Sir Pol.

18 *vents our climate*: does our part of the world publish, give out.

21 *seconded*: supported.

22 *raven*: whilst it was unpropitious for any bird to nest in the rigging of a ship, a raven was itself a bird of ill omen, and therefore the event was doubly ominous to the superstitious.
should build: is said to have built (usage conveying reported speech).

Does he gull me, trow? or is gulled? – Your name, sir?
SIR POLITIC. My name is Politic Would-be.
PEREGRINE. [*aside*] Oh, that speaks him. –
A knight, sir?
SIR POLITIC. A poor knight, sir.
PEREGRINE. Your lady
Lies here, in Venice, for intelligence
Of tires, and fashions, and behaviour,
Among the courtesans? the fine Lady Would-be?
SIR POLITIC. Yes, sir, the spider, and the bee, oft-times,
Suck from one flower.
PEREGRINE. Good Sir Politic!
I cry you mercy; I have heard much of you:
'Tis true, sir, of your raven.
SIR POLITIC. On your knowledge?
PEREGRINE. Yes, and your lion's whelping, in the Tower.
SIR POLITIC. Another whelp!
PEREGRINE. Another, sir.
SIR POLITIC. Now, Heaven!
What prodigies be these? The fires at Berwick!
And the new star! these things concurring, strange!
And full of omen! Saw you those meteors?
PEREGRINE. I did, sir.
SIR POLITIC. Fearful! Pray you sir, confirm me,
Were there three porcpisces seen, above the bridge,
As they give out?
PEREGRINE. Six, and a sturgeon, sir.

---

24 *gull*: attempt to make a fool of.
trow: do you suppose.
28 *tires*: headdresses, attires.
29 *courtesans*: Venetian courtesans were famous for their beauty and their culture.
30–1 *the spider . . . from one flower*: proverbial.
35 *Another whelp*: lion cubs were born in the Tower of London in August 1604 and February 1605.
36 *prodigies*: marvels.
fires at Berwick: in January 1605, apparitions of fighting armies were reported as causing fright on both sides of the border.
37 *new star*: discovered in October 1604 by Kepler in the Serpent constellation. It disappeared two years later.
40 *porcpisces*: porpoises (see *Sejanus*, V.[vii].638 n.). A porpoise and a whale were found in the Thames in January 1605/6.

SIR POLITIC. I am astonished!
PEREGRINE. Nay, sir, be not so;
I'll tell you a greater prodigy, than these –
SIR POLITIC. What should these things portend!
PEREGRINE. The very day
(Let me be sure) I put forth from London,
There was a whale discovered, in the river,
As high as Woolwich, that had waited there
(Few know how many months) for the subversion
Of the Stode fleet.
SIR POLITIC. Is't possible? Believe it,
'Twas either sent from Spain, or the archdukes!
Spinola's whale, upon my life, my credit!
Will they not leave these projects? Worthy sir,
Some other news.
PEREGRINE. Faith, Stone, the fool, is dead;
And they do lack a tavern fool extremely.
SIR POLITIC. Is Mas' Stone dead!
PEREGRINE. H'is dead, sir, why? I hope
You thought him not immortal? [*Aside*] Oh, this knight
(Were he well known) would be a precious thing
To fit our English stage: he that should write
But such a fellow, should be thought to feign
Extremely, if not maliciously.
SIR POLITIC. Stone dead!
PEREGRINE. Dead. Lord! how deeply, sir, you apprehend it!
He was no kinsman to you?
SIR POLITIC. That I know of.
Well! that same fellow was an unknown fool.
PEREGRINE. And yet you knew him, it seems?

---

49 *Stode fleet*: the English Merchant Adventurers' fleet sailed from Stade, at the mouth of the Elbe.
50 *archdukes*: title of the Infanta Isabella and her husband Albert as rulers of the Spanish Netherlands (see Textual Note, p. 432 below).
51 *Spinola's whale*: Spinola, commander of the Spanish army in the Netherlands, was popularly supposed to have hired a whale to drown London by spouting over it water from the Thames which he had snuffed up.
53 *Stone, the fool*: mentioned in 1605 as having been whipped for a tactless political joke.
60 *maliciously*: i.e. to caricature an actual person.
61 *apprehend*: feel; also, 'understand by'.
62 *That*: i.e. not that.
63 *unknown*: not known for what he was.

SIR POLITIC. I did so. Sir,
I knew him one of the most dangerous heads
Living within the state, and so I held him.
PEREGRINE. Indeed, sir?
SIR POLITIC. While he lived, in action.
He has received weekly intelligence,
Upon my knowledge, out of the Low Countries
(For all parts of the world) in cabbages;
And those dispensed again, t'ambassadors,
In oranges, musk-melons, apricots,
Lemons, pome-citrons, and suchlike: sometimes,
In Colchester oysters, and your Selsey cockles.
PEREGRINE. You make me wonder!
SIR POLITIC. Sir, upon my knowledge.
Nay, I have observed him, at your public ordinary,
Take his advertisement from a traveller
(A còncealed statesman) in a trencher of meat:
And, instantly, before the meal was done,
Convey an answer in a toothpick.
PEREGRINE. Strange!
How could this be, sir?
SIR POLITIC. Why, the meat was cut
So like his character, and so laid, as he
Must easily read the cipher.
PEREGRINE. I have heard,
He could not read, sir.
SIR POLITIC. So 'twas given out
(In policy) by those that did employ him:
But he could read, and had your languages,
And to't, as sound a noddle –

---

67 *in action*: at work (as a secret agent).
70 *cabbages*: first imported from Holland in the seventeenth century.
72 *musk-melons*: melons.
73 *pome-citrons*: citrons or limes.
74 *Colchester . . . cockles*: like the fruits of 72–3, delicacies of the court.
76 *ordinary*: tavern which charged fixed prices for meals.
77 *advertisement*: instructions.
78 *còncealed statesman*: disguised agent.
80 *toothpick*: elegant use of the toothpick was one of the foppish affectations of the time; presumably, Stone would imitate such display.
82 *character*: cipher.
85 *In policy*: out of statecraft.
87 *to't*: on top of that.
noddle: head (jocular).

PEREGRINE. I have heard, sir,
That your baboons were spies; and that they were
A kind of subtle nation, near to China.
SIR POLITIC. Ay, ay, your *Mamaluchi*. Faith, they had
Their hand in a French plot, or two; but they
Were so extremely given to women, as
They made discovery of all: yet I
Had my advices here (on Wednesday last)
From one of their own coat, they were returned,
Made their relations (as the fashion is)
And now stand fair for fresh employment.
PEREGRINE. [*aside*] 'Heart!
This Sir Pol will be ignorant of nothing. –
It seems, sir, you know all?
SIR POLITIC. Not all, sir. But
I have some general notions; I do love
To note, and to observe: though I live out,
Free from the active torrent, yet I'd mark
The currents, and the passages of things,
For mine own private use; and know the ebbs,
And flows of state.
PEREGRINE. Believe it, sir, I hold
Myself in no small tie unto my fortunes,
For casting me thus luckily, upon you;
Whose knowledge (if your bounty equal it)
May do me great assistance, in instruction
For my behaviour, and my bearing, which
Is yet so rude, and raw –
SIR POLITIC. Why? came you forth
Empty of rules, for travel?
PEREGRINE. Faith, I had

---

88 *baboons*: one of the sights of London about the time of *Volpone*.
90 *Mamaluchi*: Italian form of 'Mamelukes', former Turkish slaves who became rulers of Egypt in the thirteenth century, and nothing at all to do with baboons or China.
93 *made discovery of all*: revealed everything, gave the game away.
94 *advices*: dispatches.
95 *coat*: faction.
96 *relations*: reports.
as the fashion is: in the usual manner.
97 *stand fair*: are well set.
101 *out*: abroad; perhaps with a play on 'in error'.
106 *in no small tie*: greatly bound, indebted.
111 *rude*: unpolished.

Some common ones, from out that vulgar
grammar,
Which he, that cried Italian to me, taught me.
SIR POLITIC. Why, this it is that spoils all our brave
bloods;
Trusting our hopeful gentry unto pedants:
Fellows of outside, and mere bark. You seem
To be a gentleman, of ingenuous race –
I not profess it, but my fate hath been
To be where I have been consulted with,
In this high kind, touching some great men's sons,
Persons of blood, and honour –
PEREGRINE. Who be these, sir?

SCENE II

[*Enter*] MOSCA [*and*] NANO [*disguised as a mountebank's attendants, with properties for erecting a scaffold stage*].

MOSCA. Under that window, there't must be. The
same.
SIR POLITIC. Fellows, to mount a bank! Did your
instructor
In the dear tongues, never discourse to you
Of the Italian mountebanks?
PEREGRINE. Yes, sir.
SIR POLITIC. Why,
Here shall you see one.
PEREGRINE. They are quack-salvers,

113 *vulgar grammar*: grammar in ordinary use; or perhaps John Florio's *Second Fruits* (1591), which combined teaching the Italian language with useful precepts for travellers to Italy.
114 *cried*: pronounced, intoned.
115 *brave bloods*: excellent young men of spirit.
117 *outside*: superficiality.
bark: outward show; perhaps with a pun suggested by 'cried'.
118 *ingenuous race*: noble family.
119 *profess*: make a profession (of instructing travellers).
121 *high kind*: important role.
2 *mount a bank*: from Italian *monta in banco*, to mount the bench or stage (on which the mountebank performed).
3 *dear*: highly esteemed.
5 *quack-salvers*: quacks, who boast or cry up their ointments (salves).

Fellows that live by venting oils, and drugs?
SIR POLITIC. Was that the character he gave you of them?
PEREGRINE. As I remember.
SIR POLITIC. Pity his ignorance.
They are the only knowing men of Europe!
Great general scholars, excellent physicians,
Most admired statesmen, professed favourites,
And cabinet-counsellors, to the greatest princes!
The only languaged men, of all the world!
PEREGRINE. And I have heard, they are most lewd impostors;
Made all of terms, and shreds; no less beliers
Of great men's favours, than their own vile medicines;
Which they will utter, upon monstrous oaths:
Selling that drug for twopence, ere they part,
Which they have valued at twelve crowns, before.
SIR POLITIC. Sir, calumnies are answered best with silence:
Yourself shall judge. Who is it mounts, my friends?
MOSCA. Scoto of Mantua, sir.
SIR POLITIC. Is't he? Nay, then
I'll proudly promise, sir, you shall behold
Another man than has been fant'sied to you.
I wonder, yet, that he should mount his bank
Here, in this nook, that has been wont t'appear
In face of the Piazza! Here he comes.

---

6 *venting*: probably both 'vending, selling' and 'crying up'.
9 *knowing*: learned.
12 *cabinet-counsellors*: close advisers.
13 *only languaged*: finest spoken.
14 *lewd*: ignorant.
15 *terms, and shreds*: technical jargon and scraps of quotations, tags.
17 *utter*: describe; pass off (like false coin); barter, sell.
18 *part*: depart.
19 *crowns*: coins worth about five shillings, or a quarter of a pound sterling.
22 *Scoto of Mantua*: leader of a Mantuan *commedia dell' arte* acting troupe, who had performed conjuring tricks before Queen Elizabeth in 1576, and whose name had become a by-word for clever deception.
24 *fant'sied*: fancifully represented.
27 *In face of the Piazza*: facing the main square (St Mark's).

[Enter] VOLPONE *[disguised as a mountebank, followed by the crowd or* GREGE*].*

VOLPONE. *[to* NANO*]* Mount, zany.
GREGE. Follow, follow, follow, follow, follow.
SIR POLITIC. See how the people follow him! H'is a man
May write ten thousand crowns in bank, here.
*[*VOLPONE *mounts the stage.]*
Note,
Mark but his gesture: I do use to observe
The state he keeps, in getting up!
PEREGRINE. 'Tis worth it, sir.

VOLPONE. Most noble gentlemen and my worthy patrons, it may seem strange, that I, your Scoto Mantuano, who was ever wont to fix my bank in face of the public Piazza, near the shelter of the portico to the Procuratìa, should, now (after eight months' absence, from this illustrous city of Venice) humbly retire myself, into an obscure nook of the Piazza.

SIR POLITIC. Did not I, now object the same?
PEREGRINE. Peace, sir.

VOLPONE. Let me tell you: I am not (as your Lombard proverb saith) cold on my feet; or content to part with my commodities at a cheaper rate, than I accustomed: look not for it. Nor that the calumnious reports of that impudent detractor, and shame to our profession (Alessandro Buttone, I mean) who gave out, in public, I was condemned a *sforzato* to the galleys, for poisoning the Cardinal

---

28 *zany*: mountebank's comic servant, who imitated his master's actions and gestures.

30 *write*: reckon up.

32 *state*: ceremoniousness.

37 *portico to the Procuratìa*: the arcade of the Procuratie Vecchie, residence of the Venetian procurators in St Mark's Square.

38 *illustrous*: famous.

41 *object*: bring forward, raise.

43 *cold on my feet*: Italian *aver freddo a' piedi*, to be forced by poverty to sell cheaply.

47 *Buttone*: 'A button. Also, a quip or taunt' (Florio, 1598): a rival invented for the occasion.

49 *sforzato*: '*Sforzati*, galley-slaves, prisoners perforce' (Florio, 1598).

Bembo's – cook, hath at all attached, much less dejected me. No, no, worthy gentlemen (to tell you true) I cannot endure to see the rabble of these ground *ciarlitani*, that spread their cloaks on the pavement, as if they meant to do feats of activity, and then come in, lamely, with their mouldy tales out of Boccaccio, like stale Tabarine, the fabulist: some of them discoursing their travels, and of their tedious captivity in the Turk's galleys, when indeed (were the truth known) they were the Christians' galleys, where very temperately, they ate bread, and drunk water, as a wholesome penance (enjoined them by their confessors) for base pilferies.

SIR POLITIC. Note but his bearing, and contempt of these.

VOLPONE. These turdy-facy-nasty-paty-lousy-fartical rogues, with one poor groatsworth of unprepared antimony, finely wrapped up in several *scartoccios*, are able, very well, to kill their twenty a week, and play; yet these meagre, starved spirits, who have half stopped the organs of their minds with earthy oppilations, want not their favourers among your shrivelled, salad-eating artisans: who are overjoyed, that they may have

---

49–50 *Cardinal Bembo's – cook*: Pietro Bembo (1470–1547), humanist and poet, an authority on love in Book IV of Castiglione's *The Courtier*. The pause before 'cook' implies 'mistress'.

53 *ground ciarlitani*: charlatans who, unlike the mountebanks, performed their patter standing on their cloaks spread on the pavement.

54 *feats of activity*: tumbling, acrobatics.

56 *Boccaccio*: 1313–75; poet and humanist, author of the *Decameron*, a collection of tales much resorted to by later story-tellers.
Tabarine: famous zany of the same era as Scoto, but of a rival troupe.
fabulist: professional story-teller.

65–6 *turdy-facy-nasty-paty-lousy-fartical*: modelled on the abusive compound epithets of Aristophanes.

66 *groatsworth*: a groat was a coin worth fourpence, a third of a shilling.

68 *scartoccios*: 'A coffin of paper for spice, as apothecaries use' (Florio, 1598).

70 *organs*: faculties.

71 *earthy oppilations*: gross obstructions.

72 *salad*: uncooked vegetables.

their ha'porth of physic, though it purge 'em into another world, 't makes no matter.

SIR POLITIC. Excellent! ha'you heard better language, sir?

VOLPONE. Well, let 'em go. And gentlemen, honourable gentlemen, know, that for this time, our bank, being thus removed from the clamours of the *canaglia*, shall be the scene of pleasure, and delight: for I have nothing to sell, little or nothing to sell.

SIR POLITIC. I told you, sir, his end.

PEREGRINE. You did so, sir.

VOLPONE. I protest, I, and my six servants, are not able to make of this precious liquor so fast as it is fetched away from my lodging, by gentlemen of your city; strangers of the Terra Firma; worshipful merchants; ay, and senators too: who, ever since my arrival, have detained me to their uses, by their splendidous liberalities. And worthily. For what avails your rich man to have his magazines stuffed with *moscadelli*, or of the purest grape, when his physicians prescribe him (on pain of death) to drink nothing but water, cocted with aniseeds? Oh, health! health! the blessing of the rich! the riches of the poor! who can buy thee at too dear a rate, since there is no enjoying this world, without thee? Be not then so sparing of your purses, honourable gentlemen, as to abridge the natural course of life –

PEREGRINE. You see his end?

SIR POLITIC. Ay, is't not good?

VOLPONE. For, when a humid flux, or catarrh, by the mutability of air, falls from your head, into an arm, or shoulder, or any other part; take you a ducat, or your chequeen of gold, and apply to the

---

74 *physic*: purgative medicine.
80 *canaglia*: rabble, 'only fit for dogs' company' (Florio, 1598).
87 *Terra Firma*: Venice's mainland possessions.
90 *splendidous*: magnificent.
91 *magazines*: storehouses.
92 *moscadelli*: muscatel wines.
94 *cocted*: boiled.
102 *humid flux*: flow of bodily fluids (see Additional Note to II.ii.109, p. 439 below).
105 *ducat*: silver coin worth about 3 shillings and fourpence, or one-sixth of a pound sterling.

place affected: see what good effect it can work. No, no, 'tis this blessed *unguento*, this rare extraction, that hath only power to disperse all malignant humours, that proceed either of hot, cold, moist, or windy causes –

PEREGRINE. I would he had put in dry too.

SIR POLITIC. Pray you, observe.

VOLPONE. To fortify the most indigest, and crude stomach, ay, were it of one, that (through extreme weakness) vomited blood, applying only a warm napkin to the place, after the unction, and fricace; for the *vertigine* in the head, putting but a drop into your nostrils, likewise behind the ears; a most sovereign, and approved remedy: the *mal-caduco*, cramps, convulsions, paralyses, epilepsies, *tremor cordia*, retired nerves, ill vapours of the spleen, stoppings of the liver, the stone, the strangury, *hernia ventosa*, *iliaca passio*; stops a *dysenteria*, immediately; easeth the torsion of the small guts; and cures *melancholia hypochondriaca*, being taken and applied according to my printed receipt.

Pointing to his bill and his glass.

For this is the physician, this the medicine; this counsels, this cures; this gives the direction, this

---

107 *unguento*: ointment.
108 *only*: alone.
109 *humours*: see Additional Note, p. 439 below.
112 *indigest*: failing to digest.
crude: sour.
115 *unction*: (application of) ointment.
fricace: massage.
116 *vertigine*: giddiness, dizziness.
118 *sovereign*: absolutely efficacious.
approved: proved by experience, tried.
mal-caduco: epilepsy, falling sickness.
119–20 *tremor cordia*: palpitations of the heart.
120 *retired nerves*: shrunken sinews.
121 *strangury*: painful disease of the urinary organs.
122 *hernia ventosa*: rupture.
iliaca passio: intestinal pains.
dysenteria: dysentery.
123 *torsion of the small guts*: griping in the bowels.
124 *melancholia hypochondriaca*: the *hypochondria*, the abdomen immediately beneath the ribs, was thought to be the seat of melancholy.
125 *receipt*: prescription.
125 s.d. *bill*: prescription.

works the effect: and (in sum) both together may be termed an abstract of the theoric, and practic in the Aesculapian art. 'Twill cost you eight crowns. And Zan Fritada, pray thee sing a verse, extempore, in honour of it.

SIR POLITIC. How do you like him, sir?

PEREGRINE. Most strangely, I!

SIR POLITIC. Is not his language rare?

PEREGRINE. But alchemy,
I never heard the like: or Broughton's books.

[NANO *sings*.]

Song

Had old Hippocrates, or Galen
(That to their books put medicines all in),
But known this secret, they had never
(Of which they will be guilty ever)
Been murderers of so much paper,
Or wasted many a hurtless taper:
No Indian drug had e'er been famèd,
Tobacco, sassafras not namèd;
Ne yet of guacum one small stick, sir,
Nor Raymond Lully's great elixir.

---

129 *abstract*: epitome.
theoric, and practic: theoretical and practical parts.
130 *Aesculapian*: medical (from Aesculapius, classical god of medicine).
131 *Zan Fritada*: name of a famous Italian zany (*Zan* = *Gian'*, John; *Fritata* = pancake).
133 *Most strangely, I!*: i.e. I'm absolutely astonished.
134 *But*: except for.
135 *Broughton's books*: Hugh Broughton (1549–1612), Puritan divine and rabbinical scholar, whose language is again satirised by Jonson in *The Alchemist*, II.iii.238, IV.v.1–32.
136 *Hippocrates . . . Galen*: Greek physicians: Hippocrates (460–?350 BC) and Galen (*c*. AD 130–?200) invented and developed the theory of humours.
141 *hurtless*: harmless.
142 *Indian*: from the Indies.
143 *sassafras*: dried bark of the sassafras tree; like tobacco, recently imported from America, and used for medicinal purposes.
144 *Ne*: nor.
guacum: a drug made from the resin of the guaiacum tree.
145 *Lully*: or Lull (*c*. 1235–1315), Catalan author, mystic, and missionary. He was credited with the discovery of the *elixir vitae*, a substance for prolonging life indefinitely.

Ne had been known the Danish Gonswart,
Or Paracelsus, with his long sword.

PEREGRINE. All this, yet, will not do, eight crowns is high.

VOLPONE. No more. Gentlemen, if I had but time to discourse to you the miraculous effects of this my oil, surnamed *oglio del Scoto*; with the countless catalogue of those I have cured of th'aforesaid, and many more diseases; the patents and privileges of all the princes, and commonwealths of Christendom; or but the depositions of those that appeared on my part, before the signiory of the *sanità*, and most learned college of physicians; where I was authorised, upon notice taken of the admirable virtues of my medicaments, and mine own excellency, in matter of rare, and unknown secrets, not only to disperse them publicly in this famous city, but in all the territories, that happily joy under the government of the most pious and magnificent states of Italy. But may some other gallant fellow say, 'Oh, there be divers that make profession to have as good, and as experimented receipts, as yours.' Indeed, very many have assayed, like apes, in imitation of that, which is really and essentially in me, to make of this oil; bestowed great cost in furnaces, stills, alembics, continual fires, and preparation of the ingredients (as indeed there goes to it six hundred several simples, besides some quantity of human fat, for the conglutination, which we buy of the anatomists) but when these practitioners come to the last decoction, blow, blow, puff, puff, and all flies *in fumo*: ha, ha, ha!

---

146 *Gonswart*: not identified; but possibly Cornelius Hamsfort, physician-in-chief to King Christian III of Denmark, grandfather of James I's queen, Anne.

147 *Paracelsus*: 1493–1541; German physician, who carried his quintessences and drugs in the handle of his sword.

151 *oglio del Scoto*: 'Scoto's Oil'.

156 *signiory of the sanità*: department of Venetian government concerned with health; they licensed mountebanks, etc.

165 *divers*: various (men).

166 *experimented*: proven.

170 *alembics*: distilling apparatus, early counterpart of the retort or still.

172 *several simples*: different herbs.

175 *decoction*: boiling down of ingredients.

176 *in fumo*: in smoke.

Poor wretches! I rather pity their folly, and indiscretion, than their loss of time, and money; for those may be recovered by industry: but to be a fool born, is a disease incurable. For myself, I always from my youth have endeavoured to get the rarest secrets, and book them; either in exchange, or for money: I spared nor cost, nor labour, where anything was worthy to be learned. And gentlemen, honourable gentlemen, I will undertake (by virtue of chemical art) out of the honourable hat that covers your head, to extract the four elements; that is to say, the fire, air, water, and earth, and return you your felt without burn, or stain. For whilst others have been at the balloo, I have been at my book: and am now past the craggy paths of study, and come to the flowery plains of honour, and reputation.

SIR POLITIC. I do assure you, sir, that is his aim.

VOLPONE. But, to our price.

PEREGRINE. And that withal, Sir Pol.

VOLPONE. You all know (honourable gentlemen) I never valued this *ampulla*, or vial, at less than eight crowns, but for this time, I am content to be deprived of it for six; six crowns is the price; and less in courtesy, I know you cannot offer me: take it, or leave it, howsoever, both it, and I, am at your service. I ask you not, as the value of the thing, for then I should demand of you a thousand crowns; so the Cardinals Montalto, Farnese, the great Duke of Tuscany, my gossip, with divers other princes have given me; but I despise money. Only to show my affection to you, honourable gentlemen, and your illustrous state here, I have neglected the messages of these princes, mine own offices, framed my journey hither, only to present

---

182 *book*: write down.
191 *balloo*: or balloon, a Venetian ball game in which young men struck a large ball with pieces of wood bound to their arms.
197 *vial*: phial.
204 *Montalto*: became Pope Sixtus V in 1585.
Farnese: there were two cardinals of the name of Farnese in the sixteenth century; Alessandro became Pope Paul III in 1534.
205 *Duke of Tuscany*: title bestowed on Cosimo de' Medici in 1569.
gossip: intimate friend.
210 *offices*: duties, responsibilities.

you with the fruits of my travels. [*To* NANO *and* MOSCA] Tune your voices once more to the touch of your instruments, and give the honourable assembly some delightful recreation.

PEREGRINE. What monstrous, and most painful circumstance
Is here, to get some three or four gazets!
Some threepence, i'th'whole, for that 'twill come to.

Song

You that would last long, list to my song,
Make no more coil, but buy of this oil.
Would you be ever fair? and young?
Stout of teeth? and strong of tongue?
Tart of palate? quick of ear?
Sharp of sight? of nostril clear?
Moist of hand? and light of foot?
(Or I will come nearer to't)
Would you live free from all diseases?
Do the act, your mistress pleases;
Yet fright all aches from your bones?
Here's a medicine, for the nones.

VOLPONE. Well, I am in a humour (at this time) to make a present of the small quantity my coffer contains: to the rich, in courtesy, and to the poor, for God's sake. Wherefore, now mark; I asked you six crowns; and six crowns, at other times, you have paid me; you shall not give me six crowns, nor five, nor four, nor three, nor two, nor one; nor half a ducat; no, nor a *moccenigo*: six — pence it will cost you, or six hundred pound – expect no lower price, for by the banner of my front, I will

---

215 *circumstance*: 'beating about the bush'; or perhaps, 'ceremoniousness'.

216 *gazets*: Venetian coins. One pound sterling was worth 320 gazets.

219 *coil*: ado.

222 *Tart*: keen.

224 *Moist of hand*: a moist palm was held to indicate youthfulness and a sensuous disposition.

228 *aches*: pronounced 'aitches' (two syllables).

229 *nones*: nonce, occasion.

237 *moccenigo*: Venetian coin, worth sixpence, or half a shilling. *six—pence*: the long dash indicates a dramatic pause.

239 *banner of my front*: banner hanging on the front of the mountebank's stage, listing diseases and his cures for them.

not bate a *bagatine*, that I will have only a pledge of your loves, to carry something from amongst you, to show I am not contemned by you. Therefore, now, toss your handkerchiefs, cheerfully, cheerfully; and be advertised, that the first heroic spirit, that deigns to grace me, with a handkerchief, I will give it a little remembrance of something beside, shall please it better, than if I had presented it with a double pistolet.

PEREGRINE. Will you be that heroic spark, Sir Pol?

CELIA *at the window throws down her handkerchief.*

Oh, see! the window has prevented you.

VOLPONE. Lady, I kiss your bounty: and for this timely grace you have done your poor Scoto of Mantua, I will return you, over and above my oil, a secret of that high, and inestimable nature, shall make you forever enamoured on that minute, wherein your eye first descended on so mean (yet not altogether to be despised) an object. Here is a powder, concealed in this paper, of which, if I should speak to the worth, nine thousand volumes were but as one page, that page as a line, that line as a word: so short is this pilgrimage of man (which some call life) to the expressing of it. Would I reflect on the price? why, the whole world were but as an empire, that empire as a province, that province as a bank, that bank as a private purse, to the purchase of it. I will only tell you: it is the powder, that made Venus a goddess (given her by Apollo) that kept her perpetually young, cleared her wrinkles, firmed her gums, filled her skin, coloured her hair; from her, derived to Helen, and at the sack of Troy (unfortunately) lost: till now, in this our age, it was as happily recovered, by a studious antiquary, out of some ruins of Asia, who

---

240 *bate*: abate, 'knock down'.
bagatine: tiny, almost worthless, Venetian coin.

243 *toss your handkerchiefs*: i.e. with the money tied in a corner. The purchase was returned in the same manner.

244 *advertised*: informed.

248 *double pistolet*: Spanish coin worth about 18 shillings.

249 *spark*: gallant.

265 *bank*: both 'mountebank's stage' and 'place where monetary transactions are made'.

sent a moiety of it to the court of France (but much sophisticated) wherewith the ladies there, now, colour their hair. The rest (at this present) remains with me; extracted, to a quintessence; so that, wherever it but touches, in youth it perpetually preserves, in age restores the complexion; seats your teeth, did they dance like virginal jacks, firm as a wall; makes them as white, as ivory, that were black, as –

SCENE III

[*Enter*] CORVINO.

CORVINO. Spite o'the devil, and my shame! Come down, here;
Come down: no house but mine to make your scene?
He beats away the mountebank, etc.
Signior Flaminio, will you down, sir? down?
What, is my wife your Franciscina? sir?
No windows on the whole Piazza, here,
To make your properties, but mine? but mine?
Heart! Ere tomorrow, I shall be new christened,
And called the Pantalone di Besogniosi
About the town. [*Exit.*]
PEREGRINE. What should this mean, Sir Pol?

274 *moiety*: half or part.
275 *sophisticated*: adulterated:
280 *virginal jacks*: commonly used erroneously (as here) for the keys of the virginals; properly, the pieces of wood to which were attached the quills which plucked the strings.
1 *Spite o'*: see Textual Note, p. 432 below.
2 *scene*: in contemporary critical theory, a public place with houses at the rear; and in the *commedia dell' arte*, to which Corvino likens the performance he interrupts, window scenes were frequent.
3 *Signior Flaminio*: Flaminio Scala, famous actor and director of a Venetian *commedia* troupe, who took the role of the gallant lover. See Additional Note, p. 439 below.
4 *Franciscina*: stock character of the maid in *commedia*.
6 *properties*: stage props.
8 *Pantalone di Besogniosi*: 'Pantaloon of the Paupers', a Venetian *commedia* figure, a foolish old dotard, often with a young wife by whom he is cuckolded. See Additional Note, p. 439 below.

SIR POLITIC. Some trick of state, believe it. I will home.
PEREGRINE. It may be some design, on you.
SIR POLITIC. I know not.
I'll stand upon my guard.
PEREGRINE. It is your best, sir.
SIR POLITIC. This three weeks, all my advices, all my letters,
They have been intercepted.
PEREGRINE. Indeed, sir?
Best have a care.
SIR POLITIC. Nay, so I will.
PEREGRINE. [*aside*] This knight,
I may not lose him, for my mirth, till night.
[*Exeunt.*]

SCENE IV

[*Enter*] VOLPONE, MOSCA.

VOLPONE. Oh, I am wounded.
MOSCA. Where, sir?
VOLPONE. Not without;
Those blows were nothing: I could bear them ever.
But angry Cupid, bolting from her eyes,
Hath shot himself into me, like a flame;
Where, now, he flings about his burning heat,
As in a furnace, an ambitious fire
Whose vent is stopped. The fight is all within me.
I cannot live, except thou help me, Mosca;
My liver melts, and I, without the hope
Of some soft air, from her refreshing breath,
Am but a heap of cinders.
MOSCA. 'Las, good sir!
Would you had never seen her.
VOLPONE. Nay, would thou
Hadst never told me of her.
MOSCA. Sir, 'tis true;
I do confess, I was unfortunate,

---

10 *trick*: stratagem.
1 *without*: externally.
3 *bolting*: shooting his arrows (bolts); also, 'darting, springing'.
6 *ambitious*: swelling, rolling.
9 *liver*: held to be the seat of violent passions.

And you unhappy: but I'm bound in conscience,
No less than duty, to effect my best
To your release of torment, and I will, sir.
VOLPONE. Dear Mosca, shall I hope?
MOSCA. Sir, more than dear,
I will not bid you to despair of aught,
Within a human compass.
VOLPONE. Oh, there spoke
My better angel. Mosca, take my keys,
Gold, plate, and jewels, all's at thy devotion;
Employ them, how thou wilt; nay, coin me, too:
So thou, in this, but crown my longings. Mosca?
MOSCA. Use but your patience.
VOLPONE. So I have.
MOSCA. I doubt not
To bring success to your desires.
VOLPONE. Nay, then,
I not repent me of my late disguise.
MOSCA. If you can horn him, sir, you need not.
VOLPONE. True:
Besides, I never meant him for my heir.
Is not the colour o'my beard, and eyebrows,
To make me known?
MOSCA. No jot.
VOLPONE. I did it well.
MOSCA. So well, would I could follow you in mine,
With half the happiness; and yet, I would
Escape your epilogue.
VOLPONE. But were they gulled
With a belief that I was Scoto?
MOSCA. Sir,
Scoto himself could hardly have distinguished!
I have not time to flatter you, now, we'll part:
And as I prosper, so applaud my art.
[*Exeunt.*]

---

21 *better angel*: finely ironic, since Mosca's spiritual master is Beelzebub, Lord of the Flies.
22 *devotion*: disposal.
24 *crown*: bring to fruition.
Mosca?: punctuation indicates Volpone's impatience.
28 *horn him*: cuckold him, give him cuckold's horns.
30 *colour*: red, the fox's colour.
33 *happiness*: success; also, 'felicitous aptitude'.
34 *epilogue*: the beating which ended Volpone's performance.

SCENE V

[*Enter*] CORVINO, CELIA.

CORVINO. Death of mine honour, with city's fool?
A juggling, tooth-drawing, prating mountebank?
And at a public window? where whilst he,
With his strained action, and his dole of faces,
To his drug lecture draws your itching ears,
A crew of old, unmarried, noted lechers
Stood leering up, like satyrs: and you smile,
Most graciously! and fan your favours forth,
To give your hot spectators satisfaction!
What, was your mountebank their call? their
whistle?
Or were y'enamoured on his copper rings?
His saffron jewel, with the toadstone in't?
Or his embroidered suit, with the cope-stitch,
Made of a hearse cloth? or his old tilt-feather?
Or his starched beard? Well! you shall have him,
yes.
He shall come home, and minister unto you
The fricace, for the mother. Or, let me see,
I think y'had rather mount? would you not mount?
Why, if you'll mount, you may; yes truly, you may:
And so you may be seen, down to th'foot.

---

2 *juggling*: doing conjuring tricks; also, 'cheating'.
4 *strained action*: exaggerated gestures.
dole of faces: stock of facial expressions.
5 *itching*: eager, craving.
7 *satyrs*: mythological creatures, part man, part goat; type figures of lust.
9 *hot*: lustful.
10 *call . . . whistle*: cries to lure birds.
12 *toadstone*: supposedly found in the head of toads; thought to be an antidote to poisons and to have magical powers.
13 *cope-stitch*: used to embroider the edge of copes.
14 *tilt-feather*: feather from a tilting-helmet recovered after jousting.
15 *starched*: fashionably stiffened with gums or wax.
17 *fricace, for the mother*: massage for hysteria; with an indecent pun: the womb (Latin *matrix*) was considered the seat of hysteria.
18 *mount*: join the mountebank's team of performers on stage; also, 'copulate'.

Get you a cittern, Lady Vanity,
And be a dealer, with the virtuous man;
Make one: I'll but protest myself a cuckold,
And save your dowry. I am a Dutchman, I!
For if you thought me an Italian,
You would be damned, ere you did this, you whore:
Thou'dst tremble, to imagine that the murder
Of father, mother, brother, all thy race,
Should follow, as the subject of my justice!
CELIA. Good sir, have patience!
CORVINO. What couldst thou propose
Less to thyself, than, in this heat of wrath,
And stung with my dishonour, I should strike
[*Drawing his sword.*]
This steel into thee, with as many stabs
As thou wert gazed upon with goatish eyes?
CELIA. Alas, sir, be appeased! I could not think
My being at the window should more, now,
Move your impatience, than at other times.
CORVINO. No? not to seek, and entertain a parley,
With a known knave? before a multitude?
You were an actor, with your handkerchief!
Which he, most sweetly, kissed in the receipt,
And might (no doubt) return it, with a letter,
And 'point the place, where you might meet: your sister's,
Your mother's, or your aunt's might serve the turn.

---

21 *cittern*: guitar-like instrument, often played by mountebank's wenches and prostitutes; also, kept in barbers' shops for the amusement of customers. Through these associations of entertainment and availability, becomes synonymous with 'prostitute'.
Lady Vanity: figure in the morality plays.

22 *be a dealer*: take part in his transactions; also, 'have sexual dealings'.
virtuous: having powers of healing; morally good (ironical); also one of the *virtuosi*.

23 *Make one*: join the mountebank (with an indecent innuendo).
protest: proclaim.

24 *Dutchman*: considered phlegmatic and slow to be aroused.

33 *into*: see Textual Note, p. 432 below.

34 *goatish*: lustful (the goat was an emblem of lechery).

38 *entertain a parley*: carry on a conversation.

44 *aunt's*: with a play on the cant term meaning 'bawd'.
serve the turn: answer the purpose (with an indecent innuendo).

CELIA. Why, dear sir, when do I make these excuses?
Or ever stir abroad, but to the church?
And that so seldom –
CORVINO. Well, it shall be less;
And thy restraint, before, was liberty
To what I now decree: and therefore, mark me.
First, I will have this bawdy light dammed up;
And till't be done, some two, or three yards off,
I'll chalk a line: o'er which, if thou but chance
To set thy desperate foot, more Hell, more horror,
More wild, remorseless rage shall seize on thee,
Than on a conjurer, that had heedless left
His circle's safety, ere his devil was laid.
Then here's a lock, which I will hang upon thee;
And now I think on't, I will keep thee backwards;
Thy lodging shall be backwards; thy walks backwards;
Thy prospect – all be backwards; and no pleasure,
That thou shalt know, but backwards: nay, since you force
My honest nature, know it is your own
Being too open, makes me use you thus.
Since you will not contain your subtle nostrils
In a sweet room, but they must snuff the air
Of rank, and sweaty passengers –
Knock within.
One knocks.
Away, and be not seen, pain of thy life;
Not look toward the window: if thou dost –
(Nay stay, hear this) let me not prosper, whore,
But I will make thee an anatomy,
Dissect thee mine own self, and read a lecture
Upon thee, to the city, and in public.
Away.

---

50 *light*: window.
56 *circle*: magic circle within which a magician was protected until the spirit he raised was made to disappear.
57 *lock*: chastity belt.
58 *backwards*: at the back of the house.
61 *backwards*: with an indecent innuendo, intentional or otherwise.
64 *subtle*: acute; cunning.
66 *rank*: smelly; also 'lustful'.
passengers: passers-by.
70 *anatomy*: body for dissection; also, 'analysis'.

[*Exit* CELIA.]
Who's there?

[*Enter* SERVITORE.]

SERVITORE. 'Tis Signior Mosca, sir.

SCENE VI

CORVINO. Let him come in.
[*Exit* SERVITORE.]
His master's dead: there's yet
Some good, to help the bad.

[*Enter* MOSCA.]

My Mosca, welcome,
I guess your news.
MOSCA. I fear you cannot, sir.
CORVINO. Is't not his death?
MOSCA. Rather the contrary.
CORVINO. Not his recovery?
MOSCA. Yes, sir.
CORVINO. I am cursed,
I am bewitched, my crosses meet to vex me.
How? how? how? how?
MOSCA. Why, sir, with Scoto's oil!
Corbaccio and Voltore brought of it,
Whilst I was busy in an inner room –
CORVINO. Death! that damned mountebank! But for the law,
Now I could kill the rascal: 't cannot be,
His oil should have that virtue. Ha'not I
Known him a common rogue, come fiddling in
To th'*osterìa*, with a tumbling whore,
And when he has done all his forced tricks, been glad
Of a poor spoonful of dead wine, with flies in't?
It cannot be. All his ingredients

---

6 *crosses*: troubles, afflictions.
12 *virtue*: power of healing.
14 *osterìa*: inn.
tumbling whore: debauched acrobat (with an indecent innuendo).
15 *forced*: constrained by poverty; also, 'done with an effort'.
16 *dead*: flat, insipid.

Are a sheep's gall, a roasted bitch's marrow,
Some few sod earwigs, pounded caterpillars,
A little capon's grease, and fasting spittle:
I know 'em, to a dram.
MOSCA. I know not, sir,
But some on't, there they poured into his ears,
Some in his nostrils, and recovered him;
Applying but the fricace.
CORVINO. Pox o'that fricace.
MOSCA. And since, to seem the more officious,
And flattering of his health, there they have had
(At extreme fees) the college of physicians
Consulting on him, how they might restore him;
Where, one would have cataplasm of spices,
Another, a flayed ape clapped to his breast,
A third would ha'it a dog, a fourth an oil
With wild cats' skins: at last, they all resolved
That, to preserve him, was no other means,
But some young woman must be straight sought out,
Lusty, and full of juice, to sleep by him;
And to this service (most unhappily,
And most unwillingly) am I now employed,
Which, here, I thought to pre-acquaint you with,
For your advice, since it concerns you most,
Because I would not do that thing might cross
Your ends, on whom I have my whole dependence, sir:
Yet, if I do it not, they may delate
My slackness to my patron, work me out
Of his opinion; and there, all your hopes,
Ventures, or whatsoever, are all frustrate.
I do but tell you, sir. Besides, they are all
Now striving, who shall first present him. Therefore –
I could entreat you, briefly conclude somewhat:

---

19 *sod*: boiled.
25 *officious*: zealous, dutiful.
29 *cataplasm*: plaster.
39 *advice*: information.
42 *delate*: report.
47 *Therefore* –: F's long dash indicates a dramatic pause.
48 *briefly conclude somewhat*: quickly decide on some course of action.

Prevent 'em if you can.
CORVINO. Death to my hopes!
This is my villainous fortune! Best to hire
Some common courtesan?
MOSCA. Ay, I thought on that, sir.
But they are all so subtle, full of art,
And age, again, doting, and flexible,
So as – I cannot tell – we may perchance
Light on a quean, may cheat us all.
CORVINO. 'Tis true.
MOSCA. No, no: it must be one that has no tricks, sir,
Some simple thing, a creature, made unto it;
Some wench you may command. Ha'you no kinswoman?
God's so – Think, think, think, think, think, think, think, sir.
One o'the doctors offered there his daughter.
CORVINO. How!
MOSCA. Yes, Signior Lupo, the physician.
CORVINO. His daughter?
MOSCA. And a virgin, sir. Why? Alas,
He knows the state of's body, what it is;
That nought can warm his blood, sir, but a fever;
Nor any incantation raise his spirit:
A long forgetfulness hath seized that part.
Besides, sir, who shall know it? Some one, or two –
CORVINO. I pray thee give me leave.
[*Walks aside.*]
If any man
But I had had this luck – The thing in't self,
I know, is nothing – Wherefore should not I
As well command my blood, and my affections,
As this dull doctor? In the point of honour,

---

49 *Prevent*: forestall.
53 *again*: on the other hand.
55 *quean*: harlot.
57 *creature*: dependant.
unto it: for the part; perhaps also, 'to do it' (by Corvino).
59 *God's so*: 'God's soul'; but also a corruption of Italian *cazzo*, penis.
61 *Lupo*: wolf – an invented figure, quite at home in the world of the play.
64 *blood*: also, 'passion'.
65 *spirit*: semen (with a play on the magical rites of calling up the devil).

The cases are all one, of wife, and daughter.
MOSCA. [*aside*] I hear him coming.
CORVINO. She shall do't. 'Tis done.
'Slight, if this doctor, who is not engaged,
Unless't be for his counsel (which is nothing)
Offer his daughter, what should I, that am
So deeply in? I will prevent him: wretch!
Covetous wretch! Mosca, I have determined.
MOSCA. How, sir?
CORVINO. We'll make all sure. The party, you wot of,
Shall be mine own wife, Mosca.
MOSCA. Sir, the thing
(But that I would not seem to counsel you)
I should have motioned to you, at the first:
And make your count, you have cut all their throats.
Why! 'tis directly taking a possession!
And in his next fit, we may let him go.
'Tis but to pull the pillow, from his head,
And he is throttled: 't had been done before,
But for your scrupulous doubts.
CORVINO. Ay, a plague on't,
My conscience fools my wit. Well, I'll be brief,
And so be thou, lest they should be before us;
Go home, prepare him, tell him with what zeal,
And willingness, I do it: swear it was,
On the first hearing (as thou mayst do, truly),
Mine own free motion.
MOSCA. Sir, I warrant you,
I'll so possess him with it, that the rest
Of his starved clients shall be banished, all;
And only you received. But come not, sir,

---

74 *coming*: coming round.
75 *engaged*: financially committed.
78 *deeply in*: heavily committed financially.
80 *you wot of*: you know whom I mean. (Corvino uses a little delicacy for his honour's sake.)
83 *motioned*: proposed.
84 *make your count*: count your gains.
85 *directly taking a possession*: entering without difficulty into a property which you have a legal right to possess.
89 *doubts*: fears.
90 *wit*: good sense.
95 *free motion*: voluntary suggestion.
96 *so possess him with it*: make him so taken with it.

Until I send, for I have something else
To ripen, for your good (you must not know't).
CORVINO. But do you not forget to send, now.
MOSCA. Fear not.
[*Exit.*]

SCENE VII

CORVINO. Where are you, wife? my Celia? wife?

[*Enter*] CELIA.

What, blubbering?
Come, dry those tears. I think thou thought'st me in earnest?
Ha? by this light, I talked so but to try thee.
Methinks, the lightness of the occasion
Should ha'confirmed thee. Come, I am not jealous.
CELIA. No?
CORVINO. Faith, I am not, I, nor never was:
It is a poor, unprofitable humour.
Do not I know, if women have a will,
They'll do 'gainst all the watches o'the world?
And that the fiercest spies are tamed with gold?
Tut, I am confident in thee, thou shalt see't:
And see, I'll give thee cause too, to believe it.
Come, kiss me. Go, and make thee ready straight,
In all thy best attire, thy choicest jewels,
Put 'em all on, and with 'em, thy best looks:
We are invited to a solemn feast
At old Volpone's, where it shall appear
How far I am free, from jealousy, or fear.
[*Exeunt.*]

---

3 *try*: test.
7 *humour*: vagary.
8 *will*: carnal desires.
16 *solemn*: grand.

ACT III

SCENE I

[*Enter*] MOSCA.

MOSCA. I fear, I shall begin to grow in love
With my dear self, and my most prosperous parts,
They do so spring, and burgeon; I can feel
A whimsy i'my blood: I know not how,
Success hath made me wanton. I could skip
Out of my skin, now, like a subtle snake,
I am so limber. Oh! your parasite
Is a most precious thing, dropped from above,
Not bred 'mongst clods, and clotpolls, here on earth.
I muse the mystery was not made a science,
It is so liberally professed! Almost
All the wise world is little else, in nature,
But parasites, or sub-parasites. And yet,
I mean not those, that have your bare town-art,
To know who's fit to feed 'em; have no house,
No family, no care, and therefore mould
Tales for men's ears, to bait that sense; or get
Kitchen-invention, and some stale receipts
To please the belly, and the groin; nor those,
With their court-dog-tricks, that can fawn, and fleer,

---

2 *prosperous parts*: thriving talents.
4 *whimsy*: capriciousness.
5 *wanton*: playful.
7 *limber*: lithe, nimble.
9 *clotpolls*: blockheads.
10 *mystery*: trade, craft.
science: branch of learning.
11 *liberally*: freely; also, 'by educated gentlemen' (who have followed their 'liberal studies').
14 *bare town-art*: paltry skills with which to get by in town society.
16 *No family*: i.e. do not belong to any household.
care: charge, responsibility.
17 *bait*: feed; also, 'excite'.
18 *Kitchen-invention*: newly devised culinary dishes.
receipts: recipes.
19 *To please . . . the groin*: i.e. aphrodisiacs.
20 *fleer*: smirk, smile obsequiously.

Make their revènue out of legs, and faces,
Echo my lord, and lick away a moth:
But your fine, elegant rascal, that can rise,
And stoop (almost together) like an arrow;
Shoot through the air, as nimbly as a star;
Turn short, as doth a swallow; and be here,
And there, and here, and yonder, all at once;
Present to any honour, all occasion;
And change a visor, swifter than a thought!
This is the creature, had the art born with him;
Toils not to learn it, but doth practise it
Out of most excellent nature: and such sparks
Are the true parasites, others but their zanies.

SCENE II

[*Enter*] BONARIO.

Who's this? Bonario? old Corbaccio's son?
The person I was bound to seek. – Fair sir,
You are happ'ly met.
BONARIO. That cannot be, by thee.
MOSCA. Why, sir?
BONARIO. Nay, pray thee know thy way, and leave me:
I would be loath to interchange discourse
With such a mate, as thou art.
MOSCA. Courteous sir,
Scorn not my poverty.
BONARIO. Not I, by Heaven:
But thou shall give me leave to hate thy baseness.
MOSCA. Baseness?

---

21 *legs, and faces*: bowing and flattering smiles.
22 *lick away a moth*: i.e. fuss obsequiously about his person: *moth* = vermin, flea. (Flatterers were commonly characterised by their eagerness to remove threads or specks from a patron's clothes: Mosca's lower parasites go beyond this.)
28 *Present . . . occasion*: ready to satisfy any whim, and deal with every situation.
29 *visor*: mask; disguise; hence, 'appearance, role'.
32 *sparks*: gallant fellows.
33 *zanies*: comic mimics.
2 *bound*: on my way.
3 *happ'ly*: fortunately.
6 *mate*: fellow (contemptuous).

BONARIO. Ay, answer me, is not thy sloth
Sufficient argument? thy flattery?
Thy means of feeding?
MOSCA. Heaven, be good to me.
These imputations are too common, sir,
And eas'ly stuck on virtue, when she's poor;
You are unequal to me, and howe'er
Your sentence may be righteous, yet you are not,
That ere you know me, thus proceed in censure:
St Mark bear witness 'gainst you, 'tis inhuman.
[*Weeps.*]
BONARIO. [*aside*] What? does he weep? the sign is soft, and good!
I do repent me, that I was so harsh.
MOSCA. 'Tis true, that, swayed by strong necessity,
I am enforced to eat my careful bread
With too much obsequy; 'tis true, beside,
That I am fain to spin mine own poor raiment,
Out of my mere observance, being not born
To a free fortune: but that I have done
Base offices, in rending friends asunder,
Dividing families, betraying counsels,
Whispering false lies, or mining men with praises,
Trained their credulity with perjuries,
Corrupted chastity, or am in love
With mine own tender ease, but would not rather
Prove the most rugged, and laborious course,
That might redeem my present estimation;
Let me here perish, in all hope of goodness.
BONARIO. [*aside*] This cannot be a personated passion! –
I was to blame, so to mistake thy nature;
Pray thee forgive me: and speak out thy business.
MOSCA. Sir, it concerns you; and though I may seem,

---

14 *unequal*: unjust; also, 'socially superior'.
16 *censure*: judgement.
18 *soft*: indicative of a gentle character.
21 *careful*: won by care and anxiety.
22 *obsequy*: obsequiousness.
24 *observance*: obsequious service.
26–8 neatly ironic: these classic roles of the parasite are all in Mosca's repertoire.
28 *mining*: undermining, secretly destroying.
29 *Trained*: snared.
32 *Prove*: endure.
35 *personated*: counterfeited.

At first, to make a main offence, in manners,
And in my gratitude, unto my master,
Yet, for the pure love, which I bear all right,
And hatred of the wrong, I must reveal it.
This very hour, your father is in purpose
To disinherit you –

BONARIO. How!

MOSCA. And thrust you forth,
As a mere stranger to his blood; 'tis true, sir:
The work no way engageth me, but as
I claim an interest in the general state
Of goodness, and true virtue, which I hear
T'abound in you: and for which mere respect,
Without a second aim, sir, I have done it.

BONARIO. This tale hath lost thee much of the late trust
Thou hadst with me; it is impossible:
I know not how to lend it any thought,
My father should be so unnatural.

MOSCA. It is a confidence, that well becomes
Your piety; and formed (no doubt) it is,
From your own simple innocence: which makes
Your wrong more monstrous, and abhorred. But, sir,
I now, will tell you more. This very minute,
It is, or will be doing: and if you
Shall be but pleased to go with me, I'll bring you
(I dare not say where you shall see, but) where
Your ear shall be a witness of the deed;
Hear yourself written bastard: and professed
The common issue of the earth.

BONARIO. I'm 'mazed!

MOSCA. Sir, if I do it not, draw your just sword,
And score your vengeance, on my front, and face;
Mark me your villain: you have too much wrong,
And I do suffer for you, sir. My heart
Weeps blood, in anguish –

---

39 *main offence*: great impropriety.
49 *for which mere respect*: for that reason alone.
56 *piety*: filial duty.
64 *written*: designated.
professed: publicly proclaimed.
65 *common issue of the earth*: Latin *terrae filius*, a man of unknown or obscure birth.
67 *front*: forehead.

BONARIO. Lead. I follow thee.
[*Exeunt.*]

SCENE III

[*Enter*] VOLPONE, NANO, ANDROGYNO, CASTRONE.

VOLPONE. Mosca stays long, methinks. Bring forth your sports
And help to make the wretched time more sweet.
NANO. Dwarf, fool, and eunuch, well met here we be.
A question it were now, whether of us three,
Being, all, the known delicates of a rich man,
In pleasing him, claim the precedency can?
CASTRONE. I claim for myself.
ANDROGYNO. And so doth the fool.
NANO. 'Tis foolish indeed: let me set you both to school.
First, for your dwarf, he's little, and witty,
And everything, as it is little, is pretty;
Else why do men say to a creature of my shape,
So soon as they see him, 'It's a pretty little ape'?
And why a pretty ape? but for pleasing imitation
Of greater men's action, in a ridiculous fashion.
Beside, this feat body of mine doth not crave
Half the meat, drink, and cloth, one of your bulks will have.
Admit, your fool's face be the mother of laughter,
Yet, for his brain, it must always come after:
And though that do feed him, it's a pitiful case,
His body is beholding to such a bad face.
One knocks.
VOLPONE. Who's there? My couch, away, look, Nano, see:
Give me my caps, first – go, enquire.
[*Exeunt* NANO, ANDROGYNO, CASTRONE.]
Now, Cupid

---

4 *whether*: which.
5 *Being, all,*: see Textual Note, p. 432 below.
known delicates: acknowledged favourites, creatures that give pleasure.
15 *feat*: agile, comely.

Send it be Mosca, and with fair return.

[*Enter* NANO.]

NANO. It is the beauteous Madam –
VOLPONE. Would-be – is it?
NANO. The same.
VOLPONE. Now, torment on me; squire her in:
For she will enter, or dwell here for ever.
Nay, quickly, that my fit were past.

[*Exit* NANO.]

I fear
A second Hell too, that my loathing this
Will quite expel my appetite to the other:
Would she were taking, now, her tedious leave.
Lord, how it threats me, what I am to suffer!

SCENE IV

[*Enter*] NANO, LADY WOULD-BE.

LADY WOULD-BE. I thank you, good sir. Pray you signify
Unto your patron, I am here. This band
Shows not my neck enough (I trouble you, sir,
Let me request you, bid one of my women
Come hither to me) in good faith, I am dressed
Most favourably, today, it is no matter,
'Tis well enough.

[*Enter* FIRST WOMAN.]

Look, see, these petulant things!
How they have done this!
VOLPONE. I do feel the fever
Entering, in at mine ears; oh, for a charm,
To fright it hence.
LADY WOULD-BE. Come nearer: is this curl
In his right place? or this? why is this higher
Than all the rest? you ha'not washed your eyes, yet?

---

23 *fair return*: favourable answer; also, 'good profit'.
31 *threats me*: rises ominously before me.
2 *band*: collar, ruff.
7 *petulant*: insolent.

Or do they not stand even i'your head?
Where's your fellow? call her.
[*Exit* FIRST WOMAN.]
NANO. [*aside*] Now, St Mark
Deliver us: anon she'll beat her women,
Because her nose is red.

[*Enter* FIRST, SECOND WOMEN.]

LADY WOULD-BE. I pray you, view
This tire, forsooth: are all things apt, or no?
[SECOND] WOMAN. One hair a little, here, sticks out, forsooth.
LADY WOULD-BE. Does't so forsooth? and where was your dear sight
When it did so, forsooth? what now? bird-eyed?
And you, too? pray you both approach, and mend it.
Now (by that light) I muse yo'are not ashamed!
I, that have preached these things, so oft, unto you,
Read you the principles, argued all the grounds,
Disputed every fitness, every grace,
Called you to counsel of so frequent dressings –
NANO. [*aside*] (More carefully, than of your fame, or honour.)
LADY WOULD-BE. Made you acquainted, what an ample dowry
The knowledge of these things would be unto you,
Able, alone, to get you noble husbands
At your return: and you, thus, to neglect it?
Besides, you seeing what a curious nation
Th'Italians are, what will they say of me?
'The English lady cannot dress herself';
Here's a fine imputation, to our country!
Well, go your ways, and stay i'the next room.
This fucus was too coarse too, it's no matter.
Good sir, you'll give 'em entertainment?

---

15 *anon*: presently.
17 *tire*: headdress.
forsooth: a pseudo-genteel oath.
18 SECOND: see Textual Note, p. 432 below.
20 *bird-eyed*: startled, with the look of a frightened bird (as the woman retreats in anticipation of receiving a blow).
27 *fame*: reputation.
32 *curious*: fastidious.
37 *fucus*: cosmetic wash.

[*Exeunt* NANO, FIRST, SECOND WOMEN.]

VOLPONE. The storm comes toward me.
LADY WOULD-BE. How does my Volp?
VOLPONE. Troubled with noise, I cannot sleep; I dreamt
That a strange fury entered, now, my house,
And with the dreadful tempest of her breath,
Did cleave my roof asunder.
LADY WOULD-BE. Believe me, and I
Had the most fearful dream, could I remember't –
VOLPONE. [*aside*] Out on my fate; I ha'given her the occasion
How to torment me: she will tell me hers.
LADY WOULD-BE. Methought, the golden mediocrity
Polite, and delicate –
VOLPONE. Oh, if you do love me,
No more; I sweat, and suffer, at the mention
Of any dream: feel, how I tremble yet.
LADY WOULD-BE. Alas, good soul! the passion of the heart.
Seed-pearl were good now, boiled with syrup of apples,
Tincture of gold, and coral, citron-pills,
Your elecampane root, myrobalanes –
VOLPONE. [*aside*] Ay me, I have ta'en a grasshopper by the wing.
LADY WOULD-BE. Burnt silk, and amber, you have muscadel
Good i'the house –

---

41 *fury*: avenging deity of classical mythology.
47 *golden mediocrity*: golden mean, signifying in classical ethics the avoidance of all excess.
51 *passion of the heart*: heartburn.
52 *Seed-pearl*: used as a heart stimulant.
53 *coral*: a charm against melancholy and bad dreams.
citron-pills: aid to digestion.
54 *elecampane*: plant with aromatic leaves and root, used for the stomach and relieving convulsions.
myrobalanes: plum-like fruit used to alleviate melancholy and agues.
55 *I have . . . wing*: a Greek proverb; compare *Poetaster*, 'Apologetical Dialogue', 113–14: 'And like so many screaming grasshoppers / Held by the wings, fill every ear with noise.'
56 *Burnt silk*: a popular remedy for smallpox.
amber: good for the stomach.

VOLPONE. You will not drink, and part?
LADY WOULD-BE. No, fear not that. I doubt we shall not get
Some English saffron (half a dram would serve)
Your sixteen cloves, a little musk, dried mints,
Bugloss, and barley-meal –
VOLPONE. [*aside*] She's in again,
Before I feigned diseases, now I have one.
LADY WOULD-BE. And these applied, with a right scarlet cloth –
VOLPONE. [*aside*] Another flood of words! a very torrent!
LADY WOULD-BE. Shall I, sir, make you a poultice?
VOLPONE. No, no, no;
I'm very well: you need prescribe no more.
LADY WOULD-BE. I have, a little, studied physic; but, now,
I'm all for music: save, i'the forenoons,
An hour, or two, for painting. I would have
A lady, indeed, t'have all, letters, and arts,
Be able to discourse, to write, to paint,
But principal (as Plato holds) your music
(And so does wise Pythagoras, I take it)
Is your true rapture; when there is concent
In face, in voice, and clothes: and is, indeed
Our sex's chiefest ornament.
VOLPONE. The poet,
As old in time as Plato, and as knowing,
Says that your highest female grace is silence.

---

58 *doubt*: fear.
59 *saffron*: grown around Saffron Walden; taken in wine for shortness of breath and for the stomach.
60 *cloves*: good for the heart and stomach.
musk, dried mints: stimulants and antispasmodic medicines.
61 *Bugloss*: used as a heart stimulant.
barley-meal: used in poultices and for skin diseases.
63 *scarlet cloth*: used to wrap smallpox patients in.
67 *studied physic*: a knowledge of common remedies was part of a gentlewoman's accomplishments.
72–3 Lady Would-Be distorts wildly the interest in the doctrine of the music of the spheres of both philosophers, and the educational interest in music of Plato.
74 *concent*: harmony, concord (typically trivialised).
76 *poet*: Sophocles, *Ajax*, 293.

LADY WOULD-BE. Which o'your poets? Petrarch? or Tasso? or Dante?
Guarini? Ariosto? Aretine?
Cieco di Hadria? I have read them all.
VOLPONE. [*aside*] Is everything a cause to my destruction?
LADY WOULD-BE. I think, I ha'two or three of 'em, about me.
VOLPONE. [*aside*] The sun, the sea will sooner, both, stand still,
Than her eternal tongue! Nothing can 'scape it.
LADY WOULD-BE. Here's *Pastor Fido* –
VOLPONE. [*aside*] Profess obstinate silence,
That's, now, my safest.
LADY WOULD-BE. All our English writers,
I mean such as are happy in th'Italian,
Will deign to steal out of this author, mainly;
Almost as much as from Montagnié;
He has so modern, and facile a vein,
Fitting the time, and catching the court ear.
Your Petrarch is more passionate, yet he,
In days of sonneting, trusted 'em with much:

---

79 *Petrarch*: 1304–74; most honoured in the Renaissance as the author of a sonnet sequence in which Laura was celebrated.
Tasso: 1544–95; Counter-Reformation poet and critic.
Dante: 1265–1321; author of *The Divine Comedy*.

80 *Guarini*: 1537–1612; author of the pastoral drama, *Il Pastor Fido* (*The Faithful Shepherd*), 1590.
Ariosto: 1474–1533; author of the romance epic, *Orlando Furioso*.
Aretine: i.e. Aretino, 1492–1556, famous for his witty and scurrilous verses.

81 *Cieco di Hadria*: 'The blind man of Hadria', Luigi Groto, 1541–85; his work does not compare with that of the major poets just named.

89 see Additional Note, p. 440 below.
mainly: a great deal.

90 *Montagnié*: see Textual Note, p. 433 below. The *Essays* of Montaigne (1533–92) had been translated into English by Florio in 1603. For Jonson's dislike of essayists, see Additional Note, p. 440 below.

91 *modern, and facile*: up-to-date and fluent (both are new meanings; Lady Would-be's language is typically 'modern'); but also, 'commonplace and requiring little effort', which reflects Jonson's own attitude to essayists.

94 *In days of sonneting*: the fashion for writing Petrarchan sonnet sequences, deriving directly or indirectly from Petrarch's, reached its peak in England in the 1590s.

Dante is hard, and few can understand him.
But for a desperate wit, there's Aretine!
Only, his pictures are a little obscene –
You mark me not?

VOLPONE. Alas, my mind's perturbed.

LADY WOULD-BE. Why, in such cases, we must cure ourselves,
Make use of our philosophy –

VOLPONE. O'y me.

LADY WOULD-BE. And as we find our passions do rebel,
Encounter 'em with reason; or divert 'em,
By giving scope unto some other humour
Of lesser danger: as in politic bodies,
There's nothing, more, doth overwhelm the judgement,
And clouds the understanding, than too much
Settling, and fixing, and (as 'twere) subsiding
Upon one object. For the incorporating
Of these same outward things, into that part
Which we call mental, leaves some certain faeces,
That stop the organs, and, as Plato says,
Assassinates our knowledge.

VOLPONE. [*aside*] Now the spirit
Of patience help me.

LADY WOULD-BE. Come, in faith, I must

---

96 *desperate*: reckless, outrageous.

97 *pictures*: Aretino wrote sixteen *sonnetti lussuriosi* to accompany the drawings of Giulio Romano; this work attained great notoriety in the Renaissance.

100 *O'y me*: alas (Italian *ohimè*).

103 *By . . . humour*: i.e. by encouraging a bodily 'humour' or fluid with different physical and psychological operations to counteract the disturbance, and thus achieve a balance of humours and restore full health. See Additional Note to II.ii.109, p. 439 below.

104 *politic bodies*: government of states (Lady Would-be is comparing health in the human body and the body politic).

107 *Settling*: separation of sediment from liquid (a chemical term, like the two following).
fixing: congealing of liquids or volatile spirits.
subsiding: precipitation of sediment. Lady Would-be is 'explaining' obsession scientifically.

110 *faeces*: sediment.

111 *Plato*: a grotesque rendering of Plato's theory of perception: i.e. concentration on the material destroys our awareness of the reality, the ideal.

Visit you more a-days; and make you well:
Laugh, and be lusty.

VOLPONE. [*aside*] My good angel save me.

LADY WOULD-BE. There was but one sole man, in all the world,
With whom I e'er could sympathise; and he
Would lie you often, three, four hours together,
To hear me speak; and be (sometime) so rapt,
As he would answer me, quite from the purpose,
Like you, and you are like him, just. I'll discourse
(An't be but only, sir, to bring you asleep)
How we did spend our time, and loves, together,
For some six years.

VOLPONE. Oh, oh, oh, oh, oh, oh.

LADY WOULD-BE. For we were *coaetanei*, and brought up –

VOLPONE. [*aside*] Some power, some fate, some fortune rescue me.

SCENE V

[*Enter*] MOSCA.

MOSCA. God save you, madam.

LADY WOULD-BE. Good sir.

VOLPONE. Mosca? welcome,
Welcome to my redemption.

MOSCA. Why, sir?

VOLPONE. Oh,
Rid me of this my torture, quickly, there;
My madam, with the everlasting voice:
The bells, in time of pestilence, ne'er made
Like noise, or were in that perpetual motion;
The cockpit comes not near it. All my house,

---

114 *more a-days*: more often.
117 *sympathise*: have an affinity.
118 *you*: ethic dative.
121 *just*: exactly.
122 *An'*: if.
125 *coaetanei*: the same age (Latin).
5 *The bells, in time of pestilence*: the frequent tolling of the passing bells during the recurrent epidemics.
7 *cockpit*: noisy with punters; there were three cockpits in London at this time.

But now, steamed like a bath, with her thick breath.
A lawyer could not have been heard; nor scarce
Another woman, such a hail of words
She has let fall. For Hell's sake, rid her hence.

MOSCA. Has she presented?

VOLPONE. Oh, I do not care,
I'll take her absence, upon any price,
With any loss.

MOSCA. Madam –

LADY WOULD-BE. I ha'brought your patron
A toy, a cap here, of mine own work –

MOSCA. 'Tis well,
I had forgot to tell you, I saw your knight,
Where you'd little think it –

LADY WOULD-BE. Where?

MOSCA. Marry,
Where yet, if you make haste, you may apprehend him,
Rowing upon the water in a *gondole*,
With the most cunning courtesan of Venice.

LADY WOULD-BE. Is't true?

MOSCA. Pursue 'em, and believe your eyes:
Leave me, to make your gift.

[*Exit* LADY WOULD-BE.]

I knew 'twould take.
For lightly, they that use themselves most licence,
Are still most jealous.

VOLPONE. Mosca, hearty thanks,
For thy quick fiction, and delivery of me.
Now, to my hopes, what say'st thou?

[*Enter* LADY WOULD-BE.]

LADY WOULD-BE. But do you hear, sir? –

VOLPONE. Again! I fear a paroxysm.

LADY WOULD-BE. Which way
Rowed they together?

MOSCA. Toward the Rialto.

LADY WOULD-BE. I pray you lend me your dwarf.

MOSCA. I pray you, take him.

---

12 *presented*: made a presentation, made her gift.
15 *toy*: trifling thing.
19 *gondole*: gondola.
23 *lightly*: commonly, ordinarily.
24 *still*: always.

[*Exit* LADY WOULD-BE.]
Your hopes, sir, are like happy blossoms, fair,
And promise timely fruit, if you will stay
But the maturing; keep you at your couch,
Corbaccio will arrive straight, with the will:
When he is gone, I'll tell you more. [*Exit.*]

VOLPONE. My blood,
My spirits are returned; I am alive:
And like your wanton gamester at primero,
Whose thought had whispered to him, not go less,
Methinks I lie, and draw – for an encounter.

SCENE VI

[*Enter*] MOSCA, BONARIO. [MOSCA *hides him.*]

MOSCA. Sir, here concealed you may hear all. But pray you
Have patience, sir;

One knocks.

the same's your father, knocks:
I am compelled to leave you.

BONARIO. Do so. Yet,

[*Exit* MOSCA.]

Cannot my thought imagine this a truth.

SCENE VII

[*Enter*] MOSCA, CORVINO, CELIA.

MOSCA. Death on me! you are come too soon, what meant you?
Did not I say, I would send?

---

31 *timely*: in due course, in season.
31–2 *stay But*: only wait for.
36 *wanton*: reckless; also, 'lecherous'.
gamester: gambler.
primero: a gambling card-game, resembling poker.
37 *go less*: bet a smaller stake.
38 *lie, and draw*: place a bet, and draw a card from the pack.
encounter: drawing a winning card; also, 'sexual encounter'.
III.vi.s.d. *hides him*: behind one of the side doors of the Globe stage, or its curtained aperture.

CORVINO. Yes, but I feared
You might forget it, and then they prevent us.
MOSCA. Prevent? [*Aside*] Did e'er man haste so, for his horns?
A courtier would not ply it so, for a place. –
Well, now there's no helping it, stay here;
I'll presently return.
[*Crosses to* BONARIO*'s hiding-place.*]
CORVINO. Where are you, Celia?
You know not wherefore I have brought you hither?
CELIA. Not well, except you told me.
CORVINO. Now, I will:
Hark hither.
[*They talk apart.*]
MOSCA. (*to* BONARIO) Sir, your father hath sent word,
It will be half an hour, ere he come;
And therefore, if you please to walk the while,
Into that gallery – at the upper end,
There are some books, to entertain the time:
And I'll take care, no man shall come unto you, sir.
BONARIO. Yes, I will stay there. [*Aside*] I do doubt this fellow.
[*Exit* BONARIO.]
MOSCA. There, he is far enough; he can hear nothing:
And for his father, I can keep him off.
[*Crosses to* VOLPONE.]
CORVINO. Nay, now, there is no starting back; and therefore
Resolve upon it: I have so decreed.
It must be done. Nor would I move't afore,
Because I would avoid all shifts and tricks,
That might deny me.
CELIA. Sir, let me beseech you,
Affect not these strange trials; if you doubt
My chastity, why, lock me up, for ever:
Make me the heir of darkness. Let me live
Where I may please your fears, if not your trust.
CORVINO. Believe it, I have no such humour, I.

---

7 *presently*: at once.
13 *gallery*: supposed to lie beyond the door.
16 *doubt*: suspect.
22 *shifts*: subterfuges.
24 *Affect not*: do not go on with.

All that I speak, I mean; yet I am not mad:
Not horn-mad, see you? Go to, show yourself
Obedient, and a wife.
CELIA. O Heaven!
CORVINO. I say it,
Do so.
CELIA. Was this the train?
CORVINO. I've told you reasons:
What the physicians have set down; how much,
It may concern me; what my engagements are;
My means; and the necessity of those means,
For my recovery: wherefore, if you be
Loyal, and mine, be won, respect my venture.
CELIA. Before your honour?
CORVINO. Honour? tut, a breath;
There's no such thing, in nature; a mere term
Invented to awe fools. What is my gold
The worse, for touching? clothes, for being looked on?
Why, this's no more. An old, decrepit wretch,
That has no sense, no sinew; takes his meat
With others' fingers; only knows to gape,
When you do scald his gums; a voice; a shadow;
And what can this man hurt you?
CELIA. Lord! what spirit
Is this hath entered him?
CORVINO. And for your fame,
That's such a jig; as if I would go tell it,
Cry it, on the Piazza! Who shall know it?
But he, that cannot speak it; and this fellow,
Whose lips are i'my pocket: save yourself,
If you'll proclaim't, you may. I know no other,
Should come to know it.
CELIA. Are Heaven, and saints then nothing?
Will they be blind, or stupid?
CORVINO. How?

---

30 *horn-mad*: stark mad; also, 'mad with rage at being made a cuckold' (or perhaps, mad with a desire to be cuckolded – Corvino believes that Volpone is impotent).

32 *train*: trap, snare.

36 *recovery*: financial recovery.

39 *There's no such thing, in nature*: see Additional Note, p. 440 below.

43 *sense*: faculty of perception and feeling.

48 *jig*: trifle.

CELIA. Good sir,
Be jealous still, emulate them; and think
What hate they burn with, toward every sin.
CORVINO. I grant you: if I thought it were a sin,
I would not urge you. Should I offer this
To some young Frenchman, or hot Tuscan blood,
That had read Aretine, conned all his prints,
Knew every quirk within lust's labyrinth,
And were professed critic, in lechery,
An' I would look upon him, and applaud him,
This were a sin: but here, 'tis contrary,
A pious work, mere charity, for physic,
And honest policy, to assure mine own.
CELIA. O Heaven! canst thou suffer such a change?
VOLPONE. Thou art mine honour, Mosca, and my pride,
My joy, my tickling, my delight! Go, bring 'em.
MOSCA. Please you draw near, sir.
CORVINO. Come on, what –
You will not be rebellious? By that light –
[*Drags* CELIA *towards the bed*.]
MOSCA. Sir, Signior Corvino, here, is come to see you.
VOLPONE. Oh.
MOSCA. And hearing of the consultation had,
So lately, for your health, is come to offer,
Or rather, sir, to prostitute –
CORVINO. Thanks, sweet Mosca.
MOSCA. Freely, unasked, or unentreated –
CORVINO. Well.
MOSCA. (As the true, fervent instance of his love),
His own most fair and proper wife; the beauty,
Only of price, in Venice –
CORVINO. 'Tis well urged.

---

61 *quirk*: sudden twist.
62 *critic*: connoisseur.
63 *An'*: if.
look upon: regard favourably; perhaps also, 'watch'.
66 *policy*: prudence; also, 'device'.
69 *tickling*: pleasure.
75 *prostitute*: offer with complete devotion (a rare, now obsolete meaning, which Corvino takes); but Mosca is really using the word in its usual sense.
78 *proper*: honourable; lovely; suitable for the occasion.
79 *of price*: excellent (and, of course, valuable).

MOSCA. To be your comfortress, and to preserve you.
VOLPONE. Alas, I am past already! Pray you, thank him,
For his good care, and promptness; but for that,
'Tis a vain labour, e'en to fight 'gainst heaven;
Applying fire to a stone (uh, uh, uh, uh!),
Making a dead leaf grow again. I take
His wishes gently, though; and you may tell him,
What I've done for him. Marry, my state is hopeless!
Will him, to pray for me; and t'use his fortune,
With reverence, when he comes to't.
MOSCA. Do you hear, sir?
Go to him, with your wife.
CORVINO. Heart of my father!
Wilt thou persist thus? Come, I pray thee, come.
Thou seest 'tis nothing. Celia! By this hand,
I shall grow violent. Come, do't, I say.
CELIA. Sir, kill me rather: I will take down poison,
Eat burning coals, do anything –
CORVINO. Be damned.
(Heart) I will drag thee hence, home, by the hair;
Cry thee a strumpet, through the streets; rip up
Thy mouth, unto thine ears; and slit thy nose,
Like a raw rochet – Do not tempt me, come.
Yield, I am loath – (Death) I will buy some slave,
Whom I will kill, and bind thee to him, alive;
And at my window, hang you forth: devising
Some monstrous crime, which I, in capital letters,
Will eat into thy flesh, with *aquafortis*,
And burning corsives, on this stubborn breast.
Now, by the blood thou hast incensed, I'll do't.
CELIA. Sir, what you please, you may, I am your martyr.
CORVINO. Be not thus obstinate, I ha'not deserved it:
Think, who it is entreats you. Pray thee, sweet;

---

80 *comfortress*: from the various meanings of the verb: 'a woman who brings relief to a sick person'; also, 'one who brings pleasure', and 'one who invigorates'.
84 *stone*: also the slang term for 'testicle'.
86 *gently*: kindly.
95 *Eat burning coals*: like Portia, wife of Brutus (see *Julius Caesar*, IV.iii.156).
99 *rochet*: the red gurnet (a fish).
104 *aquafortis*: nitric acid, used in engraving.
105 *corsives*: corrosives.

(Good faith), thou shalt have jewels, gowns, attires,
What thou wilt think, and ask. Do, but, go kiss him.
Or touch him, but. For my sake. At my suit.
This once. No? not? I shall remember this.
Will you disgrace me thus? do you thirst m'undoing?

MOSCA. Nay, gentle lady, be advised.

CORVINO. No, no.
She has watched her time. God's precious, this is scurvy;
'Tis very scurvy: and you are –

MOSCA. Nay, good sir.

CORVINO. An arrant locust, by Heaven, a locust. Whore,
Crocodile, that hast thy tears prepared,
Expecting, how thou'lt bid 'em flow.

MOSCA. Nay, pray you, sir,
She will consider.

CELIA. Would my life would serve
To satisfy.

CORVINO. ('S death) if she would but speak to him,
And save my reputation, 'twere somewhat;
But spitefully to affect my utter ruin!

MOSCA. Ay, now you've put your fortune, in her hands.
Why i'faith, it is her modesty, I must quit her;
If you were absent, she would be more coming;
I know it: and dare undertake for her.
What woman can, before her husband? Pray you,
Let us depart, and leave her here.

CORVINO. Sweet Celia,
Thou may'st redeem all yet; I'll say no more:
If not, esteem yourself as lost. Nay, stay there.
[*Exeunt* MOSCA, CORVINO.]

CELIA. O God, and his good angels! whither, whither,
Is shame fled human breasts? that with such ease,

---

116 *God's precious*: by God's precious blood.
118 *locust*: consuming plague (H&S).
120 *Expecting*: anticipating.
124 *affect*: desire.
126 *quit*: acquit, excuse.

Men dare put off your honours, and their own?
Is that, which ever was a cause of life,
Now placed beneath the basest circumstance?
And modesty an exile made, for money?

VOLPONE. Ay, in Corvino, and such earth-fed minds,
He leaps off from his couch.
That never tasted the true heaven of love.
Assure thee, Celia, he that would sell thee,
Only for hope of gain, and that uncertain,
He would have sold his part of paradise
For ready money, had he met a cope-man.
Why art thou 'mazed, to see me thus revived?
Rather applaud thy beauty's miracle;
'Tis thy great work: that hath, not now alone,
But sundry times, raised me, in several shapes,
And but this morning, like a mountebank,
To see thee at thy window. Ay, before
I would have left my practice for thy love,
In varying figures, I would have contended
With the blue Proteus, or the hornèd flood.
Now, art thou welcome.

CELIA. Sir!

VOLPONE. Nay, fly me not.
Nor let thy false imagination
That I was bed-rid, make thee think I am so:
Thou shalt not find it. I am, now, as fresh,
As hot, as high, and in as jovial plight,
As when (in that so celebrated scene,
At recitation of our comedy,

---

136 *that*: i.e. honour.

137 *circumstance*: insignificant matter.

144 *cope-man*: dealer, merchant.

147 *great work*: the *magnum opus* of alchemy, which resulted in the philosophers' stone and the elixir of life.

151 *practice for*: scheme to gain.

152 *figures*: shapes.

153 *blue*: colour of the sea; Proteus is termed 'cerulean' in Virgil. *Proteus*: sea god who, in contests, changed shape at will to elude capture.
hornèd flood: the river god Achelous, whom Hercules overcame to win Deïaneira for his bride; he assumed several shapes. As sea gods were traditionally portrayed as blue, river gods were portrayed as horned (symbolic of life-giving powers).

158 *jovial plight*: merry state (as one born under the planet Jupiter); also referring to Jove as a seducer of women.

159 *scene*: performance.

For entertainment of the great Valois)
I acted young Antinous; and attracted
The eyes, and ears of all the ladies, present,
T'admire each graceful gesture, note, and footing.

Song

Come, my Celia, let us prove,
While we can, the sports of love;
Time will not be ours, for ever,
He, at length, our good will sever;
Spend not then his gifts, in vain.
Suns, that set, may rise again:
But if, once, we lose this light,
'Tis with us perpetual night.
Why should we defer our joys?
Fame, and rumour are but toys.
Cannot we delude the eyes
Of a few poor household spies?
Or his easier ears beguile,
Thus removèd, by our wile?
'Tis no sin, love's fruits to steal;
But the sweet thefts to reveal:
To be taken, to be seen,
These have crimes accounted been.

CELIA. Some sèrene blast me, or dire lightning strike
This my offending face.

VOLPONE. Why droops my Celia?
Thou hast in place of a base husband found
A worthy lover: use thy fortune well,
With secrecy, and pleasure. See, behold,
What thou art queen of; not in expectation,
As I feed others; but possessed, and crowned.
See, here, a rope of pearl; and each, more orient
Than that the brave Egyptian queen caroused:

---

161 *Valois*: Henri III of France, entertained in Venice in 1574 (thirty years before the action of *Volpone*).

162 *Antinous*: beautiful young man, favourite of the Emperor Hadrian (a figure to please the transvestite Henri); or the suitor to Odysseus's wife, Penelope, in the *Odyssey* (more appropriate to this scene).

164 *footing*: step.

165 *prove*: make trial of, put to the test.

183 *sèrene*: a light mist or fine rain falling after sunset in hot countries; considered harmful.

191 *brave*: magnificently attired.
Egyptian queen: Cleopatra, who drank off a priceless pearl dissolved in wine at a banquet.

Dissolve, and drink 'em. See, a carbuncle,
May put out both the eyes of our St Mark;
A diamond, would have bought Lollia Paulina,
When she came in, like star-light, hid with jewels,
That were the spoils of provinces; take these,
And wear, and lose 'em: yet remains an ear-ring
To purchase them again, and this whole state.
A gem, but worth a private patrimony,
Is nothing: we will eat such at a meal.
The heads of parrots, tongues of nightingales,
The brains of peacocks, and of estriches
Shall be our food: and could we get the phoenix
(Though nature lost her kind), she were our dish.

CELIA. Good sir, these things might move a mind affected
With such delights; but I, whose innocence
Is all I can think wealthy, or worth th'enjoying,
And which once lost, I have nought to lose beyond it,
Cannot be taken with these sensual baits:
If you have conscience –

VOLPONE. 'Tis the beggar's virtue,
If thou hast wisdom, hear me, Celia.
Thy baths shall be the juice of July-flowers,
Spirit of roses, and of violets,
The milk of unicorns, and panthers' breath
Gathered in bags, and mixed with Cretan wines.

---

193 *eyes of our St Mark*: see Additional Note, p. 440 below.

194 *Lollia Paulina*: wife of Emperor Caligula; her wealth came from her father's extortion in the provinces.

195 This spectacular appearance occurred at a betrothal party.

199 *private patrimony*: the inheritance of a single individual.

201–2 dishes served to the Emperor Heliogabalus.

202 *estriches*: ostriches.

204 *her kind*: i.e. the species of the phoenix, a mythical Arabian bird of which there was only one, and which every 500 years rose anew from its own ashes after immolating itself.

205 *affected*: moved.

212 *July-flowers*: clove-scented pinks, gilly flowers, 'nature's bastards' which Perdita excludes from her garden (*The Winter's Tale*, IV.iii.82–8).

213 *violets*: ironically, emblematic of modesty.

214 *The milk of unicorns*: there is no precedent for this exotic ingredient.
panthers' breath: panthers were held to lure their prey by the sweetness of their breath.

Our drink shall be preparèd gold, and amber;
Which we will take, until my roof whirl round
With the vertigo: and my dwarf shall dance,
My eunuch sing, my fool make up the antic.
Whilst we, in changèd shapes, act Ovid's tales,
Thou, like Europa now, and I like Jove,
Then I like Mars, and thou like Erycine,
So, of the rest, till we have quite run through
And wearied all the fables of the gods.
Then will I have thee in more modern forms,
Attirèd like some sprightly dame of France,
Brave Tuscan lady, or proud Spanish beauty;
Sometimes, unto the Persian Sophy's wife;
Or the Grand Signior's mistress; and, for change,
To one of our most artful courtesans,
Or some quick Negro, or cold Russian;
And I will meet thee, in as many shapes:
Where we may, so, transfuse our wandering souls
Out at our lips, and score up sums of pleasures,
That the curious shall not know,
How to tell them as they flow;
And the envious, when they find
What their number is, be pined.

CELIA. If you have ears that will be pierced; or eyes,
That can be opened; a heart, may be touched;
Or any part, that yet sounds man, about you:
If you have touch of holy saints, or Heaven,
Do me the grace, to let me 'scape. If not,
Be bountiful, and kill me. You do know,
I am a creature, hither ill betrayed,
By one, whose shame I would forget it were.

---

216 *preparèd*: dissolved.
219 *antic*: grotesque dance.
220 *Ovid's tales*: the *Metamorphoses*, which tells of lovers and their transformations.
221 *Europa*: carried off by Jove disguised as a bull.
222 *Erycine*: Venus (named here after her temple at Eryx in Sicily).
228 *Persian Sophy*: the Shah of Persia.
229 *Grand Signior*: the Sultan of Turkey.
231 *quick*: lively.
cold: frigid.
233 *transfuse*: cause to flow from one to another (lovers breathed their souls into each other as they kissed).
235 *curious*: interested connoisseurs.
238 *pined*: tormented.
241 *sounds man, about you*: declares you to be a man.
242 *touch of*: trace of reverence for.

If you will deign me neither of these graces,
Yet feed your wrath, sir, rather than your lust
(It is a vice comes nearer manliness);
And punish that unhappy crime of nature,
Which you miscall my beauty: flay my face,
Or poison it, with ointments, for seducing
Your blood to this rebellion. Rub these hands,
With what may cause an eating leprosy,
E'en to my bones, and marrow; anything,
That may disfavour me, save in my honour.
And I will kneel to you, pray for you, pay down
A thousand hourly vows, sir, for your health,
Report, and think you virtuous –

VOLPONE. Think me cold,
Frozen, and impotent, and so report me?
That I had Nestor's hernia, thou wouldst think.
I do degenerate, and abuse my nation,
To play with opportunity, thus long:
I should have done the act, and then have parleyed.
Yield, or I'll force thee.

CELIA. Oh! just God!

VOLPONE. In vain –

[BONARIO] *leaps out from where* MOSCA *had placed him.*

BONARIO. Forbear, foul ravisher, libidinous swine,
Free the forced lady, or thou diest, impostor.
But that I am loath to snatch thy punishment
Out of the hand of justice, thou should'st, yet,
Be made the timely sacrifice of vengeance,
Before this altar, and this dross, thy idol.
Lady, let's quit the place, it is the den
Of villainy; fear nought, you have a guard:
And he, ere long, shall meet his just reward.

[*Exeunt* BONARIO, CELIA.]

VOLPONE. Fall on me, roof, and bury me in ruin,
Become my grave, that wert my shelter. Oh!
I am unmasked, unspirited, undone,
Betrayed to beggary, to infamy –

---

256 *disfavour*: disfigure.

261 *Nestor's hernia*: Nestor was the oldest king at the siege of Troy; a symbol of impotent old age. The hernia was added by Juvenal (*Satires*, VI).

262 *degenerate*: act in a manner unworthy of my race.

277 *unspirited*: dejected; deprived of liveliness; also, 'unmanned'.

SCENE VIII

[*Enter*] MOSCA.

MOSCA. Where shall I run, most wretched shame of men,
To beat out my unlucky brains?
VOLPONE. Here, here.
What! dost thou bleed?
MOSCA. Oh, that his well-driven sword
Had been so courteous to have cleft me down
Unto the navel; ere I lived to see
My life, my hopes, my spirits, my patron, all
Thus desperately engagèd, by my error.
VOLPONE. Woe, on thy fortune.
MOSCA. And my follies, sir.
VOLPONE. Th'hast made me miserable.
MOSCA. And myself, sir.
Who would have thought, he would have hearkened so?
VOLPONE. What shall we do?
MOSCA. I know not; if my heart
Could expiate the mischance, I'd pluck it out.
Will you be pleased to hang me? or cut my throat?
And I'll requite you, sir. Let's die like Romans,
Since we have lived like Grecians.
They knock without.
VOLPONE. Hark, who's there?
I hear some footing, officers, the *saffi*,
Come to apprehend us! I do feel the brand
Hissing already, at my forehead: now,
Mine ears are boring.
MOSCA. To your couch, sir, you
Make that place good, however. Guilty men
Suspect, what they deserve still.

[*Enter* CORBACCIO.]

Signior Corbaccio!

---

7 *engagèd*: entangled, exposed to risk.
14 *like Romans*: fearlessly, by our own hands.
15 *like Grecians*: dissipatedly.
16 *footing*: footsteps.
saffi: officers of the law; '*Saffo*, a catchpole, or sergeant' (Florio, 1598).
19 *boring*: presumably a punishment for criminals.
20 *Make that place good*: keep up your part of invalid ('make good' = 'defend', a military term).

SCENE IX

CORBACCIO. Why! how now? Mosca!
MOSCA. Oh, undone, amazed, sir.
Your son (I know not by what accident)
Acquainted with your purpose to my patron,
Touching your will, and making him your heir;
Entered our house with violence, his sword drawn,
Sought for you, called you wretch, unnatural,
Vowed he would kill you.
CORBACCIO. Me?
MOSCA. Yes, and my patron.
CORBACCIO. This act shall disinherit him indeed:
Here is the will.
MOSCA. 'Tis well, sir.
CORBACCIO. Right and well.
Be you as careful now, for me.

[*Enter* VOLTORE, *unnoticed.*]

MOSCA. My life, sir,
Is not more tendered, I am only yours.
CORBACCIO. How does he? will he die shortly, think'st thou?
MOSCA. I fear
He'll outlast May.
CORBACCIO. Today?
MOSCA. No, last out May, sir.
CORBACCIO. Could'st thou not gi'him a dram?
MOSCA. Oh, by no means, sir.
CORBACCIO. Nay, I'll not bid you.
VOLTORE. This is a knave, I see.
MOSCA. [*aside*] How, Signior Voltore! did he hear me?
VOLTORE. Parasite.
MOSCA. Who's that? Oh, sir, most timely welcome –
VOLTORE. Scarce,
To the discovery of your tricks, I fear.
You are his, only? and mine, also? are you not?
MOSCA. Who? I, sir!
VOLTORE. You, sir. What device is this
About a will?
MOSCA. A plot for you, sir.

---

1 *amazed*: confounded.
11 *tendered*: cherished.

VOLTORE. Come,
Put not your foists upon me, I shall scent 'em.
MOSCA. Did you not hear it?
VOLTORE. Yes, I hear, Corbaccio
Hath made your patron, there, his heir.
MOSCA. 'Tis true,
By my device, drawn to it by my plot,
With hope –
VOLTORE. Your patron should reciprocate?
And you have promised?
MOSCA. For your good, I did, sir.
Nay more, I told his son, brought, hid him here,
Where he might hear his father pass the deed;
Being persuaded to it, by this thought, sir,
That the unnaturalness, first, of the act,
And then his father's oft disclaiming in him
(Which I did mean t'help on), would sure enrage him
To do some violence upon his parent.
On which the law should take sufficient hold,
And you be stated in a double hope:
Truth be my comfort, and my conscience,
My only aim was to dig you a fortune
Out of these two, old rotten sepulchres –
VOLTORE. (I cry thee mercy, Mosca.)
MOSCA. Worth your patience,
And your great merit, sir. And see the change!
VOLTORE. Why? what success?
MOSCA. Most hapless! you must help, sir.
Whilst we expected th'old raven, in comes
Corvino's wife, sent hither, by her husband –
VOLTORE. What, with a present?
MOSCA. No, sir, on visitation
(I'll tell you how, anon), and staying long,
The youth, he grows impatient, rushes forth,
Seizeth the lady, wounds me, makes her swear
(Or he would murder her, that was his vow)

---

22 *foists*: tricks; also, a pervasive musty smell – hence 'scent'; Mosca's musty tricks smell.
32 *disclaiming in*: renouncing any part in, repudiating legally.
36 *stated*: instated, settled.
39 *sepulchres*: the image is from grave-robbing.
40 *cry thee mercy*: beg your pardon.
42 *success*: outcome.
hapless: unfortunate.

T'affirm my patron to have done her rape:
Which how unlike it is, you see! and hence,
With that pretext, he's gone, t'accuse his father;
Defame my patron; defeat you –

VOLTORE. Where's her husband?
Let him be sent for, straight.

MOSCA. Sir, I'll go fetch him.

VOLTORE. Bring him to the *Scrutineo*.

MOSCA. Sir, I will.

VOLTORE. This must be stopped.

MOSCA. Oh, you do nobly, sir.
Alas, 'twas laboured all, sir, for your good;
Nor was there want of counsel, in the plot.
But Fortune can, at any time, o'erthrow
The projects of a hundred learned clerks, sir.

CORBACCIO. What's that?

VOLTORE. Wilt please you, sir, to go along?
[*Exeunt* CORBACCIO, VOLTORE.]

MOSCA. Patron, go in, and pray for our success.

VOLPONE. Need makes devotion: Heaven your labour bless.
[*Exeunt*.]

ACT IV

SCENE I

[*Enter*] SIR POLITIC WOULD-BE, PEREGRINE.

SIR POLITIC. I told you, sir, it was a plot: you see
What observation is. You mentioned me,
For some instructions: I will tell you, sir
(Since we are met, here in this height of Venice),
Some few particulars I have set down,
Only for this meridian; fit to be known
Of your crude traveller, and they are these.

---

50 *to*: see Textual Note, p. 433 below.
55 *Scrutineo*: the court of law in the senate house.
58 *counsel*: judgement, sagacity.
60 *clerks*: scholars.
3 *instructions*: rules for travel.
4 *height*: latitude.
6 *meridian*: particular locality.
7 *crude*: raw, inexperienced.

I will not touch, sir, at your phrase, or clothes,
For they are old.
PEREGRINE. Sir, I have better.
SIR POLITIC. Pardon,
I meant, as they are themes.
PEREGRINE. Oh, sir, proceed:
[*Aside*] I'll slander you no more of wit, good sir.
SIR POLITIC. First, for your garb, it must be grave, and serious;
Very reserved, and locked; not tell a secret,
On any terms, not to your father; scarce
A fable, but with caution; make sure choice
Both of your company, and discourse; beware,
You never speak a truth –
PEREGRINE. How!
SIR POLITIC. Not to strangers,
For those be they you must converse with, most;
Others I would not know, sir, but at distance,
So as I still might be a saver, in 'em:
You shall have tricks, else, passed upon you, hourly.
And then, for your religion, profess none;
But wonder, at the diversity of all;
And, for your part, protest, were there no other
But simply the laws o'th'land, you could content you:
Nick Machiavel, and Monsieur Bodin, both,
Were of this mind. Then, must you learn the use,
And handling of your silver fork, at meals;
The metal of your glass (these are main matters,
With your Italian), and to know the hour
When you must eat your melons, and your figs.
PEREGRINE. Is that a point of state, too?

---

8 *phrase*: manner of speaking.
12 *garb*: demeanour.
15 *fable*: fictitious story.
17 *speak*: see Textual Note, p. 433 below.
strangers: foreigners.
20 *be a saver*: not stand to lose (gambling term).
26 *Nick Machiavel, and Monsieur Bodin*: a misrepresentation; Niccolò Machiavelli (1469–1527) saw the claims of religion as secondary to those of the state, and Jean Bodin (1530–96), who did not dismiss religion, advocated religious toleration to keep the state peaceful.
28 *fork*: first introduced in Italy, and not yet common in England.
29 *metal*: the materials used for glass, in a molten state.

SIR POLITIC. Here it is.
For your Venetian, if he see a man
Preposterous in the least, he has him straight;
He has: he strips him. I'll acquaint you, sir,
I now have lived here ('tis some fourteen months);
Within the first week, of my landing here,
All took me for a citizen of Venice:
I knew the forms, so well –
PEREGRINE. [*aside*] And nothing else.
SIR POLITIC. I had read Contarine, took me a house,
Dealt with my Jews, to furnish it with movables –
Well, if I could but find one man, one man,
To mine own heart, whom I durst trust, I would –
PEREGRINE. What? what, sir?
SIR POLITIC. Make him rich; make him a fortune:
He should not think, again. I would command it.
PEREGRINE. As how?
SIR POLITIC. With certain projects, that I have:
Which, I may not discover.
PEREGRINE. [*aside*] If I had
But one to wager with, I would lay odds, now,
He tells me, instantly.
SIR POLITIC. One is (and that
I care not greatly, who knows) to serve the state
Of Venice, with red herrings, for three years,
And at a certain rate, from Rotterdam,
Where I have correspondence. There's a letter,
Sent me from one o'th'States, and to that purpose;
He cannot write his name, but that's his mark.
PEREGRINE. He is a chandler?
SIR POLITIC. No, a cheesemonger.
There are some other too, with whom I treat,

---

34 *Preposterous*: (acting) contrary to convention.
40 *Contarine*: Gasparo Contarini's book on the Venetian constitution had been translated into English in 1599 as *The Commonwealth and Government of Venice*.
41 *movables*: furnishings (not fixtures).
45 *think*: i.e. about money.
51 *red herrings*: see Additional Note, p. 440 below.
53 *correspondence*: connections.
54 *one o'th'States*: probably, someone in the United Provinces, or (less likely), a member of the States General, the Dutch assembly.
56 *chandler*: candle-maker or dealer (a surmise made from the greasy state of the letter).
57 *too*: see Textual Note, p. 433 below.

About the same negotiation;
And I will undertake it: for, 'tis thus,
I'll do't with ease, I've cast it all. Your hoy
Carries but three men in her, and a boy;
And she shall make me three returns a year:
So, if there come but one of three, I save,
If two, I can defalk. But this is now,
If my main project fail.

PEREGRINE. Then, you have others?

SIR POLITIC. I should be loath to draw the subtle air
Of such a place, without my thousand aims.
I'll not dissemble, sir, where'er I come,
I love to be considerative; and 'tis true,
I have, at my free hours, thought upon
Some certain goods, unto the state of Venice,
Which I do call my cautions: and, sir, which
I mean (in hope of pension) to propound
To the Great Council, then unto the Forty,
So to the Ten. My means are made already –

PEREGRINE. By whom?

SIR POLITIC. Sir, one, that though his place b'obscure,
Yet he can sway, and they will hear him. H'is
A *commendatore*.

PEREGRINE. What, a common sergeant?

---

58 *negotiation*: business transaction (six syllables).
59 *undertake*: carry it through; also, 'act as surety for'.
60 *cast*: calculated the cost.
hoy: small Dutch coastal vessel.
62 *returns*: return voyages.
63 *save*: recoup the outlay.
64 *defalk*: reduce the price (of the fish).
66 *draw the subtle air*: breathe the atmosphere of intrigue (Venice was a centre for the collection and assessment of intelligence at this time).
67 *aims*: designs.
69 *to be considerative*: to deliberate (upon the affairs of the country).
71 *goods*: benefits.
72 *cautions*: precautions; or perhaps, 'securities', pledges to prove his good will to the Venetian state.
74–5 *Great Council . . . the Forty . . . the Ten*: the ascending orders of the Venetian government.
78 *sergeant*: officer who carried out orders of the judiciary, arresting and summoning offenders.

SIR POLITIC. Sir, such, as they are, put in their mouths,
What they should say, sometimes: as well as greater.
I think I have my notes, to show you –
PEREGRINE. Good, sir.
SIR POLITIC. But you shall swear unto me, on your gentry,
Not to anticipate –
PEREGRINE. I, sir?
SIR POLITIC. Nor reveal
A circumstance – My paper is not with me.
PEREGRINE. Oh, but you can remember, sir.
SIR POLITIC. My first is,
Concerning tinder-boxes. You must know,
No family is, here, without its box.
Now sir, it being so portable a thing,
Put case, that you, or I were ill affected
Unto the state; sir, with it in our pockets,
Might not I go into the *Arsenale*?
Or you? come out again? and none the wiser?
PEREGRINE. Except yourself, sir.
SIR POLITIC. Go to, then. I therefore,
Advèrtise to the state, how fit it were
That none, but such as were known patriots,
Sound lovers of their country, should be suffered
T'enjoy them in their houses: and even those,
Sealed, at some office, and at such a bigness,
As might not lurk in pockets.
PEREGRINE. Admirable!
SIR POLITIC. My next is, how t'enquire, and be resolved,
By present demonstration, whether a ship,
Newly arrived from Soría, or from

---

83 *anticipate*: forestall (me).
84 *circumstance*: detail.
86 *tinder-boxes*: boxes containing combustible material, and flint and steel, with which to kindle a spark or flame.
89 *affected*: disposed.
91 *Arsenale*: arsenal (Italian form); the store of ships and weapons in Venice.
93 *Go to*: just so.
94 *Advèrtise*: inform.
98 *Sealed*: marked with a seal of authorisation.
101 *present*: immediate.
102 *Soría*: Syria (Sir Pol uses the Italian form).

Any suspected part of all the Levant,
Be guilty of the plague: and where they use
To lie out forty, fifty days, sometimes,
About the *Lazaretto*, for their trial,
I'll save that charge, and loss unto the merchant,
And, in an hour, clear the doubt.
PEREGRINE. Indeed, sir?
SIR POLITIC. Or – I will lose my labour.
PEREGRINE. My faith, that's much.
SIR POLITIC. Nay, sir, conceive me. 'Twill cost me, in onions,
Some thirty livres –
PEREGRINE. Which is one pound sterling.
SIR POLITIC. Beside my waterworks: for this I do, sir.
First, I bring in your ship 'twixt two brick walls
(But those the state shall venture); on the one
I strain me a fair tarpaulin; and, in that,
I stick my onions, cut in halves: the other
Is full of loopholes, out at which I thrust
The noses of my bellows; and those bellows
I keep, with waterworks, in perpetual motion
(Which is the easiest matter of a hundred).
Now, sir, your onion, which doth naturally
Attract th'infection, and your bellows, blowing
The air upon him, will show (instantly)
By his changed colour, if there be contagion,
Or else remain as fair, as at the first.
Now 'tis known, 'tis nothing.
PEREGRINE. You are right, sir.
SIR POLITIC. I would I had my note.
PEREGRINE. Faith, so would I:
But you ha'done well, for once, sir.
SIR POLITIC. Were I false,
Or would be made so, I could show you reasons,
How I could sell this state, now, to the Turk;

---

104 *use*: are accustomed to.
106 *Lazaretto*: plague hospital; there were two, established on islands in the Gulf of Venice after outbreaks of the plague in 1423 and 1576.
110 *conceive*: understand.
111 *livres*: French coins.
112 *waterworks*: machinery operated by water.
115 *strain*: stretch.
120 Sir Pol modestly claims to have the secret of perpetual motion.
130 *Turk*: Venice was still Europe's bulwark against the Turkish threat.

Spite of their galleys, or their –
PEREGRINE. Pray you, Sir Pol.
SIR POLITIC. I have 'em not, about me.
PEREGRINE. That I feared.
They're there, sir?
SIR POLITIC. No, this is my diary,
Wherein I note my actions of the day.
PEREGRINE. Pray you, let's see, sir. What is here?
'*Notandum*,
A rat had gnawn my spur-leathers;
notwithstanding,
I put on new, and did go forth; but first,
I threw three beans over the threshold. *Item*,
I went and bought two toothpicks, whereof one
I burst, immediately, in a discourse
With a Dutch merchant, 'bout *ragion del stato*.
From him I went, and paid a *moccenigo*
For piecing my silk stockings; by the way,
I cheapened sprats: and at St Mark's, I urined.'
Faith, these are politic notes!
SIR POLITIC. Sir, I do slip
No action of my life, thus, but I quote it.
PEREGRINE. Believe me, it is wise!
SIR POLITIC. Nay, sir, read forth.

SCENE II

[*Enter*] LADY WOULD-BE, NANO, [*two*] WOMEN.

LADY WOULD-BE. Where should this loose knight
be, trow? Sure, h'is housed.
NANO. Why, then he's fast.
LADY WOULD-BE. Ay, he plays both, with me:
I pray you, stay. This heat will do more harm
To my complexion, than his heart is worth.

136–8 superstition (details adapted from Theophrastus's character of 'The Superstitious Man') is added to Sir Pol's follies.
141 *ragion del stato*: policy of state: the justification for carrying out immoral acts for political purposes.
143 *piecing*: mending.
144 *cheapened*: bargained for.
146 *quote*: make a note of.
2 *fast*: secure.
both: i.e. 'fast and loose' (see I.ii.8 n.).

(I do not care to hinder, but to take him.)
How it comes off!
[FIRST] WOMAN. My master's yonder.
LADY WOULD-BE. Where?
[SECOND] WOMAN. With a young gentleman.
LADY WOULD-BE. That same's the party!
In man's apparel! Pray you, sir, jog my knight:
I will be tender to his reputation,
However he demerit.
SIR POLITIC. My lady!
PEREGRINE. Where?
SIR POLITIC. 'Tis she indeed, sir, you shall know her. She is,
Were she not mine, a lady of that merit,
For fashion, and behaviour; and for beauty
I durst compare –
PEREGRINE. It seems, you are not jealous,
That dare commend her.
SIR POLITIC. Nay, and for discourse –
PEREGRINE. Being your wife, she cannot miss that.
SIR POLITIC. Madam,
Here is a gentleman, pray you, use him fairly,
He seems a youth, but he is –
LADY WOULD-BE. None?
SIR POLITIC. Yes, one
Has put his face, as soon, into the world –
LADY WOULD-BE. You mean, as early? but today?
SIR POLITIC. How's this!
LADY WOULD-BE. Why, in this habit, sir, you apprehend me.
Well, Master Would-be, this doth not become you;
I had thought, the odour, sir, of your good name
Had been more precious to you; that you would not
Have done this dire massàcre, on your honour;
One of your gravity, and rank, besides!
But knights, I see, care little for the oath
They make to ladies; chiefly, their own ladies.
SIR POLITIC. Now by my spurs (the symbol of my knighthood) –

---

6 *it*: cosmetic paint.
10 *demerit*: deserves blame.
13 *behaviour*: elegant deportment.
21 *habit*: costume.
23 *odour*: fragrance, savour (religious associations); 'sweetness'.
26 *gravity*: dignity.

PEREGRINE. [*aside*] (Lord! how his brain is humbled,
for an oath!)
SIR POLITIC. I reach you not.
LADY WOULD-BE. Right, sir, your policy
May bear it through, thus. [*To* PEREGRINE] Sir, a word with you.
I would be loth to còntest publicly,
With any gentlewoman; or to seem
Froward, or violent (as *The Courtier* says),
It comes too near rusticity, in a lady,
Which I would shun, by all means: and however
I may deserve from Master Would-be, yet
T'have one fair gentlewoman, thus, be made
Th'unkind instrument, to wrong another,
And one she knows not, ay, and to persèver;
In my poor judgement, is not warranted
From being a solecism in our sex,
If not in manners.
PEREGRINE. How is this!
SIR POLITIC. Sweet madam,
Come nearer to your aim.
LADY WOULD-BE. Marry, and will, sir.
Since you provoke me, with your impudence,
And laughter of your light land-siren, here,
Your Sporus, your hermaphrodite –
PEREGRINE. What's here?
Poetic fury, and historic storms!

---

30 *humbled*: 'brought low – down to his spurs' (Brockbank); possibly a cutting reference to James I's lavish dubbing of knights (see *The Alchemist*, II.ii.86–7).
31 *policy*: politic cunning.
35 *Froward*: perverse.
The Courtier: by Castiglione, translated into English by Sir Thomas Hoby in 1561. Book III treats of the courtly behaviour appropriate to women.
36 *rusticity*: lack of refinement.
43 *solecism*: properly, a grammatical mistake; technically, the meaning of 'impropriety' is itself a solecism. See Additional Note, p. 440 below.
47 *light land-siren*: wanton seductress, woman-of-the-streets. In classical myth, sirens, sea monsters with the body of a bird and a woman's head, lured sailors to their destruction by the sweetness of their voices.
48 *Sporus*: a favourite of Nero, who had him castrated and 'married' him.
49 *Poetic . . . historic*: Lady Would-be's excited imagination draws on fiction and fact: the sirens are found in classical poetry, whilst Sporus belongs to history.

SIR POLITIC. The gentleman, believe it, is of worth,
And of our nation.
LADY WOULD-BE. Ay, your Whitefriars nation!
Come, I blush for you, Master Would-be, I;
And am ashamed, you should ha'no more forehead,
Than, thus, to be the patron, or St George
To a lewd harlot, a base fricatrice,
A female devil, in a male outside.
SIR POLITIC. Nay,
An' you be such a one! I must bid adieu
To your delights. The case appears too liquid.
[*Exit.*]
LADY WOULD-BE. Ay, you may carry't clear, with your state-face!
But for your carnival concupiscence,
Who here is fled for liberty of conscience
From furious persecution of the marshal,
Her will I disc'ple.
PEREGRINE. This is fine, i'faith!
And do you use this often? is this part
Of your wit's exercise, 'gainst you have occasion?
Madam –
LADY WOULD-BE. Go to, sir.

---

51 *Whitefriars nation*: the class of outcasts, criminals and prostitutes who took refuge in Whitefriars, a 'liberty' or area outside the jurisdiction of the City of London.
53 *forehead*: modesty.
54 *St George*: England's patron saint, and patron of damsels in distress.
55 *fricatrice*: prostitute.
56 *female devil*: i.e. a *succuba*, which also means a strumpet (see *The Alchemist*, II.ii.48).
58 *case*: with a play on 'appearance', 'dress'.
liquid: manifest.
59 *state-face*: diplomatic countenance.
60 *carnival*: refers to the riotous and licentious revels of carnival preceding Lent in Roman Catholic countries; particularly apt in its associations with dressing up in outlandish costume, as well as those of abandonment.
concupiscence: wanton woman.
61 *liberty of conscience*: freedom to practise, not her religious belief, but her immoral trade.
62 *marshal*: officer of the court in charge of prisoners and frequently of the prison.
63 *disc'ple*: chastise, inflict penitential discipline upon.
64 *use*: make a habit of doing.
66 *Go to*: 'come on, now'.

PEREGRINE. Do you hear me, lady?
Why, if your knight have set you to beg shirts,
Or to invite me home, you might have done it
A nearer way, by far.
LADY WOULD-BE. This cannot work you
Out of my snare.
PEREGRINE. Why? am I in it, then?
Indeed, your husband told me you were fair,
And so you are; only your nose inclines
(That side, that's next the sun) to the queen-apple.
LADY WOULD-BE. This cannot be endured, by any patience!

SCENE III

[*Enter*] MOSCA.

MOSCA. What's the matter, madam?
LADY WOULD-BE. If the Senate
Right not my quest, in this, I will protest 'em,
To all the world, no aristocracy.
MOSCA. What is the injury, lady?
LADY WOULD-BE. Why, the callet
You told me of, here I have ta'en disguised.
MOSCA. Who? this? what means your ladyship? The creature
I mentioned to you, is apprehended, now,
Before the Senate, you shall see her –
LADY WOULD-BE. Where?
MOSCA. I'll bring you to her. This young gentleman
I saw him land, this morning, at the port.
LADY WOULD-BE. Is't possible! how has my judgement wandered!
Sir, I must, blushing, say to you, I have erred:
And plead your pardon.

---

68 *invite me home*: for immoral purposes.
70 *snare*: Lady Would-be means, 'the trap in which I have taken your masquerade'; Peregrine interprets 'the allure of my charms'.
72 *so you are*: perhaps a reference to ceruse, the white cosmetic wash, creating the impression of 'fair' skin.
73 *queen-apple*: a variety of rosy apple.
2 *quest*: enquiry.
3 *aristocracy*: true noblemen.
4 *callet*: strumpet.

PEREGRINE. What! more changes, yet?
LADY WOULD-BE. I hope you ha'not the malice to remember
A gentlewoman's passion. If you stay,
In Venice, here, please you to use me, sir –
MOSCA. Will you go, madam?
LADY WOULD-BE. Pray you, sir, use me. In faith,
The more you see me, the more I shall conceive,
You have forgot our quarrel.
[*Exeunt* LADY WOULD-BE, MOSCA, NANO, WOMEN.]
PEREGRINE. This is rare!
Sir Politic Would-be? no, Sir Politic Bawd!
To bring me, thus, acquainted with his wife!
Well, wise Sir Pol, since you have practised, thus,
Upon my freshmanship, I'll try your salt-head,
What proof it is against a counter-plot. [*Exit.*]

SCENE IV

[*Enter*] VOLTORE, CORBACCIO, CORVINO, MOSCA.

VOLTORE. Well, now you know the carriage of the business,
Your constancy is all that is required
Unto the safety of it.
MOSCA. Is the lie
Safely conveyed amongst us? is that sure?
Knows every man his burden?
CORVINO. Yes.
MOSCA. Then shrink not.
CORVINO. [*aside to* MOSCA] But knows the advocate the truth?
MOSCA. Oh, sir,

---

15 *passion*: angry outburst; Peregrine interprets as 'amorousness'.
16 *use me*: use my acquaintance socially; Peregrine takes it as an invitation to 'use sexually'.
18 *see*: see Textual Note, p. 433 below.
conceive: understand; also, 'become pregnant'.
22 *practised*: played a trick.
23 *salt-head*: seasoned experience; also, 'salaciousness'.
5 *burden*: refrain (of a song).

By no means. I devised a formal tale,
That salved your reputation. But be valiant, sir.
CORVINO. I fear no one, but him; that this his pleading
Should make him stand for a co-heir –
MOSCA. Co-halter.
Hang him: we will but use his tongue, his noise,
As we do Croaker's here.
CORVINO. Ay, what shall he do?
MOSCA. When we ha'done, you mean?
CORVINO. Yes.
MOSCA. Why, we'll think;
Sell him for mummia, he's half dust already.
(*To* VOLTORE) Do not you smile, to see this buffalo,
How he doth sport it with his head? [*Aside*] I should,
If all were well, and past. (*To* CORBACCIO) Sir, only you
Are he, that shall enjoy the crop of all,
And these know not for whom they toil.
CORBACCIO. Ay, peace.
MOSCA. (*to* CORVINO) But you shall eat it. [*Aside*] Much! (*then to* VOLTORE *again*) Worshipful sir,
Mercury sit upon your thundering tongue,
Or the French Hercules, and make your language
As conquering as his club, to beat along
(As with a tempest) flat, our adversaries:
But much more yours, sir.
VOLTORE. Here they come, ha'done.
MOSCA. I have another witness, if you need, sir,
I can produce.
VOLTORE. Who is it?
MOSCA. Sir, I have her.

---

7 *formal*: elaborate, circumstantial.

12 *Croaker*: Corbaccio.

14 *mummia*: medicinal preparation made from Egyptian mummies (or from dead bodies faked as mummies).

15 *buffalo*: referring to Corvino's supposed cuckold's horns, and his stupidity.

21 *Mercury*: god of eloquence and business; known for his tricks.

22 *French Hercules*: symbol of eloquence. The Gauls claimed descent from Hercules, who returned home through Gallia (France) after capturing Geryon's cattle.

SCENE V

[*Enter*] *four* AVOCATORI, BONARIO, CELIA, NOTARIO, COMMENDATORI [*and others*].

FIRST AVOCATORE. The like of this the Senate never heard of.

SECOND AVOCATORE. 'Twill come most strange to them, when we report it.

FOURTH AVOCATORE. The gentlewoman has been ever held
Of unreprovèd name.

THIRD AVOCATORE. So, the young man.

FOURTH AVOCATORE. The more unnatural part that of his father.

SECOND AVOCATORE. More of the husband.

FIRST AVOCATORE. I not know to give
His act a name, it is so monstrous!

FOURTH AVOCATORE. But the impostor, he is a thing created
T'exceed example!

[FIRST] AVOCATORE. And all after times!

SECOND AVOCATORE. I never heard a true voluptuary
Described, but him.

THIRD AVOCATORE. Appear yet those were cited?

NOTARIO. All, but the old magnifico, Volpone.

FIRST AVOCATORE. Why is not he here?

MOSCA. Please your fatherhoods,
Here is his advocate. Himself's so weak,
So feeble –

FOURTH AVOCATORE. What are you?

BONARIO. His parasite,
His knave, his pander: I beseech the court,
He may be forced to come, that your grave eyes
May bear strong witness of his strange impostures.

VOLTORE. Upon my faith and credit, with your virtues,
He is not able to endure the air.

SECOND AVOCATORE. Bring him, however.

THIRD AVOCATORE. We will see him.

FOURTH AVOCATORE. Fetch him.

---

9 *example*: precedent.
FIRST: see Textual Note, p. 433 below.

[*Exeunt* COMMENDATORI.]

VOLTORE. Your fatherhoods' fit pleasures be obeyed,
But sure, the sight will rather move your pities,
Than indignation. May it please the court,
In the meantime, he may be heard in me:
I know this place most void of prejudice,
And therefore crave it, since we have no reason
To fear our truth should hurt our cause.

THIRD AVOCATORE. Speak free.

VOLTORE. Then know, most honoured fathers, I must now
Discover, to your strangely abusèd ears,
The most prodigious, and most frontless piece
Of solid impudence, and treachery,
That ever vicious nature yet brought forth
To shame the state of Venice. This lewd woman
(That wants no artificial looks, or tears,
To help the visor she has now put on)
Hath long been known a close adulteress,
To that lascivious youth there; not suspected,
I say, but known; and taken, in the act;
With him; and by this man, the easy husband,
Pardoned: whose timeless bounty makes him, now,
Stand here, the most unhappy, innocent person,
That ever man's own goodness made accused.
For these, not knowing how to owe a gift
Of that dear grace, but with their shame; being placed
So'above all powers of their gratitude,
Began to hate the benefit: and in place
Of thanks, devise t'extirp the memory
Of such an act. Wherein, I pray your fatherhoods
To observe the malice, yea, the rage of creatures

---

30 *Discover*: make known.
31 *frontless*: shameless.
35 *artificial*: cunningly contrived.
37 *close*: secret; also, 'intimate'.
40 *easy*: lenient.
41 *timeless*: untimely.
44 *owe*: acknowledge.
45 *dear*: precious; also, 'loving'.
grace: mercy.
47 *benefit*: good deed.
48 *extirp*: root out.

Discovered in their evils; and what heart
Such take, even from their crimes. But that, anon,
Will more appear. This gentleman, the father,
Hearing of this foul fact, with many others,
Which daily struck at his too tender ears,
And grieved in nothing more, than that he could not
Preserve himself a parent (his son's ills
Growing to that strange flood) at last decreed
To disinherit him.

FIRST AVOCATORE. These be strange turns!

SECOND AVOCATORE. The young man's fame was ever fair, and honest.

VOLTORE. So much more full of danger is his vice,
That can beguile so, under shade of virtue.
But, as I said (my honoured sires) his father
Having this settled purpose (by what means
To him betrayed, we know not), and this day
Appointed for the deed; that parricide
(I cannot style him better), by confederacy
Preparing this his paramour to be there,
Entered Volpone's house (who was the man
Your fatherhoods must understand, designed
For the inheritance); there, sought his father:
But with what purpose sought he him, my lords?
(I tremble to pronounce it, that a son
Unto a father, and to such a father,
Should have so foul, felonious intent.)
It was, to murder him. When, being prevented
By his more happy absence, what then did he?
Not check his wicked thoughts; no, now new deeds
(Mischief doth ever end, where it begins):
An act of horror, fathers! He dragged forth
The agèd gentleman, that had there lain, bed-rid,
Three years, and more, out off his innocent couch,
Naked, upon the floor, there left him; wounded
His servant in the face; and with this strumpet,
The stale to his forged practice, who was glad

---

54 *fact*: crime.

67 *confederacy*: collusion.

79 *Mischief . . . begins*: wickedness is always true to its nature; but see Additional Note, p. 440 below.

85 *stale*: decoy; also, the lowest class of prostitute, in league with thieves and used by them as a decoy.
forged: contrived.

To be so active (I shall here desire
Your fatherhoods to note but my collections,
As most remarkable) thought, at once, to stop
His father's ends; discredit his free choice
In the old gentleman; redeem themselves
By laying infamy upon this man,
To whom, with blushing, they should owe their
lives.

FIRST AVOCATORE. What proofs have you of this?

BONARIO. Most honoured fathers,
I humbly crave, there be no credit given
To this man's mercenary tongue.

SECOND AVOCATORE. Forbear.

BONARIO. His soul moves in his fee.

THIRD AVOCATORE. Oh, sir.

BONARIO. This fellow,
For six sols more, would plead against his Maker.

FIRST AVOCATORE. You do forget yourself.

VOLTORE. Nay, nay, grave fathers,
Let him have scope: can any man imagine
That he will spare his accuser, that would not
Have spared his parent?

FIRST AVOCATORE. Well, produce your proofs.

CELIA. I would I could forget I were a creature.

VOLTORE. Signior Corbaccio.

FOURTH AVOCATORE. What is he?

VOLTORE. The father.

SECOND AVOCATORE. Has he had an oath?

NOTARIO. Yes.

CORBACCIO. What must I do now?

NOTARIO. Your testimony's craved.

CORBACCIO. Speak to the knave?
I'll ha'my mouth, first, stopped with earth; my
heart
Abhors his knowledge: I disclaim in him.

FIRST AVOCATORE. But for what cause?

CORBACCIO. The mere portent of nature:

---

87 *collections*: conclusions.
91 *this man*: i.e. Corvino.
97 *six sols*: or sous, small French coins, i.e. about threepence.
102 *creature*: created being; dependant (of Corvino, and therefore owing him loyalty); also, 'instrument'.
107 *his knowledge*: knowledge of him.
108 *The mere portent of nature*: nothing less than the omen of nature's destruction.

He is an utter stranger to my loins.
BONARIO. Have they made you to this!
CORBACCIO. I will not hear thee,
Monster of men, swine, goat, wolf, parricide,
Speak not, thou viper.
BONARIO. Sir, I will sit down,
And rather wish my innocence should suffer,
Than I resist the authority of a father.
VOLTORE. Signior Corvino.
SECOND AVOCATORE. This is strange!
FIRST AVOCATORE. Who's this?
NOTARIO. The husband.
FOURTH AVOCATORE. Is he sworn?
NOTARIO. He is.
THIRD AVOCATORE. Speak then.
CORVINO. This woman (please your fatherhoods) is a whore,
Of most hot exercise, more than a partridge,
Upon recòrd –
FIRST AVOCATORE. No more.
CORVINO. Neighs, like a jennet.
NOTARIO. Preserve the honour of the court.
CORVINO. I shall,
And modesty of your most reverend ears.
And yet, I hope that I may say, these eyes
Have seen her glued unto that piece of cedar;
That fine, well-timbered gallant; and that, here,
The letters may be read, thorough the horn,
That make the story perfect.
MOSCA. [*aside to* CORVINO] Excellent! sir.
CORVINO. There is no shame in this, now, is there?
MOSCA. None.

---

110 *made*: wrought.
111 *swine, goat, wolf*: symbols of self-indulgence, lechery, and cruelty respectively.
112 *viper*: symbol of filial ingratitude.
118 *hot exercise*: lecherous and habitual practice.
partridge: held to be the most lustful of creatures.
119 *Upon recòrd*: well-known and acknowledged.
jennet: small, mettlesome Spanish horse.
123 *cedar*: its qualities are strength, height, and straightness.
124 *well-timbered*: well-built.
here: holding his first and second fingers to his forehead in a V shape, the sign of the cuckold's horns.
125 *The letters . . . horn*: punning on the cuckold's horns, and the horn-book, a child's primer with the alphabet, the ten digits, and the Lord's prayer, covered by a piece of translucent horn.

CORVINO. Or if I said, I hoped that she were onward
To her damnation, if there be a Hell
Greater than whore, and woman; a good Catholic
May make the doubt.
THIRD AVOCATORE. His grief hath made him frantic.
FIRST AVOCATORE. Remove him, hence.
She [CELIA] *swoons.*
SECOND AVOCATORE. Look to the woman.
CORVINO. Rare!
Prettily feigned! again!
FOURTH AVOCATORE. Stand from about her.
FIRST AVOCATORE. Give her the air.
THIRD AVOCATORE. [*to* MOSCA] What can you say?
MOSCA. My wound
(May't please your wisdoms) speaks for me, received
In aid of my good patron, when he missed
His sought-for father, when that well-taught dame
Had her cue given her, to cry out a rape.
BONARIO. Oh, most laid impudence! Fathers –
THIRD AVOCATORE. Sir, be silent,
You had your hearing free, so must they theirs.
SECOND AVOCATORE. I do begin to doubt th'imposture here.
FOURTH AVOCATORE. This woman has too many moods.
VOLTORE. Grave fathers,
She is a creature of a most professed,
And prostituted lewdness.
CORVINO. Most impetuous!
Unsatisfied, grave fathers!
VOLTORE. May her feignings
Not take your wisdoms: but this day, she baited
A stranger, a grave knight, with her loose eyes,
And more lascivious kisses. This man saw 'em
Together, on the water, in a gondola.
MOSCA. Here is the lady herself, that saw 'em too,
Without; who, then, had in the open streets
Pursued them, but for saving her knight's honour.

---

130 *Catholic*: see Textual Note, p. 433 below.
139 *laid*: plotted, planned beforehand.
146 *take*: captivate.
but: only.
baited: enticed.
151 *Without*: outside.

FIRST AVOCATORE. Produce that lady.
[*Exit* MOSCA.]
SECOND AVOCATORE. Let her come.
FOURTH AVOCATORE. These things,
They strike, with wonder!
THIRD AVOCATORE. I am turned a stone!

SCENE VI

[*Enter*] MOSCA, LADY WOULD-BE.

MOSCA. Be resolute, madam.
LADY WOULD-BE. Ay, this same is she.
Out, thou chameleon harlot; now thine eyes
Vie tears with the hyena: dar'st thou look
Upon my wrongèd face? – I cry your pardons.
I fear, I have (forgettingly) transgressed
Against the dignity of the court –
SECOND AVOCATORE. No, madam.
LADY WOULD-BE. And been exorbitant –
SECOND AVOCATORE. You have not, lady.
FOURTH AVOCATORE. These proofs are strong.
LADY WOULD-BE. Surely, I had no purpose:
To scandalise your honours, or my sex's.
THIRD AVOCATORE. We do believe it.
LADY WOULD-BE. Surely, you may believe it.
SECOND AVOCATORE. Madam, we do.
LADY WOULD-BE. Indeed, you may; my breeding
Is not so coarse –
FOURTH AVOCATORE. We know it.
LADY WOULD-BE. To offend
With pertinacy –
THIRD AVOCATORE. Lady –
LADY WOULD-BE. Such a presence:
No, surely.
FIRST AVOCATORE. We well think it.

---

2 *chameleon*: symbol of fraud and cunning (from its ability to change its colour).

3 *hyena*: supposed to lure its victims by adopting a human voice, not by tears.

7 *been exorbitant*: gone beyond the bounds of (linguistic) propriety.
SECOND: see Textual Note, p. 433 below.

13 *pertinacy*: pertinacity; an erroneous form for 'impertinence'; also (ironically), 'what is relevant'.

LADY WOULD-BE. You may think it.
FIRST AVOCATORE. Let her o'ercome. [*To* BONARIO]
What witnesses have you,
To make good your report?
BONARIO. Our consciences.
CELIA. And Heaven, that never fails the innocent.
FOURTH AVOCATORE. These are no testimonies.
BONARIO. Not in your courts,
Where multitude, and clamour overcomes.
FIRST AVOCATORE. Nay, then you do wax insolent.

VOLPONE *is brought in, as impotent.*

VOLTORE. Here, here,
The testimony comes, that will convince,
And put to utter dumbness their bold tongues.
See here, grave fathers, here's the ravisher,
The rider on men's wives, the great impostor,
The grand voluptuary! do you not think,
These limbs should affect venery? or these eyes
Covet a concubine? pray you, mark these hands.
Are they not fit to stroke a lady's breasts?
Perhaps he doth dissemble?
BONARIO. So he does.
VOLTORE. Would you ha'him tortured?
BONARIO. I would have him proved.
VOLTORE. Best try him, then, with goads, or burning irons;
Put him to the strappado: I have heard
The rack hath cured the gout, faith, give it him,
And help him of a malady, be courteous.
I'll undertake, before these honoured fathers,
He shall have, yet, as many left diseases,
As she has known adulterers, or thou strumpets.
Oh, my most equal hearers, if these deeds,
Acts of this bold, and most exorbitant strain,

---

15 *o'ercome*: prevail (in having the last word).
20 *wax*: grow.
20 s.d. *impotent*: helpless, decrepit.
21 *convince*: prove conclusively; also, 'convict'.
26 *affect venery*: be fond of sexual pleasure.
30 *proved*: put to the test.
32 *strappado*: a form of Venetian torture in which the victim's hands were bound behind him, and he was raised and lowered by a rope attached to them.
37 *known*: in the biblical sense of 'had carnal knowledge of'.
38 *equal*: just.

May pass with sufferance, what one citizen
But owes the forfeit of his life, yea, fame,
To him that dares traduce him? which of you
Are safe, my honoured fathers? I would ask
(With leave of your grave fatherhoods) if their plot
Have any face, or colour like to truth?
Or if, unto the dullest nostril, here,
It smell not rank, and most abhorrèd slander?
I crave your care of this good gentleman,
Whose life is much endangered, by their fable;
And as for them, I will conclude with this,
That vicious persons, when they are hot, and fleshed
In impious acts, their constancy abounds:
Damned deeds are done with greatest confidence.

FIRST AVOCATORE. Take 'em to custody, and sever them.

[CELIA, BONARIO *are taken out.*]

SECOND AVOCATORE. 'Tis pity, two such prodigies should live.

FIRST AVOCATORE. Let the old gentleman be returned, with care:
I'm sorry, our credulity wronged him.

[VOLPONE *is carried out.*]

FOURTH AVOCATORE. These are two creatures!

THIRD AVOCATORE. I have an earthquake in me!

SECOND AVOCATORE. Their shame (even in their cradles) fled their faces.

FOURTH AVOCATORE [*to* VOLTORE] Yo'have done a worthy service to the state, sir,
In their discovery.

FIRST AVOCATORE. You shall hear, ere night,
What punishment the court decrees upon 'em.

VOLTORE. We thank your fatherhoods.

---

41 *fame*: reputation.
45 *face, or colour*: appearance or semblance.
47 *rank*: foul.
49 *fable*: falsehood; also, 'plot'.
51 *hot, and fleshed*: eager and inured – having 'tasted blood'.
52 *constancy*: fortitude; resolution; consistency (in their evil); persistence.
55 *prodigies*: monsters.
58 *creatures*: unspeakable wretches.
61 *their discovery*: revealing their true nature.

[*Exeunt* AVOCATORI,
NOTARIO, COMMENDATORI.]
How like you it?
MOSCA. Rare.
I'd ha'your tongue, sir, tipped with gold, for this;
I'd ha'you be the heir to the whole city;
The earth I'd have want men, ere you want living:
They're bound to erect your statue, in St Mark's.
Signior Corvino, I would have you go,
And show yourself, that you have conquered.
CORVINO. Yes.
MOSCA. It was much better, that you should profess
Yourself a cuckold, thus, than that the other
Should have been proved.
CORVINO. Nay, I considered that:
Now, it is her fault.
MOSCA. Then, it had been yours.
CORVINO. True; I do doubt this advocate, still.
MOSCA. I'faith,
You need not, I dare ease you of that care.
CORVINO. I trust thee, Mosca.
MOSCA. As your own soul, sir.
[*Exit* CORVINO.]
CORBACCIO. Mosca!
MOSCA. Now for your business, sir.
CORBACCIO. How? ha'you business?
MOSCA. Yes, yours, sir.
CORBACCIO. Oh, none else?
MOSCA. None else, not I.
CORBACCIO. Be careful then.
MOSCA. Rest you, with both your eyes, sir.
CORBACCIO. Dispatch it.
MOSCA. Instantly.
CORBACCIO. And look, that all
Whatever be put in, jewels, plate, moneys,
Household stuff, bedding, curtains.
MOSCA. Curtain-rings, sir;
Only, the advocate's fee must be deducted.
CORBACCIO. I'll pay him now: you'll be too prodigal.
MOSCA. Sir, I must tender it.
CORBACCIO. Two chequeens is well?

---

66 *want living*: lack the means of getting a living.
71 *other*: i.e. that Corvino was a bawd.
79 *Rest . . . eyes*: relax; perhaps also, 'keep your eyes shut'.

MOSCA. No, six, sir.
CORBACCIO. 'Tis too much.
MOSCA. He talked a great while,
You must consider that, sir.
CORBACCIO. Well, there's three –
MOSCA. I'll give it him.
CORBACCIO. Do so, and there's for thee.
[*Exit.*]
MOSCA. Bountiful bones! What horrid strange offence
Did he commit 'gainst nature, in his youth,
Worthy this age? [*To* VOLTORE] You see, sir, how I work
Unto your ends; take you no notice.
VOLTORE. No,
I'll leave you.
MOSCA. All, is yours –
[*Exit* VOLTORE.]
the devil, and all:
Good advocate. [*To* LADY WOULD-BE] Madam, I'll bring you home.
LADY WOULD-BE. No, I'll go see your patron.
MOSCA. That you shall not:
I'll tell you why. My purpose is, to urge
My patron to reform his will; and for
The zeal yo'have shown today, whereas before
You were but third, or fourth, you shall be now
Put in the first: which would appear as begged,
If you were present. Therefore –
LADY WOULD-BE. You shall sway me.
[*Exeunt.*]

---

92 *take you no notice*: do not acknowledge it (as Lady Would-be is near).
93 *the devil, and all*: the whole confounded lot (a phrase associated with the rapaciousness of lawyers).
97 *reform*: reshape, revise.

ACT V

SCENE I

[*Enter*] VOLPONE.

VOLPONE. Well, I am here; and all this brunt is past:
I ne'er was in dislike with my disguise,
Till this fled moment; here, 'twas good, in private,
But in your public – *Cavè*, whilst I breathe.
'Fore God, my left leg 'gan to have the cramp;
And I apprehended, straight, some power had struck me
With a dead palsy: well, I must be merry,
And shake it off. A many of these fears
Would put me into some villainous disease,
Should they come thick upon me: I'll prevent 'em.
Give me a bowl of lusty wine, to fright
This humour from my heart. (*He drinks*) Hum, hum, hum!
'Tis almost gone, already: I shall conquer.
Any device, now, of rare, ingenious knavery,
That would possess me with a violent laughter,
Would make me up again! (*Drinks again*) So, so, so, so.
This heat is life; 'tis blood, by this time: Mosca!

---

1 *brunt*: crisis.
4 *Cavè*: beware (Latin); watch out!
7 *dead palsy*: palsy causing complete immobility of the affected part.
16 *make me up*: restore me.
17 *This heat . . . time*: according to Renaissance physiology, wine quickly converted into blood, went to the heart and created 'vital heat', and made the drinker bold.

SCENE II

[*Enter*] MOSCA.

MOSCA. How now, sir? does the day look clear again?
Are we recovered? and wrought out of error,
Into our way? to see our path, before us?
Is our trade free, once more?
VOLPONE. Exquisite Mosca!
MOSCA. Was it not carried learnedly?
VOLPONE. And stoutly.
Good wits are greatest in extremities.
MOSCA. It were a folly, beyond thought, to trust
Any grand act unto a cowardly spirit:
You are not taken with it enough, methinks?
VOLPONE. Oh, more, than if I had enjoyed the wench:
The pleasure of all womankind's not like it.
MOSCA. Why, now you speak, sir. We must, here, be fixed;
Here, we must rest; this is our masterpiece:
We cannot think, to go beyond this.
VOLPONE. True,
Thou'st played thy prize, my precious Mosca.
MOSCA. Nay, sir,
To gull the court –
VOLPONE. And quite divert the torrent,
Upon the innocent.
MOSCA. Yes, and to make
So rare a music out of discords –
VOLPONE. Right.
That, yet, to me's the strangest! how th'hast borne it!
That these (being so divided 'mongst themselves)
Should not scent somewhat, or in me, or thee,
Or doubt their own side.
MOSCA. True, they will not see't.
Too much light blinds 'em, I think. Each of 'em

2–3 *wrought . . . before us*: Mosca sports with the biblical image of life as a pilgrimage.
5 *learnedly*: expertly.
stoutly: courageously.
15 *prize*: star part.
16 *gull*: dupe.
19 *borne*: managed.

Is so possessed, and stuffed with his own hopes,
That anything unto the contrary,
Never so true, or never so apparent,
Never so palpable, they will resist it –
VOLPONE. Like a temptation of the devil.
MOSCA. Right, sir.
Merchants may talk of trade, and your great signiors
Of land, that yields well; but if Italy
Have any glebe more fruitful than these fellows,
I am deceived. Did not your advocate rare?
VOLPONE. Oh ('My most honoured fathers, my grave fathers,
Under correction of your fatherhoods,
What face of truth is here? If these strange deeds
May pass, most honoured fathers') – I had much ado
To forbear laughing.
MOSCA. 'T seemed to me, you sweat, sir.
VOLPONE. In troth, I did a little.
MOSCA. But confess, sir,
Were you not daunted?
VOLPONE. In good faith, I was
A little in a mist; but not dejected:
Never, but still myself.
MOSCA. I think it, sir.
Now (so truth help me) I must needs say this, sir,
And out of conscience, for your advocate:
He's taken pains, in faith, sir, and deserved
(In my poor judgement, I speak it, under favour,
Not to contrary you, sir) very richly –
Well – to be cozened.
VOLPONE. Troth, and I think so too,
By that I heard him, in the latter end.
MOSCA. Oh, but before, sir; had you heard him, first,
Draw it to certain heads, then aggravate,

---

31 *glebe*: soil.
32 *Did . . . rare?*: didn't your advocate perform excellently?
40 *in a mist*: uncertain.
45 *under favour*: in all deference.
47 *cozened*: cheated.
50 *Draw it to certain heads*: organise his speech under particular topics.
aggravate: bring charges; or possibly, 'increase the seriousness of the offence' (supposedly committed by Bonario and Celia); or, 'exaggerate'.

Then use his vehement figures – I looked still,
When he would shift a shirt; and doing this
Out of pure love, no hope of gain –
VOLPONE. 'Tis right.
I cannot answer him, Mosca, as I would,
Not yet; but for thy sake, at thy entreaty,
I will begin, e'en now, to vex 'em all:
This very instant.
MOSCA. Good, sir.
VOLPONE. Call the dwarf,
And eunuch, forth.
MOSCA. Castrone, Nano.

[*Enter* CASTRONE, NANO.]

NANO. Here.
VOLPONE. Shall we have a jig, now?
MOSCA. What you please, sir.
VOLPONE. Go,
Straight give out, about the streets, you two,
That I am dead; do it with constancy,
Sadly, do you hear? Impute it to the grief
Of this late slander.

[*Exeunt* CASTRONE, NANO.]

MOSCA. What do you mean, sir?
VOLPONE. Oh,
I shall have, instantly, my vulture, crow,
Raven, come flying hither (on the news)
To peck for carrion, my she-wolf, and all,
Greedy, and full of expectation –
MOSCA. And then to have it ravished from their mouths?
VOLPONE. 'Tis true; I will ha'thee put on a gown,
And take upon thee, as thou wert mine heir;
Show 'em a will: open that chest, and reach
Forth one of those, that has the blanks. I'll straight
Put in thy name.
MOSCA. It will be rare, sir.

---

51 *vehement figures*: impassioned rhetoric; perhaps also a reference to the accompanying gestures.
I looked still: I kept waiting to see.
52 *shift*: change (Voltore's exertions made him perspire).
59 *jig*: comic interlude; also, 'trick'.
61 *with constancy*: resolutely.
62 *Sadly*: gravely, seriously.
72 *blanks*: blank spaces for the insertion of the heirs' names.

VOLPONE. Ay,
When they e'en gape, and find themselves deluded –
MOSCA. Yes.
VOLPONE. And thou use them scurvily. Dispatch,
Get on thy gown.
MOSCA. But what, sir, if they ask
After the body?
VOLPONE. Say, it was corrupted.
MOSCA. I'll say, it stunk, sir; and was fain t'have it
Coffined up instantly, and sent away.
VOLPONE. Anything, what thou wilt. Hold, here's my will.
Get thee a cap, a count-book, pen and ink,
Papers afore thee; sit, as thou wert taking
An inventory of parcels: I'll get up,
Behind the curtain, on a stool, and hearken;
Sometime, peep over; see, how they do look;
With what degrees, their blood doth leave their faces!
Oh, 'twill afford me a rare meal of laughter.
MOSCA. Your advocate will turn stark dull, upon it.
VOLPONE. It will take off his oratory's edge.
MOSCA. But your *clarissimo*, old round-back, he
Will crump you, like a hog-louse, with the touch.
VOLPONE. And what Corvino?
MOSCA. Oh, sir, look for him,
Tomorrow morning with a rope, and a dagger,
To visit all the streets; he must run mad.
My lady too, that came into the court,
To bear false witness for your worship –
VOLPONE. Yes,
And kissed me 'fore the fathers; when my face
Flowed all with oils.
MOSCA. And sweat, sir. Why, your gold
Is such another medicine, it dries up

---

78 *fain*: obliged.
81 *count-book*: account book.
83 *parcels*: items.
88 *dull*: dejected (Volpone's response plays on the meaning, 'not sharp, having lost its keenness').
90 *clarissimo*: Venetian grandee.
91 *crump*: curl up.
hog-louse: wood-louse.
93 *rope, and a dagger*: emblems of suicidal or homicidal despair.

All those offensive savours! It transforms
The most deformèd, and restores 'em lovely,
As 'twere the strange poetical girdle. Jove
Could not invent, t'himself, a shroud more subtle,
To pass Acrisius' guards. It is the thing
Makes all the world her grace, her youth, her beauty.
VOLPONE. I think, she loves me.
MOSCA. Who? the lady, sir?
She's jealous of you.
VOLPONE. Dost thou say so?
[*Knocking without.*]
MOSCA. Hark,
There's some already.
VOLPONE. Look.
MOSCA. It is the vulture:
He has the quickest scent.
VOLPONE. I'll to my place,
Thou, to thy posture. [*Hides himself.*]
MOSCA. I am set.
VOLPONE. But Mosca,
Play the artificer now, torture 'em, rarely.

SCENE III

[*Enter*] VOLTORE.

VOLTORE. How now, my Mosca?
MOSCA. [*writing*] Turkey carpets, nine –
VOLTORE. Taking an inventory? that is well.
MOSCA. Two suits of bedding, tissue –
VOLTORE. Where's the will?
Let me read that, the while.

---

102 *poetical girdle*: 'Cestus' (Jonson's marginal note), the girdle of Venus, which made the wearer desirable.
104 *Acrisius*: father of Danaë, whom he locked in a tower of brass. Jove transformed himself into a shower of gold and fell into Danaë's lap, thus eluding the guards.
107 *jealous of you*: zealous for your welfare; also, 'envious of your fortune'.
110 *posture*: role, pose.
111 *artificer*: skilful craftsman; also, 'trickster'.
3 *suits of bedding, tissue*: sets of bed-hangings of rich cloth, interwoven with gold and silver.

[*Enter Servants with* CORBACCIO *in a chair.*]

CORBACCIO. So, set me down:
And get you home.
[*Exeunt Servants.*]
VOLTORE. Is he come, now, to trouble us?
MOSCA. Of cloth of gold, two more –
CORBACCIO. Is it done, Mosca?
MOSCA. Of several velvets, eight –
VOLTORE. I like his care.
CORBACCIO. Dost thou not hear?

[*Enter* CORVINO.]

CORVINO. Ha? is the hour come, Mosca?
VOLPONE *peeps from behind a traverse.*
VOLPONE. [*aside*] Ay, now they muster.
CORVINO. What does the advocate here?
Or this Corbaccio?
CORBACCIO. What do these here?

[*Enter* LADY WOULD-BE.]

LADY WOULD-BE. Mosca?
Is his thread spun?
MOSCA. Eight chests of linen –
VOLPONE. [*aside*] Oh,
My fine Dame Would-be, too!
CORVINO. Mosca, the will,
That I may show it these, and rid 'em hence.
MOSCA. Six chests of diaper, four of damask – There.
[*Hands them the will.*]
CORBACCIO. Is that the will?
MOSCA. Down-beds, and bolsters –
VOLPONE. [*aside*] Rare!
Be busy still. Now they begin to flutter:
They never think of me. Look, see, see, see!
How their swift eyes run over the long deed,
Unto the name, and to the legacies,
What is bequeathed them, there –
MOSCA. Ten suits of hangings –

---

7 *several*: i.e. separate hangings.
8 s.d. *traverse*: curtain or screen; see Additional Note, p. 440 below.
11 *Is his thread spun*: in classical mythology, the thread of a man's life was spun, measured, and cut by the three Fates.
14 *diaper*: like damask, a costly cloth.

VOLPONE. [*aside*] Ay, i'their garters, Mosca. Now
their hopes
Are at the gasp.
VOLTORE. Mosca the heir!
CORBACCIO. What's that?
VOLPONE. [*aside*] My advocate is dumb; look to my
merchant,
He has heard of some strange storm, a ship is lost,
He faints: my lady will swoon. Old glazen-eyes,
He hath not reached his despair yet.
CORBACCIO. All these
Are out of hope, I am sure the man.
CORVINO. But, Mosca –
MOSCA. Two cabinets –
CORVINO. Is this in earnest?
MOSCA. One
Of ebony –
CORVINO. Or do you but delude me?
MOSCA. The other, mother of pearl – I am very busy.
Good faith, it is a fortune thrown upon me –
Item, one salt of agate – not my seeking.
LADY WOULD-BE. Do you hear, sir?
MOSCA. A perfumed box – pray you, forbear,
You see I am troubled – made of an onyx –
LADY WOULD-BE. How!
MOSCA. Tomorrow, or next day, I shall be at leisure,
To talk with you all.
CORVINO. Is this my large hope's issue?
LADY WOULD-BE. Sir, I must have a fairer answer.
MOSCA. Madam!
Marry, and shall: pray you, fairly quit my house.
Nay, raise no tempest with your looks; but hark
you:
Remember what your ladyship offered me,
To put you in, an heir; go to, think on't.
And what you said, e'en your best madams did
For maintenance, and why not you? Enough.

---

21 *i'their garters*: alluding to the proverb, 'He may go hang himself in his own garters.'
22 *gasp*: last gasp.
25 *glazen-eyes*: referring to Corbaccio's spectacles.
32 *salt*: salt-cellar.
38 *fairly*: respectfully, courteously; in a decent manner; also, 'quietly'.

Go home, and use the poor Sir Pol, your knight, well,
For fear I tell some riddles: go, be melancholic.
[*Exit* LADY WOULD-BE.]
VOLPONE. [*aside*] Oh, my fine devil!
CORVINO. Mosca, pray you a word.
MOSCA. Lord! will not you take your dispatch hence, yet?
Methinks (of all) you should have been th'example.
Why should you stay here? with what thought? what promise?
Hear you, do not you know, I know you an ass?
And that you would, most fain, have been a wittol,
If Fortune would have let you? that you are
A declared cuckold, on good terms? This pearl,
You'll say, was yours? Right: this diamond?
I'll not deny't, but thank you. Much here, else?
It may be so. Why, think that these good works
May help to hide your bad: I'll not betray you,
Although you be but extraordinary,
And have it only in title, it sufficeth.
Go home, be melancholic too, or mad.
[*Exit* CORVINO.]
VOLPONE. [*aside*] Rare, Mosca! how his villainy becomes him!
VOLTORE. Certain, he doth delude all these, for me.
CORBACCIO. Mosca, the heir?
VOLPONE. [*aside*] Oh, his four eyes have found it!
CORBACCIO. I am cozened, cheated, by a parasite slave;
Harlot, th'hast gulled me.
MOSCA. Yes, sir. Stop your mouth,
Or I shall draw the only tooth is left.
Are not you he, that filthy covetous wretch,
With the three legs, that here, in hope of prey,

---

51 *fain*: eagerly.
wittol: conniving cuckold.
53 *on good terms*: expressly and plainly.
57 *your*: see Textual Note, p. 433 below.
58 *extraordinary*: supernumerary.
65 *Harlot*: rascal, wretch.
67 *filthy*: disgusting, contemptible.
68 *three legs*: referring to Corbaccio's walking-stick; also, a comment on his extreme age: in the Sphinx's riddle, the old man walks with three legs.

Have, any time this three year, snuffed about,
With your most grovelling nose; and would have
hired
Me to the poisoning of my patron? Sir?
Are not you he, that have, today, in court,
Professed the disinheriting of your son?
Perjured yourself? Go home, and die, and stink;
If you but croak a syllable, all comes out:
Away and call your porters, go, go, stink.
[*Exit* CORBACCIO.]

VOLPONE. [*aside*] Excellent varlet!
VOLTORE. Now, my faithful Mosca,
I find thy constancy –
MOSCA. Sir?
VOLTORE. Sincere.
MOSCA. [*writing*] A table
Of porphyry – I mar'l, you'll be thus troublesome.
VOLTORE. Nay, leave off now, they are gone.
MOSCA. Why? who are you?
What? who did send for you? Oh, cry you mercy,
Reverend sir! Good faith, I am grieved for you,
That any chance of mine should thus defeat
Your (I must needs say) most deserving travails:
But I protest, sir, it was cast upon me,
And I could, almost, wish to be without it,
But that the will o'th'dead must be observed.
Marry, my joy is, that you need it not,
You have a gift, sir (thank your education),
Will never let you want, while there are men,
And malice, to breed causes. Would I had
But half the like, for all my fortune, sir.
If I have any suits (as I do hope,
Things being so easy, and direct, I shall not)
I will make bold with your obstreperous aid
(Conceive me) for your fee, sir. In meantime,
You, that have so much law, I know ha'the
conscience
Not to be covetous of what is mine.
Good sir, I thank you for my plate: 'twill help

79 *mar'l*: marvel.
81 *cry you mercy*: I beg your pardon.
91 *causes*: law suits.
94 *Things*: the points of the will.
95 *obstreperous*: clamorous, vociferous.
96 *(Conceive me) for your fee*: I'll pay your fee, you understand.

To set up a young man. Good faith, you look
As you were costive; best go home, and purge, sir.
[*Exit* VOLTORE.]

[VOLPONE *comes from behind the traverse.*]

VOLPONE. Bid him eat lettuce well: my witty mischief,
Let me embrace thee. Oh, that I could now
Transform thee to a Venus – Mosca, go,
Straight, take my habit of *clarissimo*,
And walk the streets; be seen, torment 'em more:
We must pursue, as well as plot. Who would
Have lost this feast?
MOSCA. I doubt it will lose them.
VOLPONE. Oh, my recovery shall recover all.
That I could now but think on some disguise,
To meet 'em in: and ask 'em questions.
How I would vex 'em still, at every turn!
MOSCA. Sir, I can fit you.
VOLPONE. Canst thou?
MOSCA. Yes, I know
One o'the *commendatori*, sir, so like you,
Him will I straight make drunk, and bring you his habit.
VOLPONE. A rare disguise, and answering thy brain!
O, I will be a sharp disease unto 'em.
MOSCA. Sir, you must look for curses –
VOLPONE. Till they burst;
The Fox fares ever best, when he is cursed.
[*Exeunt.*]

---

101 *costive*: constipated.
105 *habit of clarissimo*: the black gown of a Venetian gentleman.
113 *fit you*: satisfy your requirements, i.e. provide a costume; but also ironical: 'fix you'.
119 *The Fox . . . cursed*: proverbial; the fox is cursed when he escapes capture.

SCENE IV

[*Enter*] PEREGRINE [*disguised*], *three* MERCHANTS.

PEREGRINE. Am I enough disguised?

FIRST MERCHANT. I warrant you.

PEREGRINE. All my ambition is to fright him, only.

SECOND MERCHANT. If you could ship him away, 'twere excellent.

THIRD MERCHANT. To Zant, or to Aleppo?

PEREGRINE. Yes, and ha'his
Adventures put i'th'Book of Voyages,
And his gulled story registered, for truth?
Well, gentlemen, when I am in a while,
And that you think us warm in our discourse,
Know your approaches.

FIRST MERCHANT. Trust it to our care.

[*Exeunt* MERCHANTS.]

[*Enter* WOMAN.]

PEREGRINE. Save you, fair lady. Is Sir Pol within?

WOMAN. I do not know, sir.

PEREGRINE. Pray you, say unto him,
Here is a merchant, upon earnest business,
Desires to speak with him.

WOMAN. I will see, sir.

PEREGRINE. Pray you.

[*Exit* WOMAN.]

I see the family is all female, here.

[*Enter* WOMAN.]

WOMAN. He says, sir, he has weighty affairs of state,
That now require him whole; some other time
You may possess him.

---

1 *warrant*: assure.

4 *Zant*: Zante, one of the Greek islands.
Aleppo: in Syria.

5 *Book of Voyages*: i.e. one of the popular accounts of voyages, such as Hakluyt's *Principal Navigations*.

9 *Know your approaches*: make your approach obvious; or perhaps, 'make your entrance at that point'.

14 *family*: household (Peregrine implies that the house is a brothel).

17 *possess him*: acquaint him (with your business); or 'have his full attention'.

PEREGRINE. Pray you say again,
If those require him whole, these will exact him,
Whereof I bring him tidings.
[*Exit* WOMAN.]
What might be
His grave affair of state, now? how to make
Bolognian sausages, here, in Venice, sparing
One o'th'ingredients?

[*Enter* WOMAN.]

WOMAN. Sir, he says, he knows
By your word, 'tidings', that you are no statesman,
And therefore, wills you stay.
PEREGRINE. Sweet, pray you return him,
I have not read so many proclamations,
And studied them, for words, as he has done,
But – Here he deigns to come.

[*Enter* SIR POLITIC WOULD-BE.]

SIR POLITIC. Sir, I must crave
Your courteous pardon. There hath chanced (today)
Unkind disaster, 'twixt my lady, and me:
And I was penning my apology
To give her satisfaction, as you came, now.
PEREGRINE. Sir, I am grieved I bring you worse disaster;
The gentleman you met at th'port, today,
That told you, he was newly arrived –
SIR POLITIC. Ay, was
A fugitive punk?
PEREGRINE. No, sir, a spy, set on you:
And he has made relation to the Senate,
That you professed to him, to have a plot,
To sell the state of Venice to the Turk.
SIR POLITIC. O me!
PEREGRINE. For which, warrants are signed by this time,

---

18 *exact*: extract, force out.

23 *tidings*: 'intelligence' is the statesman's word (compare II.i.68).

24 *stay*: remain, not go away; but Peregrine interprets 'wait until he deigns to come'.

35 *punk*: prostitute.

To apprehend you, and to search your study,
For papers –

SIR POLITIC. Alas, sir. I have none, but notes,
Drawn out of play-books –

PEREGRINE. All the better, sir.

SIR POLITIC. And some essays. What shall I do?

PEREGRINE. Sir, best
Convey yourself into a sugar-chest,
Or, if you could lie round, a frail were rare:
And I could send you aboard.

SIR POLITIC. Sir, I but talked so,
For discourse sake, merely.

They knock without.

PEREGRINE. Hark, they are there.

SIR POLITIC. I am a wretch, a wretch.

PEREGRINE. What will you do, sir?
Ha'you ne'er a currant-butt to leap into?
They'll put you to the rack, you must be sudden.

SIR POLITIC. Sir, I have an engine –

THIRD MERCHANT. [*off stage*] (Sir Politic Would-be?

SECOND MERCHANT. [*off stage*] Where is he?)

SIR POLITIC. That I have thought upon, before time.

PEREGRINE. What is it?

SIR POLITIC. (I shall ne'er endure the torture.)
Marry, it is, sir, of a tortoise-shell,
Fitted for these extremities: pray you sir, help me.
Here I've a place, sir, to put back my legs
(Please you to lay it on, sir). With this cap,
And my black gloves, I'll lie, sir, like a tortoise,
Till they are gone.

PEREGRINE. And call you this an engine?

---

42 *play-books*: from which the pretentious gull drew his knowledge.
better: i.e. more incriminating, as plays were closely scrutinised by the authorities for seditious material.

43 *essays*: another source of undigested knowledge; see III.iv.90 n. and 91 n.

44 *sugar-chest*: a stock prop for comic escapes (compare Falstaff's experience in the laundry-basket in *The Merry Wives of Windsor*, III.iii and v); as also *frail*: a rush basket for conveying figs and raisins (45); and *currant-butt*: a cask for currants, or currant wine (49).

45 *round*: curled up.
rare: just the thing.

51 *engine*: contrivance.

55 *Fitted*: adapted. See Textual Note, p. 433 below.

SIR POLITIC. Mine own device – Good sir, bid my wife's women
To burn my papers.

They [the three MERCHANTS*] rush in.*

FIRST MERCHANT. Where's he hid?
THIRD MERCHANT. We must,
And will, sure, find him.
SECOND MERCHANT. Which is his study?
FIRST MERCHANT. What
Are you, sir?
PEREGRINE. I'm a merchant, that came here
To look upon this tortoise.
THIRD MERCHANT. How?
FIRST MERCHANT. St Mark!
What beast is this?
PEREGRINE. It is a fish.
SECOND MERCHANT. Come out, here.
PEREGRINE. Nay, you may strike him, sir, and tread upon him:
He'll bear a cart.
FIRST MERCHANT. What, to run over him?
PEREGRINE. Yes.
THIRD MERCHANT. Let's jump upon him.
SECOND MERCHANT. Can he not go?
PEREGRINE. He creeps, sir.
FIRST MERCHANT. [*goading him.*] Let's see him creep.
PEREGRINE. No, good sir, you will hurt him.
SECOND MERCHANT. (Heart) I'll see him creep; or prick his guts.
THIRD MERCHANT. Come out, here.
PEREGRINE. Pray you sir – [*Aside to* SIR POLITIC] (Creep a little.)
FIRST MERCHANT. Forth.
SECOND MERCHANT. Yet further.
PEREGRINE. Good sir – [*To* SIR POLITIC] (Creep.)
SECOND MERCHANT. We'll see his legs.
THIRD MERCHANT. Godso, he has garters!
FIRST MERCHANT. Ay, and gloves!

They pull off the shell and discover him.

---

60 *device*: contrivance (Sir Pol's meaning); emblem (Jonson's meaning): see Additional Note, p. 440 below.

68 *go*: walk.

SECOND MERCHANT. Is this
Your fearful tortoise?
PEREGRINE. Now, Sir Pol, we are even;
For your next project, I shall be prepared:
I am sorry for the funeral of your notes, sir.
FIRST MERCHANT. 'Twere a rare motion, to be seen in Fleet Street!
SECOND MERCHANT. Ay, i'the term.
FIRST MERCHANT. Or Smithfield, in the fair.
THIRD MERCHANT. Methinks 'tis but a melancholic sight!
PEREGRINE. Farewell, most politic tortoise.
[*Exeunt* PEREGRINE, MERCHANTS.]

[*Enter* WOMAN.]

SIR POLITIC. Where's my lady?
Knows she of this?
WOMAN. I know not, sir.
SIR POLITIC. Enquire.
[*Exit* WOMAN.]
Oh, I shall be the fable of all feasts;
The freight of the *gazetti*; ship-boys' tale;
And, which is worst, even talk for ordinaries.

[*Enter* WOMAN.]

WOMAN. My lady's come most melancholic home,
And says, sir, she will straight to sea, for physic.
SIR POLITIC. And I, to shun this place, and clime forever;
Creeping, with house, on back: and think it well,
To shrink my poor head, in my politic shell.
[*Exeunt.*]

---

77 *motion*: puppet show.
78 *i'the term*: law term, when lawyers and their clients were in residence in London.
Smithfield: site of Bartholomew Fair, held on 24 August and the two following days. Jonson's later play, *Bartholomew Fair*, features a puppet play.
82 *fable*: subject of common talk, 'by-word'.
83 *freight of the gazetti*: topic of the Venetian news-sheets (notoriously unreliable and gossipy).
86 *for physic*: as a cure.

SCENE V

[Enter] VOLPONE, MOSCA; *the first, in the habit of a commendatore; the other, of a clarissimo.*

VOLPONE. Am I then like him?
MOSCA. O sir, you are he:
No man can sever you.
VOLPONE. Good.
MOSCA. But what am I?
VOLPONE. 'Fore Heav'n, a brave *clarissimo*, thou becom'st it!
Pity, thou wert not born one.
MOSCA. If I hold
My made one, 'twill be well.
VOLPONE. I'll go, and see
What news, first, at the court. *[Exit.]*
MOSCA. Do so. My Fox
Is out on his hole, and ere he shall re-enter,
I'll make him languish, in his borrowed case,
Except he come to composition, with me:
Androgyno, Castrone, Nano!

[Enter ANDROGYNO, CASTRONE, NANO.*]*

ALL. Here.
MOSCA. Go, recreate yourselves abroad; go, sport:
[Exeunt ANDROGYNO, CASTRONE, NANO.*]*
So, now I have the keys, and am possessed.
Since he will needs be dead, afore his time,
I'll bury him, or gain by him. I am his heir:
And so will keep me, till he share at least.
To cozen him of all, were but a cheat
Well placed; no man would cònstrue it a sin;
Let his sport pay for't, this is called the Fox-trap.
[Exit.]

---

2 *sever you*: tell you apart.
4 *hold*: keep up; also, 'hold on to'.
6–7 *My Fox . . . hole*: alluding to the children's game, Fox-in-the-Hole.
18 *Fox-trap*: see Additional Note, p. 441 below.

SCENE VI

[*Enter*] CORBACCIO, CORVINO.

CORBACCIO. They say, the court is set.
CORVINO. We must maintain
Our first tale good, for both our reputations.
CORBACCIO. Why, mine's no tale: my son would, there, have killed me.
CORVINO. That's true, I had forgot: mine is, I am sure.
But for your will, sir.
CORBACCIO. Ay, I'll come upon him
For that, hereafter, now his patron's dead.

[*Enter* VOLPONE, *disguised*.]

VOLPONE. Signior Corvino! and Corbaccio! Sir,
Much joy unto you.
CORVINO. Of what?
VOLPONE. The sudden good,
Dropped down upon you –
CORBACCIO. Where?
VOLPONE. (And none knows how)
From old Volpone, sir.
CORBACCIO. Out, arrant knave.
VOLPONE. Let not your too much wealth, sir, make you furious.
CORBACCIO. Away, thou varlet.
VOLPONE. Why, sir?
CORBACCIO. Dost thou mock me?
VOLPONE. You mock the world, sir, did you not change wills?
CORBACCIO. Out, harlot.
VOLPONE. Oh! belike you are the man,
Signior Corvino? Faith, you carry it well;
You grow not mad withal: I love your spirit.
You are not over-leavened, with your fortune.
You should ha'some would swell, now, like a wine-vat,
With such an autumn – Did he gi'you all, sir?

---

5 *come upon*: make my claim upon.
12 *varlet*: rogue; but also, 'sergeant'.
13 *change*: exchange.
17 *over-leavened*: puffed up.

CORVINO. Avoid, you rascal.
VOLPONE. Troth, your wife has shown
Herself a very woman: but you are well,
You need not care, you have a good estate
To bear it out, sir, better by this chance.
Except Corbaccio have a share?
CORBACCIO. Hence, varlet.
VOLPONE. You will not be a'known, sir: why, 'tis wise.
Thus do all gamesters, at all games, dissemble.
No man will seem to win.
[*Exeunt* CORBACCIO, CORVINO.]
Here comes my vulture,
Heaving his beak up i'the air, and snuffing.

SCENE VII

[*Enter* VOLTORE.]

VOLTORE. Outstripped thus, by a parasite? a slave?
Would run on errands? and make legs, for crumbs?
Well, what I'll do –
VOLPONE. The court stays for your worship.
I e'en rejoice, sir, at your worship's happiness,
And that it fell into so learnèd hands,
That understand the fingering.
VOLTORE. What do you mean?
VOLPONE. I mean to be a suitor to your worship,
For the small tenement, out of reparations;
That, at the end of your long row of houses,
By the Piscaria: it was, in Volpone's time,
Your predecessor, ere he grew diseased,
A handsome, pretty, customed, bawdy-house,
As any was in Venice (none dispraised)
But fell with him; his body, and that house
Decayed, together.

---

20 *Avoid*: go away!
21 *very*: true.
25 *be a'known*: i.e. 'be acknown', acknowledge, confess to (your good fortune).
2 *make legs*: bow and scrape.
8 *out of reparations*: in disrepair.
10 *Piscaria*: fish market.
12 *customed*: well patronised.

VOLTORE. Come, sir, leave your prating.
VOLPONE. Why, if your worship give me but your hand,
That I may ha'the refusal, I have done.
'Tis a mere toy, to you, sir; candle-rents:
As your learned worship knows –
VOLTORE. What do I know?
VOLPONE. Marry, no end of your wealth, sir, God decrease it.
VOLTORE. Mistaking knave! what, mock'st thou my misfortune?
VOLPONE. His blessing on your heart, sir, would 'twere more.
[*Exit* VOLTORE.]
(Now to my first again; at the next corner.)

SCENE VIII

[*Enter*] CORBACCIO, CORVINO; MOSCA *passant*.

CORBACCIO. See, in our habit! see the impudent varlet!
CORVINO. That I could shoot mine eyes at him, like gun-stones.
VOLPONE. But is this true, sir, of the parasite?
CORBACCIO. Again, t'afflict us? monster!
VOLPONE. In good faith, sir,
I'm heartily grieved, a beard of your grave length
Should be so over-reached. I never brooked
That parasite's hair, methought his nose should cozen:
There still was somewhat, in his look, did promise
The bane of a *clarissimo*.
CORBACCIO. Knave –

---

16 *hand*: to seal the bargain.
18 *candle-rents*: rents from deteriorating property.
21 *Mistaking*: using the wrong word; see Additional Note, p. 441 below.
V.viii.s.d. *passant*: passing over the stage.
2 *gun-stones*: cannon balls.
6 *over-reached*: outsmarted.
brooked: could endure.
9 *bane*: ruin.

VOLPONE. Methinks,
Yet you, that are so traded i'the world,
A witty merchant, the fine bird, Corvino,
That have such moral emblems on your name,
Should not have sung your shame; and dropped your cheese:
To let the Fox laugh at your emptiness.
CORVINO. Sirrah, you think the privilege of the place,
And your red saucy cap, that seems (to me)
Nailed to your jolt-head, with those two chequeens,
Can warrant your abuses; come you, hither:
You shall perceive, sir, I dare beat you. Approach.
VOLPONE. No haste, sir, I do know your valour, well:
Since you durst publish what you are, sir.
CORVINO. Tarry,
I'd speak with you.
VOLPONE. Sir, sir, another time –
CORVINO. Nay, now.
VOLPONE. O God, sir! I were a wise man,
Would stand the fury of a distracted cuckold.

MOSCA *walks by 'em.*

CORBACCIO. What! come again?
VOLPONE. Upon 'em, Mosca; save me.
CORBACCIO. The air's infected, where he breathes.
CORVINO. Let's fly him.
[*Exeunt* CORBACCIO, CORVINO.]
VOLPONE. Excellent basilisk! turn upon the vulture.

---

10 *traded*: experienced.

12 *emblems*: symbolic engravings with verse or prose explanations; the following lines make it clear that Volpone is referring to Aesop's fable of the crow tricked by the fox's flattery into dropping his piece of cheese.

15 *privilege of the place*: immunity (from being given a beating) conferred by the precincts of the court; see Additional Note, p. 441 below.

17 *jolt-head*: blockhead.
chequeens: coin-like gilt buttons.

20 *I do know your valour, well*: i.e. from the beating received in II.iii, as well as the insolent reason given in the following line.

27 *basilisk*: legendary reptile, able to kill by its glance.

SCENE IX

[*Enter*] VOLTORE.

VOLTORE. Well, flesh-fly, it is summer with you, now;
Your winter will come on.
MOSCA. Good advocate,
Pray thee, not rail, nor threaten out of place, thus;
Thou'lt make a solecism (as madam says).
Get you a biggen more: your brain breaks loose.
[*Exit.*]
VOLTORE. Well, sir.
VOLPONE. Would you ha'me beat the insolent slave?
Throw dirt, upon his first good clothes?
VOLTORE. This same
Is, doubtless, some familiar!
VOLPONE. Sir, the court,
In troth, stays for you. I am mad, a mule,
That never read Justinian, should get up,
And ride an advocate. Had you no quirk
To avoid gullage, sir, by such a creature?
I hope you do but jest; he has not done't:
This's but confederacy, to blind the rest.
You are the heir?
VOLTORE. A strange, officious,
Troublesome knave! thou dost torment me.
VOLPONE. I know –
It cannot be, sir, that you should be cozened;
'Tis not within the wit of man, to do it:
You are so wise, so prudent, and 'tis fit,
That wealth, and wisdom, still, should go together.
[*Exeunt.*]

---

1 *flesh-fly*: blow-fly, a play on Mosca's name.
5 *biggen more*: another (or perhaps, a larger) lawyer's cap.
8 *familiar*: attendant evil spirit.
10 *Justinian*: the *Corpus Juris Civilis*, Roman code of law compiled under the direction of the Emperor Justinian I.
11 *quirk*: trick, shift.

SCENE X

[*Enter*] *Four* AVOCATORI, NOTARIO, COMMENDATORI, BONARIO, CELIA, CORBACCIO, CORVINO.

FIRST AVOCATORE. Are all the parties here?
NOTARIO. All, but the advocate.
SECOND AVOCATORE. And here he comes.

[*Enter* VOLTORE, VOLPONE.]

[FIRST] AVOCATORE. Then bring 'em forth to sentence.
VOLTORE. O my most honoured fathers, let your mercy
Once win upon your justice, to forgive –
I am distracted –
VOLPONE. [*aside*] (What will he do now?)
VOLTORE. Oh,
I know not which t'address myself to, first,
Whether your fatherhoods, or these innocents –
CORVINO. [*aside*] (Will he betray himself?)
VOLTORE. Whom, equally,
I have abused, out of most covetous ends –
CORVINO. [*to* CORBACCIO] (The man is mad!
CORBACCIO. [*to* CORVINO] What's that?
CORVINO. [*to* CORBACCIO] He is possessed.)
VOLTORE. For which, now struck in conscience, here I prostrate
Myself, at your offended feet, for pardon.
FIRST, SECOND AVOCATORI. Arise.
CELIA. O Heav'n, how just thou art!
VOLPONE. [*aside*] I'm caught
I'mine own noose –
CORVINO. [*to* CORBACCIO] Be constant, sir, nought now
Can help, but impudence.
FIRST AVOCATORE. Speak forward.
COMMENDATORE. Silence.
VOLTORE. It is not passion in me, reverend fathers,

---

2 FIRST: see Textual Note, p. 433 below.
4 *win*: prevail.
5 VOLTORE: see Textual Note, p. 433 below.
10 *possessed*: i.e. by the devil.
16 *passion*: overpowering emotion.

But only conscience, conscience, my good sires,
That makes me, now, tell truth. That parasite,
That knave hath been the instrument of all.
[SECOND] AVOCATORE. Where is that knave? Fetch him.
VOLPONE. I go. [*Exit.*]
CORVINO. Grave fathers,
This man's distracted; he confessed it, now:
For, hoping to be old Volpone's heir,
Who now is dead –
THIRD AVOCATORE. How?
SECOND AVOCATORE. Is Volpone dead?
CORVINO. Dead since, grave fathers –
BONARIO. Oh, sure vengeance!
FIRST AVOCATORE. Stay,
Then he was no deceiver?
VOLTORE. Oh no, none:
The parasite, grave fathers.
CORVINO. He does speak
Out of mere envy, 'cause the servant's made
The thing he gaped for; please your fatherhoods,
This is the truth: though I'll not justify
The other, but he may be some-deal faulty.
VOLTORE. Ay, to your hopes, as well as mine, Corvino:
But I'll use modesty. Pleaseth your wisdoms
To view these certain notes, and but confer them;
As I hope favour, they shall speak clear truth.
CORVINO. The devil has entered him!
BONARIO. Or bides in you.
FOURTH AVOCATORE. We have done ill, by a public officer
To send for him, if he be heir.
SECOND AVOCATORE. For whom?
FOURTH AVOCATORE. Him, that they call the parasite.
THIRD AVOCATORE. 'Tis true;
He is a man of great estate, now left.
FOURTH AVOCATORE. Go you, and learn his name; and say, the court

---

20 SECOND: see Textual Note, p. 433 below.
30 *some-deal*: in some part.
32 *modesty*: moderation.
33 *certain*: few; particular; also, 'reliable'.
confer: put the sense together, construe.

Entreats his presence, here; but to the clearing
Of some few doubts.

[*Exit* NOTARIO.]

SECOND AVOCATORE. This same's a labyrinth!
FIRST AVOCATORE. Stand you unto your first report?
CORVINO. My state,
My life, my fame –
BONARIO. (Where is't?)
CORVINO. Are at the stake.
FIRST AVOCATORE. Is yours so too?
CORBACCIO. The advocate's a knave:
And has a forkèd tongue –
SECOND AVOCATORE. (Speak to the point.)
CORBACCIO. So is the parasite, too.
FIRST AVOCATORE. This is confusion.
VOLTORE. I do beseech your fatherhoods, read but those.
CORVINO. And credit nothing the false spirit hath writ:
It cannot be, but he is possessed, grave fathers.

SCENE XI

[*Enter*] VOLPONE.

VOLPONE. To make a snare, for mine own neck! and run
My head into it, wilfully! with laughter!
When I had newly 'scaped, was free, and clear!
Out of mere wantonness! Oh, the dull devil
Was in this brain of mine, when I devised it;
And Mosca gave it second: he must now
Help to sear up this vein, or we bleed dead.

[*Enter*] NANO, ANDROGYNO, CASTRONE.

How now! who let you loose? whither go you, now?

---

43 *state*: estate, standing.
46 *forkèd*: equivocal.
48 *those*: i.e. the notes he handed them at 33.
4 *wantonness*: capricious playfulness; insolent triumph.
dull devil: devil of stupidity (Creaser).
6 *second*: support.
7 *sear up*: cauterise.

What? to buy gingerbread? or to drown kitlings?
NANO. Sir, Master Mosca called us out of doors,
And bid us all go play, and took the keys.
ANDROGYNO. Yes.
VOLPONE. Did Master Mosca take the keys? why, so!
I am farther in. These are my fine conceits!
I must be merry, with a mischief to me!
What a vile wretch was I, that could not bear
My fortune soberly? I must ha'my crotchets!
And my conundrums! Well, go you, and seek him:
His meaning may be truer, than my fear.
Bid him, he straight come to me, to the court;
Thither will I, and, if't be possible,
Unscrew my advocate, upon new hopes:
When I provoked him, then I lost myself.
[*Exeunt.*]

SCENE XII

[*The Scrutineo*]

[*Four* AVOCATORI, NOTARIO, VOLTORE, BONARIO, CELIA, CORBACCIO, CORVINO, COMMENDATORI.]

FIRST AVOCATORE. These things can ne'er be reconciled. He, here,
Professeth, that the gentleman was wronged;
And that the gentlewoman was brought thither,
Forced by her husband: and there left.
VOLTORE. Most true.
CELIA. How ready is Heaven to those that pray!
FIRST AVOCATORE. But that
Volpone would have ravished her, he holds
Utterly false; knowing his impotence.
CORVINO. Grave fathers, he is possessed; again I say,

---

9 *kitlings*: kittens.
13 *in*: involved, entangled.
conceits: ideas, notions.
14 *with a mischief to me!*: confound me!
16 *crotchets*: perverse whims.
17 *conundrums*: caprices.
21 *Unscrew*: 'wind down'.
upon: on promise of.
2 *gentleman*: i.e. Bonario.

Possessed: nay, if there be possession,
And obsession, he has both.
THIRD AVOCATORE. Here comes our officer.

[*Enter* VOLPONE.]

VOLPONE. The parasite will straight be here, grave fathers.
FOURTH AVOCATORE. You might invent some other name, sir varlet.
THIRD AVOCATORE. Did not the notary meet him?
VOLPONE. Not that I know.
FOURTH AVOCATORE. His coming will clear all
SECOND AVOCATORE. Yet it is misty.
VOLTORE. May't please your fatherhoods –

VOLPONE *whispers the advocate.*

VOLPONE. Sir, the parasite
Willed me to tell you, that his master lives;
That you are still the man; your hopes the same;
And this was only a jest –
VOLTORE. How?
VOLPONE. Sir, to try
If you were firm, and how you stood affected.
VOLTORE. Art sure he lives?
VOLPONE. Do I live, sir?
VOLTORE. O me!
I was too violent.
VOLPONE. Sir, you may redeem it,
They said, you were possessed; fall down, and seem so:
I'll help to make it good.

VOLTORE *falls.*

God bless the man!
(Stop your wind hard, and swell.) See, see, see, see!
He vomits crooked pins! his eyes are set,

---

9 *possession*: in which the demon entered the body.
10 *obsession*: in which the demon worked on the victim from outside him.
12 *invent*: find.
14 *misty*: confused.
19 *affected*: disposed.
20 *Do I live*: 'as true as I'm alive'; but also, unknown to Voltore, literally the truth.
21 *violent*: vehement.
24–31 Such details can be found in contemporary accounts of false exorcisms.

Like a dead hare's, hung in a poulter's shop!
His mouth's running away! do you see, signior?
Now, 'tis in his belly.
CORVINO. (Ay, the devil!)
VOLPONE. Now, in his throat.
CORVINO. (Ay, I perceive it plain.)
VOLPONE. 'Twill out, 'twill out; stand clear. See, where it flies!
In shape of a blue toad, with a bat's wings!
Do not you see it, sir?
CORBACCIO. What? I think I do.
CORVINO. 'Tis too manifest.
VOLPONE. Look! he comes t'himself!
VOLTORE. Where am I?
VOLPONE. Take good heart, the worst is past, sir.
You are dispossessed.
FIRST AVOCATORE. What accident is this?
[SECOND] AVOCATORE. Sudden, and full of wonder!
THIRD AVOCATORE. If he were
Possessed, as it appears, all this is nothing.
CORVINO. He has been, often, subject to these fits.
FIRST AVOCATORE. Show him that writing. Do you know it, sir?
VOLPONE. [*aside to* VOLTORE] Deny it, sir, forswear it, know it not.
VOLTORE. Yes, I do know it well, it is my hand:
But all, that it contains, is false.
BONARIO. O practice!
SECOND AVOCATORE. What maze is this!
FIRST AVOCATORE. Is he not guilty, then,
Whom you, there, name the parasite?
VOLTORE. Grave fathers,
No more than his good patron, old Volpone.
FOURTH AVOCATORE. Why, he is dead?
VOLTORE. Oh no, my honoured fathers.
He lives –
FIRST AVOCATORE. How! lives?
VOLTORE. Lives.

---

26 *poulter*: poulterer.
27 *running away*: contorting.
35 *accident*: unforeseen event.
36 SECOND: see Textual Note, p. 433 below.
37 *this*: i.e. Voltore's notes.
42 *practice*: a plot.

SECOND AVOCATORE. This is subtler, yet!
THIRD AVOCATORE. You said, he was dead?
VOLTORE. Never.
THIRD AVOCATORE. [*to* CORVINO] You said so?
CORVINO. I heard so.
FOURTH AVOCATORE. Here comes the gentleman, make him way.

[*Enter* MOSCA.]

THIRD AVOCATORE. A stool.
FOURTH AVOCATORE. A proper man! and were Volpone dead,
A fit match for my daughter.
THIRD AVOCATORE. Give him way.
VOLPONE. [*aside to* MOSCA] Mosca, I was a'most lost, the advocate
Had betrayed all; but, now, it is recovered:
All's o'the hinge again – say I am living.
MOSCA. What busy knave is this! Most reverend fathers,
I sooner had attended your grave pleasures,
But that my order, for the funeral
Of my dear patron did require me –
VOLPONE. [*aside*] (Mosca!)
MOSCA. Whom I intend to bury, like a gentleman.
VOLPONE. [*aside*] Ay, quick, and cozen me of all.
SECOND AVOCATORE. Still stranger!
More intricate!
FIRST AVOCATORE. And come about again!
FOURTH AVOCATORE. [*aside*] It is a match, my daughter is bestowed.
MOSCA. [*aside to* VOLPONE] (Will you gi'me half?
VOLPONE. [*aside to* MOSCA] First, I'll be hanged.
MOSCA. [*aside to* VOLPONE] I know
Your voice is good, cry not so loud.)
FIRST AVOCATORE. Demand
The advocate. Sir, did not you affirm
Volpone was alive?

---

47 *subtler*: more intricate, complicated.
50 *proper*: handsome.
54 *o'the hinge*: running smoothly.
55 *busy*: troublesome.
57 *order*: arrangements.
60 *quick*: alive.
61 *come about*: reversed, veered round.

VOLPONE. Yes, and he is;
This gent'man told me so. [*Aside to* MOSCA] (Thou shalt have half.)
MOSCA. Whose drunkard is this same? speak some, that know him:
I never saw his face. [*Aside to* VOLPONE] (I cannot now
Afford it you so cheap.
VOLPONE. [*aside to* MOSCA] No?)
FIRST AVOCATORE. [*to* VOLTORE] What say you?
VOLTORE. The officer told me.
VOLPONE. I did, grave fathers,
And will maintain he lives, with mine own life.
And that this creature told me. [*Aside*] (I was born,
With all good stars my enemies.)
MOSCA. Most grave fathers,
If such an insolence, as this, must pass
Upon me, I am silent: 'twas not this
For which you sent, I hope.
SECOND AVOCATORE. Take him away.
VOLPONE. [*aside*] (Mosca!)
THIRD AVOCATORE. Let him be whipped.
VOLPONE. [*aside to* MOSCA] (Wilt thou betray me? Cozen me?)
THIRD AVOCATORE. And taught to bear himself
Toward a person of his rank.
FOURTH AVOCATORE. Away.
[VOLPONE *is seized.*]
MOSCA. I humbly thank your fatherhoods.
VOLPONE. [*aside*] Soft, soft: whipped?
And lose all that I have? if I confess,
It cannot be much more.
FOURTH AVOCATORE. [*to* MOSCA] Sir, are you married?
VOLPONE. [*aside*] They'll be allied, anon; I must be resolute:
The Fox shall, here, uncase.
He puts off his disguise.
MOSCA. (Patron!)

---

74 *good*: propitious, fortunate.
75 *pass*: pass judgement.
81 *Soft*: wait.
84 *allied*: related (by marriage).
85 *uncase*: remove his disguise.

VOLPONE. Nay, now
My ruins shall not come alone; your match
I'll hinder sure: my substance shall not glue you,
Nor screw you, into a family.
MOSCA. (Why, patron!)
VOLPONE. I am Volpone, and this [*indicating* MOSCA] is my knave;
This, [VOLTORE] his own knave; this, [CORBACCIO] avarice's fool;
This, [CORVINO] a chimaera of wittol, fool, and knave;
And, reverend fathers, since we all can hope
Nought, but a sentence, let's not now despair it.
You hear me brief.
CORVINO. May it please your fatherhoods –
COMMENDATORE. Silence.
FIRST AVOCATORE. The knot is now undone, by miracle!
SECOND AVOCATORE. Nothing can be more clear.
THIRD AVOCATORE. Or can more prove
These innocent.
FIRST AVOCATORE. Give 'em their liberty.
BONARIO. Heaven could not, long, let such gross crimes be hid.
SECOND AVOCATORE. If this be held the highway to get riches,
May I be poor.
THIRD AVOCATORE. This's not the gain, but torment.
FIRST AVOCATORE. These possess wealth, as sick men possess fevers,
Which trulier may be said to possess them.
SECOND AVOCATORE. Disrobe that parasite.
CORVINO, MOSCA. Most honoured fathers.
FIRST AVOCATORE. Can you plead aught to stay the course of justice?
If you can, speak.
CORVINO, VOLTORE. We beg favour.
CELIA. And mercy.
FIRST AVOCATORE. You hurt your innocence, suing for the guilty.
Stand forth; and first, the parasite. You appear

---

91 *chimaera*: mythical beast, composed of three different animals, having the head of a lion, body of a goat, and tail of a dragon. *wittol*: conniving cuckold.

95 *knot*: tangle (of a mystery); also, the complication of a plot.

T'have been the chiefest minister, if not plotter,
In all these lewd impostures; and now, lastly,
Have, with your impudence, abused the court,
And habit of a gentleman of Venice,
Being a fellow of no birth, or blood:
For which, our sentence is, first thou be whipped;
Then live perpetual prisoner in our galleys.
VOLPONE. I thank you, for him.
MOSCA. Bane to thy wolfish nature.
FIRST AVOCATORE. Deliver him to the *saffi*.
[MOSCA *is taken aside.*]
Thou, Volpone,
By blood, and rank a gentleman, canst not fall
Under like censure; but our judgement on thee
Is, that thy substance all be straight confiscate
To the hospital of the *Incurabili*:
And, since the most was gotten by imposture,
By feigning lame, gout, palsy, and such diseases,
Thou art to lie in prison, cramped with irons,
Till thou be'st sick, and lame indeed. Remove him.
VOLPONE. This is called mortifying of a Fox.
[VOLPONE *is taken aside.*]
FIRST AVOCATORE. Thou, Voltore, to take away the scandal
Thou hast given all worthy men of thy profession,
Art banished from their fellowship, and our state.
Corbaccio, – bring him near. We here possess
Thy son, of all thy state; and confine thee
To the monastery of *San Spirito*:
Where, since thou knew'st not how to live well here,
Thou shalt be learned to die well.
CORBACCIO. Ha! what said he?
COMMENDATORE. You shall know anon, sir.
[FIRST] AVOCATORE. Thou, Corvino, shalt
Be straight embarked from thine own house, and rowed

---

109 *lewd*: base.
118 *censure*: sentence.
120 *hospital of the Incurabili*: for beggars and prostitutes. Dependent on private benevolence, it also provided dowries for orphans to keep them from prostitution.
125 *mortifying*: see Additional Note, p. 441 below.
133 *learned*: taught.
134 FIRST: see Textual Note, p. 433 below.

Round about Venice, through the *Grand Canale*,
Wearing a cap with fair, long ass's ears,
Instead of horns: and so to mount (a paper
Pinned on thy breast) to the *berlino* –

CORVINO. Yes,
And have mine eyes beat out with stinking fish,
Bruised fruit, and rotten eggs – 'Tis well. I'm glad,
I shall not see my shame, yet.

FIRST AVOCATORE. And to expiate
Thy wrongs done to thy wife, thou art to send her
Home, to her father, with her dowry trebled:
And these are all your judgements.

ALL. (Honoured fathers.)

FIRST AVOCATORE. Which may not be revoked. Now you begin,
When crimes are done, and past, and to be punished,
To think what your crimes are: away with them.
Let all, that see these vices thus rewarded,
Take heart, and love to study 'em. Mischiefs feed
Like beasts, till they be fat, and then they bleed.

VOLPONE [*comes forward*].

VOLPONE. The seasoning of a play is the applause.
Now, though the Fox be punished by the laws,
He, yet, doth hope there is no suffering due
For any fact, which he hath done 'gainst you;
If there be, censure him: here he, doubtful, stands.
If not, fare jovially, and clap your hands.

THE END

---

136 *Grand Canale*: the Italian form.
137 *cap . . . ears*: i.e. to proclaim his folly.
139 *berlino*: pillory.
155 *fact*: crime.
156 *doubtful*: apprehensive.
157 *fare jovially*: behave cheerfully.

This comedy was first
acted in the year
1605
by the King's Majesty's
Servants.
The principal comedians were

Richard Burbage	John Heminges
Henry Condell	John Lowin
William Sly	Alexander Cook

With the allowance of the Master of the Revels.

Endnote: *This comedy . . . Revels*: see Textual Note, p. 433 below.

EPICOENE,

OR

The ſilent VVoman.

A Comœdie.

Acted in the yeere 1609. By
the Children of her Maieſties
REVELLS.

The Author B. I.

HORAT.

Vt ſis tu ſimilis Cæli, Byrrhiq́; latronum,
Non ego ſim Capri, neq́; Sulci. Cur metuas me?

LONDON,
Printed by VVILLIAM STANSBY.

M. DC. XVI.

Title-page from the 1616 folio, reproduced by permission of the British Library

Motto
'Although you may be like Caelius and Birrius, the robbers, I am not like Caprius or Sulcius [who attack all and sundry publicly]. Why should you fear me?' (Horace, *Satires*, I.iv.69–70)

INTRODUCTORY NOTE

Sources

The central plot device of tricking an old man into marrying a youth disguised as a girl goes back to Plautus's *Casina*, and has an analogue in Machiavelli's *Clizia*; but Jonson's immediate dramatic source is Aretino's comedy, *Il Marescalco* (*The Stablemaster*). Both Aretino's and Jonson's victims are unsuited to marriage – the stable-master is a homosexual, and Morose a confirmed misanthrope – and both suffer indignities, including the humiliation of declaring themselves impotent, to escape from their 'marriages'. The main and pervasive source of *Epicoene*, however, is Libanius of Antioch's sixth declamation, *The Loquacious Woman*, on which Jonson had drawn previously in *Volpone*. From the Latin translation which accompanied the 1606 Paris edition of Libanius's works comes Morose's name; and Libanius's speaker and his account of his married life provide Morose's abnormal hatred of noise and some of the details of his eccentricity: his dislike of noisy trades and vendors (I.i.167 ff.), the commotion of the law courts (IV.vii.16 ff.), the use of forms of address (V.iii.29 ff.), and his account of his upbringing (V.iii.53 ff.), as well as the torments he endures on his wedding day. Morose's intention to disinherit his nephew appears to have been suggested by Libanius's *The Peevish Father*; in this declamation another speaker, also called Morosus in the Latin translation, disinherits his son for laughing at him.[1]

Ovid's *Art of Love* is used wittily and ironically by Truewit to point the play's concerns with appearance and self-presentation: the praise of artifice in beauty (I.i.115 ff.) comes from book III; the advice on disguising physical defects (IV.i.40 ff.) from books II and III; the skills with which to win women (IV.i.65 ff.) from books I and II. Truewit's admiration of proportion in IV.i.57 ff. (from book III) draws attention to the lack of it in the women of the play; whilst in IV.iii.34 ff., the Collegiate ladies justify their promiscuity with arguments from the same book. Juvenal's anti-feminist Satire VI on the miseries of marriage is brilliantly adapted by Truewit in II.i, and many of its lessons are illustrated in the play. Ironically, Morose, who does not benefit from Truewit's attempted dis-suasions, is the most Juvenalian figure in the play in temper

---

1 See R. V. Holdsworth's edition of *Epicoene*, pp. xxiii ff.

and attitudes. The scholarly pretensions of the Collegiates, like those of Lady Would-be in *Volpone*, derive in part from the learned wife of Satire VI. Other debts indicate the range of material Jonson blended into his plays: Clerimont's song of I.i.103 ff. is one of several seventeenth-century versions of 'Semper munditias, semper, Basilissa, decores', actually from the *Anthologia Latina* but in the late sixteenth century sometimes appended to the works of Virgil and Petronius; the twelve impediments to marriage in V.iii are taken from St Thomas Aquinas's *Summa Theologiae*; and Truewit's plot to make the Collegiates fall in love with Dauphine may derive from an anecdote in book II of Castiglione's *The Courtier* (translated by Sir Thomas Hoby in 1561) in which ladies are made to fall in love with a gentleman from hearing another's good report of him.[2]

Although there are some verbal echoes of Plautus's plays, Jonson's debt to classical comedy is more general than specific. Intrigues in which the younger generation outwits the older with the help of one servant or more had long been absorbed into English comedy, along with comic professional types – these made funnier in *Epicoene* V.iii by the lawyer and divine being bogus. The Collegiates' manner is close to that of the formidable Plautine wife, and their way of life analogous to that of the women in Aristophanes' *Ecclesiazusae*. Here, and elsewhere in the play, Jonson develops character types he had used before: 'learned' women in the comical satires and *Volpone*; clever young men who have their fun at the expense of fools in *Every Man in his Humour*; affected fops in that play and *Cynthia's Revels*; the bullying wife and hen-pecked husband in *Poetaster*. Contemporary drama furnishes the near-encounter of Daw and La Foole arranged by Truewit in IV.v from the duel between Viola and Sir Andrew Aguecheek engineered by Sir Toby and his accomplices in III.ii and III.iv of *Twelfth Night*; whilst with his effeminate men and masculine women, so fulminated against in the contemporary pulpit and Puritan writings, Jonson develops the theme of the reversal of sexual roles found in comedies which satirised homosexuality in high places, using the device of a man disguised as a woman – as in Thomas

---

2 W. David Kay, 'Jonson's urbane gallants: humanistic contexts for *Epicoene*', *Huntington Library Quarterly*, 39 (1975–6), p. 261.

Arthus's *L'Isle des Hermaphrodites* (1605), which satirised the court of Henri III (referred to in IV.vi.33–4), and influenced John Day's satire on the court of James I, *The Isle of Gulls* (1606), performed as *Epicoene* by the Children of Blackfriars, the same company that, under its later name, acted Jonson's play. It is, however, the contemporary acting convention that boys should play women's parts that gives rise to Jonson's neatest *coup de théâtre*, the discovery kept from the audience until the end of the play of Epicoene's true identity when, with typical Jonsonian adherence to truth, it is revealed that the convention is the reality: the 'girl' really *is* a boy.

Stage history

The folio states that *Epicoene* was first acted in 1609; that is, December 1609 after the theatres reopened, or January 1609/10 when the children's company for whom it was written became the Children of Her Majesty's Revels and moved into their new private playhouse, the Whitefriars. The cast included Nathan Field, later to join the King's Men, and William Barsted and Hugh Attwell who were probably the play's first Morose and La Foole.[3] *Epicoene* was banned by early February 1609/10, after the king's cousin Lady Arabella Stuart complained that 'an allusion was made to her person, and the part played by the Prince of Moldavia'.[4] The complaint arises from the ambiguous wording of V.i.26–7 which, despite Jonson's protestations of innocence of 'application' in the Second Prologue, could be interpreted as referring to the claims made by the impostor 'prince', Stephano Janiculo, that he had become engaged to Lady Arabella whilst on a visit to the English court in 1607. The play survived official displeasure and became the property of the King's Men, probably by 1619; John Lowin and Joseph Taylor were associated with the roles of Morose and Truewit respectively. *Epicoene*'s popularity is attested by its being linked with *Volpone* and

---

3 James A. Riddell, 'Some actors in Ben Jonson's plays', *Shakespeare Survey*, 5 (1969), p. 296.

4 Letter of the Venetian Ambassador, 8 February 1609/10, *Calendar of State Papers Venetian* (London: H.M.S.O., 1864), XI, no. 794, p. 427.

The Alchemist,[5] and in 1636 it was twice performed at court.

Appropriately, *Epicoene*, the Jonsonian comedy which most strikingly prefigures that of the Restoration, was the first play to be performed after the theatres were reopened in 1660. It held its popularity through the rest of the century. It was much admired by Pepys, who recorded the success of the boy actor Edward Kynaston as Epicoene in Killigrew's company in 1661, and was equally enthusiastic about the 1663 production in which Mrs Knepp became the first of a line of actresses to play Epicoene. Kynaston had moved to the role of Dauphine, and William Cartwright and Michael Mohun played Morose and Truewit. As well as being performed regularly in London by Killigrew's and the King's company, *Epicoene* was staged at the universities; at Cambridge in 1662, and, with prologue and epilogue by Dryden, at Oxford in 1673. A performance before the king and queen took place in 1685.

Epicoene continued to be popular in the first half of the eighteenth century. In the early years Thomas Betterton played Morose three times – it was to be his only Jonsonian part. In 1707 Betterton's company combined with that of Drury Lane to give *Epicoene* its most outstanding cast, and many of the actors retained their associations with their parts: Ben Johnson played Morose until 1742, 'an exhibition of comic distress';[6] Colley Cibber played Daw up to 1735; Wilks was Truewit until his death in 1732; and Booth was Dauphine until 1729. Mrs Oldfield was Epicoene. The play was performed at least once a year from 1711 to 1733; thirteen times between 1733 and 1736; and between 1745 and 1748 there were seven performances by Rich's company at Covent Garden, with Mrs Pritchard in the title role.

However, taste and the drama were changing, and not even Garrick could make his 1752 revival succeed, in a cast with Richard Yates as Morose, William Palmer as Truewit, Ned Shuter as La Foole, and Mrs Pritchard and Mrs Clive as Epicoene and Lady Haughty. Garrick next produced *Epicoene* in 1776 in a version by George Colman, modern-

---

5 See G. E. Bentley, *Shakespeare and Jonson* (Chicago: 1945), II, p. 273; J. F. Bradley and J. Q. Adams (eds.), *The Jonson Allusion-Book* (New Haven: Cornell University Press, 1922).

6 T. Davies, *Dramatic Miscellanies*, 3 vols. (London: 1783–4), II, p. 106.

ised, bowdlerised, with the harshness softened and the learned allusions removed. Bensley played Morose, and Palmer Truewit; and for the first performance, Mrs Siddons took the part of Epicoene, although Garrick afterwards restored tradition and an important point of Jonson's play by using a male actor for the silent woman. The last performance of the eighteenth century, in 1784, was in Colman's adaptation.

The only nineteenth-century performance, in a version devised on similar lines to Colman's, was given at Harvard by students of the American Academy of Dramatic Arts in 1895, and foreshadowed the mainly academic productions of the twentieth century. The Marlowe Society produced *Epicoene* at Cambridge in 1909, and Nevill Coghill put the play on at Oxford in 1938. Written for a children's company, *Epicoene* is suited to young actors, and there have been numerous student productions since the war. The play has regained little ground in the professional theatre. It was performed by the Mermaid Repertory Company in 1905, with Cyril Cattley as Epicoene; by the influential Phoenix Company in 1924, with Cedric Hardwicke as Morose and Godfrey Winn as Epicoene; by Cygnet Productions in 1967; and by Frank Hauser's Oxford Playhouse Company at Oxford in 1968, a production with great pace and comic energy. The Manchester Umbrella Theatre's 1980 *Epicoene* brought out the nastiness and cruelty of the gallants, making Morose too sympathetic; but paid careful attention to Jonson's stagecraft.

Foreign interest this century produced a French adaptation by Marcel Achard, performed at the Théâtre Atelier in Paris in 1926; and Stefan Zweig, the adapter of *Volpone*, wrote the libretto for Richard Strauss's comic opera, *Die schweigsame Frau*, in 1935.

Definitive and individual editions

Although Gifford claimed to have seen a 1612 quarto of *Epicoene*, the play appears to have been first published in the 1616 folio;[7] all editions follow this authoritative text.

---

7 J. Gerritsen, 'Stansby and Jonson produce a folio: a preliminary account', *English Studies*, 40 (1959), p. 54; L. A. Beaurline's edition of *Epicoene*, pp. xx–xxi; W. W. Greg, 'Was there a 1612 quarto of *Epicoene*?', *The Library*, 4th ser., 15 (1935), pp. 306–15.

However, gathering Yy of the folio (pp. 529–40), which contains the prologues to *Epicoene* and the play to II.ii.72, survives in two states: the original, and one reset during printing to accommodate corrections of the original setting and some authorial alterations. In their edition of *Epicoene*, Herford and Simpson print the reset version (vol. V), and list the variants in vol. IX, pp. 21–30; but they believe the reset to be the original setting and the variants are presented accordingly. Their discussion of the folio text in the introduction to *Epicoene* (vol. II) is similarly affected by this misconception. The actual standing of the two gatherings was established by Professors Gerritsen and Beaurline.[8] Herford and Simpson's usually impeccable text contains a few errors derived from Dr Henry's edition, which they used as copy text for the last three acts.[9] These are corrected in the new Oxford edition by G. A. Wilkes based on Herford and Simpson, *The Complete Plays of Ben Jonson*, vol. III, 1982. Vol. X of Herford and Simpson contains stage history, and commentary and notes which are still indispensable.

The first modern critical edition is Aurelia Henry's, Yale Studies in English, 31 (New York: Yale University Press, 1906). Despite some textual errors, this provided useful groundwork for future discussion of the play. There are three recent individual editions, each with modernised spelling and punctuation: L. A. Beaurline's for Regent's Renaissance Drama Series (London: Edward Arnold, 1967); Edward Partridge's in the Yale Ben Jonson, vol. VI (New Haven and London: Yale University Press, 1971); and R. V. Holdsworth's New Mermaid edition (London: Ernest Benn, 1979). All have good, and Partridge and Holdsworth full, annotation; and useful critical introductions; Beaurline later develops his in 'Ben Jonson and the illusion of completeness', *PMLA*, LXXXIV (1969), pp. 51–9, and chapter 6 of *Jonson and Elizabethan Comedy* (San Marino: the Huntington Library, 1978); and in his introduction Partridge draws on his discussion of *Epicoene* in *The Broken Compass*, chapter 7 (London: Chatto & Windus, 1958).

8 Gerritsen, 'Stansby and Jonson', pp. 52–5; Beaurline, pp. xx–xxi.

9 See Beaurline's edition, Appendix A, pp. 150–2.

[DEDICATORY EPISTLE]

TO THE TRULY
NOBLE, BY ALL
TITLES,
Sir Francis Stuart

Sir,

My hope is not so nourished by example, as it will conclude this dumb piece should please you, by cause it hath pleased others before: but by trust, that when you have read it, you will find it worthy to have displeased none. This makes that I now number you, not only in the names of favour, but the names of justice, to what I write; and do, presently, call you to the exercise of that noblest, and manliest virtue: as coveting rather to be freed in my fame by the authority of a judge, than the credit of an undertaker. Read therefore, I pray you, and censure. There is not a line, or syllable in it changed from the simplicity of the first copy. And when you shall consider, through the certain hatred of some, how much a man's innocency may be endangered by an uncertain accusation; you will, I doubt not, so begin to hate the iniquity of such natures, as I shall love the contumely done me, whose end was so honourable, as to be wiped off by your sentence.

Your unprofitable, but true lover,
BEN. JONSON.

Sir Francis Stuart: grandson of Mary, Queen of Scots's half-brother, James; one of the learned gentlemen and wits who gathered at the Mermaid Tavern.

3 *dumb piece*: silent play (because its performance had been banned by the authorities); also, 'silent woman' (for *piece* = woman, see *Volpone*, I.ii.18).

8 *presently*: now, straightaway.

11 *undertaker*: guarantor; also, political 'fixer'.

12 *censure*: judge.

13 *simplicity*: straightforwardness, plainness.

17 *accusation*: i.e. that *Epicoene* made reference to the engagement which the bogus Prince of Moldavia claimed to have contracted with King James's cousin, Lady Arabella Stuart; see p. 297 above; Second Prologue, and V.i.26–7 and n.

21 *lover*: friend, well-wisher.

THE PERSONS OF THE PLAY

MOROSE. *A gentleman that loves no noise*
DAUP[HINE] EUGENIE. *A knight his nephew*
CLERIMONT. *A gentleman his friend*
TRUEWIT. *Another friend*
EPICOENE. *A young gentleman, supposed the silent woman*
JOH[N] DAW. *A knight, her servant*
AMOROUS LA FOOLE. *A knight also*
THOM. OTTER. *A land and sea captain*
CUTBEARD. *A barber*
MUTE. *One of Morose his servants*

MAD[AM] HAUGHTY MAD[AM] CENTAUR MISTRESS MAVIS	*Ladies Collegiates*
MISTRESS TRUSTY. *The Lady Haughty's woman* MISTRESS OTTER. *The captain's wife*	*Pretenders*

PARSON
PAGES
SERVANTS
[*Musicians*]

THE PERSONS: see Additional Note, p. 441 below.

1 MOROSE: sour-tempered, sullen, gloomy, unsocial (Latin *morosus*, peevish, fretful, wayward).

2 DAUP[HINE] EUGENIE: well-born heir (Greek ἐυγενίος, French *dauphin*); also, 'good wit or spirit' (ἐυ + *génie*).

3 CLERIMONT: ?from French *clairemont*, clearly, plainly (Partridge, *The Broken Compass*).

5 EPICOENE: having the characteristics of both sexes (derived playfully from the grammatical term for Latin and Greek nouns which, without changing their gender, may denote either sex). For the modern reader, the pronunciation 'Epi-sée-nee' (four syllables) conveys both the clue and the element of disguise in Jonson's joke.

7 JOH[N] DAW: i.e. jackdaw, a bird known for its thievishness and noisy chatter ('Cornachione: a great jackdaw. Also a detracting prattler', John Florio, *Queen Anna's World of Words*, 1611).
servant: lover devoted to his mistress.

8 LA FOOLE: i.e. the feminine form of the name.

9 OTTER: amphibious animal (I.iv.29); a creature of two elements, 'neither one thing nor the other'.

13 CENTAUR: mythical beast, half man, half horse; symbolic of wildness and lustfulness. See Textual Note, p. 433 below.
Collegiates: belonging to a college (i.e. a collective society).

14 MAVIS: 'an ill face' (Florio, 1611); also, a song-thrush.

16 *Pretenders*: claimants, those who aspire to.

THE SCENE
LONDON

PROLOGUE

Truth says, of old, the art of making plays
  Was to content the people; and their praise
  Was to the poet money, wine, and bays.
But in this age, a sect of writers are,
  That only for particular likings care,
  And will taste nothing that is popular.
With such we mingle neither brains, nor breasts;
  Our wishes, like to those (make public feasts)
  Are not to please the cooks' tastes, but the guests'.
Yet if those cunning palates hither come,
  They shall find guests' entreaty, and good room;
  And though all relish not, sure, there will be some,
That, when they leave their seats, shall make 'em say,
  'Who wrote that piece, could so have wrote a play:
  But that he knew this was the better way.'
For to present all custard, or all tart,
  And have no other meats to bear a part,
  Or to want bread, and salt, were but coarse art.
The poet prays you then, with better thought
  To sit; and when his cates are all in brought,
  Though there be none far-fet, there will dear-
    bought
Be fit for ladies: some for lords, knights, squires,
  Some for your waiting wench, and city-wires,

---

2 *to content the people*: from Terence, opening lines of the prologue to *Andria*. Contrast Jonson's Second Prologue, 2.
3 *bays*: laurel wreath of acclaim; hence, figuratively, 'fame'.
5 *particular likings*: special tastes (as of the private theatre audiences).
6 *taste*: relish, enjoy.
popular: pertaining to the people.
7 *mingle neither brains, nor breasts*: share neither ideas nor feelings.
8 *those (make*: those who make (omitted relative, frequent in Jonson).
10 *cunning*: skilful, expert.
11 *entreaty*: entertainment.
12 *all relish not*: every part does not please.
14 *piece*: specimen of a work of art.
14–15 Compare *Volpone*, Epistle, 122–33.
16 *custard*: open fruit or meat pie, covered with a broth of eggs, milk, and spices.
20 *cates*: delicacies.
21 *far-fet*: far-fetched.
21–2 *far-fet . . . ladies*: 'far-fet and dear-bought are good for ladies' (proverb).
23 *city-wires*: fashionably dressed citizens' wives. Wires were used in styling the hair and shaping ruffs.

Some for your men, and daughters of Whitefriars.
Nor is it, only, while you keep your seat
Here, that his feast will last; but you shall eat
A week at ord'naries, on his broken meat:
If his muse be true,
Who commends her to you.

ANOTHER

Occasioned by some person's impertinent exception

The ends of all, who for the scene do write,
Are, or should be, to profit, and delight.
And still't hath been the praise of all best times,
So persons were not touched, to tax the crimes.
Then, in this play, which we present tonight,
And make the object of your ear, and sight,
On forfeit of yourselves, think nothing true:
Lest so you make the maker to judge you.
For he knows, poet never credit gained
By writing truths, but things (like truths) well
feigned.
If any, yet, will (with particular sleight
Of application) wrest what he doth write;
And that he meant or him, or her, will say:
They make a libel, which he made a play.

---

24 *Whitefriars*: an area in the City of London outside the jurisdiction of the city authorities, a 'liberty', hence a haven for thieves and prostitutes (see *Volpone*, IV.ii.51); also, the theatre in which *Epicoene* was performed.
27 *ord'naries*: taverns which provided meals at a fixed price.
Heading: see Textual Note, p. 433 below.
impertinent exception: irrelevant or incongruous complaint.
1 *scene*: stage (Latin *scena*).
2 *to profit, and delight*: a famous dictum from Horace's *The Art of Poetry*, 333–4; an important critical tenet of the Renaissance.
4 *touched*: accused.
tax: censure.
7 *On forfeit of yourselves*: compare *Bartholomew Fair*, Induction 168–71.
8 *maker*: poet (literal meaning of Greek ποιητής).
9–10 *poet . . . feigned*: 'Let what thou feign'st for pleasure's sake be near / The truth' (Jonson's translation of *The Art of Poetry*, 338).
12 *application*: interpreting literature as referring to contemporary events or living persons (Jonson is defending himself against the construction put on *Epicoene* by Lady Arabella Stuart and her friends).

EPICOENE, OR THE SILENT WOMAN

ACT I

SCENE I

[*Enter*] CLERIMONT: *he comes out making himself ready;* BOY.

CLERIMONT. Ha'you got the song yet perfect I ga'you, boy?

BOY. Yes, sir.

CLERIMONT. Let me hear it.

BOY. You shall, sir, but i'faith let nobody else.

CLERIMONT. Why, I pray?

BOY. It will get you the dangerous name of a poet in town, sir, besides me a perfect deal of ill-will at the mansion you wot of, whose lady is the argument of it: where now I am the welcom'st thing under a man that comes there.

CLERIMONT. I think, and above a man too, if the truth were racked out of you.

BOY. No faith, I'll confess before, sir. The gentlewomen play with me, and throw me o'the bed; and carry me in to my lady; and she kisses me with her oiled face; and puts a peruke o'my head; and asks me an' I will wear her gown; and I say 'No': and then she hits me a blow o'the ear, and calls me innocent, and lets me go.

CLERIMONT. No marvel, if the door be kept shut against your master, when the entrance is so easy to you – well sir, you shall go there no more, lest I be fain to seek your voice in my lady's rushes, a fortnight hence. Sing, sir.

I.i.s.d. *making . . . ready*: dressing.

7 *dangerous name of a poet*: because society, offended by the poets satirising its follies, repaid them with contempt: 'Thou call'st me poet as a term of shame' (Jonson, *Epigrams*, 10.1).

9 *argument*: subject.

10 *under*: less than; but also with a sexual pun (see 28).

17 *oiled*: greasy.

18 *an'*: if.

20 *innocent*: child; also, 'simpleton'.

24 *to seek your voice in my lady's rushes*: see Additional Note, p. 442 below.

BOY *sings*.

[*Enter* TRUEWIT.]

TRUEWIT. Why, here's the man that can melt away his time, and never feels it! What, between his mistress abroad, and his ingle at home, high fare, soft lodging, fine clothes, and his fiddle; he thinks the hours ha'no wings, or the day no post-horse. Well, sir gallant, were you struck with the plague this minute, or condemned to any capital punishment tomorrow, you would begin then to think, and value every article o'your time, esteem it at the true rate, and give all for't.

CLERIMONT. Why, what should a man do?

TRUEWIT. Why, nothing: or that, which when 'tis done, is as idle. Hearken after the next horse race, or hunting match; lay wagers, praise Puppy, or Peppercorn, Whitefoot, Franklin; swear upon Whitemane's party; spend aloud, that my lords may hear you; visit my ladies at night, and be able to give 'em the character of every bowler, or better o'the green. These be the things, wherein your fashionable men exercise themselves, and I for company.

CLERIMONT. Nay, if I have thy authority, I'll not leave yet. Come, the other are considerations when we come to have grey heads, and weak hams, moist eyes, and shrunk members. We'll think on 'em then; then we'll pray, and fast.

TRUEWIT. Ay, and destine only that time of age to goodness, which our want of ability will not let us employ in evil?

CLERIMONT. Why, then 'tis time enough.

---

25 s.d. BOY *sings*: i.e. 'Still to be neat', printed at line 103 below.
28 *abroad*: away from home.
ingle: catamite, boy kept for immoral purposes.
30 *no post-horse*: i.e. had no swift passage from hour to hour. Post-horses completed a stage of ten miles in an hour.
34 *article*: moment.
38 *idle*: vain, useless.
Hearken: enquire.
39–41 *Puppy . . . Peppercorn, Whitefoot, Franklin . . . Whitemane*: 'Horses o'the time' (Jonson's marginal note).
41 *spend aloud*: talk noisily, as hounds bark when they sight the game.
50 *moist*: watery, 'rheumy'; indicative of old age.
52 *destine*: devote, allot.

TRUEWIT. Yes: as if a man should sleep all the term, and think to effect his business the last day. Oh, Clerimont, this time, because it is an incorporeal thing, and not subject to sense, we mock ourselves the fineliest out of it, with vanity, and misery indeed: not seeking an end of wretchedness, but only changing the matter still.

CLERIMONT. Nay, thou'lt not leave now –

TRUEWIT. See but our common disease! with what justice can we complain that great men will not look upon us, nor be at leisure to give our affairs such dispatch as we expect, when we will never do it to ourselves: nor hear, nor regard ourselves.

CLERIMONT. Foh, thou hast read Plutarch's *Morals*, now, or some such tedious fellow; and it shows so vilely with thee: 'fore God, 'twill spoil thy wit utterly. Talk me of pins, and feathers, and ladies, and rushes, and such things: and leave this stoicity alone till thou mak'st sermons.

TRUEWIT. Well, sir. If it will not take, I have learned to lose as little of my kindness as I can. I'll do good to no man against his will, certainly. When were you at the college?

CLERIMONT. What college?

TRUEWIT. As if you knew not!

CLERIMONT. No faith, I came but from court yesterday.

TRUEWIT. Why, is it not arrived there yet, the news? A new foundation, sir, here i'the town, of ladies, that call themselves the Collegiates, an order between courtiers, and country madams, that live

---

56 *term*: one of the four legal terms, during which court cases were heard.

60 *fineliest*: most subtly.

62 *still*: continually.

64 *disease*: discontent, about the lack of patronage.

69 *Plutarch's Morals*: the *Moral Essays*, widely used in Renaissance education.

70 *some such tedious fellow*: actually, Truewit has been drawing on *Of the Brevity of Life* by Seneca, whose Stoic ethics were highly regarded in the Renaissance.

72–3 *pins . . . feathers . . . rushes*: i.e. trivialities; so, by implication, are all 'ladies'.

75 *take*: succeed.

86 *courtiers, and country madams*: ladies of the court and ladies from the country.

from their husbands; and give entertainment to all the Wits, and Braveries o'the time, as they call 'em; cry down, or up, what they like, or dislike in a brain, or a fashion, with most masculine, or rather hermaphroditical authority: and, every day, gain to their college some new probationer.

CLERIMONT. Who is the president?

TRUEWIT. The grave, and youthful matron, the Lady Haughty.

CLERIMONT. A pox of her autumnal face, her pieced beauty: there's no man can be admitted till she be ready, nowadays, till she has painted, and perfumed, and washed, and scoured, but the boy here; and him she wipes her oiled lips upon, like a sponge. I have made a song, I pray thee hear it, o'the subject.

[BOY *sings again.*]

Song

Still to be neat, still to be dressed,
As you were going to a feast;
Still to be powdered, still perfumed:
Lady, it is to be presumed,
Though art's hid causes are not found,
All is not sweet, all is not sound.

Give me a look, give me a face,
That makes simplicity a grace;
Robes loosely flowing, hair as free:
Such sweet neglect more taketh me,
Than all th'adulteries of art.
They strike mine eyes, but not my heart.

TRUEWIT. And I am, clearly, o'the other side: I love

---

87 *from*: apart from.

88 *Wits, and Braveries*: gallants well versed in the current fashions of witty talk and of dress respectively.

89 *cry down, or up*: decry or praise.

90–1 *or rather hermaphroditical*: i.e. because the ladies deny their own sexual roles by their mannish behaviour, this makes them a curious amalgam of male and female.

96 *pieced*: patched.

103 *still*: always.
neat: finely or elegantly dressed.

110 *simplicity*: lack of adornment.

112 *taketh*: captivates.

113 *adulteries*: adulterations.

115 *clearly*: unreservedly.

a good dressing, before any beauty o'the world. Oh, a woman is, then, like a delicate garden; nor is there one kind of it: she may vary, every hour; take often counsel of her glass, and choose the best. If she have good ears, show 'em; good hair, lay it out; good legs, wear short clothes; a good hand, discover it often; practise any art, to mend breath, cleanse teeth, repair eyebrows, paint, and profess it.

CLERIMONT. How? publicly?

TRUEWIT. The doing of it, not the manner: that must be private. Many things, that seem foul i'the doing, do please, done. A lady should, indeed, study her face, when we think she sleeps; nor when the doors are shut, should men be enquiring; all is sacred within, then. Is it for us to see their perukes put on, their false teeth, their complexion, their eyebrows, their nails? you see gilders will not work, but enclosed. They must not discover how little serves, with the help of art, to adorn a great deal. How long did the canvas hang afore Aldgate? were the people suffered to see the city's 'Love' and 'Charity', while they were rude stone, before they were painted, and burnished? No. No more should servants approach their mistresses, but when they are complete, and finished.

CLERIMONT. Well said, my Truewit.

TRUEWIT. And a wise lady will keep a guard always upon the place, that she may do things securely. I once followed a rude fellow into a chamber, where the poor madam, for haste, and troubled, snatched at her peruke, to cover her baldness: and put it on, the wrong way.

CLERIMONT. O prodigy!

TRUEWIT. And the unconscionable knave held her in

---

116 *dressing*: adornment.

121 *lay it out*: display it.

122 *discover*: reveal.

124 *profess*: declare; also, 'declare herself expert in', 'proficient at'.

137 *Aldgate*: this principal eastern gate of London was rebuilt in 1609–10, and flanked by two statues representing Peace and Charity.

140 *servants*: lovers (term derived from the courtly love convention), admirers.

149 *prodigy*: monstrous thing.

compliment an hour, with that reversed face, when I still looked when she should talk from the t'other side.

CLERIMONT. Why, thou shouldst ha'relieved her.

TRUEWIT. No faith, I let her alone, as we'll let this argument, if you please, and pass to another. When saw you Dauphine Eugenie?

CLERIMONT. Not these three days. Shall we go to him this morning? He is very melancholic, I hear.

TRUEWIT. Sick o'the uncle? is he? I met that stiff piece of formality, his uncle, yesterday, with a huge turban of nightcaps on his head, buckled over his ears.

CLERIMONT. Oh, that's his custom when he walks abroad. He can endure no noise, man.

TRUEWIT. So I have heard. But is the disease so ridiculous in him, as it is made? They say he has been upon divers treaties with the fishwives, and orange-women; and articles propounded between them: marry, the chimney-sweepers will not be drawn in.

CLERIMONT. No, nor the broom-men: they stand out stiffly. He cannot endure a costardmonger, he swoons if he hear one.

TRUEWIT. Methinks, a smith should be ominous.

CLERIMONT. Or any hammerman. A brazier is not suffered to dwell in the parish, nor an armourer. He would have hanged a pewterer's 'prentice once upon a Shrove Tuesday's riot, for being o'that trade, when the rest were quit.

TRUEWIT. A trumpet should fright him terribly, or the hautboys?

---

160 *Sick o'the uncle*: coined after 'sick of the mother' (hysteria).
168 *been upon divers*: been engaged in making various.
168–9 *fishwives, and orange-women*: notoriously raucous. Morose attempts to silence street criers.
171 *drawn in*: induced (to make an agreement).
172 *broom-men*: broom-sellers.
173 *stiffly*: resolutely.
costardmonger: fruit-seller (costard = apple).
175 *ominous*: inauspicious.
176 *hammerman*: metal-worker.
brazier: worker in brass.
179 *Shrove Tuesday*: when apprentices traditionally went on the rampage and wrecked brothels and theatres.
180 *quit*: acquitted.
182 *hautboys*: oboes (French *hautbois*).

CLERIMONT. Out of his senses. The waits of the city have a pension of him, not to come near that ward. This youth practised on him, one night, like the bell-man; and never left till he had brought him down to the door, with a long sword: and there left him flourishing with the air.

BOY. Why, sir! he hath chosen a street to lie in, so narrow at both ends, that it will receive no coaches, nor carts, nor any of these common noises: and therefore, we that love him, devise to bring him in such as we may, now and then, for his exercise, to breathe him. He would grow resty else in his ease. His virtue would rust without action. I entreated a bearward, one day, to come down with the dogs of some four parishes that way, and I thank him, he did; and cried his games under Master Morose's window: till he was sent crying away, with his head made a most bleeding spectacle to the multitude. And another time, a fencer, marching to his prize, had his drum most tragically run through, for taking that street in his way, at my request.

TRUEWIT. A good wag. How does he for the bells?

CLERIMONT. Oh, i'the queen's time, he was wont to go out of town every Saturday at ten o'clock, or on holiday eves. But now, by reason of the sickness, the perpetuity of ringing has made him devise a room with double walls, and treble ceilings; the windows close shut, and caulked: and there he

---

183 *waits*: band of street musicians maintained at public expense to play on holidays and festivals.
184 *ward*: district.
185 *practised*: played a trick.
186 *bell-man*: nightwatchman who called the hours and rang a bell.
189 *lie*: live.
194 *breathe him*: exercise him, 'give him a good run'.
resty: lazy (used of horses).
195 *virtue*: distinctive quality (Morose's eccentric obsession with noise); also, 'vigour'.
196 *bearward*: keeper of bears for bear-baiting.
198 *cried his games*: gave public notice of a bear-baiting.
201 *marching*: see Textual Note, p. 433 below.
prize: fencing-match.
202 *drum*: beaten to announce the match.
207 *sickness*: plague, particularly virulent in 1609.
208 *perpetuity of ringing*: continual tolling of church bells for the dead (compare *Volpone*, III.v.5).

lives by candlelight. He turned away a man, last week, for having a pair of new shoes that creaked. And this fellow waits on him, now, in tennis-court socks, or slippers soled with wool: and they talk each to other in a trunk. See, who comes here.

SCENE II

[*Enter*] DAUPHINE.

DAUPHINE. How now! what ail you, sirs? dumb?

TRUEWIT. Struck into stone, almost, I am here, with tales o'thine uncle! There was never such a prodigy heard of.

DAUPHINE. I would you would once lose this subject, my masters, for my sake. They are such as you are, that have brought me into that predicament I am with him.

TRUEWIT. How is that?

DAUPHINE. Marry, that he will disinherit me, no more. He thinks, I and my company are authors of all the ridiculous acts, and monuments are told of him.

TRUEWIT. 'Slid, I would be the author of more, to vex him; that purpose deserves it: it gives thee law of plaguing him. I'll tell thee what I would do. I would make a false almanac; get it printed: and then ha'him drawn out on a coronation day to the Tower Wharf, and kill him with the noise of the ordnance. Disinherit thee! he cannot, man. Art not thou next of blood, and his sister's son?

---

211 *turned away*: dismissed.
215 *trunk*: speaking-tube.
1 *ail*: present subjunctive tense, used in interrogative sentences.
3 *prodigy*: monster.
5 *once*: once for all.
12 *acts, and monuments*: John Foxe's *Book of Martyrs* was entitled *Acts and Monuments* in its first English edition (1563); the reference implies the incongruity of Morose's martyrdom – to noise, exploited later in the play.
14 *'Slid*: God's (eye)lid, a common form of oath.
15 *gives thee law*: authorises you.
19 *Tower Wharf*: where a salute of gunfire marked the anniversary of King James's coronation.

DAUPHINE. Ay, but he will thrust me out of it, he vows, and marry.

TRUEWIT. How! that's a more portent. Can he endure no noise, and will venture on a wife?

CLERIMONT. Yes: why, thou art a stranger, it seems, to his best trick, yet. He has employed a fellow this half year, all over England, to hearken him out a dumb woman; be she of any form, or any quality, so she be able to bear children: her silence is dowry enough, he says.

TRUEWIT. But I trust to God, he has found none.

CLERIMONT. No, but he has heard of one that's lodged i'the next street to him, who is exceedingly soft-spoken; thrifty of her speech; that spends but six words a day. And her he's about now, and shall have her.

TRUEWIT. Is't possible! who is his agent i'the business?

CLERIMONT. Marry, a barber, one Cutbeard: an honest fellow, one that tells Dauphine all here.

TRUEWIT. Why, you oppress me with wonder! A woman, and a barber, and love no noise!

CLERIMONT. Yes faith. The fellow trims him silently, and has not the knack with his shears, or his fingers: and that continence in a barber he thinks so eminent a virtue, as it has made him chief of his counsel.

TRUEWIT. Is the barber to be seen? or the wench?

CLERIMONT. Yes, that they are.

TRUEWIT. I pray thee, Dauphine, let's go thither.

DAUPHINE. I have some business now: I cannot, i'faith.

TRUEWIT. You shall have no business shall make you neglect this, sir, we'll make her talk, believe it; or if she will not, we can give out at least so much as shall interrupt the treaty: we will break it. Thou art bound in conscience, when he suspects thee without cause, to torment him.

---

24 *more*: greater.
29 *quality*: rank.
40 *one Cutbeard*: see Textual Note, p. 433 below.
42–3 *A woman, and a barber*: proverbially, both notorious talkers.
45 *knack*: snapping, clicking noise.
47–8 *chief of his counsel*: his chief confidant.

DAUPHINE. Not I, by any means. I'll give no suffrage to't. He shall never ha'that plea against me, that I opposed the least fant'sy of his. Let it lie upon my stars to be guilty, I'll be innocent.

TRUEWIT. Yes, and be poor, and beg; do, innocent: when some groom of his has got him an heir, or this barber, if he himself cannot. Innocent! I pray thee, Ned, where lies she? let him be innocent, still.

CLERIMONT. Why, right over against the barber's; in the house where Sir John Daw lies.

TRUEWIT. You do not mean to confound me!

CLERIMONT. Why?

TRUEWIT. Does he, that would marry her, know so much?

CLERIMONT. I cannot tell.

TRUEWIT. 'Twere enough of imputation to her, with him.

CLERIMONT. Why?

TRUEWIT. The only talking sir i'the town! Jack Daw! And he teach her not to speak – God b'w'you. I have some business too.

CLERIMONT. Will you not go thither then?

TRUEWIT. Not with the danger to meet Daw, for mine ears.

CLERIMONT. Why? I thought you two had been upon very good terms.

TRUEWIT. Yes, of keeping distance.

CLERIMONT. They say he is a very good scholar.

TRUEWIT. Ay, and he says it first. A pox on him, a fellow that pretends only to learning, buys titles, and nothing else of books in him.

CLERIMONT. The world reports him to be very learned.

TRUEWIT. I am sorry the world should so conspire to belie him.

---

60 *suffrage*: approval.

62 *fant'sy*: fancy, imagination; also, fantasy – whim, desire, delusion.
lie upon: be ordained by.

64 *innocent*: simpleton, fool.

65 *groom*: servant.

71 *confound*: astound.

76 *imputation to*: accusation against.

79 *only*: outstanding.

CLERIMONT. Good faith, I have heard very good things come from him.

TRUEWIT. You may. There's none so desperately ignorant to deny that: would they were his own. God b'w'you, gentlemen. [*Exit.*]

CLERIMONT. This is very abrupt!

SCENE III

DAUPHINE. Come, you are a strange open man, to tell everything thus.

CLERIMONT. Why, believe it, Dauphine, Truewit's a very honest fellow.

DAUPHINE. I think no other: but this frank nature of his is not for secrets.

CLERIMONT. Nay, then, you are mistaken, Dauphine; I know where he has been well trusted, and discharged the trust very truly, and heartily.

DAUPHINE. I contend not, Ned, but with the fewer a business is carried, it is ever the safer. Now we are alone, if you'll go thither, I am for you.

CLERIMONT. When were you there?

DAUPHINE. Last night: and such a *Decameron* of sport fallen out! Boccace never thought of the like. Daw does nothing but court her; and the wrong way. He would lie with her, and praises her modesty; desires that she would talk, and be free, and commends her silence in verses: which he reads, and swears are the best that ever man made. Then rails at his fortunes, stamps, and mutines why he is not made a councillor, and called to affairs of state.

CLERIMONT. I pray thee let's go. I would fain partake this. Some water, boy.

[*Exit* BOY.]

DAUPHINE. We are invited to dinner together, he

14–15 *Decameron of sport*: masterpiece of fun (H&S). Boccaccio's hundred tales contain many about the follies of love.

18 *free*: uninhibited, talkative; also, 'free with her sexual favours'.

21–2 *mutines why*: rebels because.

25 *Some water*: summon a boat to carry us on the Thames (popular form of travel up or down river).

and I, by one that came thither to him, Sir La Foole.

CLERIMONT. Oh, that's a precious manikin!

DAUPHINE. Do you know him?

CLERIMONT. Ay, and he will know you too, if ere he saw you but once, though you should meet him at church in the midst of prayers. He is one of the Braveries, though he be none o'the Wits. He will salute a judge upon the bench, and a bishop in the pulpit, a lawyer when he is pleading at the bar, and a lady when she is dancing in a masque, and put her out. He does give plays, and suppers, and invites his guests to 'em aloud, out of his window, as they ride by in coaches. He has a lodging in the Strand for the purpose. Or to watch when ladies are gone to the china-houses, or the Exchange, that he may meet 'em by chance, and give 'em presents, some two or three hundred pounds worth of toys, to be laughed at. He is never without a spare banquet, or sweetmeats in his chamber, for their women to alight at, and come up to, for a bait.

DAUPHINE. Excellent! He was a fine youth last night, but now he is much finer! What is his christen name? I ha'forgot.

[*Enter* BOY.]

CLERIMONT. Sir Amorous La Foole.

BOY. The gentleman is here below, that owns that name.

CLERIMONT. 'Heart, he's come to invite me to dinner, I hold my life.

DAUPHINE. Like enough: pray thee, let's ha'him up.

---

29 *manikin*: little man, puppet.

38 *give plays*: pays for private performances by professional companies.

42 *china-houses*: shops selling eastern goods; fashionable places of resort and assignation.
Exchange: the New Exchange, opened in 1609, which housed fashionable milliners' and jewellers' shops.

45 *toys*: trifles, trumpery.

46 *banquet*: course of sweetmeats, fruit, and wine.
for: see Textual Note, p. 433 below.

47 *their women*: womenservants of the ladies.
bait: snack taken by travellers; break in a journey for refreshments; also, 'food used to lure or entice'.

50 *christen*: Christian.

52 *below*: see Textual Note, p. 433 below.

CLERIMONT. Boy, marshal him.

BOY. With a truncheon, sir?

CLERIMONT. Away, I beseech you.

[*Exit* BOY.]

I'll make him tell us his pedigree, now; and what meat he has to dinner; and, who are his guests; and, the whole course of his fortunes: with a breath.

SCENE IV

[*Enter*] LA FOOLE.

LA FOOLE. 'Save, dear Sir Dauphine, honoured Master Clerimont.

CLERIMONT. Sir Amorous! you have very much honested my lodging, with your presence.

LA FOOLE. Good faith, it is a fine lodging! almost as delicate a lodging, as mine.

CLERIMONT. Not so, sir.

LA FOOLE. Excuse me, sir, if it were i'the Strand, I assure you. I am come, Master Clerimont, to entreat you wait upon two or three ladies, to dinner, today.

CLERIMONT. How, sir! wait upon 'em? did you ever see me carry dishes?

LA FOOLE. No, sir, dispense with me; I meant, to bear 'em company.

CLERIMONT. Oh, that I will, sir. The doubtfulness o'your phrase, believe it, sir, would breed you a quarrel once an hour with the terrible boys, if you

---

57 *marshal*: conduct ceremoniously.
58 *truncheon*: a play on 'marshal's baton' and 'cudgel'.
61 *meat*: food.
61–2 *and, . . . and,*: see Textual Note, p. 433 below.
62–3 *with a breath*: all in one breath. Clerimont is mocking (and probably imitating) La Foole's manner of speech.
1 *'Save*: God save you.
4 *honested*: honoured.
14 *dispense with*: excuse (an affected usage); but also, 'do away with', 'put up with absence of'.
16 *doubtfulness*: ambiguity.
18 *terrible boys*: 'roaring boys', bands of sword-happy young men ready to quarrel at the slightest provocation.

should but keep 'em fellowship a day.

LA FOOLE. It should be extremely against my will, sir, if I contested with any man.

CLERIMONT. I believe it, sir; where hold you your feast?

LA FOOLE. At Tom Otter's, sir.

DAUPHINE. Tom Otter? what's he?

LA FOOLE. Captain Otter, sir; he is a kind of gamester: but he has had command, both by sea, and by land.

DAUPHINE. Oh, then he is *animal amphibium*?

LA FOOLE. Ay, sir: his wife was the rich china-woman, that the courtiers visited so often, that gave the rare entertainment. She commands all at home.

CLERIMONT. Then she is Captain Otter?

LA FOOLE. You say very well, sir: she is my kins-woman, a La Foole by the mother side, and will invite any great ladies, for my sake.

DAUPHINE. Not of the La Fooles of Essex?

LA FOOLE. No, sir, the La Fooles of London.

CLERIMONT. [*aside to* DAUPHINE] Now h'is in.

LA FOOLE. They all come out of our house, the La Fooles o'the north, the La Fooles of the west, the La Fooles of the east, and south – we are as ancient a family, as any is in Europe – but I myself am descended lineally of the French La Fooles – and, we do bear for our coat yellow, or *or*, checkered *azure*, and *gules*, and some three or four colours more, which is a very noted coat, and has, sometimes, been solemnly worn by divers nobility of our

---

19 *but*: see Textual Note, p. 433 below.

27 *gamester*: devotee of a game (in this case, bear-baiting); gambler.

29 *animal amphibium*: creature able to live on land and in water; also, creature of two natures, as a man effeminately subjected to his wife.

30–1 *china-woman*: owner of a china-house.

36 *mother*: mother's.

40 *in*: launched on a favourite subject.

46 *for*: see Textual Note, p. 433 below.

coat: coat-of-arms; but also, parti-coloured coat worn by a professional fool or jester.

46–7 *or . . . azure . . . gules*: heraldic terms for gold, blue, and red respectively.

48 *noted*: celebrated.

house – but let that go, antiquity is not respected now – I had a brace of fat does sent me, gentlemen, and half a dozen of pheasants, a dozen or two of godwits, and some other fowl, which I would have eaten, while they are good, and in good company – there will be a great lady, or two, my Lady Haughty, my Lady Centaur, Mistress Dol Mavis – and they come a'purpose, to see the silent gentlewoman, Mistress Epicoene, that honest Sir John Daw has promised to bring thither – and then, Mistress Trusty, my lady's woman, will be there too, and this honourable knight, Sir Dauphine, with yourself, Master Clerimont – and we'll be very merry, and have fiddlers, and dance – I have been a mad wag, in my time, and have spent some crowns since I was a page in court, to my Lord Lofty, and after, my lady's gentleman-usher, who got me knighted in Ireland, since it pleased my elder brother to die – I had as fair a gold jerkin on that day, as any was worn in the Island Voyage, or at Caliz, none dispraised, and I came over in it hither, showed myself to my friends, in court, and after went down to my tenants, in the country, and surveyed my lands, let new leases, took their money, spent it in the eye o'the land here, upon ladies – and now I can take up at my pleasure.

DAUPHINE. Can you take up ladies, sir?

CLERIMONT. Oh, let him breath, he has not recovered.

DAUPHINE. Would I were your half, in that commodity –

---

53 *godwits*: marsh birds, a delicacy.

58 *Epicoene*: four syllables.

66 *gentleman-usher*: gentleman who attended on a person of high rank.

67 *knighted in Ireland*: the Earl of Essex created so many knights on his Irish expedition of 1599 that the honour was held to have been cheapened.

69 *Island Voyage*: Essex's unsuccessful expedition to the Azores in 1597.

70 *Caliz*: Cadiz, captured by Essex and the English fleet in 1596.

75 *take up*: borrow (at interest); Dauphine takes it as 'buy up, or hire', the sense in 82.

77 *breath*: take breath.

79 *half*: partner.

80 *commodity*: the practice by which borrowers had to receive part

LA FOOLE. No, sir, excuse me: I meant money, which can take up anything. I have another guest, or two, to invite, and say as much to, gentlemen. I'll take my leave abruptly, in hope you will not fail – Your servant. [*Exit.*]

DAUPHINE. We will not fail you, Sir precious La Foole; but she shall, that your ladies come to see: if I have credit afore Sir Daw.

CLERIMONT. Did you ever hear such a wind-fucker as this?

DAUPHINE. Or such a rook, as the other! that will betray his mistress to be seen. Come, 'tis time we prevented it.

CLERIMONT. Go.

[*Exeunt.*]

ACT II

SCENE I

[*Enter*] MOROSE, MUTE.

MOROSE. Cannot I, yet, find out a more compendious method, than by this trunk, to save my servants the labour of speech, and mine ears the discord of sounds? Let me see: all discourses, but mine own, afflict me, they seem harsh, impertinent, and irksome. Is it not possible that thou shouldst answer me by signs, and I apprehend thee, fellow? Speak not, though I question you. You have taken

---

of a loan in worthless goods, which were bought back by the moneylender at a much lower price.

81 LA FOOLE: see Textual Note, p. 433 below.

89 *wind-fucker*: kestrel; used as a term of opprobrium.

91 *rook*: simpleton.

1 *compendious*: expeditious, direct.

5 *impertinent*: irrelevant.

the ring off from the street door, as I bade you? Answer me not by speech, but by silence; unless it be otherwise.

At the breaches, still the fellow makes legs, or signs.

Very good. And you have fastened on a thick quilt, or flock-bed, on the outside of the door; that if they knock with their daggers, or with brickbats, they can make no noise? But with your leg, your answer, unless it be otherwise. [MUTE *makes a leg*] Very good. This is not only fit modesty in a servant, but good state, and discretion in a master. And you have been with Cutbeard, the barber, to have him come to me? [MUTE *makes a leg*] Good. And he will come presently? Answer me not but with your leg, unless it be otherwise: if it be otherwise, shake your head, or shrug. [MUTE *makes a leg*] So. Your Italian, and Spaniard, are wise in these! and it is a frugal, and comely gravity. How long will it be, ere Cutbeard come? Stay, if an hour, hold up your whole hand; if half an hour, two fingers; if a quarter, one; [MUTE *holds up one finger bent*] good: half a quarter? 'Tis well. And have you given him a key, to come in without knocking? [MUTE *makes a leg*] Good. And is the lock oiled, and the hinges, today? [MUTE *makes a leg*] Good. And the quilting of the stairs nowhere worn out, and bare? [MUTE *makes a leg*] Very good. I see, by much doctrine, and impulsion, it may be effected. Stand by. The Turk, in this divine discipline, is admirable, exceeding all the potentates of the earth; still waited on by

---

9 *ring*: circular knocker.

11 s.d. *breaches*: breaks in the text; see Textual Note, p. 433 below.
still: always.
makes legs: bows.

14 *brickbats*: pieces of brick, used as missiles.

15 *But*: only.

17 *modesty*: deference.

18 *state*: dignified manner.
discretion: judgement (in the exercise of power).

21 *presently*: immediately.

25 *these*: i.e. ceremonious observances.
gravity: sober demeanour.

35 *doctrine*: teaching (Latin *doctrina*).

35–6 *impulsion*: prompting.

36 *by*: aside.

mutes; and all his commands so executed; yea, even in the war (as I have heard) and in his marches, most of his charges and directions given by signs, and with silence: an exquisite art! And I am heartily ashamed, and angry oftentimes, that the princes of Christendom should suffer a barbarian to transcend 'em in so high a point of felicity. I will practise it, hereafter.

One winds a horn without.

How now? Oh! Oh! What villain? what prodigy of mankind is that? Look.

[*Exit* MUTE.]

[*Horn sounds*] *again.*

Oh! Cut his throat, cut his throat: what murderer, hell-hound, devil, can this be?

[*Enter* MUTE.]

MUTE. It is a post from the court –

MOROSE. Out rogue, and must thou blow thy horn, too?

MUTE. Alas, it is a post from the court, sir, that says he must speak with you, pain of death –

MOROSE. Pain of thy life, be silent.

SCENE II

[*Enter*] TRUEWIT [*with a post-horn and halter.*]

TRUEWIT. By your leave, sir (I am a stranger here): is your name Master Morose? Is your name Master Morose? Fishes! Pythagoreans all! This is strange! What say you, sir, nothing? Has Harpocrates been here, with his club, among you? Well sir, I will believe you to be the man, at this time: I will

---

46 s.d. *winds*: blows.
without: outside; off stage.
51 *post*: messenger who travelled express.
55 *with*: see Textual Note, p. 433 below.
3 *Fishes*: i.e. as dumb as fishes.
Pythagoreans: kept a five-year silence on first joining the sect.
4 *Harpocrates*: god of silence and secrecy, sometimes represented with a club, apparently acquired from Hercules in an iconographic confusion.

venture upon you, sir. Your friends at court commend 'em to you, sir –

MOROSE. [*aside*] (O men! O manners! Was there ever such an impudence?)

TRUEWIT. And are extremely solicitous for you, sir.

MOROSE. Whose knave are you?

TRUEWIT. Mine own knave, and your compeer, sir.

MOROSE. Fetch me my sword –

TRUEWIT. You shall taste the one half of my dagger if you do (groom) and you the other, if you stir, sir; be patient, I charge you, in the king's name, and hear me without insurrection. They say, you are to marry? to marry! Do you mark, sir?

MOROSE. How then, rude companion!

TRUEWIT. Marry, your friends do wonder, sir, the Thames being so near, wherein you may drown so handsomely; or London Bridge, at a low fall, with a fine leap, to hurry you down the stream; or such a delicate steeple i'the town, as Bow, to vault from; or a braver height, as Paul's; or if you affected to do it nearer home, and a shorter way, an excellent garret window, into the street; or a beam, in the said garret, with this halter;

He shows him a halter.

which they have sent, and desire that you would sooner commit your grave head to this knot, than to the wedlock noose; or take a little sublimate, and go out of the world, like a rat; or a fly (as one said) with a straw i'your arse: any way, rather than to follow this goblin matrimony. Alas, sir, do you ever think to find a chaste wife, in these times? now? when there are so many masques, plays,

---

7 *venture upon*: dare to approach; make trial of.

9 *O men! O manners*: adapted from Cicero's exclamation in *Against Catiline*, I.2: *O tempora! O mores!* 'O times! O manners!'

10 *impudence*: shamelessness.

13 *compeer*: equal.

20 *companion*: fellow (contemptuous).

23 *fall*: ebb tide.

25 *Bow*: St Mary-le-Bow, in Cheapside.

26 *Paul's*: St Paul's.

32 *sublimate*: arsenic, used as rat poison.

34 *straw*: thrust into the tail of a fly in spider and fly fights, a pastime affected by gallants.

Puritan preachings, mad folks, and other strange sights to be seen daily, private and public? If you had lived in King Ethelred's time, sir, or Edward the Confessor's, you might, perhaps, have found in some cold country hamlet, then, a dull frosty wench, would have been contented with one man: now, they will as soon be pleased with one leg, or one eye. I'll tell you, sir, the monstrous hazards you shall run with a wife.

MOROSE. Good sir! have I ever cozened any friends of yours of their land? bought their possessions? taken forfeit of their mortgage? begged a reversion from 'em? bastarded their issue? What have I done, that may deserve this?

TRUEWIT. Nothing, sir, that I know, but your itch of marriage.

MOROSE. Why, if I had made an assassinate upon your father; vitiated your mother; ravished your sisters –

TRUEWIT. I would kill you, sir, I would kill you, if you had.

MOROSE. Why, you do more in this, sir: it were a vengeance centuple, for all facinorous acts that could be named, to do that you do –

TRUEWIT. Alas, sir, I am but a messenger: I but tell you what you must hear. It seems your friends are careful after your soul's health, sir, and would have you know the danger (but you may do your pleasure, for all them, I persuade not, sir). If, after you are married, your wife do run away with a

---

38 *preachings*: see Textual Note, p. 433 below.
mad folks: at Bedlam, the hospital for the insane, which was visited for entertainment, as one of the sights of the town.
40 *Ethelred*: the Unready, 978–1016; father of Edward the Confessor, 1042–66: figures of legendary virtue from a near-mythical past.
49 *taken forfeit*: foreclosed on, for breach of contract.
49–50 *begged a reversion from*: secured away from those who might expect to succeed to it either an estate which has returned to the grantor, or the right to an office.
52 *itch of*: restless desire after.
54 *made an assassinate*: committed a murder.
55 *vitiated*: corrupted.
60 *facinorous*: criminal (Latin *facinorosus*).
64 *careful*: concerned.

vaulter, or the Frenchman that walks upon ropes, or him that dances the jig, or a fencer for his skill at his weapon, why it is not their fault; they have discharged their consciences: when you know what may happen. Nay, suffer valiantly, sir, for I must tell you all the perils that you are obnoxious to. If she be fair, young, and vegetous, no sweet-meats ever drew more flies; all the yellow doublets, and great roses i'the town will be there. If foul, and crooked, she'll be with them, and buy those doublets and roses, sir. If rich, and that you marry her dowry, not her, she'll reign in your house, as imperious as a widow. If noble, all her kindred will be your tyrants. If fruitful, as proud as May, and humorous as April; she must have her doctors, her midwives, her nurses, her longings every hour: though it be for the dearest morsel of man. If learned, there was never such a parrot; all your patrimony will be too little for the guests that must be invited, to hear her speak Latin and Greek: and you must lie with her in those languages too, if you will please her. If precise, you must feast all the silenced brethren, once in three days; salute the sisters; entertain the whole family, or wood of 'em; and hear long-winded exercises, singings, and catechisings, which you are not given to, and yet must give for: to please

---

68 *Frenchman that walks upon ropes*: one performed before Queen Elizabeth in 1600.
70 *weapon*: with an indecent double entendre: penis.
73 *obnoxious*: liable (Latin *obnoxius*).
74 *vegetous*: lively, vigorous.
76 *roses*: ribbons gathered into a knot, adorning the shoe.
77 *foul*: ugly.
82 *humorous*: capricious.
84 *dearest*: most loved; also, 'most expensive'.
morsel: tit-bit, delicate dish.
85 *parrot*: compare Lady Would-be, wife of Sir Pol, in *Volpone*.
89 *precise*: Puritanical.
90 *silenced brethren*: Puritan clergy whose licence to preach was taken away after the Hampton Court Conference of 1604. See *The Alchemist*, III.i.38; *Bartholomew Fair*, V.ii.74.
92 *family*: probably a side reference to the Family of Love, an Anabaptist sect, proscribed in England in 1580.
wood: crowd (Latin *silva*, 'a dense mass, collection'); also, a pun on *wood* = mad.
93 *exercises*: religious devotions.

the zealous matron your wife, who, for the holy cause, will cozen you, over and above. You begin to sweat, sir? but this is not half, i'faith: you may do your pleasure notwithstanding, as I said before, I come not to persuade you.

The MUTE *is stealing away.*

Upon my faith, master serving-man, if you do stir, I will beat you.

MOROSE. Oh, what is my sin! what is my sin?

TRUEWIT. Then if you love your wife, or rather dote on her, sir: Oh, how she'll torture you! and take pleasure i'your torments! You shall lie with her but when she lists; she will not hurt her beauty, her complexion; or it must be for that jewel, or that pearl, when she does; every half hour's pleasure must be bought anew: and with the same pain, and charge, you wooed her at first. Then you must keep what servants she please; what company she will; that friend must not visit you without her licence; and him she loves most she will seem to hate eagerliest, to decline your jealousy; or feign to be jealous of you first; and for that cause go live with her she-friend, or cousin at the college, that can instruct her in all the mysteries of writing letters, corrupting servants, taming spies; where she must have that rich gown for such a great day; a new one for the next; a richer for the third; be served in silver; have the chamber filled with a succession of grooms, footmen, ushers, and other messengers; besides embroiderers, jewellers, tirewomen, sempsters, feathermen, perfumers; while she feels not how the land drops away; nor the acres melt; nor foresees the change, when the mercer has your woods for her velvets; never

---

95 *zealous*: connoting Puritan zeal.
96 *cause*: (Puritan) movement.
110 *charge*: expense.
114 *eagerliest*: most fiercely, bitterly.
decline: avert.
116 *she-friend*: female friend; also 'prostitute'.
cousin: intimate friend; also, 'strumpet'.
124 *tirewomen*: dressmakers.
sempsters: tailors (male and female).
feathermen: feather salesmen.
125 *feels*: is aware of.
127 *mercer*: dealer in expensive materials.

weighs what her pride costs, sir: so she may kiss a page, or a smooth chin, that has the despair of a beard; be a stateswoman, know all the news, what was done at Salisbury, what at the Bath, what at court, what in progress; or so she may censure poets, and authors, and styles, and compare 'em, Daniel with Spenser, Jonson with the t'other youth, and so forth; or be thought cunning in controversies, or the very knots of divinity; and have often in her mouth the state of the question: and then skip to the mathematics, and demonstration; and answer in religion to one; in state, to another; in bawdry to a third.

MOROSE. Oh, Oh!

TRUEWIT. All this is very true, sir. And then her going in disguise to that conjurer, and this cunning woman: where the first question is, how soon you shall die? next, if her present servant love her? next that, if she shall have a new servant? and how many? which of her family would make the best bawd, male or female? what precedence she shall have by her next match? and sets down the answers, and believes 'em above the Scriptures. Nay, perhaps she'll study the art.

MOROSE. Gentle sir, ha'you done? ha'you had your pleasure o'me? I'll think of these things.

---

130 *stateswoman*: pretender to knowledge of affairs of state; female counterpart to Sir Pol of *Volpone*, or the statesmen of 'The New Cry' (*Epigrams*, 92).

131 *Salisbury*: where fashionable race-meetings were held.
Bath: fashionable resort for medicinal bathing in the springs.

132 *progress*: state journey made by the monarch through different parts of the kingdom.
censure: judge.

134 *Daniel*: Samuel Daniel, 1562–1619; important Elizabethan poet; compared with Spenser by contemporaries, but a rival scorned by Jonson; see Additional Note to this line, p. 442, and *Volpone*, III.iv.89, Additional Note, p. 440.
t'other youth: see Additional Note, p. 442 below.

135 *cunning*: learned, skilful.

136 *knots*: intricate problems.

137 *state of the question*: the main issue of a controversy.

143 *conjurer*: astrologer.

143–4 *cunning woman*: fortune-teller, woman possessed of magical knowledge.

148 *precedence*: the right of preceding others at public ceremonies and social functions.

151 *art*: fortune-telling.

TRUEWIT. Yes, sir: and then comes reeking home of vapour and sweat, with going afoot, and lies in a month of a new face, all oil, and birdlime; and rises in asses' milk, and is cleansed with a new fucus: God b'w'you, sir. One thing more (which I had almost forgot). This too, with whom you are to marry, may have made a conveyance of her virginity aforehand, as your wise widows do of their states before they marry, in trust to some friend, sir: who can tell? Or if she have not done it yet, she may do, upon the wedding day, or the night before, and antedate you cuckold. The like has been heard of, in nature. 'Tis no devised impossible thing, sir. God b'w'you: I'll be bold to leave this rope with you, sir, for a remembrance. Farewell, Mute. [*Exit.*]

MOROSE. Come, ha'me to my chamber: but first shut the door.

The horn again.

O, shut the door, shut the door: is he come again?

[*Enter* CUTBEARD.]

CUTBEARD. 'Tis I, sir, your barber.

MOROSE. Oh, Cutbeard, Cutbeard, Cutbeard! Here has been a cut-throat with me: help me in to my bed, and give me physic with thy counsel.

[*Exeunt.*]

---

154 *reeking*: steaming (from heat).
155 *lies in*: is confined (as in childbirth).
156 *birdlime*: sticky substance smeared on twigs to snare birds; here a cosmetic ingredient.
rises: see Textual Note, p. 433 below.
157 *fucus*: cosmetic wash.
158 *God b'w'you*: 'Goodbye', God be with you.
160 *conveyance*: legal transfer of property from one person to another; here, to prevent it from falling into the hands of the husband, to one who would administer it faithfully ('in trust') for the benefit of the owner.
162 *states*: estates, possessions.
163 *friend*: lover.
170 *ha'*: take.
176 *give me physic*: barbers were also surgeons and medical men.

SCENE III

[*Enter*] DAW, CLERIMONT, DAUPHINE, EPICOENE.

DAW. Nay, an' she will, let her refuse, at her own charges: 'tis nothing to me, gentlemen. But she will not be invited to the like feasts, or guests, every day.

CLERIMONT. Oh, by no means, she may not refuse –
They dissuade her, privately.
to stay at home, if you love your reputation. 'Slight, you are invited thither o'purpose to be seen, and laughed at by the lady of the college, and her shadows. This trumpeter hath proclaimed you.

DAUPHINE. You shall not go; let him be laughed at in your stead, for not bringing you: and put him to his extemporal faculty of fooling, and talking loud to satisfy the company.

CLERIMONT. He will suspect us, talk aloud. – Pray, Mistress Epicoene, let's see your verses; we have Sir John Daw's leave: do not conceal your servant's merit, and your own glories.

EPICOENE. They'll prove my servant's glories, if you have his leave so soon.

DAUPHINE. [*aside to* EPICOENE] His vainglories, lady!

DAW. Show 'em, show 'em, mistress, I dare own 'em.

EPICOENE. Judge you, what glories?

DAW. Nay, I'll read 'em myself, too: an author must recite his own works. It is a madrigal of modesty.

'Modest and fair, for fair and good are near
Neighbours, howe'er – '

DAUPHINE. Very good.

CLERIMONT. Ay, is't not?

DAW. 'No noble virtue ever was alone,
But two in one.'

---

1 *an'*: if.
1–2 *at . . . charges*: to . . . cost.
9 *shadows*: those who reflect; parasites.
This trumpeter: Daw. (Ironically, Epicoene has already been 'proclaimed' by the horn-blowing Truewit in II.ii.)
12 *extemporal*: extempore.
fooling: acting the fool.
25 *madrigal*: short lyrical poem about love.
26 ff. see Additional Note, p. 442 below.

DAUPHINE. Excellent!
CLERIMONT. That again, I pray, Sir John.
DAUPHINE. It has something in't like rare wit, and sense.
CLERIMONT. Peace.
DAW. 'No noble virtue ever was alone,
But two in one.
Then when I praise sweet modesty, I praise
Bright beauty's rays:
And having praised both beauty'and modesty,
I have praised thee.'
DAUPHINE. Admirable!
CLERIMONT. How it chimes, and cries tink i'the close, divinely!
DAUPHINE. Ay, 'tis Seneca.
CLERIMONT. No, I think 'tis Plutarch.
DAW. The dor on Plutarch, and Seneca, I hate it: they are mine own imaginations, by that light. I wonder those fellows have such credit with gentlemen!
CLERIMONT. They are very grave authors.
DAW. Grave asses! mere essayists! a few loose sentences, and that's all. A man would talk so, his whole age; I do utter as good things every hour, if they were collected, and observed, as either of 'em.
DAUPHINE. Indeed! Sir John?
CLERIMONT. He must needs, living among the Wits, and Braveries, too.
DAUPHINE. Ay, and being president of 'em, as he is.

---

34 *rare*: fine; also, 'hard to discover' – Dauphine's real meaning.

41 *beauty'*: the apostrophe indicates that the second syllable should be elided for the sake of the verse line.

44 *chimes*: jingles.
cries tink: rhymes, tinkles.

45 *close*: conclusion of a musical phrase – drawing attention to the unmusical phrasing of Daw's conclusion.

48 *The dor on*: a dismissive scoff: 'a fig for'.
Plutarch, and Seneca: compare Clerimont's rejection in I.i.69–70.

53 *essayists*: Jonson himself had a scathing view of modern essayists; see Additional Note to *Volpone*, III.iv.90, p. 440 below.

54 *sentences*: maxims, sententious sayings; ironically 'a few loose sentences' describes the structure of Daw's own manner of talking.

DAW. There's Aristotle, a mere commonplace fellow; Plato, a discourser; Thucydides and Livy, tedious and dry; Tacitus, an entire knot: sometimes worth the untying, very seldom.

CLERIMONT. What do you think of the poets, Sir John?

DAW. Not worthy to be named for authors. Homer, an old tedious prolix ass, talks of curriers, and chines of beef. Virgil, of dunging of land, and bees. Horace, of I know not what.

CLERIMONT. I think so.

DAW. And so Pindarus, Lycophron, Anacreon, Catullus, Seneca the tragedian, Lucan, Propertius, Tibullus, Martial, Juvenal, Ausonius, Statius, Politian, Valerius Flaccus, and the rest –

CLERIMONT. What a sack full of their names he has got!

DAUPHINE. And how he pours 'em out! Politian, with Valerius Flaccus!

62–5 see Additional Note, p. 442 below.

62 *commonplace*: trite, trivial; but also, Latin *locus communis*, a general theme applicable to many particular cases, a universal truth.

63 *discourser*: (mere) talker; but also, writer of discourses, notably the Socratic dialogues, in which truth is pursued through the medium of informed conversation.
Thucydides: *c.* 460–*c.*400 BC; greatest Greek historian.
Livy: 59 BC–AD 17; Roman historian.

64 *dry*: Livy's name suggests 'livid' (Latin *liveo*), blue or black, the colour of melancholy, the dry humour (noted by Partridge); and the humour associated with creativity and composition.
Tacitus: *c.* AD 55–*c.* 117; Roman historian; notorious for the curtness and obscurity of his Latin, though his name (= 'secret, concealed') also suggests 'knot'.
knot: tangle; but also, 'essential points'.

69 *curriers*: grooms of horses.

70 *chines*: backbones; in *The Iliad*, VII.321, Ajax is given the whole chine of an ox.

70–1 *dunging of land, and bees*: in *The Georgics*, I.79–81 and IV.

73–6 an indiscriminate jumble of foremost and mediocre Latin and Greek poets, and an Italian humanist (Politian); see Additional Note, p. 442 below.

77–82 perhaps spoken ironically in Daw's hearing.

79 *Politian*: Angelo Poliziano, 1454–94, brilliant Florentine humanist.

80 *Valerius Flaccus*: Latin poet of the first century AD; author of an unfinished, learned and mediocre epic, *Argonautica*.

CLERIMONT. Was not the character right of him?

DAUPHINE. As could be made, i'faith.

DAW. And Persius, a crabbed coxcomb, not to be endured.

DAUPHINE. Why, whom do you account for authors, Sir John Daw?

DAW. *Syntagma juris civilis*, *Corpus juris civilis*, *Corpus juris canonici*, the King of Spain's Bible.

DAUPHINE. Is the King of Spain's Bible an author?

CLERIMONT. Yes, and *Syntagma*.

DAUPHINE. What was that *Syntagma*, sir?

DAW. A civil lawyer, a Spaniard.

DAUPHINE. Sure, *Corpus* was a Dutchman.

CLERIMONT. Ay, both the *Corpuses*, I knew 'em: they were very corpulent authors.

DAW. And then there's Vatablus, Pomponatius, Symancha; the other are not to be received within the thought of a scholar.

DAUPHINE. 'Fore God, you have a simple learned servant, lady, in titles.

CLERIMONT. I wonder that he is not called to the helm, and made a councillor!

DAUPHINE. He is one extraordinary.

CLERIMONT. Nay, but in ordinary! To say truth, the state wants such.

DAUPHINE. Why, that will follow.

---

81 *character*: detailed report of a person's qualities; character sketch (compare I.ii.89 ff.).

83 *Persius*: AD 34–62; Roman satirist whose style was noted for its intricacy and obscurity.

87 *Syntagma juris civilis, Corpus juris civilis*: titles of collections of Roman civil law: *syntagma* (Greek) = a systematically arranged treatise; *corpus* (Latin) = the whole body of literature on a subject.

88 *Corpus juris canonici*: the collection of canon law. *King of Spain's Bible*: the polyglot Bible sponsored by Philip II of Spain, published in 1569–72.

95 *corpulent*: fleshy, fat (of people: the Dutch were held to be fat from their liking for drink and butter); thick, solid (of works).

96–7 *Vatablus, Pomponatius, Symancha*: respectively, Hebrew scholar and authority on Aristotle; philosopher and author of a tract on the immortality of the soul; Spanish jurist and authority on canon law; minor scholars of the sixteenth century.

99 *simple*: absolutely; but also, 'deficiently'.

103 *extraordinary*: outside the regular staff; but with an ironic pun.

104 *in ordinary*: of the regular officials; but also, 'undistinguished'.

105 *wants*: lacks; also (ironically) 'needs'.

CLERIMONT. I muse a mistress can be so silent to the dotes of such a servant.

DAW. 'Tis her virtue, sir. I have written somewhat of her silence too.

DAUPHINE. In verse, Sir John?

CLERIMONT. What else?

DAUPHINE. Why, how can you justify your own being of a poet, that so slight all the old poets?

DAW. Why, every man that writes in verse is not a poet; you have of the Wits that write verses, and yet are no poets: they are poets that live by it, the poor fellows that live by it.

DAUPHINE. Why, would not you live by your verses, Sir John?

CLERIMONT. No, 'twere pity he should. A knight live by his verses? He did not make 'em to that end, I hope.

DAUPHINE. And yet the noble Sidney lives by his, and the noble family not ashamed.

CLERIMONT. Ay, he professed himself; but Sir John Daw has more caution: he'll not hinder his own rising i'the state so much! do you think he will? Your verses, good Sir John, and no poems.

DAW. 'Silence in woman is like speech in man,
Deny't who can.'

DAUPHINE. Not I, believe it: your reason, sir.

DAW. 'Nor is't a tale,
That female vice should be a virtue male,
Or masculine vice a female virtue be:
You shall it see
Proved with increase,
I know to speak, and she to hold her peace.'
Do you conceive me, gentlemen?

---

108 *dotes*: natural endowments (Latin *dotes*); also, 'pieces of folly'.

121–2 *live by*: earn his living by; but Dauphine picks up the other meaning, 'gain immortality by'. See Additional Note, p. 442 below.

124 *Sidney*: 1554–86; his works were published after his death by his sister, the Countess of Pembroke.

126 *professed*: declared (in *The Apology for Poetry*, published in 1595).

127–8 *hinder his own rising*: through being considered too frivolous for affairs of state on account of his interest in poetry.

130 DAW: see Textual Note, p. 433 below.

139 *conceive*: understand; also, an appropriate pun of procreation.

DAUPHINE. No, faith; how mean you 'with increase', Sir John?

DAW. Why, 'with increase' is when I court her for the common cause of mankind; and she says nothing, but *consentire videtur*: and in time is *gravida*.

DAUPHINE. Then this is a ballad of procreation?

CLERIMONT. A madrigal of procreation, you mistake.

EPICOENE. Pray give me my verses again, servant.

DAW. If you'll ask 'em aloud, you shall.

[EPICOENE, DAW *walk aside*.]

CLERIMONT. See, here's Truewit again!

SCENE IV

[*Enter*] TRUEWIT [*with his post-horn*].

[CLERIMONT.] Where hast thou been, in the name of madness! thus accoutred with thy horn?

TRUEWIT. Where the sound of it might have pierced your senses with gladness, had you been in ear-reach of it. Dauphine, fall down and worship me: I have forbid the banns, lad. I have been with thy virtuous uncle, and have broke the match.

DAUPHINE. You ha'not, I hope.

TRUEWIT. Yes, faith; an' thou shouldst hope otherwise, I should repent me: this horn got me entrance, kiss it. I had no other way to get in, but by feigning to be a post; but when I got in once, I proved none, but rather the contrary, turned him into a post, or a stone, or what is stiffer, with thundering into him the incommodities of a wife, and the miseries of marriage. If ever Gorgon were seen in the shape of a woman, he hath seen her in my description. I have put him off o'that scent forever. Why do you not applaud, and adore me,

---

143 *common cause of mankind*: procreation.

144 *consentire videtur*: seems to consent.

gravida: pregnant.

13 *none*: Truewit is playing on two senses of *post*: 'messenger'; and also, 'block' (and therefore dumb).

16 *Gorgon*: one of three monstrous sisters of Greek myth, whose look turned people to stone.

sirs? Why stand you mute? Are you stupid? You are not worthy o'the benefit.

DAUPHINE. Did not I tell you? mischief! –

CLERIMONT. I would you had placed this benefit somewhere else.

TRUEWIT. Why so?

CLERIMONT. 'Slight, you have done the most inconsiderate, rash, weak thing, that ever man did to his friend.

DAUPHINE. Friend! If the most malicious enemy I have had studied to inflict an injury upon me, it could not be a greater.

TRUEWIT. Wherein? for God's sake! Gentlemen, come to yourselves again.

DAUPHINE. But I presaged thus much afore, to you.

CLERIMONT. Would my lips had been soldered, when I spake on't. 'Slight, what moved you to be thus impertinent?

TRUEWIT. My masters, do not put on this strange face to pay my courtesy: off with this visor. Have good turns done you, and thank 'em this way?

DAUPHINE. 'Fore heaven, you have undone me. That which I have plotted for, and been maturing now these four months, you have blasted in a minute: now I am lost, I may speak. This gentlewoman was lodged here by me o'purpose, and, to be put upon my uncle, hath professed this obstinate silence for my sake, being my entire friend; and one, that for the requital of such a fortune as to marry him, would have made me very ample conditions: where now, all my hopes are utterly miscarried by this unlucky accident.

CLERIMONT. Thus 'tis, when a man will be ignorantly officious; do services, and not know his why: I wonder what courteous itch possessed you! You never did absurder part i'your life, nor a greater

---

20 *stupid*: stupefied (Latin *stupidus* = stunned); also, 'slow-witted', 'dull'.

36–7 *to be thus impertinent*: to act out of turn so.

44 *now I am lost, I may speak*: proverbial: 'give losers leave to speak' (M. P. Tilley, *A Dictionary of Proverbs in England*, Ann Arbor: University of Michigan Press, 1950, L458).

46 *put upon*: imposed on; also, 'delude'.

47 *entire*: sincere.

55 *did*: played.

trespass to friendship, to humanity.

DAUPHINE. Faith, you may forgive it best: 'twas your cause principally.

CLERIMONT. I know it, would it had not.

[*Enter* CUTBEARD.]

DAUPHINE. How now, Cutbeard? what news?

CUTBEARD. The best, the happiest that ever was, sir. There has been a mad gentleman with your uncle this morning (I think this be the gentleman) that has almost talked him out of his wits, with threatening him from marriage –

DAUPHINE. On, I pray thee.

CUTBEARD. And your uncle, sir, he thinks 'twas done by your procurement; therefore he will see the party you wot of, presently: and if he like her, he says, and that she be so inclining to dumb as I have told him, he swears he will marry her today, instantly, and not defer it a minute longer.

DAUPHINE. Excellent! beyond our expectation!

TRUEWIT. Beyond your expectation? By this light, I knew it would be thus.

DAUPHINE. Nay, sweet Truewit, forgive me.

TRUEWIT. No, I was 'ignorantly officious', 'impertinent': this was 'the absurd, weak part'.

CLERIMONT. Wilt thou ascribe that to merit, now, was mere fortune?

TRUEWIT. Fortune? mere providence. Fortune had not a finger in't. I saw it must necessarily in nature fall out so: my genius is never false to me in these things. Show me how it could be otherwise.

DAUPHINE. Nay, gentlemen, contend not, 'tis well now.

TRUEWIT. Alas, I let him go on with 'inconsiderate', and 'rash', and what he pleased.

---

58 *cause*: fault.
69 *wot*: know.
presently: at once.
80 *mere*: downright.
81 *providence*: foresight (Latin *providentia*).
83 *genius*: attendant spirit 'Who wondrous things concerning our welfare . . . doth let us see' (Spenser, *Faerie Queene*, II.xii.47: 5–6).

CLERIMONT. Away, thou strange justifier of thyself, to be wiser than thou wert, by the event.

TRUEWIT. Event! By this light, thou shalt never persuade me but I foresaw it, as well as the stars themselves.

DAUPHINE. Nay, gentlemen, 'tis well now: do you two entertain Sir John Daw with discourse, while I send her away with instructions.

TRUEWIT. I'll be acquainted with her, first, by your favour.

[EPICOENE, DAW *come forward.*]

CLERIMONT. Master Truewit, lady, a friend of ours.

TRUEWIT. I am sorry I have not known you sooner, lady, to celebrate this rare virtue of your silence.

CLERIMONT. Faith, an' you had come sooner, you should ha'seen and heard her well celebrated in Sir John Daw's madrigals.

TRUEWIT. Jack Daw, God save you; when saw you La Foole?

[*Exeunt* DAUPHINE, EPICOENE, CUTBEARD.]

DAW. Not since last night, Master Truewit.

TRUEWIT. That's miracle! I thought you two had been inseparable.

DAW. He's gone to invite his guests.

TRUEWIT. Gods so! 'tis true! What a false memory have I towards that man! I am one: I met him e'en now, upon that he calls his delicate fine black horse, rid into a foam with posting from place to place, and person to person, to give 'em the cue –

CLERIMONT. Lest they should forget?

TRUEWIT. Yes: there was never poor captain took more pains at a muster to show men, than he, at this meal, to show friends.

DAW. It is his quarter-feast, sir.

CLERIMONT. What! do you say so, Sir John?

---

90 *event*: outcome.

111 *Gods so*: a corruption of either 'God's soul', or Italian *cazzo*, penis.

113 *delicate*: exquisite.

118 *show*: assemble for inspection.

120 *quarter-feast*: see Additional Note, p. 443 below.

TRUEWIT. Nay, Jack Daw will not be out, at the best friends he has, to the talent of his wit: where's his mistress, to hear and applaud him? Is she gone?

DAW. Is Mistress Epicoene gone?

CLERIMONT. Gone afore, with Sir Dauphine, I warrant, to the place.

TRUEWIT. Gone afore! That were a manifest injury; a disgrace and a half: to refuse him at such a festival time as this, being a Bravery, and a Wit too.

CLERIMONT. Tut, he'll swallow it like cream: he's better read in *jure civili* than to esteem anything a disgrace is offered him from a mistress.

DAW. Nay, let her e'en go; she shall sit alone, and be dumb in her chamber a week together, for John Daw, I warrant her: does she refuse me?

CLERIMONT. No, sir, do not take it so to heart: she does not refuse you, but a little neglect you. Good faith, Truewit, you were to blame to put it into his head that she does refuse him.

TRUEWIT. She does refuse him, sir, palpably: however you mince it. An' I were as he, I would swear to speak ne'er a word to her today, for't.

DAW. By this light, no more I will not.

TRUEWIT. Nor to anybody else, sir.

DAW. Nay, I will not say so, gentlemen.

CLERIMONT. [*aside to* TRUEWIT] It had been an excellent happy condition for the company, if you could have drawn him to it.

DAW. I'll be very melancholic, i'faith.

CLERIMONT. As a dog, if I were as you, Sir John.

TRUEWIT. Or a snail, or a hog-louse: I would roll myself up for this day, in troth, they should not unwind me.

DAW. By this pick-tooth, so I will.

CLERIMONT. [*aside to* TRUEWIT] 'Tis well done: he begins already to be angry with his teeth.

122–3 *be out . . . wit*: lose his jest which reveals the natural capacity of his wit to the full, even at the expense of his best friends.

130 *Bravery*: with an ironic glance at 'courage'.

132 *jure civili*: civil law.

139 *to blame*: see Textual Note, p. 433 below.

142 *mince*: minimise.

151 *dog*: proverbially melancholy.

152 *hog-louse*: wood-louse.

155 *pick-tooth*: toothpick, a fashionable affectation.

DAW. Will you go, gentlemen?

CLERIMONT. Nay, you must walk alone, if you be right melancholic, Sir John.

TRUEWIT. Yes sir, we'll dog you, we'll follow you afar off.

[*Exit* DAW.]

CLERIMONT. Was there ever such a two yards of knighthood, measured out by time, to be sold to laughter?

TRUEWIT. A mere talking mole! hang him: no mushroom was ever so fresh. A fellow so utterly nothing, as he knows not what he would be.

CLERIMONT. Let's follow him: but first, let's go to Dauphine, he's hovering about the house, to hear what news.

TRUEWIT. Content.

[*Exeunt.*]

SCENE V

[*Enter*] MOROSE, EPICOENE, CUTBEARD, MUTE.

MOROSE. Welcome, Cutbeard; draw near with your fair charge: and in her ear, softly entreat her to unmask. [*She unmasks*] So. Is the door shut? [MUTE *makes a leg*] Enough. Now, Cutbeard, with the same discipline I use to my family, I will question you. As I conceive, Cutbeard, this gentlewoman is she you have provided, and brought, in hope she will fit me in the place and person of a wife? Answer me not, but with your leg, unless it be otherwise. [CUTBEARD *makes a leg*] Very well done, Cutbeard. I conceive besides, Cutbeard, you have been pre-acquainted with her birth, education, and qualities, or else you would not prefer her to my acceptance, in the weighty consequence of marriage. [*Makes a leg*] This I conceive,

---

166 *mole*: proverbially blind.

166–7 *mushroom*: upstart; 'these mushroom gentlemen, / That shoot up in a night' (*Every Man out of his Humour*, I.ii.162–3).

167 *fresh*: insipid (H&S); raw, inexperienced.

3 s.d. see Textual Note, p. 433 below.

5 *family*: household (Latin *familia*).

Cutbeard. Answer me not but with your leg, unless it be otherwise. [*Makes another leg*] Very well done, Cutbeard. Give aside now a little, and leave me to examine her condition, and aptitude to my affection.

He goes about her, and views her.

She is exceeding fair, and of a special good favour; a sweet composition, or harmony of limbs: her temper of beauty has the true height of my blood. The knave hath exceedingly well fitted me without: I will now try her within. – Come near, fair gentlewoman: let not my behaviour seem rude, though unto you, being rare, it may haply appear strange.

She curtsies.

Nay, lady, you may speak, though Cutbeard, and my man, might not: for of all sounds, only the sweet voice of a fair lady has the just length of mine ears. I beseech you, say, lady, out of the first fire of meeting eyes (they say) love is stricken: do you feel any such motion, suddenly shot into you, from any part you see in me? ha, lady?

Curtsy.

Alas, lady, these answers by silent curtsies, from you, are too courtless, and simple. I have ever had my breeding in court; and she that shall be my wife must be accomplished with courtly, and audacious ornaments. Can you speak, lady?

EPICOENE. (*she speaks softly*) Judge you, forsooth.

MOROSE. What say you, lady? Speak out, I beseech you.

---

18 *Give aside*: condensed from 'give way' and 'stand aside'.
19 *condition*: disposition.
20 *affection*: liking.
21 *favour*: loveliness.
22–3 *composition . . . harmony . . . temper*: see Additional Note, p. 443 below.
23 *temper*: delicate balance (from tuning a musical instrument). *has . . . blood*: is exactly attuned to the high pitch of my appetite.
24–5 *without*: in external appearance.
25 *try her within*: test her temper, disposition.
27 *rare*: exceptionally excellent.
31 *just length of*: exact attunement to.
34 *motion*: stirring of the soul, emotion.
37 *courtless*: uncourtly.
39 *audacious*: spirited (Gifford); but also 'bold'.

EPICOENE. Judge you, forsooth.

MOROSE. O'my judgement, a divine softness! But can you naturally, lady, as I enjoin these by doctrine and industry, refer yourself to the search of my judgement, and (not taking pleasure in your tongue, which is a woman's chiefest pleasure) think it plausible to answer me by silent gestures, so long as my speeches jump right with what you conceive?

Curtsy.

Excellent! divine! If it were possible she should hold out thus! Peace, Cutbeard, thou art made forever, as thou hast made me, if this felicity have lasting: but I will try her further. – Dear lady, I am courtly, I tell you, and I must have mine ears banqueted with pleasant, and witty conferences, pretty girds, scoffs, and dalliance in her that I mean to choose for my bed-phere. The ladies in court think it a most desperate impair to their quickness of wit, and good carriage, if they cannot give occasion for a man to court 'em; and when an amorous discourse is set on foot, minister as good matter to continue it, as himself: and do you alone so much differ from all them, that what they (with so much circumstance) affect, and toil for, to seem learned, to seem judicious, to seem sharp, and conceited, you can bury in yourself, with silence? and rather trust your graces to the fair conscience of virtue, than to the world's, or your own proclamation?

EPICOENE. I should be sorry else.

MOROSE. What say you, lady? Good lady, speak out.

EPICOENE. I should be sorry, else.

MOROSE. That sorrow doth fill me with gladness! O

---

47 *industry*: diligence.
search: extent.
51 *jump right*: exactly tally.
59 *pretty girds*: ingenious taunts.
60 *bed-phere*: bedfellow.
61 *desperate impair*: irremediable injury.
62 *carriage*: behaviour, bearing (with an unconscious innuendo).
67 *circumstance*: ado.
affect: aspire to.
69 *conceited*: witty.
70 *conscience*: inward knowledge.

Morose! thou art happy above mankind! pray that thou mayst contain thyself. I will only put her to it once more, and it shall be with the utmost touch, and test of their sex. – But hear me, fair lady, I do also love to see her, whom I shall choose for my heifer, to be the first and principal in all fashions; precede all the dames at court by a fortnight; have her council of tailors, lineners, lace-women, embroiderers, and sit with 'em sometimes twice a day, upon French intelligences; and then come forth, varied like Nature, or oftener than she, and better, by the help of Art, her emulous servant. This do I affect. And how will you be able, lady, with this frugality of speech, to give the manifold (but necessary) instructions for that bodice, these sleeves, those skirts, this cut, that stitch, this embroidery, that lace, this wire, those knots, that ruff, those roses, this girdle, that fan, the t'other scarf, these gloves? ha! what say you, lady?

EPICOENE. I'll leave it to you, sir.

MOROSE. How, lady? pray you, rise a note.

EPICOENE. I leave it to wisdom, and you, sir.

MOROSE. Admirable creature! I will trouble you no more: I will not sin against so sweet a simplicity. Let me now be bold to print, on those divine lips, the seal of being mine. Cutbeard, I give thee the lease of thy house free: thank me not, but with thy leg. [*Makes a leg*] I know what thou wouldst say, she's poor, and her friends deceased; she has brought a wealthy dowry in her silence, Cutbeard: and in respect of her poverty, Cutbeard, I shall have her more loving, and obedient, Cutbeard. Go thy ways, and get me a minister presently, with a soft, low voice to marry us, and pray him he will not be impertinent, but brief as he can; away:

---

79 *touch*: trial.
82 *heifer*: bride; literally, a young cow that has not yet had a calf. See Additional Note, p. 443 below.
principal: foremost.
84 *lineners*: drapers.
86 *French intelligences*: (fashion) dispatches from France.
89 *affect*: like.
92 *cut*: fashionable slash in gowns through which the silk showed.
93 *wire*: to support ruff or hair.
knots: bows.
111 *be impertinent*: introduce unnecessary matter.

softly, Cutbeard.

[*Exit* CUTBEARD.]

Sirrah, conduct your mistress into the dining room, your now-mistress.

[*Exeunt* MUTE, EPICOENE.]

O my felicity! How I shall be revenged on mine insolent kinsman, and his plots to fright me from marrying! This night I will get an heir, and thrust him out of my blood like a stranger; he would be knighted, forsooth, and thought by that means to reign over me, his title must do it: no, kinsman, I will now make you bring me the tenth lord's and the sixteenth lady's letter, kinsman; and it shall do you no good, kinsman. Your knighthood itself shall come on its knees, and it shall be rejected; it shall be sued for its fees to execution, and not be redeemed; it shall cheat at the twelvepenny ordinary, it knighthood, for its diet all the term time, and tell tales for it in the vacation, to the hostess: or it knighthood shall do worse, take sanctuary in Coleharbour, and fast. It shall fright all it friends with borrowing letters; and when one of the fourscore hath brought it knighthood ten shillings, it knighthood shall go to the Cranes, or the Bear at the Bridge foot, and be drunk in fear: it shall not have money to discharge one tavern reckoning, to invite the old creditors to forbear it knighthood; or the new that should be, to trust it knighthood. It shall be the tenth name in the bond, to take up the

---

121–2 *tenth . . . letter*: recommendations by (presumably) obscure court patrons; or by patrons obtained after fruitless application to nine and fifteen other lords and ladies (?).

125 *to execution*: as far as seizure by writ of possession (for debt).

126–7 *twelvepenny ordinary*: one of the better eating-houses.

127 *it*: archaic form of 'its' or 'his'; used in baby talk; throughout this passage used contemptuously.

128 *tell tales for it*: earn his food by witty conversation which draws customers.

130 *Coleharbour*: Coldharbour, where debtors found sanctuary.

131 *borrowing*: begging.

133 *Cranes . . . Bear*: the Three Cranes in the Vintry, and the Bear below London Bridge, popular taverns.

136 *forbear*: refrain from pressing demands on.

138 *tenth name*: tenth man to be paid off (who therefore gets very little).

commodity of pipkins, and stone jugs; and the part thereof shall not furnish it knighthood forth for the attempting of a baker's widow, a brown baker's widow. It shall give it knighthood's name for a stallion to all gamesome citizens' wives, and be refused; when the master of a dancing-school, or (how do you call him) the worst reveller in the town is taken: it shall want clothes, and by reason of that, wit, to fool to lawyers. It shall not have hope to repair itself by Constantinople, Ireland, or Virginia; but the best, and last fortune to it knighthood shall be to make Dol Tearsheet, or Kate Common, a lady: and so it knighthood may eat.

[*Exit.*]

SCENE VI

[*Enter*] TRUEWIT, DAUPHINE, CLERIMONT.

TRUEWIT. Are you sure he is not gone by?

DAUPHINE. No, I stayed in the shop ever since.

CLERIMONT. But he may take the other end of the lane.

DAUPHINE. No, I told him I would be here at this end: I appointed him hither.

TRUEWIT. What a barbarian it is to stay then!

[*Enter* CUTBEARD.]

DAUPHINE. Yonder he comes.

---

139 *commodity*: consignment of worthless goods which money-lenders imposed on borrowers as part of their loan. *pipkins*: small earthenware pots.

141 *brown*: coarse, inferior (of bread); dark-complexioned, not 'fair' (of people): not much of a matrimonial catch in either respect.

145 *how*: see Textual Note, p. 434 below.

147 *fool to*: delude, trick.

148–9 *Constantinople . . . Virginia*: refuges for the needy, wastrels, and criminals, where they could try to recoup their fortune or escape the law.

150–1 *Dol Tearsheet, or Kate Common*: prostitutes. Dol Tearsheet is in *Henry IV*, Part 2; Kate perhaps becomes Dol Common in *The Alchemist*.

151 *may eat*: i.e. live off the immoral earnings of his wife.

6 *appointed him hither*: arranged to meet him here.

CLERIMONT. And his charge left behind him, which is a very good sign, Dauphine.

DAUPHINE. How now, Cutbeard, succeeds it, or no?

CUTBEARD. Past imagination, sir, *omnia secunda*; you could not have prayed to have had it so well: *saltat senex*, as it is i'the proverb, he does triumph in his felicity; admires the party! He has given me the lease of my house too! and I am now going for a silent minister to marry 'em, and away.

TRUEWIT. 'Slight, get one o'the silenced ministers, a zealous brother would torment him purely.

CUTBEARD. *Cum privilegio*, sir.

DAUPHINE. Oh, by no means, let's do nothing to hinder it now; when 'tis done and finished, I am for you: for any device of vexation.

CUTBEARD. And that shall be within this half hour, upon my dexterity, gentlemen. Contrive what you can in the meantime, *bonis avibus*. [*Exit.*]

CLERIMONT. How the slave doth Latin it!

TRUEWIT. It would be made a jest to posterity, sirs, this day's mirth, if ye will.

CLERIMONT. Beshrew his heart that will not, I pronounce.

DAUPHINE. And for my part. What is't?

TRUEWIT. To translate all La Foole's company, and his feast hither, today, to celebrate this bride-ale.

DAUPHINE. Ay, marry, but how will't be done?

TRUEWIT. I'll undertake the directing of all the lady guests thither, and then the meat must follow.

CLERIMONT. For God's sake, let's effect it: it will be an excellent comedy of affliction, so many several noises.

DAUPHINE. But are they not at the other place already, think you?

TRUEWIT. I'll warrant you for the college-honours:

12, 14 *omnia secunda . . . saltat senex*: Latin proverb: 'All's well, the old man's dancing.'

18 *silenced ministers*: Puritans banned from preaching, whose sermons would have been excessively wordy.

19 *purely*: perfectly; also, 'in the Puritan manner'.

20 *Cum privilegio*: with authority.

26 *bonis avibus*: with favourable omens.

33 *translate*: transfer; also, 'transform'.

34 *bride-ale*: old-fashioned wedding-feast, bridal. See Textual Note, p. 434 below.

39 *several*: different.

one o'their faces has not the priming colour laid on yet, nor the other her smock sleeked.

CLERIMONT. Oh, but they'll rise earlier than ordinary, to a feast.

TRUEWIT. Best go see, and assure ourselves.

CLERIMONT. Who knows the house?

TRUEWIT. I'll lead you; were you never there yet?

DAUPHINE. Not I.

CLERIMONT. Nor I.

TRUEWIT. Where ha'you lived, then? not know Tom Otter!

CLERIMONT. No: for God's sake, what is he?

TRUEWIT. An excellent animal, equal with your Daw, or La Foole, if not transcendent; and does Latin it as much as your barber: he is his wife's subject, he calls her princess, and at such times as these, follows her up and down the house like a page, with his hat off, partly for heat, partly for reverence. At this instant, he is marshalling of his bull, bear, and horse.

DAUPHINE. What be those, in the name of Sphinx?

TRUEWIT. Why, sir, he has been a great man at the Bear Garden in his time: and from that subtle sport, has ta'en the witty denomination of his chief carousing cups. One he calls his bull, another his bear, another his horse. And then he has his lesser glasses, that he calls his deer, and his ape; and several degrees of 'em too: and never is well, nor thinks any entertainment perfect, till these be brought out, and set o'the cupboard.

CLERIMONT. For God's love! We should miss this, if we should not go.

TRUEWIT. Nay, he has a thousand things as good, that will speak him all day. He will rail on his wife, with certain commonplaces, behind her back; and to her face –

---

45 *sleeked*: smoothed, ironed.

61–2 *for reverence*: out of respect. (It was a mark of respect to stand bare-headed in the presence of a superior.)

64 *Sphinx*: invoked as an asker of riddles.

66 *Bear Garden*: on the Bankside, next to Paris Garden.

68–9 *bull . . . bear . . . horse*: from the covers of the cups, shaped like the heads of these animals.

71 *degrees*: ascending (or descending) sizes.

77 *speak him*: reveal what he is.

DAUPHINE. No more of him. Let's go see him, I petition you.

[*Exeunt.*]

ACT III

SCENE I

[*Enter*] OTTER, MISTRESS OTTER: TRUEWIT, CLERIMONT, DAUPHINE [*follow shortly, unperceived*].

OTTER. Nay, good princess, hear me *pauca verba*.

MISTRESS OTTER. By that light, I'll ha'you chained up with your bull-dogs and bear-dogs, if you be not civil the sooner. I'll send you to kennel, i'faith. You were best bait me with your bull, bear, and horse! Never a time that the courtiers, or Collegiates come to the house, but you make it a Shrove Tuesday! I would have you get your Whitsuntide velvet cap, and your staff i'your hand, to entertain 'em: yes in troth, do.

OTTER. Not so, princess, neither, but under correction, sweet princess, gi'me leave – these things I am known to the courtiers by. It is reported to them for my humour, and they receive it so, and do expect it. Tom Otter's bull, bear, and horse is known all over England, *in rerum natura*.

---

1 *pauca verba*: few words; an alehouse catch-phrase: 'Talk less, drink more.'

5 *were best*: had best.

8 *Shrove Tuesday*: see I.i.179 n.

9 *velvet cap*: appropriate wear for a holiday.
staff: of office. Mistress Otter implies that Otter is the presiding fool of the festivities.

11–12 *under correction*: subject to correction; a phrase implying deference to a superior.

14 *humour*: personal oddity; an affectation, judged by the standards Jonson sets out in the Induction to *Every Man out of his Humour*. For the physio-psychological theory of humours, see Additional Note to *Volpone*, II.ii.109, p. 439 below.

16 *in rerum natura*: literally, 'in the nature of things'. (The usual meaning of this tag is found in III.ii.7.)

MISTRESS OTTER. Fore me, I will 'na-ture' 'em over to Paris Garden, and 'na-ture' you thither too, if you pronounce 'em again. Is a bear a fit beast, or a bull, to mix in society with great ladies? think i'your discretion, in any good polity?

OTTER. The horse then, good princess.

MISTRESS OTTER. Well, I am contented for the horse: they love to be well horsed, I know. I love it myself.

OTTER. And it is a delicate fine horse this. *Poetarum Pegasus*. Under correction, princess, Jupiter did turn himself into a – *taurus*, or bull, under correction, good princess.

MISTRESS OTTER. By my integrity, I'll send you over to the Bankside, I'll commit you to the Master of the Garden, if I hear but a syllable more. Must my house, or my roof, be polluted with the scent of bears, and bulls, when it is perfumed for great ladies? Is this according to the instrument, when I married you? That I would be princess, and reign in mine own house: and you would be my subject, and obey me? What did you bring me, should make you thus peremptory? Do I allow you your half crown a day, to spend where you will among your gamesters, to vex and torment me at such times as these? Who gives you your maintenance, I pray you? Who allows you your horse meat, and man's meat? your three suits of apparel a year? your four pair of stockings, one silk, three worsted? your clean linen, your bands, and cuffs

---

17 *Fore*: for. Mistress Otter characteristically takes her solemn oath upon herself.
21 *good polity*: well-ordered state; a high-flown term in context.
24 *horsed*: with sexual implications of 'mounted' and 'ride'.
26–7 *Poetarum Pegasus*: the poets' Pegasus; see Additional Note, p. 443 below.
28 *taurus*: Jupiter's transformation when he carried off Europa.
32 *Garden*: Bear Garden.
35 *instrument*: formal legal document.
39 *peremptory*: stubborn, self-willed.
41 *gamesters*: gamblers.
43 *horse meat*: horse fodder.
44 *three suits*: a servant's allowance.
45 *silk*: for special occasions.
46 *bands*: collars or ruffs.

when I can get you to wear 'em? 'Tis mar'l you ha' 'em on now. Who graces you with courtiers, or great personages, to speak to you out of their coaches, and come home to your house? Were you ever so much as looked upon by a lord, or a lady, before I married you: but on the Easter or Whitsun holidays? and then out at the Banqueting House window, when Ned Whiting, or George Stone, were at the stake?

TRUEWIT. [*aside*] (For God's sake, let's go stave her off him.)

MISTRESS OTTER. Answer me to that. And did not I take you up from thence, in an old greasy buff-doublet, with points; and green velvet sleeves, out at the elbows? You forget this.

TRUEWIT. [*aside*] (She'll worry him, if we help not in time.)

MISTRESS OTTER. Oh, here are some o'the gallants! Go to, behave yourself distinctly, and with good morality; or I protest, I'll take away your exhibition.

SCENE II

TRUEWIT, CLERIMONT, DAUPHINE [*come forward*].

TRUEWIT. By your leave, fair Mistress Otter, I'll be bold to enter these gentlemen in your acquaintance.

---

47 *mar'l*: marvel.
53 *Banqueting House*: at Whitehall. Bulls and bears were baited there at Shrovetide and Easter.
54 *Ned Whiting . . . George Stone*: famous bears.
56–7 *stave . . . off*: drive off with staves, as dogs were driven off in bull- and bear-baiting.
59–60 *buff-doublet*: leather jacket, worn by ordinary soldiers.
60 *points*: laces.
62 *worry*: as in bear-baiting.
65 *distinctly*: properly (Latin *distincte*).
66 *morality*: moral behaviour. Here, and in conversation with the gallants and Collegiates, Mistress Otter adopts an affected idiom which she thinks courtly.
67 *exhibition*: allowance.
2 *enter . . . in*: admit to.

MISTRESS OTTER. It shall not be obnoxious, or difficil, sir.

TRUEWIT. How does my noble captain? Is the bull, bear, and horse, *in rerum natura* still?

OTTER. Sir, *sic visum superis*.

MISTRESS OTTER. I would you would but intimate 'em, do. Go your ways in, and get toasts and butter made for the woodcocks. That's a fit province for you.

[*Exit* OTTER.]

CLERIMONT. [*aside to* TRUEWIT, DAUPHINE] Alas, what a tyranny is this poor fellow married to.

TRUEWIT. Oh, but the sport will be anon, when we get him loose.

DAUPHINE. Dares he ever speak?

TRUEWIT. No Anabaptist ever railed with the like licence: but mark her language in the meantime, I beseech you.

MISTRESS OTTER. Gentlemen, you are very aptly come. My cousin, Sir Amorous, will be here briefly.

TRUEWIT. In good time, lady. Was not Sir John Daw here, to ask for him, and the company?

MISTRESS OTTER. I cannot assure you, Master Truewit. Here was a very melancholy knight in a ruff, that demanded my subject for somebody, a gentleman, I think.

CLERIMONT. Ay, that was he, lady.

MISTRESS OTTER. But he departed straight, I can resolve you.

DAUPHINE. What an excellent choice phrase this lady expresses in!

---

4 *obnoxious*: offensive.
5 *difficil*: troublesome.
7 *in rerum natura*: anywhere, in the universe; the usual sense of this phrase. See III.i.16, and n.
8 *sic visum superis*: as those above decree.
9 *intimate*: either, 'get intimate with', an affected way of saying 'go and join (your animals)'; or, threateningly, 'start that topic again . . .' ('*Intimare*, to intimate, . . . to proclaim, set abroach', Florio, 1611).
10–12 see Additional Note, p. 443 below.
18 *Anabaptist*: here, synonymous with Puritan.
23 *briefly*: shortly.
32 *resolve*: assure (affected idiom).

TRUEWIT. Oh, sir! she is the only authentical courtier, that is not naturally bred one, in the city.

MISTRESS OTTER. You have taken that report upon trust, gentlemen.

TRUEWIT. No, I assure you, the court governs it so, lady, in your behalf.

MISTRESS OTTER. I am the servant of the court, and courtiers, sir.

TRUEWIT. They are rather your idolaters.

MISTRESS OTTER. Not so, sir.

[*Enter* CUTBEARD.]

DAUPHINE. How now, Cutbeard? Any cross?

CUTBEARD. Oh, no, sir: *omnia bene*. 'Twas never better o'the hinges, all's sure. I have so pleased him with a curate, that he's gone to't almost with the delight he hopes for soon.

DAUPHINE. What is he, for a vicar?

CUTBEARD. One that has catched a cold, sir, and can scarce be heard six inches off; as if he spoke out of a bulrush that were not picked, or his throat were full of pith: a fine quick fellow, and an excellent barber of prayers. I came to tell you, sir, that you might *omnem movere lapidem* (as they say) be ready with your vexation.

DAUPHINE. Gramercy, honest Cutbeard, be thereabouts with thy key to let us in.

CUTBEARD. I will not fail you, sir: *ad manum*. [*Exit.*]

TRUEWIT. Well, I'll go watch my coaches.

CLERIMONT. Do; and we'll send Daw to you, if you meet him not.

[*Exit* TRUEWIT.]

MISTRESS OTTER. Is Master Truewit gone?

DAUPHINE. Yes, lady, there is some unfortunate business fallen out.

MISTRESS OTTER. So I judged by the physiognomy of

---

39 *governs*: determines.
45 *cross*: hindrance.
46 *omnia bene*: all's well.
47 *o'the hinges*: went more smoothly.
48 *curate*: parson, one having cure (or charge) of souls.
52–3 *out of a bulrush . . . not picked*: i.e. huskily; *picked* = cleaned out, cleared.
56 *omnem movere lapidem*: leave no stone unturned.
58 *Gramercy*: thanks.
60 *ad manum*: at hand.

the fellow that came in; and I had a dream last night too of the new pageant, and my Lady Mayoress, which is always very ominous to me. I told it my Lady Haughty t'other day; when her honour came hither to see some china stuffs: and she expounded it out of Artemidorus, and I have found it since very true. It has done me many affronts.

CLERIMONT. Your dream, lady?

MISTRESS OTTER. Yes, sir, anything I do but dream o'the city. It stained me a damask tablecloth cost me eighteen pound, at one time; and burnt me a black satin gown, as I stood by the fire at my Lady Centaur's chamber in the college, another time. A third time, at the lord's masque, it dropped all my wire and my ruff with wax candle, that I could not go up to the banquet. A fourth time, as I was taking coach to go to Ware to meet a friend, it dashed me a new suit all over (a crimson satin doublet, and black velvet skirts) with a brewer's horse, that I was fain to go in and shift me, and kept my chamber a leash of days for the anguish of it.

DAUPHINE. These were dire mischances, lady.

CLERIMONT. I would not dwell in the city, and 'twere so fatal to me.

MISTRESS OTTER. Yes sir, but I do take advice of my doctor, to dream of it as little as I can.

DAUPHINE. You do well, Mistress Otter.

[*Enter* DAW: CLERIMONT *takes him aside.*]

MISTRESS OTTER. Will it please you to enter the house farther, gentlemen?

---

69 *pageant*: procession attending the installation of a new Lord Mayor.

73 *Artemidorus*: second-century Greek author of a treatise on the meaning of dreams.

78 *me*: ethic dative; similarly at 79 and 86.

85 *Ware*: twenty miles north of London, a place notorious for amorous assignations.

86–7 *crimson satin . . . velvet*: colour and expensive cloths reserved for the better classes.

87 *doublet*: strictly, man's attire; a fashion which characteristically appeals to the domineering Mistress Otter.

88 *shift me*: change my clothes.

89 *leash*: three (hunting term for a set of three hounds or hawks).

DAUPHINE. And your favour, lady: but we stay to speak with a knight, Sir John Daw, who is here come. We shall follow you, lady.

MISTRESS OTTER. At your own time, sir. It is my cousin Sir Amorous his feast –

DAUPHINE. I know it, lady.

MISTRESS OTTER. And mine together. But it is for his honour; and therefore I take no name of it, more than of the place.

DAUPHINE. You are a bounteous kinswoman.

MISTRESS OTTER. Your servant, sir. [*Exit.*]

SCENE III

CLERIMONT [*comes forward with*] DAW.

CLERIMONT. Why, do not you know it, Sir John Daw?

DAW. No, I am a rook if I do.

CLERIMONT. I'll tell you then; she's married by this time! And whereas you were put i'the head that she was gone with Sir Dauphine, I assure you, Sir Dauphine has been the noblest, honestest friend to you, that ever gentleman of your quality could boast of. He has discovered the whole plot, and made your mistress so acknowledging, and indeed, so ashamed of her injury to you, that she desires you to forgive her, and but grace her wedding with your presence today – She is to be married to a very good fortune, she says, his uncle, old Morose: and she willed me in private to tell you, that she shall be able to do you more favours, and with more security now, than before.

DAW. Did she say so, i'faith?

CLERIMONT. Why, what do you think of me, Sir John! ask Sir Dauphine.

DAW. Nay, I believe you. – Good Sir Dauphine, did she desire me to forgive her?

---

99 *And your favour*: with your permission.
106 *name of*: credit for.
107 *of the place*: for providing the place.
3 *rook*: simpleton, fool.
8 *quality*: rank.
21 DAW: see Textual Note, p. 434 below.

DAUPHINE. I assure you, Sir John, she did.

DAW. Nay then, I do with all my heart, and I'll be jovial.

CLERIMONT. Yes, for look you sir, this was the injury to you. La Foole intended this feast to honour her bridal day, and made you the property to invite the college ladies, and promise to bring her: and then at the time she should have appeared (as his friend) to have given you the dor. Whereas now, Sir Dauphine has brought her to a feeling of it, with this kind of satisfaction, that you shall bring all the ladies to the place where she is, and be very jovial; and there she will have a dinner, which shall be in your name: and so disappoint La Foole, to make you good again, and (as it were) a saver i'the man.

DAW. As I am a knight, I honour her, and forgive her heartily.

CLERIMONT. About it then presently; Truewit is gone before to confront the coaches, and to acquaint you with so much, if he meet you. Join with him, and 'tis well.

[*Enter* LA FOOLE.]

See, here comes your antagonist, but take you no notice, but be very jovial.

LA FOOLE. Are the ladies come, Sir John Daw, and your mistress?

[*Exit* DAW.]

Sir Dauphine! you are exceeding welcome, and honest Master Clerimont. Where's my cousin? Did you see no Collegiates, gentlemen?

---

25 *jovial*: cheerful, happy; literally, in the state of spirits caused by the influence of the planet Jupiter.

28 *property*: tool, cat's paw.

31 *given you the dor*: made a fool of you; see Additional Note, p. 443 below.

32 *feeling of*: sensitivity to.

36–7 *make you good again*: recoup your losses (as in gambling); also, 'recover your standing in society'.

37 *saver*: a gambling term, 'one who escapes loss, though without gain' (Dr Johnson).

i'the man: of your manhood; with a pun on *main* = main point, turning the tables on La Foole; also, fixed score in the dice game, hazard, which if thrown by the caster enabled the other players to regain their stake money. See Textual Note, p. 434 below.

DAUPHINE. Collegiates! Do you not hear, Sir Amorous, how you are abused?

LA FOOLE. How, sir!

CLERIMONT. Will you speak so kindly to Sir John Daw, that has done you such an affront?

LA FOOLE. Wherein, gentlemen? Let me be a suitor to you to know, I beseech you!

CLERIMONT. Why sir, his mistress is married today to Sir Dauphine's uncle, your cousin's neighbour, and he has diverted all the ladies, and all your company thither, to frustrate your provision, and stick a disgrace upon you. He was here, now, to have enticed us away from you too: but we told him his own, I think.

LA FOOLE. Has Sir John Daw wronged me so inhumanly?

DAUPHINE. He has done it, Sir Amorous, most maliciously, and treacherously: but if you'll be ruled by us, you shall quit him, i'faith.

LA FOOLE. Good gentlemen! I'll make one, believe it. How, I pray?

DAUPHINE. Marry, sir, get me your pheasants, and your godwits, and your best meat, and dish it in silver dishes of your cousin's presently, and say nothing, but clap me a clean towel about you, like a sewer; and bare-headed, march afore it with a good confidence ('tis but over the way, hard by) and we'll second you, where you shall set it o'the board, and bid 'em welcome to't, which shall show 'tis yours, and disgrace his preparation utterly: and for your cousin, whereas she should be troubled here at home with care of making and giving welcome, she shall transfer all that labour thither, and be a principal guest herself, sit ranked with the college-Honours, and be honoured, and have her health drunk as often, as bare, and as loud as the best of 'em.

---

61 *provision*: preparations.
64 *his own*: the truth about himself.
70 *make one*: join in.
76 *sewer*: gentleman in a noble household who overlooked the setting of the table and the placing of the dishes.
bare-headed: as a servant would be in the presence of superiors.
78 *second*: accompany, follow.
86 *bare*: bare-headed.

LA FOOLE. I'll go tell her presently. It shall be done, that's resolved. [*Exit.*]

CLERIMONT. I thought he would not hear it out, but 'twould take him.

DAUPHINE. Well, there be guests, and meat now; how shall we do for music?

CLERIMONT. The smell of the venison going through the street will invite one noise of fiddlers or other.

DAUPHINE. I would it would call the trumpeters thither.

CLERIMONT. Faith, there is hope, they have intelligence of all feasts. There's good correspondence betwixt them, and the London cooks. 'Tis twenty to one but we have 'em.

DAUPHINE. 'Twill be a most solemn day for my uncle, and an excellent fit of mirth for us.

CLERIMONT. Ay, if we can hold up the emulation betwixt Foole, and Daw, and never bring them to expostulate.

DAUPHINE. Tut, flatter 'em both (as Truewit says) and you may take their understandings in a purse-net. They'll believe themselves to be just such men as we make 'em, neither more nor less. They have nothing, not the use of their senses, but by tradition.

[LA FOOLE] *enters like a sewer.*

CLERIMONT. See! Sir Amorous has his towel on already. Have you persuaded your cousin?

LA FOOLE. Yes, 'tis very feasible: she'll do anything she says, rather than the La Fooles shall be disgraced.

DAUPHINE. She is a noble kinswoman. It will be such a pestling device, Sir Amorous! It will pound all

---

95 *noise*: band.

99 *correspondence*: communication; also, 'business relations'.

102 *solemn*: of fitting ceremoniousness; also, 'sombre', 'gloomy'.

103 *fit*: bout.

104 *emulation*: contention, ill-will between rivals.

106 *expostulate*: declare their grievance.

108–9 *purse-net*: bag-shaped net, secured by draw-strings, used for catching rabbits.

112 *tradition*: i.e. what is handed to them (Latin *traditio* = instruction or doctrine delivered).

119 *pestling*: crushing, as with a pestle.

your enemy's practices to powder, and blow him up with his own mine, his own train.

LA FOOLE. Nay, we'll give fire, I warrant you.

CLERIMONT. But you must carry it privately, without any noise, and take no notice by any means –

[*Enter* OTTER.]

OTTER. Gentlemen, my princess says you shall have all her silver dishes, *festinate*: and she's gone to alter her tire a little, and go with you –

CLERIMONT. And yourself too, Captain Otter.

DAUPHINE. By any means, sir.

OTTER. Yes sir, I do mean it: but I would entreat my cousin Sir Amorous, and you gentlemen, to be suitors to my princess, that I may carry my bull, and my bear, as well as my horse.

CLERIMONT. That you shall do, Captain Otter.

LA FOOLE. My cousin will never consent, gentlemen.

DAUPHINE. She must consent, Sir Amorous, to reason.

LA FOOLE. Why, she says they are no *decorum* among ladies.

OTTER. But they are *decora*, and that's better, sir.

CLERIMONT. Ay, she must hear argument. Did not Pasiphaë, who was a queen, love a bull? and was not Callisto, the mother of Arcas, turned into a bear, and made a star, Mistress Ursula, i'the heavens?

OTTER. O God! that I could ha'said as much! I will

---

120 *practices*: plots.
121 *train*: a gunpowder fuse, laid to explode a mine; also 'trick', 'snare'.
123 *carry*: carry off.
126 *festinate*: quickly, straightaway.
127 *tire*: headdress.
138 *no decorum*: an impropriety.
140 *decora*: handsome, adorned (Latin *decorus*); punning on the plural form of *decorum*.
142 *Pasiphaë*: wife of Minos of Crete; the Minotaur was born from her union with a bull.
143 *Callisto*: loved by Jupiter, by whom she had a son, Arcas; she was transformed into a bear by Juno, and after her death into a constellation, the Great Bear, by Jupiter.
144 *Ursula*: diminutive form of Latin *ursa* = bear; not strictly applicable to the Great Bear, *ursa major*.

have these stories painted i'the Bear Garden, *ex Ovidii Metamorphosi*.

DAUPHINE. Where is your princess, captain? Pray be our leader.

OTTER. That I shall, sir.

CLERIMONT. Make haste, good Sir Amorous.

[*Exeunt.*]

SCENE IV

[*Enter*] MOROSE, EPICOENE, PARSON, CUTBEARD.

MOROSE. Sir, there's an angel for yourself, and a brace of angels for your cold. Muse not at this manage of my bounty. It is fit we should thank Fortune double to nature, for any benefit she confers upon us; besides, it is your imperfection, but my solace.

PARSON. (*speaks as having a cold*) I thank your worship, so is it mine, now.

MOROSE. What says he, Cutbeard?

CUTBEARD. He says, *praesto*, sir, whensoever your worship needs him, he can be ready with the like. He got this cold with sitting up late, and singing catches with cloth-workers.

MOROSE. No more. I thank him.

PARSON. God keep your worship, and give you much joy with your fair spouse. (*He coughs*) Umh, umh.

MOROSE. Oh, Oh, stay, Cutbeard! Let him give me five shillings of my money back. As it is bounty to reward benefits, so is it equity to mulct injuries. I will have it. What says he?

147–8 *ex Ovidii Metamorphosi*: out of Ovid's *Metamorphoses*. Callisto's story is in book II; but Pasiphaë's comes from Ovid's *Art of Love*, I.295–326.

1 *angel*: gold coin worth ten shillings, or half a pound sterling.

3 *manage*: management.

5 *imperfection*: defect, impairment.

10 *praesto*: at your service (Latin).

13 *catches*: rounds, part songs.
cloth-workers: Flemish Protestant refugees, given to singing at their work.

18 *five shillings*: a quarter of a pound sterling, i.e. half an angel.

19 *mulct*: fine.

CUTBEARD. He cannot change it, sir.
MOROSE. It must be changed.
CUTBEARD. [*aside to* PARSON] Cough again.
MOROSE. What says he?
CUTBEARD. He will cough out the rest, sir.
PARSON. (*again*) Umh, umh, umh.
MOROSE. Away, away with him, stop his mouth, away, I forgive it.

[*Exeunt* CUTBEARD, PARSON.]

EPICOENE. Fie, Master Morose, that you will use this violence to a man of the church.
MOROSE. How!
EPICOENE. It does not become your gravity, or breeding (as you pretend in court), to have offered this outrage on a waterman, or any more boisterous creature, much less on a man of his civil coat.
MOROSE. You can speak then!
EPICOENE. Yes, sir.
MOROSE. Speak out, I mean.
EPICOENE. Ay, sir. Why, did you think you had married a statue? or a motion, only? one of the French puppets, with the eyes turned with a wire? or some innocent out of the hospital, that would stand with her hands thus, and a plaice mouth, and look upon you?
MOROSE. O immodesty! a manifest woman! What, Cutbeard!
EPICOENE. Nay, never quarrel with Cutbeard, sir, it is too late now. I confess it doth bate somewhat of the modesty I had, when I writ simply maid: but I hope I shall make it a stock still competent to the

---

32 *gravity*: dignity.
33 *pretend*: claim.
34 *waterman*: Thames boatman, notoriously obstreperous and quarrelsome.
35 *civil coat*: respectable profession.
40 *motion*: puppet.
42 *innocent*: half-wit.
hospital: Bethlehem (Bedlam), the hospital for the insane.
43 *hands thus*: crossed in front of her, a posture denoting obedience or idiocy.
plaice mouth: small puckered or wry mouth, like a fish's.
48 *bate*: lessen.
49 *writ*: called myself.
50 *stock*: capital sum; perhaps also, 'dowry'.
competent: appropriate; also, 'sufficient'.

estate, and dignity of your wife.

MOROSE. She can talk!

EPICOENE. Yes indeed, sir.

MOROSE. What, sirrah! None of my knaves, there?

[*Enter* MUTE.]

Where is this impostor, Cutbeard?

[MUTE *makes signs.*]

EPICOENE. Speak to him, fellow, speak to him. I'll have none of this coacted, unnatural dumbness in my house, in a family where I govern.

MOROSE. She is my regent already! I have married a Penthesilia, a Semiramis, sold my liberty to a distaff!

SCENE V

[*Enter*] TRUEWIT.

TRUEWIT. Where's Master Morose?

MOROSE. Is he come again! Lord have mercy upon me.

TRUEWIT. I wish you all joy, Mistress Epicoene, with your grave and honourable match.

EPICOENE. I return you the thanks, Master Truewit, so friendly a wish deserves.

MOROSE. She has acquaintance, too!

TRUEWIT. God save you, sir, and give you all contentment in your fair choice, here. Before, I was the bird of night to you, the owl, but now I am the messenger of peace, a dove, and bring you the glad wishes of many friends, to the celebration of this good hour.

MOROSE. What hour, sir?

TRUEWIT. Your marriage hour, sir. I commend your

---

57 *coacted*: compelled, enforced.

60 *Penthesilia*: queen of the Amazons, a race of female warriors in Greek mythology.
Semiramis: Assyrian warrior-queen.

61 *distaff*: staff on which flax or wool is fastened, and from which a thread is drawn for weaving; traditionally symbolic of woman's domestic occupations and hence her proper sphere of government.

11 *owl*: bird of ill omen.

resolution, that (notwithstanding all the dangers I laid afore you, in the voice of a night-crow) would yet go on, and be yourself. It shows you are a man constant to your own ends, and upright to your purposes, that would not be put off with left-handed cries.

MOROSE. How should you arrive at the knowledge of so much?

TRUEWIT. Why, did you ever hope, sir, committing the secrecy of it to a barber, that less than the whole town should know it? You might as well ha'told it the conduit, or the bake-house, or the infantry that follow the court, and with more security. Could your gravity forget so old and noted a remnant as *lippis et tonsoribus notum*? Well sir, forgive it yourself now, the fault, and be communicable with your friends. Here will be three or four fashionable ladies, from the college, to visit you presently, and their train of minions, and followers.

MOROSE. Bar my doors! bar my doors! Where are all my eaters? my mouths now?

[*Enter* SERVANTS.]

Bar up my doors, you varlets.

EPICOENE. He is a varlet that stirs to such an office. Let 'em stand open. I would see him that dares move his eyes toward it. Shall I have a barricado

---

18 *night-crow*: also a bird of ill omen; common in literature, but difficult to identify ornithologically.

21–2 *left-handed*: sinister (Latin *sinister* = left); in classical divination, the flight of birds to the left boded ill.

28 *conduit*: from which fresh water was fetched; a meeting-place for gossips.
bake-house: another meeting-place where gossip was exchanged.

29 *infantry that follow the court*: 'blackguard' or most menial drudges who rode in carts with the kitchen utensils when the court went on progress.

31 *noted*: well-known, celebrated.
remnant: tag.
lippis et tonsoribus notum: 'well known to the bleary-eyed and barbers' (Horace, *Satires*, I.vii.3).

33 *communicable*: affable.

38 *eaters . . . mouths*: servants, dependent on another for means of living.

42 *barricado*: barricade.

made against my friends, to be barred of any pleasure they can bring in to me with honourable visitation?

[*Exeunt* SERVANTS.]

MOROSE. Oh, Amazonian impudence!

TRUEWIT. Nay faith, in this, sir, she speaks but reason: and methinks is more continent than you. Would you go to bed so presently, sir, afore noon? a man of your head, and hair, should owe more to that reverend ceremony, and not mount the marriage bed like a town bull, or a mountain goat; but stay the due season; and ascend it then with religion, and fear. Those delights are to be steeped in the humour, and silence of the night; and give the day to other open pleasures, and jollities of feast, of music, of revels, of discourse: we'll have all, sir, that may make your Hymen high, and happy.

MOROSE. Oh, my torment, my torment!

TRUEWIT. Nay, if you endure the first half hour, sir, so tediously, and with this irksomeness, what comfort, or hope, can this fair gentlewoman make to herself hereafter, in the consideration of so many years as are to come –

MOROSE. Of my affliction. Good sir, depart, and let her do it alone.

TRUEWIT. I have done, sir.

MOROSE. That cursed barber!

TRUEWIT. (Yes faith, a cursed wretch indeed, sir.)

MOROSE. I have married his cittern, that's common to all men. Some plague, above the plague –

---

50 *head . . . hair*: judgement, character; with an ironic glance at Morose's appearance.

54 *religion*: pious observance.
fear: religious awe (of the obligations and sanctity of marriage).

55 *humour*: inclination; with a play on 'moisture', emphasised by 'steeped'.

58 *Hymen*: Greek god of marriage; hence, by transference, 'wedding'.
high: solemn, dignified.

63–4 *make to*: imagine.

70–105 see Textual Note, p. 434 below.

71 *cittern*: a lute-like instrument, provided in barbers' shops for customers to play on while they waited; with a sexual innuendo.

TRUEWIT. (All Egypt's ten plagues –)

MOROSE. Revenge me on him.

TRUEWIT. 'Tis very well, sir. If you laid on a curse or two, more, I'll assure you he'll bear 'em. As, that he may get the pox with seeking to cure it, sir? Or that while he is curling another man's hair, his own may drop off? Or for burning some male bawd's lock, he may have his brain beat out with the curling iron?

MOROSE. No, let the wretch live wretched. May he get the itch, and his shop so lousy, as no man dare come at him, nor he come at no man.

TRUEWIT. (Ay, and if he would swallow all his balls for pills, let not them purge him.)

MOROSE. Let his warming-pan be ever cold.

TRUEWIT. (A perpetual frost underneath it, sir.)

MOROSE. Let him never hope to see fire again.

TRUEWIT. (But in Hell, sir.)

MOROSE. His chairs be always empty, his scissors rust, and his combs mould in their cases.

TRUEWIT. Very dreadful that! (And may he lose the invention, sir, of carving lanterns in paper.)

MOROSE. Let there be no bawd carted that year, to employ a basin of his: but let him be glad to eat his sponge for bread.

TRUEWIT. And drink lotium to it, and much good do him.

MOROSE. Or for want of bread –

TRUEWIT. Eat earwax, sir. I'll help you. Or draw his own teeth, and add them to the lute string.

MOROSE. No, beat the old ones to powder, and make bread of them.

---

73 *Egypt's ten plagues*: called down on the Egyptians by Moses when Pharaoh prevaricated over his promise to allow the children of Israel to leave (Exodus 7–12).

76 *more*: greater.

77 *pox*: syphilis, which barbers treated in their role of surgeons.

80 *lock*: fashionable curled love-lock.

85 *balls*: of soap.

94 *carving lanterns in paper*: cutting lanterns out of oiled paper, which barbers then sold.

96 *basin*: metal basins were rented out by barbers and beaten by the crowd when bawds were carted through the streets.

98 *lotium*: stale urine, used as a dressing for the hair.

101–2 *earwax . . . draw . . . teeth*: barbers cleaned ears, and pulled teeth, which were strung on strings and hung in the shops.

TRUEWIT. (Yes, make meal o'the millstones.)
MOROSE. May all the botches, and burns, that he has cured on others, break out upon him.
TRUEWIT. And he now forget the cure of 'em in himself, sir: or if he do remember it, let him ha'scraped all his linen into lint for't, and have not a rag left him, to set up with.
MOROSE. Let him never set up again, but have the gout in his hands forever. Now, no more, sir.
TRUEWIT. Oh that last was too high set! you might go less with him, i'faith, and be revenged enough: as, that he be never able to new-paint his pole –
MOROSE. Good sir, no more. I forgot myself.
TRUEWIT. Or want credit to take up with a comb-maker –
MOROSE. No more, sir.
TRUEWIT. Or having broken his glass in a former despair, fall now into a much greater of ever getting another –
MOROSE. I beseech you, no more.
TRUEWIT. Or that he never be trusted with trimming of any but chimney-sweepers –
MOROSE. Sir –
TRUEWIT. Or may he cut a collier's throat with his razor by chance-medley, and yet hang for't.
MOROSE. I will forgive him, rather than hear any more. I beseech you, sir.

---

105 *millstones*: 'grinders', teeth.
106 *botches*: skin eruptions.
111 *set up with*: set up in business with.
112 *set up*: also, set hair.
114 *was too high set*: went too far (from gambling).
114–15 *go less*: go for lower stakes (gambling term); take less extreme measures.
126 *chimney-sweepers*: like colliers (128), the dirtiest possible customers; others would not wish to follow them.
129 *chance-medley*: accidental homicide.

SCENE VI

[*Enter*] DAW, HAUGHTY, CENTAUR, MAVIS, TRUSTY.

DAW. This way, madam.

MOROSE. Oh, the sea breaks in upon me! another flood! an inundation! I shall be o'erwhelmed with noise. It beats already at my shores. I feel an earthquake in myself for't.

DAW. Give you joy, mistress.

MOROSE. Has she servants too!

DAW. I have brought some ladies here to see and know you.

She kisses them severally as he presents them.

My Lady Haughty, this my Lady Centaur, Mistress Dol Mavis, Mistress Trusty my Lady Haughty's woman. Where's your husband? Let's see him: can he endure no noise? Let me come to him.

MOROSE. What *nomenclator* is this!

TRUEWIT. Sir John Daw, sir, your wife's servant, this.

MOROSE. A Daw, and her servant! Oh 'tis decreed, 'tis decreed of me, an' she have such servants.

[*He attempts to leave.*]

TRUEWIT. Nay sir, you must kiss the ladies, you must not go away, now; they come toward you, to seek you out.

HAUGHTY. I'faith, Master Morose, would you steal a marriage thus, in the midst of so many friends, and not acquaint us? Well, I'll kiss you, notwithstanding the justice of my quarrel: you shall give me leave, mistress, to use a becoming familiarity with your husband.

EPICOENE. Your ladyship does me an honour in it, to let me know he is so worthy your favour: as you have done both him and me grace, to visit so unprepared a pair to entertain you.

MOROSE. Compliment! compliment!

2-3 *another flood*: like that God sent to destroy the world in Genesis 7.

9 s.d. *severally*: one by one.

14 *nomenclator*: announcer of guests' names; with a pun on 'clatter'.

18 *decreed of me*: i.e. ordained that I shall be a cuckold.

EPICOENE. But I must lay the burden of that upon my servant, here.

HAUGHTY. It shall not need, Mistress Morose, we will all bear, rather than one shall be oppressed.

MOROSE. I know it: and you will teach her the faculty, if she be to learn it.

[*The Collegiates talk aside with* TRUEWIT.]

HAUGHTY. Is this the silent woman?

CENTAUR. Nay, she has found her tongue since she was married, Master Truewit says.

HAUGHTY. Oh, Master Truewit! save you. What kind of creature is your bride here? She speaks, methinks!

TRUEWIT. Yes, madam, believe it, she is a gentlewoman of very absolute behaviour, and of a good race.

HAUGHTY. And Jack Daw told us she could not speak.

TRUEWIT. So it was carried in plot, madam, to put her upon this old fellow, by Sir Dauphine, his nephew, and one or two more of us: but she is a woman of an excellent assurance, and an extraordinary happy wit, and tongue. You shall see her make rare sport with Daw, ere night.

HAUGHTY. And he brought us to laugh at her!

TRUEWIT. That falls out, often, madam, that he that thinks himself the master-wit, is the master-fool. I assure your ladyship, ye cannot laugh at her.

HAUGHTY. No, we'll have her to the college: an' she have wit, she shall be one of us! Shall she not, Centaur? We'll make her a Collegiate.

CENTAUR. Yes, faith, madam, and Mavis and she will set up a side.

TRUEWIT. Believe it, madam, and Mistress Mavis, she will sustain her part.

---

36 *bear*: bear the burden of the fault; also, 'bear the weight of a man'.
oppressed: also with sexual overtones: 'ravished' (Latin *opprimere*).
37 *faculty*: ability.
46 *absolute*: perfect.
47 *race*: family.
50 *carried*: managed.
64 *set up a side*: be partners (as in a card game).

MAVIS. I'll tell you that when I have talked with her, and tried her.

HAUGHTY. Use her very civilly, Mavis.

MAVIS. So I will, madam.

MOROSE. Blessed minute, that they would whisper thus ever.

TRUEWIT. In the meantime, madam, would but your ladyship help to vex him a little: you know his disease, talk to him about the wedding ceremonies, or call for your gloves, or –

HAUGHTY. Let me alone. Centaur, help me. – Master bridegroom, where are you?

MOROSE. Oh, it was too miraculously good to last!

HAUGHTY. We see no ensigns of a wedding, here; no character of a bride-ale: where be our scarves, and our gloves? I pray you, give 'em us. Let's know your bride's colours, and yours, at least.

CENTAUR. Alas, madam, he has provided none.

MOROSE. Had I known your ladyship's painter, I would.

HAUGHTY. He has given it you, Centaur, i'faith. But do you hear, Master Morose, a jest will not absolve you in this manner. You that have sucked the milk of the court, and from thence have been brought up to the very strong meats, and wine, of it; been a courtier from the biggen to the nightcap (as we say): and you, to offend in such a high point of ceremony as this! and let your nuptials want all marks of solemnity! How much plate have you lost today (if you had but regarded your profit), what gifts, what friends, through your mere rusticity?

MOROSE. Madam –

HAUGHTY. Pardon me, sir, I must insinuate your errors to you. No gloves? no garters? no scarves?

---

77 *Let me alone*: leave it to me.
80 *ensigns*: signs, tokens.
81–2 *scarves . . . gloves*: given to wedding guests.
83 *colours*: of the bride and groom, worn by their respective friends.
85 *painter*: cosmetician.
92 *biggen*: baby's bonnet, a sign of infancy.
95 *solemnity*: ceremoniousness.
97 *mere rusticity*: utter boorishness.
99 *insinuate*: subtly hint.
100 *garters*: the bride's garters, striven for by the groomsmen and bridesmaids.

no epithalamium? no masque?

DAW. Yes, madam, I'll make an epithalamium, I promised my mistress, I have begun it already: will your ladyship hear it?

HAUGHTY. Ay, good Jack Daw.

MOROSE. Will it please your ladyship command a chamber, and be private with your friend? You shall have your choice of rooms to retire to after: my whole house is yours. I know it hath been your ladyship's errand into the city, at other times, however now you have been unhappily diverted upon me: but I shall be loth to break any honourable custom of your ladyship's. And therefore, good madam –

EPICOENE. Come, you are a rude bridegroom, to entertain ladies of honour in this fashion.

CENTAUR. He is a rude groom, indeed.

TRUEWIT. By that light, you deserve to be grafted, and have your horns reach from one side of the island to the other. – Do not mistake me, sir, I but speak this to give the ladies some heart again, not for any malice to you.

MOROSE. Is this your bravo, ladies?

TRUEWIT. As God help me, if you utter such another word, I'll take mistress bride in, and begin to you in a very sad cup, do you see? Go to, know your friends, and such as love you.

SCENE VII

[*Enter*] CLERIMONT [*and musicians*].

CLERIMONT. By your leave, ladies. Do you want any music? I have brought you variety of noises. Play, sirs, all of you.

---

101 *epithalamium*: wedding song or poem praising bride and groom, and wishing them prosperity.
109 *it*: i.e. the keeping of an assignation.
117 *groom*: bridegroom; also, 'servant'.
118 *grafted*: i.e. have cuckold's horns grafted upon your head.
123 *bravo*: hired bully.
125–6 *begin . . . cup*: drink your health in a way most unpleasant to you (cuckold you).
2 *noises*: bands of musicians; also, an intimation of the cacophony which they have been instructed to produce.

Music of all sorts.

MOROSE. Oh, a plot, a plot, a plot, a plot upon me! This day, I shall be their anvil to work on, they will grate me asunder. 'Tis worse than the noise of a saw.

CLERIMONT. No, they are hair, rosin, and guts. I can give you the receipt.

TRUEWIT. Peace, boys.

CLERIMONT. Play, I say.

TRUEWIT. Peace, rascals. [*To* MOROSE] You see who's your friend now, sir? Take courage, put on a martyr's resolution. Mock down all their attemptings with patience. 'Tis but a day, and I would suffer heroically. Should an ass exceed me in fortitude? No. You betray your infirmity with your hanging dull ears, and make them insult: bear up bravely, and constantly.

LA FOOLE *passes over* [*the stage*] *sewing the meat;* [SERVANTS, MISTRESS OTTER].

Look you here, sir, what honour is done you unexpected, by your nephew; a wedding dinner come, and a knight-sewer before it, for the more reputation: and fine Mistress Otter, your neighbour, in the rump, or tail of it.

MOROSE. Is that Gorgon, that Medusa come? Hide me, hide me.

TRUEWIT. I warrant you, sir, she will not transform you. Look upon her with a good courage. Pray you entertain her, and conduct your guests in. No? Mistress bride, will you entreat in the ladies? Your bridegroom is so shamefaced, here –

---

6 *grate*: grind; also, 'fret, harass, irritate'.
8 *hair, rosin, and guts*: horsehair for the bow, rosin to rub on it, and cat gut for the strings of the violin.
9 *receipt*: formula.
15 *attemptings*: endeavours; also, 'assaults'.
16 *ass*: proverbial for bearing, and for foolishness.
17 *infirmity*: weakness.
18 *hanging dull ears*: like those of an overburdened and unwilling ass; perhaps also a glance at the tails of Morose's nightcaps. *insult*: exult.
19 s.d. *sewing*: directing the arrangement of the dishes.
22–3 *more reputation*: greater honour.
27 *transform*: turn into stone, as did the face of Medusa.
31 *shamefaced*: bashful.

EPICOENE. Will it please your ladyship, madam?
HAUGHTY. With the benefit of your company, mistress.
EPICOENE. Servant, pray you perform your duties.
DAW. And glad to be commanded, mistress.
CENTAUR. How like you her wit, Mavis?
MAVIS. Very prettily, absolutely well.
MISTRESS OTTER. [*trying to take precedence*] 'Tis my place.
MAVIS. You shall pardon me, Mistress Otter.
MISTRESS OTTER. Why, I am a Collegiate.
MAVIS. But not in ordinary.
MISTRESS OTTER. But I am.
MAVIS. We'll dispute that within.

[*Exeunt* DAW, LADIES.]

CLERIMONT. Would this had lasted a little longer.
TRUEWIT. And that they had sent for the heralds.

[*Enter* OTTER.]

Captain Otter, what news?
OTTER. I have brought my bull, bear, and horse, in private, and yonder are the trumpeters without, and the drum, gentlemen.

The drum and trumpets sound.

MOROSE. Oh, Oh, Oh.
OTTER. And we will have a rouse in each of 'em, anon, for bold Britons, i'faith.

[*Drum and trumpets sound again.*]

MOROSE. Oh, Oh, Oh. [*Exit.*]
ALL. Follow, follow, follow.

[*Exeunt.*]

---

43 *in ordinary*: regular or full member.
47 *heralds*: who decided matters of precedence.
53 *rouse*: bumper.
54 *for bold Britons*: a toast (from a ballad or drinking song?).
56 *Follow*: hunting cry.

ACT IV

SCENE I

[*Enter*] TRUEWIT, CLERIMONT.

TRUEWIT. Was there ever poor bridegroom so tormented? or man, indeed?

CLERIMONT. I have not read of the like, in the chronicles of the land.

TRUEWIT. Sure, he cannot but go to a place of rest, after all this purgatory.

CLERIMONT. He may presume it, I think.

TRUEWIT. The spitting, the coughing, the laughter, the neezing, the farting, dancing, noise of the music, and her masculine and loud commanding, and urging the whole family, makes him think he has married a Fury.

CLERIMONT. And she carries it up bravely.

TRUEWIT. Ay, she takes any occasion to speak: that's the height on't.

CLERIMONT. And how soberly Dauphine labours to satisfy him that it was none of his plot!

TRUEWIT. And has almost brought him to the faith, i'the article.

[*Enter* DAUPHINE.]

Here he comes. – Where is he now? What's become of him, Dauphine?

DAUPHINE. Oh, hold me up a little, I shall go away i'the jest else. He has got on his whole nest of nightcaps, and locked himself up i'the top o'the house, as high as ever he can climb from the noise. I peeped in at a cranny, and saw him sitting over a

---

4 *chronicles of the land*: i.e. those of Hall and Holinshed.

9 *neezing*: sneezing.

12 *Fury*: classical avenging spirit who punishes crime; hence, an avenging or tormenting infernal spirit.

15 *height*: high spot.

19 *article*: statement (as in 'article of faith').

22–3 *go away i'the jest*: die laughing.

23 *nest*: set of objects so made that the smaller fit into the larger.

crossbeam o'the roof, like him o'the saddler's horse in Fleet Street, upright: and he will sleep there.

CLERIMONT. But where are your Collegiates?

DAUPHINE. Withdrawn with the bride in private.

TRUEWIT. Oh, they are instructing her i'the college-grammar. If she have grace with them, she knows all their secrets instantly.

CLERIMONT. Methinks the Lady Haughty looks well today, for all my dispraise of her i'the morning. I think I shall come about to thee again, Truewit.

TRUEWIT. Believe it, I told you right. Women ought to repair the losses time and years have made i'their features, with dressings. And an intelligent woman, if she know by herself the least defect, will be most curious to hide it: and it becomes her. If she be short, let her sit much, lest when she stands, she be thought to sit. If she have an ill foot, let her wear her gown the longer, and her shoe the thinner. If a fat hand, and scald nails, let her carve the less, and act in gloves. If a sour breath, let her never discourse fasting: and always talk at her distance. If she have black and rugged teeth, let her offer the less at laughter, especially if she laugh wide, and open.

CLERIMONT. Oh, you shall have some women, when they laugh, you would think they brayed, it is so rude, and –

TRUEWIT. Ay, and others that will stalk i'their gait like an estrich, and take huge strides. I cannot endure such a sight. I love measure i'the feet, and number i'the voice: they are gentlenesses that ofttimes draw no less than the face.

DAUPHINE. How cam'st thou to study these

27–8 *saddler's horse*: model horse and rider, outside a saddler's shop.
37 *come about to thee*: come round to your opinion.
41 *by*: about.
42 *curious*: careful.
46 *scald*: scabbed.
carve: gesture affectedly.
47 *act*: gesture.
50 *offer . . . at laughter*: attempt to laugh.
56 *estrich*: ostrich.
57 *measure*: graceful movement (as in dancing).
58 *number*: rhythm (as in verse).
gentlenesses: elegancies.

creatures so exactly? I would thou would'st make me a proficient.

TRUEWIT. Yes, but you must leave to live i'your chamber then a month together upon *Amadis de Gaul*, or *Don Quixote*, as you are wont; and come abroad where the matter is frequent, to court, to tiltings, public shows, and feasts, to plays, and church sometimes: thither they come to show their new tires too, to see, and to be seen. In these places a man shall find whom to love, whom to play with, whom to touch once, whom to hold ever. The variety arrests his judgement. A wench to please a man comes not down dropping from the ceiling, as he lies on his back droning a tobacco pipe. He must go where she is.

DAUPHINE. Yes, and be never the near.

TRUEWIT. Out, heretic! That diffidence makes thee worthy it should be so.

CLERIMONT. He says true to you, Dauphine.

DAUPHINE. Why?

TRUEWIT. A man should not doubt to overcome any woman. Think he can vanquish 'em, and he shall: for though they deny, their desire is to be tempted. Penelope herself cannot hold out long. Ostend, you saw, was taken at last. You must persever, and hold to your purpose. They would solicit us, but that they are afraid. Howsoever, they wish in their hearts we should solicit them. Praise 'em, flatter 'em, you shall never want eloquence, or trust: even the chastest delight to feel themselves that way rubbed. With praises you must mix kisses too. If they take them, they'll take more. Though they strive, they would be overcome.

CLERIMONT. Oh, but a man must beware of force.

TRUEWIT. It is to them an acceptable violence, and

---

62 *proficient*: learner, pupil.

64–5 *Amadis de Gaul . . . Don Quixote*: chivalric romances despised by Jonson.

66 *frequent*: abundant.

74 *droning*: sucking (as on a bagpipe).

76 *near*: nearer; the comparative form of the word.

84 *Penelope*: faithful wife of Odysseus, who steadfastly resisted her suitors during the twenty years' absence of her husband. *Ostend*: fell in 1604, after a three years' siege by the Spanish.

85 *persever*: persevere.

91 *rubbed*: annoyed; pressed; also, 'troubled'.

has ofttimes the place of the greatest courtesy. She that might have been forced, an' you let her go free without touching, though she then seem to thank you, will ever hate you after; and glad i'the face is assuredly sad at the heart.

CLERIMONT. But all women are not to be taken all ways.

TRUEWIT. 'Tis true. No more than all birds, or all fishes. If you appear learned to an ignorant wench, or jocund to a sad, or witty to a foolish, why she presently begins to mistrust herself. You must approach them i'their own height, their own line: for the contrary makes many that fear to commit themselves to noble and worthy fellows, run into the embraces of a rascal. If she love wit, give verses, though you borrow 'em of a friend, or buy 'em, to have good. If valour, talk of your sword, and be frequent in the mention of quarrels, though you be staunch in fighting. If activity, be seen o'your barbary often, or leaping over stools, for the credit of your back. If she love good clothes or dressing, have your learned council about you every morning, your French tailor, barber, linener, *et cetera*. Let your powder, your glass, and your comb be your dearest acquaintance. Take more care for the ornament of your head, than the safety: and wish the commonwealth rather troubled, than a hair about you. That will take her. Then if she be covetous and craving, do you promise anything, and perform sparingly: so shall you keep her in appetite still. Seem as you would give, but be like a barren field that yields little, or unlucky dice to foolish and hoping gamesters. Let your gifts be slight, and dainty, rather than precious. Let cunning be above cost. Give cherries

99–100 *glad . . . heart*: proverbial.
101–2 *all ways*: see Textual Note, p. 434 below.
107 *height . . . line*: high and low wards in fencing; with perhaps puns on *height* = latitude, and *line* = standard of life, conduct.
114 *staunch*: restrained, cautious.
activity: exercise.
115 *barbary*: arab horse.
115–16 *for the credit of your back*: for your reputation for sexual prowess.
121–2 *than the safety*: i.e. than keeping your head on your shoulders.
130 *cunning*: ingenuity; perhaps also, 'craftiness'.

at time of year, or apricots; and say they were sent you out o'the country, though you bought 'em in Cheapside. Admire her tires; like her in all fashions; compare her in every habit to some deity; invent excellent dreams to flatter her, and riddles; or if she be a great one, perform always the second parts to her: like what she likes, praise whom she praises; and fail not to make the household and servants yours, yea the whole family, and salute 'em by their names ('tis but light cost if you can purchase 'em so) and make her physician your pensioner, and her chief woman. Nor will it be out of your gain to make love to her too, so she follow, not usher, her lady's pleasure. All blabbing is taken away, when she comes to be a part of the crime.

DAUPHINE. On what courtly lap hast thou late slept, to come forth so sudden and absolute a courtling?

TRUEWIT. Good faith, I should rather question you, that are so hearkening after these mysteries. I begin to suspect your diligence, Dauphine. Speak, art thou in love in earnest?

DAUPHINE. Yes, by my troth, am I: 'twere ill dissembling before thee.

TRUEWIT. With which of 'em, I pray thee?

DAUPHINE. With all the Collegiates.

CLERIMONT. Out on thee. We'll keep you at home, believe it, i'the stable, an' you be such a stallion.

TRUEWIT. No. I like him well. Men should love wisely, and all women: some one for the face, and let her please the eye; another for the skin, and let her please the touch; a third for the voice, and let her please the ear; and where the objects mix, let the senses so too. Thou wouldst think it strange, if I should make 'em all in love with thee afore night!

DAUPHINE. I would say thou hadst the best philtre i'the world, and couldst do more than Madam

---

134 *habit*: costume, outfit.
137 *second parts*: supporting roles (Latin *secundae partes*), a theatrical expression.
142 *pensioner*: retainer.
148 *courtling*: courtier.
150 *hearkening*: making enquiries.
166 *philtre*: love potion.

Medea, or Doctor Foreman.

TRUEWIT. If I do not, let me play the mountebank for my meat while I live, and the bawd for my drink.

DAUPHINE. So be it, I say.

SCENE II

[*Enter*] OTTER, DAW, LA FOOLE.

OTTER. Oh lord, gentlemen, how my knights and I have missed you here!

CLERIMONT. Why, captain, what service? what service?

OTTER. To see me bring up my bull, bear, and horse to fight.

DAW. Yes, faith, the captain says we shall be his dogs to bait 'em.

DAUPHINE. A good employment.

TRUEWIT. Come on, let's see a course then.

LA FOOLE. I am afraid my cousin will be offended if she come.

OTTER. Be afraid of nothing. Gentlemen, I have placed the drum and the trumpets, and one to give 'em the sign when you are ready.

[*Brings out the cups.*]

Here's my bull for myself, and my bear for Sir John Daw, and my horse for Sir Amorous. Now set your foot to mine, and yours to his, and –

LA FOOLE. Pray God my cousin come not.

OTTER. Saint George and Saint Andrew, fear no cousins. Come, sound, sound. *Et rauco strepuerunt cornua cantu.*

[*Drum and trumpets sound. They drink.*]

---

168 *Medea*: sorceress who restored his youth to Aeson, father of Jason, leader of the Argonauts.
Doctor Foreman: 1522–1611; astrologer and quack, seller of love potions.

5–84 the metaphors of the drinking scene are drawn from bull- and bear-baiting.

10 *course*: drinking round; also, encounter between dogs and baited animals.

21–2 *Et rauco . . . cornua cantu*: 'And the trumpets shrilled with a raucous sound' (Virgil, *Aeneid*, VIII.2).

TRUEWIT. Well said, captain, i'faith: well fought at the bull.

CLERIMONT. Well held at the bear.

TRUEWIT. Low, low, captain.

DAUPHINE. Oh, the horse has kicked off his dog already.

LA FOOLE. I cannot drink it, as I am a knight.

TRUEWIT. Gods so, off with his spurs, somebody.

LA FOOLE. It goes again my conscience. My cousin will be angry with it.

DAW. I ha'done mine.

TRUEWIT. You fought high and fair, Sir John.

CLERIMONT. At the head.

DAUPHINE. Like an excellent bear-dog.

CLERIMONT. [*aside to* DAW] You take no notice of the business, I hope.

DAW. Not a word, sir, you see we are jovial.

OTTER. Sir Amorous, you must not equivocate. It must be pulled down, for all my cousin.

CLERIMONT. [*aside to* LA FOOLE] 'Sfoot, if you take not your drink, they'll think you are discontented with something: you'll betray all, if you take the least notice.

LA FOOLE. Not I, I'll both drink and talk, then.

OTTER. You must pull the horse on his knees, Sir Amorous: fear no cousins. *Jacta est alea*.

TRUEWIT. Oh, now he's in his vein, and bold. The least hint given him of his wife now will make him rail desperately.

CLERIMONT. Speak to him of her.

TRUEWIT. Do you, and I'll fetch her to the hearing of it. [*Exit.*]

DAUPHINE. Captain he-Otter, your she-Otter is coming, your wife.

OTTER. Wife! Buzz. *Titivilitium*. There's no such thing in nature. I confess, gentlemen, I have a cook, a laundress, a house-drudge, that serves my necessary turns, and goes under that title: but he's an ass that will be so uxorious to tie his affections

---

23 *said*: done.
48 *Jacta est alea*: 'The die is cast'; Caesar's words as he crossed the Rubicon, declaring war on the Republic.
57 *Titivilitium*: a vile thing of no value (from Plautus, *Casina*, 347).
61–2 *ass . . . one circle*: like an ass tied to a rotary mill; with an obscene pun on *circle* = the female pudenda.

to one circle. Come, the name dulls appetite. Here, replenish again: another bout. Wives are nasty sluttish animals.

DAUPHINE. Oh, captain.

OTTER. As ever the earth bare, *tribus verbis*. Where's Master Truewit?

DAW. He's slipped aside, sir.

CLERIMONT. But you must drink, and be jovial.

DAW. Yes, give it me.

LA FOOLE. And me, too.

DAW. Let's be jovial.

LA FOOLE. As jovial as you will.

OTTER. Agreed. Now you shall ha'the bear, cousin, and Sir John Daw the horse, and I'll ha'the bull still. Sound, Tritons o'the Thames. *Nunc est bibendum, nunc pede libero –*

MOROSE. (*speaks from above* [*within*]*: the trumpets sounding*) Villains, murderers, sons of the earth, and traitors, what do you there?

CLERIMONT. Oh, now the trumpets have waked him, we shall have his company.

OTTER. A wife is a scurvy *clogdogdo*; an unlucky thing, a very foresaid bear-whelp, without any good fashion or breeding: *mala bestia*.

His wife is brought out [*unperceived*] *to hear him.*

DAUPHINE. Why did you marry one then, captain?

OTTER. A pox – I married with six thousand pound, I. I was in love with that. I ha'not kissed my Fury these forty weeks.

CLERIMONT. The more to blame you, captain.

TRUEWIT. Nay, Mistress Otter, hear him a little first.

OTTER. She has a breath worse than my grand-mother's, *profecto*.

---

66 *tribus verbis*: briefly; literally, 'in three words'.
76 *Tritons*: sea gods, who blew conch shells.
76–7 *Nunc . . . libero*: 'Now is the time to drink, now with free foot [to beat the earth]' (Horace, *Odes*, I.xxxvii.1).
78 *sons of the earth*: bastards (Latin *terrae filius*).
82 *clogdogdo*: obscure; Upton conjectured 'clog proper only for a dog', possibly Bear Garden slang?
83 *very foresaid*: truly predictable (to be bad).
84 *fashion*: demeanour, behaviour.
mala bestia: an evil beast.
92 *profecto*: truly, really, indeed.

MISTRESS OTTER. O treacherous liar! Kiss me, sweet Master Truewit, and prove him a slandering knave.

TRUEWIT. I'll rather believe you, lady.

OTTER. And she has a peruke that's like a pound of hemp, made up in shoe-threads.

MISTRESS OTTER. O viper, mandrake!

OTTER. A most vile face! and yet she spends me forty pound a year in mercury, and hogs' bones. All her teeth were made i'the Blackfriars: both her eyebrows i'the Strand, and her hair in Silver Street. Every part o'the town owns a piece of her.

MISTRESS OTTER. I cannot hold.

OTTER. She takes herself asunder still when she goes to bed, into some twenty boxes; and about next day noon is put together again, like a great German clock: and so comes forth and rings a tedious larum to the whole house, and then is quiet again for an hour, but for her quarters. Ha'you done me right, gentlemen?

She falls upon him and beats him.

MISTRESS OTTER. No, sir, I'll do you right with my quarters, with my quarters.

OTTER. Oh, hold, good princess.

TRUEWIT. Sound, sound.

[*Drum and trumpets sound.*]

CLERIMONT. A battle, a battle.

MISTRESS OTTER. You notoriously stinkardly bearward, does my breath smell?

OTTER. Under correction, dear princess: look to my bear, and my horse, gentlemen.

MISTRESS OTTER. Do I want teeth, and eyebrows, thou bulldog?

---

99 *viper*: a type of ingratitude.
mandrake: plant whose root was held to resemble a man's form; a term of abuse: 'man only in show'?

101 *mercury, and hogs' bones*: used in cosmetics.

109 *German clock*: earliest imported clock; in need of constant repair, if we are to believe the dramatists, who use it frequently in punning allusions to 'repairing' clocks and women's beauty.

110 *larum*: alarm.

111 *quarters*: struck by a clock (hence, regular outbursts); also, 'own rooms'.

112 *done me right*: drunk off a bumper.

114 *quarters*: blows, quarter-strokes of fencing.

120 *Under correction*: see III.i.11–12 n.

TRUEWIT. Sound, sound still.

[*They sound again.*]

OTTER. No, I protest, under correction –

MISTRESS OTTER. Ay, now you are under correction, you protest: but you did not protest before correction, sir. Thou Judas, to offer to betray thy princess! I'll make thee an example –

MOROSE *descends with a long sword.*

MOROSE. I will have no such examples in my house, Lady Otter.

MISTRESS OTTER. Ah –

MOROSE. Mistress Mary Ambree, your examples are dangerous.

[MISTRESS OTTER, DAW, LA FOOLE *run off.*]

Rogues, hellhounds, Stentors, out of my doors, you sons of noise and tumult, begot on an ill May Day, or when the galley-foist is afloat to Westminster!

[*Drives out musicians.*]

A trumpeter could not be conceived but then!

DAUPHINE. What ails you, sir?

MOROSE. They have rent my roof, walls, and all my windows asunder with their brazen threats. [*Exit.*]

TRUEWIT. Best follow him, Dauphine.

DAUPHINE. So I will. [*Exit.*]

CLERIMONT. Where's Daw, and La Foole?

OTTER. They are both run away, sir. Good gentlemen, help me to pacify my princess, and speak to the great ladies for me. Now must I go lie with the bears this fortnight, and keep out o'the way, till

---

125 *protest*: avow.

129 s.d. *long sword*: sword with a heavy, cutting blade.

133 *Mary Ambree*: who disguised herself as a soldier and took part in the siege of Ghent in 1584.

135 *Stentors*: 'iron-voiced' men: Stentor was the Greek herald at Troy, whose voice was as strong as those of fifty men.

136–7 *ill May Day*: from the May Day riot of 1517; but the annual celebrations would make all May Days equally painful for Morose.

137 *galley-foist*: lord mayor's state barge, used to take him to Westminster at his installation; hence accompanied with revelry.

my peace be made, for this scandal she has taken. Did you not see my bull-head, gentlemen?

CLERIMONT. Is't not on, captain?

TRUEWIT. No: [*Aside to* CLERIMONT] but he may make a new one, by that is on.

OTTER. Oh, here 'tis, An' you come over, gentlemen, and ask for Tom Otter, we'll go down to Ratcliffe, and have a course, i'faith: for all these disasters. There's *bona spes* left.

TRUEWIT. Away, captain, get off while you are well.

[*Exit* OTTER.]

CLERIMONT. I am glad we are rid of him.

TRUEWIT. You had never been, unless we had put his wife upon him. His humour is as tedious at last, as it was ridiculous at first.

SCENE III

[*Enter*] HAUGHTY, MISTRESS OTTER, MAVIS, DAW, LA FOOLE, CENTAUR, EPICOENE.

HAUGHTY. We wondered why you shrieked so, Mistress Otter.

MISTRESS OTTER. O God, madam, he came down with a huge long naked weapon in both his hands, and looked so dreadfully! Sure, he's beside himself.

MAVIS. Why, what made you there, Mistress Otter?

MISTRESS OTTER. Alas, Mistress Mavis, I was chastising my subject, and thought nothing of him.

DAW. Faith, mistress, you must do so too. Learn to chastise. Mistress Otter corrects her husband so, he dares not speak but under correction.

LA FOOLE. And with his hat off to her: 'twould do you good to see.

---

150 *scandal*: offence.
151 *bull-head*: cover for the drinking-cup.
154 *that is on*: i.e. Otter's own head, which, with his cuckold's horns, would serve as a model for a replacement cover.
156 *Ratcliffe*: one of the 'liberties' of London, not under the jurisdiction of the city; consequently, a resort for rogues.
157 *course*: see IV.ii.10 n.
158 *bona spes*: good hope.

HAUGHTY. In sadness, 'tis good and mature counsel: practise it, Morose. I'll call you Morose still now, as I call Centaur, and Mavis: we four will be all one.

CENTAUR. And you'll come to the college, and live with us?

HAUGHTY. Make him give milk, and honey.

MAVIS. Look how you manage him at first, you shall have him ever after.

CENTAUR. Let him allow you your coach and four horses, your woman, your chambermaid, your page, your gentleman-usher, your French cook, and four grooms.

HAUGHTY. And go with us, to Bedlam, to the china-houses, and to the Exchange.

CENTAUR. It will open the gate to your fame.

HAUGHTY. Here's Centaur has immortalised herself, with taming of her wild male.

MAVIS. Ay, she has done the miracle of the kingdom.

EPICOENE. But ladies, do you count it lawful to have such plurality of servants, and do 'em all graces?

HAUGHTY. Why not? Why should women deny their favours to men? Are they the poorer, or the worse?

DAW. Is the Thames the less for the dyers' water, mistress?

LA FOOLE. Or a torch, for lighting many torches?

TRUEWIT. [*aside*] Well said, La Foole; what a new one he has got!

CENTAUR. They are empty losses women fear in this kind.

HAUGHTY. Besides, ladies should be mindful of the approach of age, and let no time want his due use. The best of our days pass first.

MAVIS. We are rivers that cannot be called back, madam: she that now excludes her lovers may live to lie a forsaken beldame, in a frozen bed.

CENTAUR. 'Tis true, Mavis: and who will wait on us

---

15 *In sadness*: seriously.

16 *Morose*: i.e. the masculine form of address, relevant to the reversal of sexual roles in the play.

17–18 *all one*: altogether; as one.

21 *milk, and honey*: of the Promised Land (Exodus 3.8).

39, 41 proverbial, and clichéd.

51 *beldame*: hag.

to coach then? or write, or tell us the news then? Make anagrams of our names, and invite us to the Cockpit, and kiss our hands all the play-time, and draw their weapons for our honours?

HAUGHTY. Not one.

DAW. Nay, my mistress is not altogether unintelligent of these things; here be in presence have tasted of her favours.

CLERIMONT. [*aside*] What a neighing hobbyhorse is this!

EPICOENE. But not with intent to boast 'em again, servant. And have you those excellent receipts, madam, to keep yourselves from bearing of children?

HAUGHTY. Oh yes, Morose. How should we maintain our youth and beauty, else? Many births of a woman make her old, as many crops make the earth barren.

SCENE IV

[*Enter*] MOROSE, DAUPHINE.

MOROSE. O my cursèd angel, that instructed me to this fate!

DAUPHINE. Why, sir?

MOROSE. That I should be seduced by so foolish a devil as a barber will make!

DAUPHINE. I would I had been worthy, sir, to have partaken your counsel, you should never have trusted it to such a minister.

MOROSE. Would I could redeem it with the loss of an eye (nephew), a hand, or any other member.

DAUPHINE. Marry, God forbid, sir, that you should geld yourself, to anger your wife.

MOROSE. So it would rid me of her! and that I did

---

55 *Cockpit*: small private theatre in Whitehall, where cock-fights were also held; with a sexual innuendo.

56 *weapons*: with a sexual pun: *weapon* = slang for penis.

61 *hobbyhorse*: buffoon.

64 *receipts*: prescriptions.

supererogatory penance, in a belfry, at Westminster Hall, i'the Cockpit, at the fall of a stag; the Tower Wharf (what place is there else?), London Bridge, Paris Garden, Billingsgate, when the noises are at their height and loudest. Nay, I would sit out a play that were nothing but fights at sea, drum, trumpet, and target!

DAUPHINE. I hope there shall be no such need, sir. Take patience, good uncle. This is but a day, and 'tis well worn too now.

MOROSE. Oh, 'twill be so forever, nephew, I foresee it, forever. Strife and tumult are the dowry that comes with a wife.

TRUEWIT. I told you so, sir, and you would not believe me.

MOROSE. Alas, do not rub those wounds, Master Truewit, to blood again: 'twas my negligence. Add not affliction to affliction. I have perceived the effect of it, too late, in Madam Otter.

EPICOENE. How do you, sir?

MOROSE. Did you ever hear a more unnecessary question? as if she did not see! Why, I do as you see, empress, empress.

EPICOENE. You are not well, sir! You look very ill! Something has distempered you.

MOROSE. O horrible, monstrous impertinences! Would not one of these have served? Do you think, sir? Would not one of these have served?

TRUEWIT. Yes, sir, but these are but notes of female kindness, sir: certain tokens that she has a voice, sir.

---

14 *supererogatory*: (in a religious act) going beyond what is required.

14–15 *Westminster Hall*: which had shops and law courts.

15 *fall*: death, sounded by huntsmen's horns and accompanied by hounds barking.

17 *Billingsgate*: a general market for food.

19 *play*: e.g. Heywood and Rowley's *Fortunes by Land and Sea* (1607).

20 *target*: shield (clashing).

38 *distempered*: upset; also, 'unbalanced' (with the four bodily humours or moisture in unequal proportions, thus causing disorder emotionally and/or physically and/or mentally).

42 *notes*: signs, tokens.

43 *kindness*: also, behaviour natural (to women).

MOROSE. Oh, is't so? Come, an't be no otherwise – What say you?

EPICOENE. How do you feel yourself, sir?

MOROSE. Again, that!

TRUEWIT. Nay, look you, sir: you would be friends with your wife upon unconscionable terms, her silence –

EPICOENE. They say you are run mad, sir.

MOROSE. Not for love, I assure you, of you; do you see?

EPICOENE. Oh lord, gentlemen! Lay hold on him for God's sake: what shall I do? Who's his physician (can you tell?) that knows the state of his body best, that I might send for him? Good sir, speak. I'll send for one of my doctors else.

MOROSE. What, to poison me, that I might die intestate, and leave you possessed of all?

EPICOENE. Lord, how idly he talks, and how his eyes sparkle! He looks green about the temples! Do you see what blue spots he has?

CLERIMONT. Ay, it's melancholy.

EPICOENE. Gentlemen, for Heaven's sake counsel me. Ladies! Servant, you have read Pliny, and Paracelsus: ne'er a word now to comfort a poor gentlewoman? Ay me! what fortune had I to marry a distracted man?

DAW. I'll tell you, mistress –

TRUEWIT. [*aside*] How rarely she holds it up!

MOROSE. What mean you, gentlemen?

EPICOENE. What will you tell me, servant?

DAW. The disease in Greek is called μανία, in Latin *insania*, *furor*, *vel ecstasis melancholica*, that is, *egressio*, when a man *ex melancholico evadit fanaticus*.

62–4 Symptoms of madness comically ascribed to Menaechmus of Epidamnus in Plautus's *Menaechmi*, 829–30.

65 *melancholy*: passion; frenzy; also, 'aberration'.

67 *Pliny*: AD 23–79; author of a *Natural History*.

68 *Paracelsus*: 1493–1541; a Renaissance authority on medicine.

75 μανία: madness.

76 *insania . . . melancholica*: madness, insanity, or melancholic ecstasy.

77 *egressio*: going out (of one's mind).

77–8 *ex . . . fanaticus*: from the state of melancholy proceeds into madness.

MOROSE. Shall I have a lecture read upon me alive?

DAW. But he may be but *phreneticus* yet, mistress, and *phrenitis* is only *delirium*, or so –

EPICOENE. Ay, that is for the disease, servant: but what is this to the cure? We are sure enough of the disease.

MOROSE. Let me go.

TRUEWIT. Why, we'll entreat her to hold her peace, sir.

MOROSE. Oh, no. Labour not to stop her. She is like a conduit-pipe, that will gush out with more force when she opens again.

HAUGHTY. I'll tell you, Morose, you must talk divinity to him altogether, or moral philosophy.

LA FOOLE. Ay, and there's an excellent book of moral philosophy, madam, of Reynard the Fox, and all the beasts, called *Doni's Philosophy*.

CENTAUR. There is, indeed, Sir Amorous La Foole.

MOROSE. O misery!

LA FOOLE. I have read it, my Lady Centaur, all over to my cousin, here.

MISTRESS OTTER. Ay, and 'tis a very good book as any is, of the moderns.

DAW. Tut, he must have Seneca read to him, and Plutarch, and the ancients; the moderns are not for this disease.

CLERIMONT. Why you discommended them too, today, Sir John.

DAW. Ay, in some cases: but in these they are best, and Aristotle's *Ethics*.

MAVIS. Say you so, Sir John? I think you are deceived: you took it upon trust.

HAUGHTY. Where's Trusty, my woman? I'll end this difference. I prithee, Otter, call her. Her father

---

79 i.e. shall I be dissected before I am dead?

80 *phreneticus*: suffering from phrenitis, an inflammation of the brain.

81 *delirium*: disturbed state of mind (rather than madness); characterised by, amongst other symptoms, incoherent speech, restlessness, and frenzied excitement.

92 *altogether*: uninterruptedly; i.e. nothing but divinity.

95 *Doni's Philosophy*: collection of ancient oriental fables translated from Doni's Italian version by Sir Thomas North as *The Moral Philosophy of Doni* (1570). It does not contain the mediaeval fable of Reynard the Fox.

and mother were both mad, when they put her to me.

[*Exit* MISTRESS OTTER.]

MOROSE. I think so. – Nay, gentlemen, I am tame. This is but an exercise, I know, a marriage ceremony, which I must endure.

HAUGHTY. And one of 'em (I know not which) was cured with *The Sick Man's Salve*; and the other with *Greene's Groats-worth of Wit*.

TRUEWIT. A very cheap cure, madam.

HAUGHTY. Ay, it's very feasible.

[*Enter* MISTRESS OTTER, TRUSTY.]

MISTRESS OTTER. My lady called for you, Mistress Trusty: you must decide a controversy.

HAUGHTY. O Trusty, which was it you said, your father or your mother, that was cured with *The Sick Man's Salve*?

TRUSTY. My mother, madam, with the *Salve*.

TRUEWIT. Then it was *The Sick Woman's Salve*.

TRUSTY. And my father with the *Groats-worth of Wit*. But there was other means used: we had a preacher that would preach folk asleep still; and so they were prescribed to go to church, by an old woman that was their physician, thrice a week –

EPICOENE. To sleep?

TRUSTY. Yes forsooth: and every night they read themselves asleep on those books.

EPICOENE. Good faith, it stands with great reason. I would I knew where to procure those books.

MOROSE. Oh.

LA FOOLE. I can help you with one of 'em, Mistress Morose, the *Groats-worth of Wit*.

EPICOENE. But I shall disfurnish you, Sir Amorous: can you spare it?

---

116 *exercise*: carrying out of a ceremony; training (of an animal); also, 'discipline', 'trial' (as of a saint or martyr – which is how Morose sees himself).

119 *The Sick Man's Salve*: popular, much reprinted sixteenth-century tract by Thomas Becon, giving spiritual and practical advice to the sick.

120 *Greene's Groats-worth of Wit*: 1592; the death-bed confession of and general exhortation to repentance by the dramatist Robert Greene.

121 *cheap*: a groat (the cost of the pamphlet) = fourpence.

LA FOOLE. Oh, yes, for a week, or so; I'll read it myself to him.

EPICOENE. No, I must do that, sir: that must be my office.

MOROSE. Oh, Oh!

EPICOENE. Sure, he would do well enough, if he could sleep.

MOROSE. No, I should do well enough, if you could sleep. Have I no friend that will make her drunk? or give her a little laudanum? or opium?

TRUEWIT. Why, sir, she talks ten times worse in her sleep.

MOROSE. How!

CLERIMONT. Do you not know that, sir? Never ceases all night.

TRUEWIT. And snores like a porcpisce.

MOROSE. Oh, redeem me, fate, redeem me, fate. For how many causes may a man be divorced, nephew?

DAUPHINE. I know not truly, sir.

TRUEWIT. Some divine must resolve you in that, sir, or canon lawyer.

MOROSE. I will not rest, I will not think of any other hope or comfort, till I know.

[*Exit with* DAUPHINE.]

CLERIMONT. Alas, poor man.

TRUEWIT. You'll make him mad indeed, ladies, if you pursue this.

HAUGHTY. No, we'll let him breathe, now, a quarter of an hour, or so.

CLERIMONT. By my faith, a large truce.

HAUGHTY. Is that his keeper, that is gone with him?

DAW. It is his nephew, madam.

LA FOOLE. Sir Dauphine Eugenie.

CENTAUR. He looks like a very pitiful knight –

DAW. As can be. This marriage has put him out of all.

LA FOOLE. He has not a penny in his purse, madam –

DAW. He is ready to cry all this day.

LA FOOLE. A very shark, he set me i'the nick t'other night at primero.

---

160 *porcpisce*: porpoise (Latin *porcus piscis*, pig fish).

173 *large*: generous.

181 *shark*: swindler, cheat.

set me i'the nick: see Additional Note, p. 443 below.

182 *primero*: fashionable gambling card-game.

TRUEWIT. [*aside*] How these swabbers talk!

CLERIMONT. [*aside*] Ay, Otter's wine has swelled their humours above a spring tide.

HAUGHTY. Good Morose, let's go in again. I like your couches exceeding well: we'll go lie, and talk there.

EPICOENE. I wait on you, madam.

[*Exeunt all but* EPICOENE, TRUEWIT, CLERIMONT.]

TRUEWIT. 'Slight, I will have 'em as silent as signs, and their posts too, ere I ha'done. Do you hear, lady bride? I pray thee now, as thou art a noble wench, continue this discourse of Dauphine within: but praise him exceedingly. Magnify him with all the height of affection thou canst (I have some purpose in't) and but beat off these two rooks, Jack Daw, and his fellow, with any discontentment hither, and I'll honour thee forever.

EPICOENE. I was about it, here. It angered me to the soul, to hear 'em begin to talk so malapert.

TRUEWIT. Pray thee perform it, and thou win'st me an idolater to thee, everlasting.

EPICOENE. Will you go in, and hear me do it?

TRUEWIT. No, I'll stay here. Drive 'em out of your company, 'tis all I ask: which cannot be any way better done than by extolling Dauphine, whom they have so slighted.

EPICOENE. I warrant you: you shall expect one of 'em presently. [*Exit.*]

CLERIMONT. What a cast of kastrils are these, to hawk after ladies thus?

TRUEWIT. Ay, and strike at such an eagle as Dauphine.

CLERIMONT. He will be mad when we tell him. Here he comes.

---

183 *swabbers*: louts.
191 *posts*: i.e. the posts that support the signs.
200 *malapert*: impudently.
210 *cast of kastrils*: pair of cowardly hawks; *kastril* (kestrel) was a term of abuse. 'Kastril' is used as a proper name in *The Alchemist*.

SCENE V

[*Enter*] DAUPHINE.

[CLERIMONT.] O sir, you are welcome.

TRUEWIT. Where's thine uncle?

DAUPHINE. Run out o'doors in's nightcaps, to talk with a casuist about his divorce. It works admirably.

TRUEWIT. Thou wouldst ha'said so, an' thou hadst been here! The ladies have laughed at thee, most comically, since thou went'st, Dauphine.

CLERIMONT. And asked if thou wert thine uncle's keeper?

TRUEWIT. And the brace of baboons answered, Yes; and said thou wert a pitiful poor fellow, and didst live upon posts: and hadst nothing but three suits of apparel, and some few benevolences that lords ga'thee to fool to 'em, and swagger.

DAUPHINE. Let me not live, I'll beat 'em. I'll bind 'em both to grand madam's bedposts, and have 'em baited with monkeys.

TRUEWIT. Thou shalt not need, they shall be beaten to thy hand, Dauphine. I have an execution to serve upon 'em, I warrant thee shall serve: trust my plot.

DAUPHINE. Ay, you have many plots! So you had one, to make all the wenches in love with me.

TRUEWIT. Why, if I do not yet afore night, as near as 'tis; and that they do not every one invite thee, and be ready to scratch for thee: take the mortgage of my wit.

CLERIMONT. 'Fore God, I'll be his witness; thou shalt have it, Dauphine: thou shalt be his fool forever, if thou dost not.

TRUEWIT. Agreed. Perhaps 'twill be the better estate. Do you observe this gallery? or rather

---

4 *casuist*: theologian who decides cases of conscience; but often used with implications of sophistry.

13 *live upon posts*: make a living by running errands (like a lackey).

three suits: see III.i.44.

20 *execution*: legal writ.

33 *estate*: property in which a share is held.

lobby, indeed? Here are a couple of studies, at each end one: here will I act such a tragicomedy between the Guelphs and the Ghibellines, Daw and La Foole – which of 'em comes out first, will I seize on (you two shall be the chorus behind the arras, and whip out between the acts, and speak). If I do not make 'em keep the peace for this remnant of the day, if not of the year, I have failed once – I hear Daw coming: hide, and do not laugh, for God's sake.

[*They hide. Enter* DAW.]

DAW. Which is the way into the garden, trow?

TRUEWIT. Oh, Jack Daw! I am glad I have met with you. In good faith, I must have this matter go no further between you. I must ha'it taken up.

DAW. What matter, sir? Between whom?

TRUEWIT. Come, you disguise it – Sir Amorous and you. If you love me, Jack, you shall make use of your philosophy now, for this once, and deliver me your sword. This is not the wedding the Centaurs were at, though there be a she-one here. The bride has entreated me I will see no blood shed at her bridal, you saw her whisper me erewhile.

DAW. As I hope to finish Tacitus, I intend no murder.

TRUEWIT. Do you not wait for Sir Amorous?

DAW. Not I, by my knighthood.

TRUEWIT. And your scholarship too?

DAW. And my scholarship too.

TRUEWIT. Go to, then I return you your sword, and ask you mercy; but put it not up, for you will be assaulted. I understood that you had apprehended it, and walked here to brave him: and that you had held your life contemptible, in regard of your honour.

DAW. No, no, no such thing I assure you. He and I parted now, as good friends as could be.

---

34 *studies*: see Additional Note, p. 443 below.

36 *Guelphs . . . Ghibellines*: political parties of mediaeval Italy, whose rivalry was expressed in cruel violence.

39 *arras*: tapestry hanging; see Additional Note to IV.v.34.

47 *taken up*: settled amicably.

52–3 *wedding the Centaurs were at*: of Pirithöus and Hippodamia, where an insult to the bride by a drunken Centaur resulted in the battle of the Lapithae and Centaurs.

53 *she-one*: in classical myth, there were no female Centaurs.

TRUEWIT. Trust not you to that visor. I saw him since dinner with another face: I have known many men in my time vexed with losses, with deaths, and with abuses, but so offended a wight as Sir Amorous did I never see, or read of. For taking away his guests, sir, today, that's the cause: and he declares it behind your back, with such threatenings and contempts – he said to Dauphine you were the arrantest ass –

DAW. Ay, he may say his pleasure.

TRUEWIT. And swears you are so protested a coward, that he knows you will never do him any manly or single right, and therefore he will take his course.

DAW. I'll give him any satisfaction, sir – but fighting.

TRUEWIT. Ay, sir, but who knows what satisfaction he'll take? Blood he thirsts for, and blood he will have: and whereabouts on you he will have it, who knows, but himself?

DAW. I pray you, Master Truewit, be you a mediator.

TRUEWIT. Well, sir, conceal yourself then in this study, till I return.

He puts him up [*behind a door.*]

Nay, you must be content to be locked in: for, for mine own reputation I would not have you seen to receive a public disgrace, while I have the matter in managing. Gods so, here he comes: keep your breath close, that he do not hear you sigh. – In good faith, Sir Amorous, he is not this way, I pray you be merciful, do not murder him; he is a Christian as good as you: you are armed as if you sought a revenge on all his race. Good Dauphine, get him away from this place. I never knew a man's choler so high but he would speak to his friends, he would hear reason . – Jack Daw, Jack Daw! asleep?

DAW. [*within*] Is he gone, Master Truewit?

TRUEWIT. Ay, did you hear him?

DAW. O God, yes.

TRUEWIT. [*aside*] What a quick ear fear has!

---

69 *visor*: mask.
72 *wight*: man (archaic).
79 *protested*: avowed.
81 *single*: one-to-one; also, 'without duplicity'.

[DAW *comes out.*]

DAW. But is he so armed, as you say?

TRUEWIT. Armed? Did you ever see a fellow set out to take possession?

DAW. Ay, sir.

TRUEWIT. That may give you some light to conceive of him: but 'tis nothing to the principal. Some false brother i'the house has furnished him strangely. Or if it were out o'the house, it was Tom Otter.

DAW. Indeed, he's a captain, and his wife is his kinswoman.

TRUEWIT. He has got somebody's old two-hand sword, to mow you off at the knees. And that sword hath spawned such a dagger! – but then he is so hung with pikes, halberds, petronels, calivers, and muskets, that he looks like a justice of peace's hall: a man of two thousand a year is not sessed at so many weapons as he has on. There was never fencer challenged at so many several foils. You would think he meant to murder all St Pulchre's parish. If he could but victual himself for half a year in his breeches, he is sufficiently armed to overrun a country.

DAW. Good lord, what means he, sir! I pray you, Master Truewit, be you a mediator.

TRUEWIT. Well, I'll try if he will be appeased with a leg or an arm, if not, you must die once.

DAW. I would be loth to lose my right arm, for writing madrigals.

TRUEWIT. Why, if he will be satisfied with a thumb, or a little finger, all's one to me. You must think I'll do my best.

DAW. Good sir, do.

He puts him up again, and then [CLERIMONT, DAUPHINE] *come forth.*

---

109 *take possession*: of property with a disputed legal title; the new owner would often be accompanied by an armed band.
112 *principal*: original.
113 *brother*: associate.
120 *petronels*: large pistols.
calivers: light muskets.
122 *sessed*: assessed (for the provision of weapons for the state).
124 *at . . . several foils*: to fence with . . . different swords.
125 *St Pulchre's*: St Sepulchre's, a populous London parish.
127 *breeches*: fashionably voluminous.

CLERIMONT. What hast thou done?

TRUEWIT. He will let me do nothing, man, he does all afore me, he offers his left arm.

CLERIMONT. His left wing, for a Jack Daw.

DAUPHINE. Take it, by all means.

TRUEWIT. How! Maim a man forever, for a jest? What a conscience hast thou?

DAUPHINE. 'Tis no loss to him: he has no employment for his arms, but to eat spoon meat. Beside, as good maim his body as his reputation.

TRUEWIT. He is a scholar, and a Wit, and yet he does not think so. But he loses no reputation with us, for we all resolved him an ass before. To your places again.

CLERIMONT. I pray thee, let me be in at the other a little.

TRUEWIT. Look, you'll spoil all: these be ever your tricks.

CLERIMONT. No, but I could hit of some things that thou wilt miss, and thou wilt say are good ones.

TRUEWIT. I warrant you. I pray forbear, I'll leave it off, else.

DAUPHINE. Come away, Clerimont.

[*They hide again. Enter* LA FOOLE.]

TRUEWIT. Sir Amorous!

LA FOOLE. Master Truewit.

TRUEWIT. Whither were you going?

LA FOOLE. Down into the court, to make water.

TRUEWIT. By no means, sir, you shall rather tempt your breeches.

LA FOOLE. Why, sir?

[TRUEWIT *opens the other study door.*]

TRUEWIT. Enter here, if you love your life.

LA FOOLE. Why? Why?

TRUEWIT. Question till your throat be cut, do: dally till the enraged soul find you.

LA FOOLE. Who's that?

TRUEWIT. Daw it is: will you in?

LA FOOLE. Ay, ay, I'll in: what's the matter?

TRUEWIT. Nay, if he had been cool enough to tell us

---

147 *spoon meat*: soft food or slops, given to invalids and children.
151 *resolved him*: concluded he was.
166–7 *tempt your breeches*: test (the capacity) of your breeches.

that, there had been some hope to atone you, but he seems so implacably enraged.

LA FOOLE. 'Slight, let him rage. I'll hide myself.

TRUEWIT. Do, good sir. But what have you done to him within, that should provoke him thus? You have broke some jest upon him, afore the ladies –

LA FOOLE. Not I, never in my life broke jest upon any man. The bride was praising Sir Dauphine, and he went away in snuff, and I followed him, unless he took offence at me, in his drink erewhile, that I would not pledge all the horse full.

TRUEWIT. By my faith, and that may be, you remember well: but he walks the round up and down, through every room o'the house, with a towel in his hand, crying, 'Where's La Foole? Who saw La Foole?' and when Dauphine and I demanded the cause, we can force no answer from him, but 'O revenge, how sweet art thou! I will strangle him in this towel' – which leads us to conjecture that the main cause of his fury is for bringing your meat today, with a towel about you, to his discredit.

LA FOOLE. Like enough. Why, an' he be angry for that, I'll stay here, till his anger be blown over.

TRUEWIT. A good becoming resolution, sir. If you can put it on o'the sudden.

LA FOOLE. Yes, I can put it on. Or I'll away into the country presently.

TRUEWIT. How will you get out o'the house, sir? He knows you are i'the house, and he'll watch you this sennight but he'll have you. He'll outwait a sergeant for you.

LA FOOLE. Why, then I'll stay here.

TRUEWIT. You must think how to victual yourself in time, then.

LA FOOLE. Why, sweet Master Truewit, will you entreat my cousin Otter to send me a cold venison pasty, a bottle or two of wine, and a chamber-pot?

---

177 *atone*: reconcile.
185 *in snuff*: angrily.
189 *walks the round*: makes a circuit (of the rooms of the house), as the watch made of the sentry posts.
202 *put it on*: adopt; also, 'assume (a resolute) character'.
207 *sennight*: week (seven nights).
208 *sergeant*: arresting officer.

TRUEWIT. A stool were better, sir, of Sir A-jax his invention.

LA FOOLE. Ay, that will be better indeed: and a pallet to lie on.

TRUEWIT. Oh, I would not advise you to sleep by any means.

LA FOOLE. Would you not, sir? Why, then I will not.

TRUEWIT. Yet there's another fear –

LA FOOLE. Is there, sir? What is't?

TRUEWIT. No, he cannot break open this door with his foot, sure.

LA FOOLE. I'll set my back against it, sir. I have a good back.

TRUEWIT. But then if he should batter.

LA FOOLE. Batter! If he dare, I'll have an action of battery against him.

TRUEWIT. Cast you the worst. He has sent for powder already, and what he will do with it, no man knows: perhaps blow up the corner o'the house where he suspects you are. Here he comes, in quickly.

He feigns as if one were present, to fright the other, who is run in to hide himself.

I protest, Sir John Daw, he is not this way: what will you do? Before God, you shall hang no petard here. I'll die rather. Will you not take my word? I never knew one but would be satisfied. – Sir Amorous, there's no standing out. He has made a petard of an old brass pot, to force your door. Think upon some satisfaction, or terms, to offer him.

LA FOOLE. [*within*] Sir, I'll give him any satisfaction. I dare give any terms.

TRUEWIT. You'll leave it to me, then?

LA FOOLE. Ay, sir. I'll stand to any conditions.

TRUEWIT. (*calls forth* CLERIMONT, *and* DAUPHINE) How now, what think you, sirs? Were't not a difficult thing to determine which of these two feared most?

CLERIMONT. Yes, but this fears the bravest: the

---

215 *Sir A-jax*: the flushing toilet, with a pun on 'a jakes' = privy, coined by its inventor, Sir John Harington, in the title of his book describing it, *The Metamorphosis of A-jax* (1596).

231 *Cast*: forecast; also, 'calculate'.

240 *petard*: mine.

other a whiniling dastard, Jack Daw! but La Foole, a brave heroic coward! and is afraid in a great look, and a stout accent. I like him rarely.

TRUEWIT. Had it not been pity these two should ha'been concealed?

CLERIMONT. Shall I make a motion?

TRUEWIT. Briefly. For I must strike while 'tis hot.

CLERIMONT. Shall I go fetch the ladies to the catastrophe?

TRUEWIT. Umh? Ay, by my troth.

DAUPHINE. By no mortal means. Let them continue in the state of ignorance, and err still: think 'em wits, and fine fellows, as they have done. 'Twere sin to reform them.

TRUEWIT. Well, I will have 'em fetched, now I think on't, for a private purpose of mine: do, Clerimont, fetch 'em, and discourse to 'em all that's past, and bring 'em into the gallery here.

DAUPHINE. This is thy extreme vanity, now: thou think'st thou wert undone, if every jest thou mak'st were not published.

TRUEWIT. Thou shalt see how unjust thou art, presently. Clerimont, say it was Dauphine's plot.

[*Exit* CLERIMONT.]

Trust me not, if the whole drift be not for thy good. There's a carpet i'the next room, put it on, with this scarf over thy face, and a cushion o'thy head, and be ready when I call Amorous. Away –

[*Exit* DAUPHINE.]

John Daw.

[DAW *comes out.*]

DAW. What good news, sir?

TRUEWIT. Faith, I have followed, and argued with him hard for you. I told him you were a knight, and a scholar; and that you knew fortitude did consist *magis patiendo quam faciendo, magis ferendo quam feriendo*.

DAW. It doth so indeed, sir.

---

251 *whiniling*: whining, whimpering.
256 *motion*: suggestion.
259 *catastrophe*: dénouement (of a play).
275 *carpet*: tapestry table covering.
283–4 *magis patiendo . . . quam feriendo*: more in suffering than in doing, more in enduring than in striking.

TRUEWIT. And that you would suffer, I told him: so at first he demanded, by my troth, in my conceit, too much.

DAW. What was it, sir?

TRUEWIT. Your upper lip, and six o'your fore-teeth.

DAW. 'Twas unreasonable.

TRUEWIT. Nay, I told him plainly you could not spare 'em all. So after long argument (*pro et con*, as you know) I brought him down to your two butter-teeth, and them he would have.

DAW. Oh, did you so? Why, he shall have 'em.

[*Enter above* HAUGHTY, CENTAUR, MAVIS, MISTRESS OTTER, EPICOENE, TRUSTY, CLERIMONT.]

TRUEWIT. But he shall not, sir, by your leave. The conclusion is this, sir, because you shall be very good friends hereafter, and this never to be remembered, or upbraided; besides, that he may not boast he has done any such thing to you in his own person: he is to come here in disguise, give you five kicks in private, sir, take your sword from you, and lock you up in that study, during pleasure. Which will be but a little while, we'll get it released presently.

DAW. Five kicks? He shall have six, sir, to be friends.

TRUEWIT. Believe me, you shall not overshoot yourself to send him that word by me.

DAW. Deliver it, sir. He shall have it with all my heart, to be friends.

TRUEWIT. Friends? nay, an' he should not be so, and heartily too, upon these terms, he shall have me to enemy while I live. Come, sir, bear it bravely.

DAW. O God, sir, 'tis nothing.

TRUEWIT. True. What's six kicks to a man that reads Seneca?

DAW. I have had a hundred, sir.

TRUEWIT. Sir Amorous! – No speaking one to another, or rehearsing old matters.

DAUPHINE *comes forth* [*disguised*], *and kicks him.*

---

287 *conceit*: opinion.
294–5 *butter-teeth*: front teeth.
308 *overshoot*: overreach; also, 'fall into error'.

DAW. One, two, three, four, five. I protest, Sir Amorous, you shall have six.

TRUEWIT. Nay, I told you you should not talk. Come, give him six, an' he will needs. Your sword. Now return to your safe custody: you shall presently meet afore the ladies, and be the dearest friends one to another –

[*Exit* DAW.]

Give me the scarf, now, thou shalt beat the other bare-faced. Stand by –

[*Exit* DAUPHINE.]

Sir Amorous!

[*Enter* LA FOOLE.]

LA FOOLE. What's here? A sword!

TRUEWIT. I cannot help it, without I should take the quarrel upon myself: here he has sent you his sword –

LA FOOLE. I'll receive none on't.

TRUEWIT. And he wills you to fasten it against a wall, and break your head in some few several places against the hilts.

LA FOOLE. I will not: tell him roundly. I cannot endure to shed my own blood.

TRUEWIT. Will you not?

LA FOOLE. No. I'll beat it against a fair flat wall, if that will satisfy him: if not, he shall beat it himself, for Amorous.

TRUEWIT. Why, this is a strange starting off, when a man undertakes for you! I offered him another condition: will you stand to that?

LA FOOLE. Ay, what is't?

TRUEWIT. That you will be beaten, in private.

LA FOOLE. Yes. I am content, at the blunt.

TRUEWIT. Then you must submit yourself to be hoodwinked in this scarf, and be led to him, where he will take your sword from you, and make you

---

323 *you you*: see Textual Note, p. 434 below.
329 *by*: aside.
339 *roundly*: plainly.
345 *starting off*: swerving (as horses do).
346 *undertakes*: stands surety.
350 *at the blunt*: with the flat of the sword.
352 *hoodwinked*: blindfolded; also, 'deceived', 'fooled'.

bear a blow over the mouth, *gules*, and tweaks by the nose, *sans nombre*.

LA FOOLE. I am content. But why must I be blinded?

TRUEWIT. That's for your good, sir: because if he should grow insolent upon this, and publish it hereafter to your disgrace (which I hope he will not do) you might swear safely and protest he never beat you, to your knowledge.

LA FOOLE. Oh, I conceive.

TRUEWIT. I do not doubt but you'll be perfect good friends upon't, and not dare to utter an ill thought one of another, in future.

LA FOOLE. Not I, as God help me, of him.

TRUEWIT. Nor he of you, sir. If he should – Come sir.

[*He binds* LA FOOLE*'s eyes.*]

All hid, Sir John.

DAUPHINE *enters to tweak him.*

LA FOOLE. Oh, Sir John, Sir John. Oh, o-o-o-o-o-Oh –

TRUEWIT. Good Sir John, leave tweaking, you'll blow his nose off. 'Tis Sir John's pleasure you should retire into the study. Why, now you are friends. All bitterness between you, I hope, is buried; you shall come forth by and by, Damon and Pythias upon't: and embrace with all the rankness of friendship that can be.

[*Exit* LA FOOLE.]

I trust we shall have 'em tamer i'their language hereafter. Dauphine, I worship thee. God's will, the ladies have surprised us!

---

354 *gules*: red; i.e. La Foole will have a bloody mouth. Truewit is mocking La Foole's own language; see I.iv.47.

355 *sans nombre*: countless.

368 *All hid*: the cry in the children's game of hide-and-seek.

375–6 *Damon and Pythias*: type of loyal friendship; each offering his life for the other.

377 *rankness*: exuberance, fullness; but also, 'foulness'.

SCENE VI

[*Enter below*] HAUGHTY, CENTAUR, MAVIS, MISTRESS OTTER, EPICOENE, TRUSTY, [CLERIMONT,] *having discovered part of the past scene above.*

HAUGHTY. Centaur, how our judgements were imposed on by these adulterate knights!

CENTAUR. Nay, madam, Mavis was more deceived than we, 'twas her commendation uttered 'em in the college.

MAVIS. I commended but their wits, madam, and their braveries. I never looked toward their valours.

HAUGHTY. Sir Dauphine is valiant, and a Wit too, it seems?

MAVIS. And a Bravery too.

HAUGHTY. Was this his project?

MISTRESS OTTER. So Master Clerimont intimates, madam.

HAUGHTY. Good Morose, when you come to the college, will you bring him with you? He seems a very perfect gentleman.

EPICOENE. He is so, madam, believe it.

CENTAUR. But when will you come, Morose?

EPICOENE. Three or four days hence, madam, when I have got me a coach, and horses.

HAUGHTY. No, tomorrow, good Morose, Centaur shall send you her coach.

MAVIS. Yes, faith, do, and bring Sir Dauphine with you.

HAUGHTY. She has promised that, Mavis.

MAVIS. He is a very worthy gentleman in his exteriors, madam.

HAUGHTY. Ay, he shows he is judicial in his clothes.

CENTAUR. And yet not so superlatively neat as some, madam, that have their faces set in a brake!

HAUGHTY. Ay, and have every hair in form!

---

2 *adulterate*: spurious, counterfeit.

4 *uttered*: made known; also, 'passed into circulation' (as are counterfeit coins).

7 *braveries*: finery.

30 *set in a brake*: assume a set expression; a 'brake' = a frame in which colts were held whilst being shod.

31 *in form*: in place.

MAVIS. That wear purer linen than ourselves, and profess more neatness than the French hermaphrodite!

EPICOENE. Ay, ladies, they, what they tell one of us, have told a thousand, and are the only thieves of our fame: that think to take us with that perfume, or with that lace, and laugh at us unconscionably when they have done.

HAUGHTY. But Sir Dauphine's carelessness becomes him.

CENTAUR. I could love a man for such a nose!

MAVIS. Or such a leg!

CENTAUR. He has an exceeding good eye, madam!

MAVIS. And a very good lock!

CENTAUR. Good Morose, bring him to my chamber first.

MISTRESS OTTER. Please your honours to meet at my house, madam?

TRUEWIT. [*aside to* DAUPHINE] See how they eye thee, man! They are taken, I warrant thee.

HAUGHTY. You have unbraced our brace of knights, here, Master Truewit.

TRUEWIT. Not I, madam, it was Sir Dauphine's engine: who, if he have disfurnished your ladyship of any guard, or service by it, is able to make the place good again, in himself.

HAUGHTY. There's no suspicion of that, sir.

CENTAUR. Gods so, Mavis, Haughty is kissing.

MAVIS. Let us go too, and take part.

HAUGHTY. But I am glad of the fortune (beside the discovery of two such empty caskets) to gain the knowledge of so rich a mine of virtue, as Sir Dauphine.

CENTAUR. We would be all glad to style him of our friendship, and see him at the college.

33–4 *French hermaphrodite*: possibly a reference to a side-show attraction of the time; or to the late Henri III of France, a notorious transvestite.

37 *fame*: reputation.

52 *unbraced*: exposed.

55 *engine*: device.

56–7 *make the place good*: take up that position; 'make good' = 'defend', a military term: Truewit is presenting Dauphine as her soldier-knight.

58 *suspicion*: doubt.

MAVIS. He cannot mix with a sweeter society, I'll prophesy, and I hope he himself will think so.

DAUPHINE. I should be rude to imagine otherwise, lady.

TRUEWIT. [*aside to* DAUPHINE] Did not I tell thee, Dauphine? Why, all their actions are governed by crude opinion, without reason or cause; they know not why they do anything: but as they are informed, believe, judge, praise, condemn, love, hate, and in emulation one of another, do all these things alike. Only, they have a natural inclination sways 'em generally to the worst, when they are left to themselves. But pursue it, now thou hast 'em.

HAUGHTY. Shall we go in again, Morose?

EPICOENE. Yes, madam.

CENTAUR. We'll entreat Sir Dauphine's company.

TRUEWIT. Stay, good madam, the interview of the two friends, Pylades and Orestes: I'll fetch 'em out to you straight.

HAUGHTY. Will you, Master Truewit?

DAUPHINE. Ay, but noble ladies, do not confess in your countenance, or outward bearing to 'em any discovery of their follies, that we may see how they will bear up again, with what assurance, and erection.

HAUGHTY. We will not, Sir Dauphine.

CENTAUR, MAVIS. Upon our honours, Sir Dauphine.

TRUEWIT. Sir Amorous, Sir Amorous. The ladies are here.

LA FOOLE. [*within*] Are they?

TRUEWIT. Yes, but slip out by and by, as their backs are turned, and meet Sir John here, as by chance, when I call you. – Jack Daw.

DAW. [*within*] What say you, sir?

TRUEWIT. Whip out behind me suddenly: and no anger i'your looks to your adversary. Now, now.

[*Enter* LA FOOLE, DAW.]

LA FOOLE. Noble Sir John Daw! Where ha'you been?

---

85 *Pylades and Orestes*: like Damon and Pythias, a type of friendship. Pylades aided Orestes to avenge the murder of his father, Agamemnon.

91 *bear up again*: recover their spirits.

92 *erection*: high spirits; with a sexual pun.

DAW. To seek you, Sir Amorous.
LA FOOLE. Me! I honour you.
DAW. I prevent you, sir.
CLERIMONT. They have forgot their rapiers!
TRUEWIT. Oh, they meet in peace, man.
DAUPHINE. Where's your sword, Sir John?
CLERIMONT. And yours, Sir Amorous?
DAW. Mine! My boy had it forth, to mend the handle, e'en now.
LA FOOLE. And my gold handle was broke too, and my boy had it forth.
DAUPHINE. Indeed, sir? – How their excuses meet!
CLERIMONT. What a consent there is, i'the handles!
TRUEWIT. Nay, there is so i'the points too, I warrant you.
MISTRESS OTTER. O me! Madam, he comes again, the madman, away!

[*Exeunt* LADIES, LA FOOLE, DAW.]

SCENE VII

[*Enter*] MOROSE: *he had found the two swords drawn within.*

MOROSE. What make these naked weapons here, gentlemen?
TRUEWIT. O sir! Here hath like to been murder since you went! A couple of knights fallen out about the bride's favours: we were fain to take away their weapons, your house had been begged by this time else –
MOROSE. For what?
CLERIMONT. For manslaughter, sir, as being accessory.
MOROSE. And for her favours?
TRUEWIT. Ay, sir, heretofore, not present. Clerimont, carry 'em their swords, now. They have done all the hurt they will do.

[*Exit* CLERIMONT.]

---

107 *prevent*: anticipate.
117 *handles*: of the swords; also, 'excuses'.
6 *begged*: petitioned for (as the property of a criminal or suspected criminal forfeited to the crown was petitioned for by rapacious courtiers).

DAUPHINE. Ha'you spoke with a lawyer, sir?

MOROSE. Oh, no! There is such a noise i'the court, that they have frighted me home, with more violence than I went! such speaking, and counter-speaking, with their several voices of citations, appellations, allegations, certificates, attachments, intergatories, references, convictions, and afflictions indeed, among the doctors and proctors! that the noise here is silence to't! a kind of calm midnight!

TRUEWIT. Why, sir, if you would be resolved indeed, I can bring you hither a very sufficient lawyer, and a learned divine, that shall enquire into every least scruple for you.

MOROSE. Can you, Master Truewit?

TRUEWIT. Yes, and are very sober grave persons, that will dispatch it in a chamber, with a whisper, or two.

MOROSE. Good sir, shall I hope this benefit from you, and trust myself into your hands?

TRUEWIT. Alas, sir! your nephew and I have been ashamed, and ofttimes mad since you went, to think how you are abused. Go in, good sir, and lock yourself up till we call you, we'll tell you more anon, sir.

MOROSE. Do your pleasure with me, gentlemen; I believe in you: and that deserves no delusion – [*Exit.*]

TRUEWIT. You shall find none, sir – but heaped, heaped plenty of vexation.

DAUPHINE. What wilt thou do now, Wit?

TRUEWIT. Recover me hither Otter, and the barber, if you can by any means, presently.

DAUPHINE. Why? To what purpose?

TRUEWIT. Oh, I'll make the deepest divine, and gravest lawyer, out o'them two for him –

DAUPHINE. Thou canst not, man, these are waking dreams.

---

20 *appellations*: appeals.
20–1 *attachments*: writs of arrest.
21 *intergatories*: interrogatories (= formally written questions).
22 *doctors*: barristers.
23 *proctors*: attorneys.
25 *you would be resolved*: have your case determined.

TRUEWIT. Do not fear me. Clap but a civil gown with a welt, o'the one; and a canonical cloak with sleeves, o'the other: and give 'em a few terms i'their mouths, if there come not forth as able a doctor, and complete a parson for this turn as may be wished, trust not my election. And, I hope, without wronging the dignity of either profession, since they are but persons put on, and for mirth's sake, to torment him. The barber smatters Latin, I remember.

DAUPHINE. Yes, and Otter too.

TRUEWIT. Well then, if I make 'em not wrangle out this case, to his no comfort, let me be thought a Jack Daw, or La Foole, or anything worse. Go you to your ladies, but first send for them.

DAUPHINE. I will.

[*Exeunt.*]

ACT V

SCENE I

[*Enter*] LA FOOLE, CLERIMONT, DAW.

LA FOOLE. Where had you our swords, Master Clerimont?

CLERIMONT. Why, Dauphine took 'em from the madman.

LA FOOLE. And he took 'em from our boys, I warrant you?

CLERIMONT. Very like, sir.

LA FOOLS. Thank you, good Master Clerimont. Sir John Daw and I are both beholden to you.

CLERIMONT. Would I knew how to make you so, gentlemen.

DAW. Sir Amorous and I are your servants, sir.

52–3 *civil gown with a welt*: gown of a civil lawyer, distinguished with a border of fur.

54 *terms*: technical expressions.

57 *election*: judgement, ability to choose.

57–60 see Additional Note, p. 443 below.

[*Enter* MAVIS.]

MAVIS. Gentlemen, have any of you a pen and ink? I would fain write out a riddle in Italian, for Sir Dauphine to translate.

CLERIMONT. Not I, in troth lady, I am no scrivener.

DAW. I can furnish you, I think, lady.

[*Exeunt* DAW, MAVIS.]

CLERIMONT. He has it in the haft of a knife, I believe!

LA FOOLE. No, he has his box of instruments.

CLERIMONT. Like a surgeon!

LA FOOLE. For the mathematics: his square, his compasses, his brass pens, and black lead, to draw maps of every place, and person, where he comes.

CLERIMONT. How, maps of persons!

LA FOOLE. Yes, sir, of Nomentack, when he was here, and of the Prince of Moldavia, and of his mistress, Mistress Epicoene.

CLERIMONT. Away! He has not found out her latitude, I hope.

LA FOOLE. You are a pleasant gentleman, sir.

[*Enter* DAW.]

CLERIMONT. Faith, now we are in private, let's wanton it a little, and talk waggishly. Sir John, I am telling Sir Amorous here, that you two govern the ladies, where'er you come, you carry the feminine gender afore you.

DAW. They shall rather carry us afore them, if they will, sir.

CLERIMONT. Nay, I believe that they do withal – But that you are the prime men in their affections, and direct all their actions –

DAW. Not I: Sir Amorous is.

LA FOOLE. I protest, Sir John is.

DAW. As I hope to rise i'the state, Sir Amorous, you

---

16 *scrivener*: professional scribe.

25 *Nomentack*: Indian chief from Virginia brought to England as a hostage in 1605.

26–7 *Prince of Moldavia . . . his mistress*: see Additional Note, p. 443 below.

29 *latitude*: the geographical line; also, freedom in moral conduct – 'how far she'll go'.

30 *pleasant*: witty, facetious.

34–5 *carry . . . you*: referring to their own effeminacy.

ha'the person.

LA FOOLE. Sir John, you ha'the person, and the discourse too.

DAW. Not I, sir. I have no discourse – and then you have activity beside.

LA FOOLE. I protest, Sir John, you come as high from Tripoly as I do every whit: and lift as many joined stools, and leap over 'em, if you would use it –

CLERIMONT. Well, agree on't together, knights; for between you, you divide the kingdom, or commonwealth of ladies' affections: I see it, and can perceive a little how they observe you, and fear you, indeed. You could tell strange stories, my masters, if you would, I know.

DAW. Faith, we have seen somewhat, sir.

LA FOOLE. That we have – velvet petticoats, and wrought smocks, or so.

DAW. Ay, and –

CLERIMONT. Nay, out with it, Sir John: do not envy your friend the pleasure of hearing, when you have had the delight of tasting.

DAW. Why – a – do you speak, Sir Amorous.

LA FOOLE. No, do you, Sir John Daw.

DAW. I'faith, you shall.

LA FOOLE. I'faith, you shall.

DAW. Why, we have been –

LA FOOLE. In the Great Bed at Ware together in our time. On, Sir John.

DAW. Nay, do you, Sir Amorous.

CLERIMONT. And these ladies with you, knights?

LA FOOLE. No, excuse us, sir.

DAW. We must not wound reputation.

LA FOOLE. No matter – they were these, or others. Our bath cost us fifteen pound, when we came home.

---

44 *person*: figure; attractiveness.
49–50 *come . . . from Tripoly*: vault, tumble.
51 *use*: practise.
59–60 *velvet petticoats, and wrought smocks*: dress of courtly ladies and high-class prostitutes; see *Bartholomew Fair*, IV.vi.22–3.
70 *Great Bed at Ware*: capable of sleeping twelve people. Formerly at the Saracen's Head in Ware; now in the Victoria and Albert Museum in London.
77 *bath*: medicinal, for the cure of venereal diseases.

CLERIMONT. Do you hear, Sir John, you shall tell me but one thing truly, as you love me.

DAW. If I can, I will, sir.

CLERIMONT. You lay in the same house with the bride, here?

DAW. Yes, and conversed with her hourly, sir.

CLERIMONT. And what humour is she of? Is she coming, and open, free?

DAW. Oh, exceeding open, sir. I was her servant, and Sir Amorous was to be.

CLERIMONT. Come, you have both had favours from her? I know, and have heard so much.

DAW. Oh, no, sir.

LA FOOLE. You shall excuse us, sir: we must not wound reputation.

CLERIMONT. Tut, she is married, now; and you cannot hurt her with any report, and therefore speak plainly: how many times, i'faith? Which of you led first? Ha?

LA FOOLE. Sir John had her maidenhead, indeed.

DAW. Oh, it pleases him to say so, sir, but Sir Amorous knows what's what, as well.

CLERIMONT. Dost thou i'faith, Amorous?

LA FOOLE. In a manner, sir.

CLERIMONT. Why, I commend you lads. Little knows Don Bridegroom of this. Nor shall he, for me.

DAW. Hang him, mad ox.

CLERIMONT. Speak softly: here comes his nephew, with the Lady Haughty. He'll get the ladies from you, sirs, if you look not to him in time.

LA FOOLE. Why, if he do, we'll fetch 'em home again, I warrant you.

[*Exeunt.*]

---

85 *humour*: temperament.

86 *coming*: compliant, encouraging.
open, free: with sexual connotations of availability and easy morals.

SCENE II

[*Enter*] HAUGHTY, DAUPHINE.

HAUGHTY. I assure you, Sir Dauphine, it is the price and estimation of your virtue only, that hath embarked me to this adventure, and I could not but make out to tell you so; nor can I repent me of the act, since it is always an argument of some virtue in ourselves, that we love and affect it so in others.

DAUPHINE. Your ladyship sets too high a price on my weakness.

HAUGHTY. Sir, I can distinguish gems from pebbles –

DAUPHINE. [*aside*] (Are you so skilful in stones?)

HAUGHTY. And howsoever I may suffer in such a judgement as yours, by admitting equality of rank, or society, with Centaur, or Mavis –

DAUPHINE. You do not, madam, I perceive they are your mere foils.

HAUGHTY. Then are you a friend to truth, sir. It makes me love you the more. It is not the outward, but the inward man that I affect. They are not apprehensive of an eminent perfection, but love flat, and dully.

CENTAUR. [*within*] Where are you, my Lady Haughty?

HAUGHTY. I come presently, Centaur. – My chamber, sir, my page shall show you; and Trusty, my woman, shall be ever awake for you: you need not fear to communicate anything with her, for she is a Fidelia. I pray you wear this jewel for my sake, Sir Dauphine.

[*Enter* CENTAUR.]

Where's Mavis, Centaur?

CENTAUR. Within, madam, a-writing. I'll follow you presently. I'll but speak a word with Sir Dauphine.

---

1 *price*: worth.
4 *make out*: manage, make shift.
6 *affect*: desire; seek to obtain.
11 *stones*: gems; also, 'testicles' (slang).
16 *foils*: settings for jewels; whatever sets off to advantage.
28 *Fidelia*: Latin for 'Trusty'; also, name of a character in romances.

[*Exit* HAUGHTY.]

DAUPHINE. With me, madam?

CENTAUR. Good Sir Dauphine, do not trust Haughty, nor make any credit to her, whatever you do besides. Sir Dauphine, I give you this caution, she is a perfect courtier, and loves nobody but for her uses: and for her uses, she loves all. Besides, her physicians give her out to be none o'the clearest; whether she pay 'em or no, Heaven knows: and she's above fifty too, and pargets! See her in a forenoon. Here comes Mavis, a worse face than she! you would not like this, by candlelight. If you'll come to my chamber one o'these mornings early, or late in an evening, I'll tell you more.

[*Enter* MAVIS.]

Where's Haughty, Mavis?

MAVIS. Within, Centaur.

CENTAUR. What ha'you there?

MAVIS. An Italian riddle for Sir Dauphine [*Aside*] (you shall not see it i'faith, Centaur). Good Sir Dauphine, solve it for me. I'll call for it anon.

[*Exeunt* CENTAUR, MAVIS.]

[*Enter* CLERIMONT.]

CLERIMONT. How now, Dauphine? How dost thou quit thyself of these females?

DAUPHINE. 'Slight, they haunt me like fairies, and give me jewels here, I cannot be rid of 'em.

CLERIMONT. Oh, you must not tell, though.

DAUPHINE. Mass, I forgot that: I was never so assaulted. One loves for virtue, and bribes me with this. Another loves me with caution, and so would possess me. A third brings me a riddle here, and all are jealous: and rail each at other.

CLERIMONT. A riddle? Pray le'me see't?

He reads the paper.

'Sir Dauphine,
I chose this way of intimation for privacy. The

---

35 *make any credit*: have any opinion of.

40 *clearest*: purest, most innocent; also, 'most free from disease'.

41 *pargets*: plasters (her face with make-up).

43 *candlelight*: kindest and most becoming light for the face.

56 *you must not tell*: bad luck followed the revelation of fairy gifts.

ladies here, I know, have both hope, and purpose, to make a Collegiate and servant of you. If I might be so honoured as to appear at any end of so noble a work, I would enter into a fame of taking physic tomorrow, and continue it four or five days, or longer, for your visitation. Mavis.'
By my faith, a subtle one! Call you this a riddle? What's their plain dealing, trow?

DAUPHINE. We lack Truewit to tell us that.

CLERIMONT. We lack him for somewhat else too: his knights *reformados* are wound up as high, and insolent, as ever they were.

DAUPHINE. You jest.

CLERIMONT. No drunkards, either with wine or vanity, ever confessed such stories of themselves. I would not give a fly's leg in balance against all the women's reputations here, if they could be but thought to speak truth: and for the bride, they have made their affidavit against her directly –

DAUPHINE. What, that they have lien with her?

CLERIMONT. Yes, and tell times, and circumstances, with the cause why, and the place where. I had almost brought 'em to affirm that they had done it today.

DAUPHINE. Not both of 'em.

CLERIMONT. Yes, faith: with a sooth or two more I had effected it. They would ha'set it down under their hands.

DAUPHINE. Why, they will be our sport, I see, still! whether we will, or no.

SCENE III

[*Enter*] TRUEWIT.

TRUEWIT. Oh, are you here? Come, Dauphine. Go, call your uncle presently. I have fitted my divine,

---

68 *enter into a fame*: have it made known.
physic: purgative (providing an excuse for staying in).
75 *reformados*: disbanded soldiers who kept the titles of their rank; also, a play on 'reformed'.
84 *lien*: lain, with a pun on 'lied about'.
90 *sooth*: an exclamation: 'really! indeed!'.
91–2 *under their hands*: signed their names (to the affidavit).

and my canonist, dyed their beards and all: the knaves do not know themselves, they are so exalted, and altered. Preferment changes any man. Thou shalt keep one door, and I another, and then Clerimont in the midst, that he may have no means of escape from their cavilling, when they grow hot once. And then the women (as I have given the bride her instructions) to break in upon him, i'the *l'envoy*. Oh, 'twill be full and twanging! Away, fetch him.

[*Exit* DAUPHINE.]

[*Enter* OTTER *disguised as a divine,* CUTBEARD *as a canon lawyer.*]

Come, master doctor, and master parson, look to your parts now, and discharge 'em bravely: you are well set forth, perform it as well. If you chance to be out, do not confess it with standing still, or humming, or gaping one at another: but go on, and talk aloud, and eagerly, use vehement action, and only remember your terms, and you are safe. Let the matter go where it will: you have many will do so. But at first, be very solemn, and grave like your garments, though you loose yourselves after, and skip out like a brace of jugglers on a table. Here he comes! set your faces, and look superciliously, while I present you.

[*Enter* MOROSE, DAUPHINE.]

MOROSE. Are these the two learned men?

TRUEWIT. Yes, sir, please you salute 'em?

MOROSE. Salute 'em? I had rather do anything than wear out time so unfruitfully, sir. I wonder how these common forms, as 'God save you', and 'You are welcome', are come to be a habit in our lives! or 'I am glad to see you'! when I cannot see what the profit can be of these words, so long as it is no whit better with him whose affairs are sad, and

---

6–7 *one door . . . and another . . . in the midst*: for the stage of the Whitefriars theatre, see Additional Note to IV.v.34, p. 443 below.

11 *l'envoy*: conclusion.
twanging: splendid; with a play on 'noisy'.

16 *be out*: forget your words.

18 *action*: gesticulation.

grievous, that he hears this salutation.

TRUEWIT. 'Tis true, sir, we'll go to the matter then. Gentlemen, master doctor, and master parson, I have acquainted you sufficiently with the business for which you are come hither. And you are not now to inform yourselves in the state of the question, I know. This is the gentleman who expects your resolution, and therefore, when you please, begin.

OTTER. Please you, master doctor.

CUTBEARD. Please you, good master parson.

OTTER. I would hear the canon law speak first.

CUTBEARD. It must give place to positive divinity, sir.

MOROSE. Nay, good gentlemen, do not throw me into circumstances. Let your comforts arrive quickly at me, those that are. Be swift in affording me my peace, if so I shall hope any. I love not your disputations, or your court tumults. An' that it be not strange to you, I will tell you. My father, in my education, was wont to advise me that I should always collect, and contain my mind, not suffering it to flow loosely; that I should look to what things were necessary to the carriage of my life, and what not: embracing the one and eschewing the other. In short, that I should endear myself to rest, and avoid turmoil: which now is grown to be another nature to me. So that I come not to your public pleadings, or your places of noise; not that I neglect those things that make for the dignity of the commonwealth: but for the mere avoiding of clamours, and impertinencies of orators, that know not how to be silent. And for the cause of noise, am I now a suitor to you. You do not know in what a misery I have been exercised this day, what a torrent of evil! My very house turns round with the tumult! I dwell in a windmill! The perpetual motion is here, and not at Eltham.

40–1 *question*: subject of debate or strife between two parties.
41 *expects*: also, awaits.
42 *resolution*: answer, solution for his difficulty.
47 *positive*: dealing only with matters of fact or experience (not speculative or theoretical).
49 *circumstances*: small points of detail.
71 *perpetual motion*: a machine made by Cornelius Drebbel supposedly demonstrating this was exhibited at Eltham Palace; it was one of the sights of the time.

TRUEWIT. Well, good master doctor, will you break the ice? Master parson will wade after.

CUTBEARD. Sir, though unworthy, and the weaker, I will presume.

OTTER. 'Tis no presumption, *domine* doctor.

MOROSE. Yet again!

CUTBEARD. Your question is, for how many causes a man may have *divortium legitimum*, a lawful divorce. First, you must understand the nature of the word divorce, *a divertendo* –

MOROSE. No excursions upon words, good doctor, to the question briefly.

CUTBEARD. I answer then, the canon law affords divorce but in few cases, and the principal is in the common case, the adulterous case. But there are *duodecim impedimenta*, twelve impediments (as we call 'em) all which do not *dirimere contractum*, but *irritum reddere matrimonium*, as we say in the canon law, not take away the bond, but cause a nullity therein.

MOROSE. I understood you, before: good sir, avoid your impertinency of translation.

OTTER. He cannot open this too much, sir, by your favour.

MOROSE. Yet more!

TRUEWIT. Oh, you must give the learned men leave, sir. To your impediments, master doctor.

CUTBEARD. The first is *impedimentum erroris*.

OTTER. Of which there are several species.

CUTBEARD. Ay, as *error personae*.

OTTER. If you contract yourself to one person, thinking her another.

CUTBEARD. Then, *error fortunae*.

OTTER. If she be a beggar, and you thought her rich.

CUTBEARD. Then, *error qualitatis*.

OTTER. If she prove stubborn, or headstrong, that you thought obedient.

---

76 *domine*: master.
81 *a divertendo*: derived from 'separating'.
93 *impertinency*: irrelevance.
99 *impedimentum erroris*: impediment arising from error or mistake.
101 *error personae*: mistaken identity.
104 *error fortunae*: mistake as to fortune.
106 *error qualitatis*: mistake about character, disposition.

MOROSE. How? is that, sir, a lawful impediment? One at once, I pray you, gentlemen.

OTTER. Ay, *ante copulam*, but not *post copulam*, sir.

CUTBEARD. Master parson says right. *Nec post nuptiarum benedictionem*. It doth indeed but *irrita reddere sponsalia*, annul the contract: after marriage it is of no obstancy.

TRUEWIT. Alas, sir, what a hope are we fallen from, by this time!

CUTBEARD. The next is *conditio*: if you thought her freeborn, and she prove a bondwoman, there is impediment of estate and condition.

OTTER. Ay, but master doctor, those servitudes are *sublatae*, now, among us Christians.

CUTBEARD. By your favour, master parson –

OTTER. You shall give me leave, master doctor.

MOROSE. Nay, gentlemen, quarrel not in that question; it concerns not my case: pass to the third.

CUTBEARD. Well then, the third is *votum*. If either party have made a vow of chastity. But that practice, as master parson said of the other, is taken away among us, thanks be to discipline. The fourth is *cognatio*: if the persons be of kin, within the degrees.

OTTER. Ay: do you know what the degrees are, sir?

MOROSE. No, nor I care not, sir: they offer me no comfort in the question, I am sure.

CUTBEARD. But there is a branch of this impediment may, which is *cognatio spiritualis*. If you were her godfather, sir, then the marriage is incestuous.

OTTER. That comment is absurd, and superstitious, master doctor. I cannot endure it. Are we not all brothers and sisters, and as much akin in that, as godfathers, and goddaughters?

---

111 *ante copulam . . . post copulam*: before the union, after the union.
112–13 *Nec . . . benedictionem*: not after the sacrament of marriage.
114 *contract*: betrothal.
115 *obstancy*: judicial opposition.
118 *conditio*: social rank.
120 *estate*: rank.
122 *sublatae*: cancelled.
127 *votum*: vow.
130 *discipline*: church system (of the reformed churches).
131 *cognatio*: (blood) relationship.
132 *degrees*: i.e. of kindred, within which marriage is forbidden by the church.

MOROSE. O me! to end the controversy, I never was a godfather, I never was a godfather in my life, sir. Pass to the next.

CUTBEARD. The fifth is *crimen adulterii*: the known case. The sixth, *cultus disparitas*, difference of religion: have you ever examined her what religion she is of?

MOROSE. No, I would rather she were of none, than be put to the trouble of it!

OTTER. You may have it done for you, sir.

MOROSE. By no means, good sir, on, to the rest: shall you ever come to an end, think you?

TRUEWIT. Yes, he has done half, sir. (On, to the rest.) Be patient, and expect, sir.

CUTBEARD. The seventh is *vis*: if it were upon compulsion, or force.

MOROSE. Oh no, it was too voluntary, mine: too voluntary.

CUTBEARD. The eighth is *ordo*: if ever she have taken holy orders.

OTTER. That's superstitious, too.

MOROSE. No matter, master parson: would she would go into a nunnery yet.

CUTBEARD. The ninth is *ligamen*: if you were bound, sir, to any other before.

MOROSE. I thrust myself too soon into these fetters.

CUTBEARD. The tenth is *publica honestas*: which is *inchoata quaedam affinitas*.

OTTER. Ay, or *affinitas orta ex sponsalibus*: and is but *leve impedimentum*.

MOROSE. I feel no air of comfort blowing to me, in all this.

CUTBEARD. The eleventh is *affinitas ex fornicatione*.

OTTER. Which is no less *vera affinitas* than the other, master doctor.

CUTBEARD. True, *quae oritur ex legitimo matrimonio*.

---

146 *crimen adulterii*: crime of adultery.
166 *ligamen*: bond, tie.
169 *publica honestas*: public reputation.
170 *inchoata . . . affinitas*: (previous) unconsummated marriage.
171 *affinitas . . . sponsalibus*: relationship arising from a betrothal.
172 *leve impedimentum*: slight impediment.
175 *affinitas . . . fornicatione*: relationship arising from fornication.
176 *vera affinitas*: true relationship.
178–9 *quae . . . matrimonio*: which comes from legal marriage.

OTTER. You say right, venerable doctor. And *nascitur ex eo, quod per coniugium duae personae efficiuntur una caro* –

MOROSE. Heyday, now they begin.

CUTBEARD. I conceive you, master parson. *Ita per fornicationem aeque est verus pater, qui sic generat* –

OTTER. *Et vere filius qui sic generatur* –

MOROSE. What's all this to me?

CLERIMONT. [*aside*] Now it grows warm.

CUTBEARD. The twelfth, and last is *si forte coire nequibis*.

OTTER. Ay, that is *impedimentum gravissimum*. It doth utterly annul, and annihilate, that. If you have *manifestam frigiditatem*, you are well, sir.

TRUEWIT. Why, there is comfort come at length, sir. Confess yourself but a man unable, and she will sue to be divorced first.

OTTER. Ay, or if there be *morbus perpetuus, et insanabilis*, as paralysis, elephantiasis, or so –

DAUPHINE. Oh, but *frigiditas* is the fairer way, gentlemen.

OTTER. You say troth, sir, and as it is in the canon, master doctor.

CUTBEARD. I conceive you, sir.

CLERIMONT. [*aside*] Before he speaks.

OTTER. That a boy, or child, under years, is not fit for marriage, because he cannot *reddere debitum*. So your *omnipotentes* –

TRUEWIT. [*aside to* OTTER] Your *impotentes*, you whoreson lobster.

181–2 *nascitur . . . caro*: it follows from this, that through physical union two people are made one flesh.
184–6 *Ita . . . generat*: so with regard to fornication, he is as much a true father who thus begets.
187 *Et . . . generatur*: and he is truly a son who is so begotten.
190–1 *si . . . nequibis*: if by chance you should be unable to copulate.
192 *impedimentum gravissimum*: a most weighty impediment.
194 *manifestam frigiditatem*: evident frigidity.
198–9 *morbus . . . insanabilis*: a chronic and incurable disease.
199 *elephantiasis*: type of skin disease in which the affected part resembles an elephant's hide.
207 *reddere debitum*: render his obligation.
208 *omnipotentes*: omnipotent men (Otter's mistake for impotent).
209 *impotentes*: impotent men.

OTTER. Your *impotentes*, I should say, are *minime apti ad contrahenda matrimonium*.

TRUEWIT. [*aside to* OTTER] *Matrimonium*? We shall have most unmatrimonial Latin with you: *matrimonia*, and be hanged.

DAUPHINE. [*aside to* TRUEWIT] You put 'em out, man.

CUTBEARD. But then there will arise a doubt, master parson, in our case, *post matrimonium*: that *frigiditate praeditus* (do you conceive me, sir?) –

OTTER. Very well, sir.

CUTBEARD. Who cannot *uti uxore pro uxore* may *habere eam pro sorore*.

OTTER. Absurd, absurd, absurd, and merely apostatical.

CUTBEARD. You shall pardon me, master parson, I can prove it.

OTTER. You can prove a will, master doctor, you can prove nothing else. Does not the verse of your own canon say, *Haec socianda vetant conubia, facta retractant* –

CUTBEARD. I grant you, but how do they *retractare*, master parson?

MOROSE. (Oh, this was it I feared.)

OTTER. *In aeternum*, sir.

CUTBEARD. That's false in divinity, by your favour.

OTTER. 'Tis false in humanity to say so. Is he not *prorsus inutilis ad thorum*? Can he *praestare fidem datam*? I would fain know.

CUTBEARD. Yes: how if he do *convalere*?

211–12 *minime . . . matrimonium*: least fit to contract marriage.

214 *unmatrimonial*: because Otter's confusion of cases disrupts grammatical agreement or 'marriage'.

219 *post matrimonium*: after marriage.

220 *frigiditate praeditus*: afflicted with frigidity.

222 *uti . . . uxore*: use his wife as a wife.

223 *habere . . . sorore*: keep her as a sister.

224–5 *merely apostatical*: totally heretical.

230–1 *Haec . . . retractant*: these things forbid uniting in marriage, revoke a marriage made (Aquinas).

235 *In aeternum*: for ever.

237 *humanity*: secular learning (a common meaning, when, as here, opposed to 'divinity').

238 *prorsus . . . thorum*: absolutely useless in bed. See Additional Note, p. 444 below.

238–9 *praestare fidem datum*: fulfil the promise given.

240 *convalere*: recover.

OTTER. He cannot *convalere*, it is impossible.
TRUEWIT. [*to* MOROSE] Nay, good sir, attend the learned men, they'll think you neglect 'em else.
CUTBEARD. Or if he do *simulare* himself *frigidum*, *odio uxoris*, or so?
OTTER. I say he is *adulter manifestus*, then.
DAUPHINE. (They dispute it very learnedly, i'faith.)
OTTER. And *prostitutor uxoris*, and this is positive.
MOROSE. Good sir, let me escape.
TRUEWIT. You will not do me that wrong, sir?
OTTER. And therefore if he be *manifeste frigidus*, sir –
CUTBEARD. Ay, if he be *manifeste frigidus*, I grant you –
OTTER. Why, that was my conclusion.
CUTBEARD. And mine too.
TRUEWIT. [*to* MOROSE] Nay, hear the conclusion, sir.
OTTER. Then *frigiditatis causa* –
CUTBEARD. Yes, *causa frigiditatis* –
MOROSE. Oh, mine ears!
OTTER. She may have *libellum divortii* against you.
CUTBEARD. Ay, *divortii libellum* she will sure have.
MOROSE. Good echoes, forbear.
OTTER. If you confess it.
CUTBEARD. Which I would do, sir –
MOROSE. I will do anything –
OTTER. And clear myself *in foro conscientiae* –
CUTBEARD. Because you want indeed –
MOROSE. Yet more?
OTTER. *Exercendi potestate*.

244–5 *simulare . . . uxoris*: feign himself frigid, out of hatred of his wife.
246 *adulter manifestus*: a manifest adulterer.
248 *prostitutor uxoris*: prostitutor of his wife.
251 *manifeste*: manifestly, evidently.
257 *frigiditatis causa*: the cause of frigidity.
260 *libellum divortii*: a bill of divorce.
266 *in foro conscientiae*: at the bar of conscience (legal proverb).
267 *want*: lack.
269 *Exercendi potestate*: the power of putting to use.

SCENE IV

[*Enter*] EPICOENE, HAUGHTY, CENTAUR, MAVIS, MISTRESS OTTER, DAW, LA FOOLE.

EPICOENE. I will not endure it any longer. Ladies, I beseech you help me. This is such a wrong as never was offered to poor bride before. Upon her marriage day, to have her husband conspire against her, and a couple of mercenary companions to be brought in for form's sake, to persuade a separation! If you had blood, or virtue in you, gentlemen, you would not suffer such earwigs about a husband, or scorpions, to creep between man and wife –

MOROSE. Oh, the variety and changes of my torment!

HAUGHTY. Let 'em be cudgelled out of doors by our grooms.

CENTAUR. I'll lend you my footman.

MAVIS. We'll have our men blanket 'em i'the hall.

MISTRESS OTTER. As there was one at our house, madam, for peeping in at the door.

DAW. Content, i'faith.

TRUEWIT. Stay, ladies and gentlemen, you'll hear, before you proceed?

MAVIS. I'd ha'the bridegroom blanketed, too.

CENTAUR. Begin with him first.

HAUGHTY. Yes, by my troth.

MOROSE. Oh, mankind generation!

DAUPHINE. Ladies, for my sake forbear.

HAUGHTY. Yes, for Sir Dauphine's sake.

CENTAUR. He shall command us.

LA FOOLE. He is as fine a gentleman of his inches, madam, as any is about the town, and wears as good colours when he list.

5–6 *companions*: low fellows.
7 *persuade*: advise, advocate.
9 *earwigs*: ear whisperers, flatterers.
11 *changes*: as in bell-ringing; *variety* is also a musical quality.
15 *blanket*: toss in a blanket.
16 *one*: Otter, observing his wife at her toilet as described in IV.ii.106 ff.
24 *mankind*: masculine, virago-like; mad, furious (from *mankeen*); also, 'cruel', 'ferocious'.
28 *of his inches*: brave.
30 *colours*: a knight's heraldic colours.

TRUEWIT. Be brief, sir, and confess your infirmity, she'll be afire to be quit of you, if she but hear that named once, you shall not entreat her to stay. She'll fly you, like one that had the marks upon him.

MOROSE. Ladies, I must crave all your pardons –

TRUEWIT. Silence, ladies.

MOROSE. For a wrong I have done to your whole sex, in marrying this fair, and virtuous gentlewoman –

CLERIMONT. Hear him, good ladies.

MOROSE. Being guilty of an infirmity, which before I conferred with these learned men, I thought I might have concealed –

TRUEWIT. But now being better informed in his conscience by them, he is to declare it, and give satisfaction, by asking your public forgiveness.

MOROSE. I am no man, ladies.

ALL. How!

MOROSE. Utterly unabled in nature, by reason of frigidity, to perform the duties, or any the least office of a husband.

MAVIS. Now, out upon him, prodigious creature!

CENTAUR. Bridegroom uncarnate.

HAUGHTY. And would you offer it, to a young gentlewoman?

MISTRESS OTTER. A lady of her longings?

EPICOENE. Tut, a device, a device, this, it smells rankly, ladies. A mere comment of his own.

TRUEWIT. Why, if you suspect that, ladies, you may have him searched.

DAW. As the custom is, by a jury of physicians.

LA FOOLE. Yes faith, 'twill be brave.

MOROSE. O me, must I undergo that!

MISTRESS OTTER. No, let women search him, madam: we can do it ourselves.

---

34 *marks*: of the plague.

53 *prodigious*: monstrous.

54 *uncarnate*: not of flesh and blood (humorous coinage from 'incarnate').

55 *offer it*: attempt to carry out such a thing.

57 *longings*: wealth (belongings – a reference to Epicoene's status); also, sexual longings.

59 *rankly*: foully.
comment: lie, feigned tale (Latin *commentum*).

61 *searched*: examined.

MOROSE. Out on me, worse!

EPICOENE. No, ladies, you shall not need, I'll take him with all his faults.

MOROSE. Worst of all!

CLERIMONT. Why, then 'tis no divorce, doctor, if she consent not?

CUTBEARD. No, if the man be *frigidus*, it is *de parte uxoris* that we grant *libellum divortii*, in the law.

OTTER. Ay, it is the same in theology.

MOROSE. Worse, worse than worst!

TRUEWIT. Nay, sir, be not utterly disheartened, we have yet a small relic of hope left, as near as our comfort is blown out. Clerimont, produce your brace of knights. What was that, master parson, you told me *in errore qualitatis*, e'en now? [*Aside to* DAUPHINE] – Dauphine, whisper the bride that she carry it as if she were guilty, and ashamed.

OTTER. Marry, sir, *in errore qualitatis* (which master doctor did forbear to urge) if she be found *corrupta*, that is, vitiated or broken up, that was *pro virgine desponsa*, espoused for a maid –

MOROSE. What then, sir?

OTTER. It does *dirimere contractum*, and *irritum reddere* too.

TRUEWIT. If this be true, we are happy again, sir, once more. Here are an honourable brace of knights that shall affirm so much.

DAW. Pardon us, good Master Clerimont.

LA FOOLE. You shall excuse us, Master Clerimont.

CLERIMONT. Nay, you must make it good now, knights, there is no remedy, I'll eat no words for you, nor no men: you know you spoke it to me?

DAW. Is this gentleman-like, sir?

TRUEWIT. [*aside to* DAW] Jack Daw, he's worse than Sir Amorous: fiercer a great deal. [*Aside to* LA FOOLE] Sir Amorous, beware, there be ten Daws in this Clerimont.

LA FOOLE. I'll confess it, sir.

73–4 *de parte uxoris*: on the wife's behalf.
84 *carry it*: behave.
87 *vitiated*: deflowered.
90 *dirimere contractum*: cancel the contract.
90–1 *irritum reddere*: render it null and void.
99 *nor no men*: nor retract your names.

DAW. Will you, Sir Amorous? will you wound reputation?
LA FOOLE. I am resolved.
TRUEWIT. So should you be too, Jack Daw: what should keep you off? She is but a woman, and in disgrace. He'll be glad on't.
DAW. Will he? I thought he would ha'been angry.
CLERIMONT. You will dispatch, knights, it must be done, i'faith.
TRUEWIT. Why, an' it must it shall, sir, they say. They'll ne'er go back. [*Aside to* DAW, LA FOOLE] – Do not tempt his patience.
DAW. It is true indeed, sir.
LA FOOLE. Yes, I assure you, sir.
MOROSE. What is true, gentlemen? What do you assure me?
DAW. That we have known your bride, sir –
LA FOOLE. In good fashion. She was our mistress, or so –
CLERIMONT. Nay, you must be plain, knights, as you were to me.
OTTER. Ay, the question is, if you have *carnaliter*, or no.
LA FOOLE. *Carnaliter*? what else, sir?
OTTER. It is enough: a plain nullity.
EPICOENE. I am undone, I am undone!
MOROSE. Oh, let me worship and adore you, gentlemen!
EPICOENE. [*weeps*] I am undone!
MOROSE. Yes, to my hand, I thank these knights: master parson, let me thank you otherwise.
[*He gives him money.*]
CENTAUR. And ha'they confessed?
MAVIS. Now out upon 'em, informers!
TRUEWIT. You see what creatures you may bestow your favours on, madams.
HAUGHTY. I would except against 'em as beaten knights, wench, and not good witnesses in law.
MISTRESS OTTER. Poor gentlewoman, how she takes it!

---

127 *carnaliter*: carnally.
135 *to my hand*: into my power.
141 *except against*: object to.
141–2 *beaten knights*: proven cowards, and therefore not admissible as witnesses.

HAUGHTY. Be comforted, Morose, I love you the better for't.

CENTAUR. So do I, I protest.

CUTBEARD. But gentlemen, you have not known her since *matrimonium*?

DAW. Not today, master doctor.

LA FOOLE. No, sir, not today.

CUTBEARD. Why, then I say, for any act before, the *matrimonium* is good and perfect: unless the worshipful bridegroom did precisely, before witness, demand if she were *virgo ante nuptias*.

EPICOENE. No, that he did not, I assure you, master doctor.

CUTBEARD. If he cannot prove that, it is *ratum coniugium*, notwithstanding the premises. And they do no way *impedire*. And this is my sentence, this I pronounce.

OTTER. I am of master doctor's resolution too, sir: if you made not that demand, *ante nuptias*.

MOROSE. O my heart! wilt thou break? wilt thou break? This is worst of all worst worsts, that Hell could have devised! Marry a whore! and so much noise!

DAUPHINE. Come, I see now plain confederacy in this doctor, and this parson, to abuse a gentleman. You study his affliction. I pray be gone, companions. And gentlemen, I begin to suspect you for having parts with 'em. Sir, will it please you hear me?

MOROSE. Oh, do not talk to me, take not from me the pleasure of dying in silence, nephew.

DAUPHINE. Sir, I must speak to you. I have been long your poor despised kinsman, and many a hard thought has strengthened you against me: but now it shall appear if either I love you or your peace, and prefer them to all the world beside. I will not be long or grievous to you, sir. If I free you of this unhappy match absolutely, and instantly after all this trouble, and almost in your despair, now –

MOROSE. (It cannot be.)

---

155 *virgo ante nuptias*: a virgin before marriage.
158–9 *ratum coniugium*: a valid union.
159 *premises*: previous happenings.
168 *confederacy*: conspiracy.

DAUPHINE. Sir, that you be never troubled with a murmur of it more, what shall I hope for, or deserve of you?

MOROSE. Oh, what thou wilt, nephew! Thou shalt deserve me, and have me.

DAUPHINE. Shall I have your favour perfect to me, and love hereafter?

MOROSE. That, and anything beside. Make thine own conditions. My whole estate is thine. Manage it, I will become thy ward.

DAUPHINE. Nay, sir, I will not be so unreasonable.

EPICOENE. Will Sir Dauphine be mine enemy too?

DAUPHINE. You know I have been long a suitor to you, uncle, that out of your estate, which is fifteen hundred a year, you would allow me but five hundred during life, and assure the rest upon me after: to which I have often by myself and friends tendered you a writing to sign, which you would never consent, or incline to. If you please but to effect it now –

MOROSE. Thou shalt have it, nephew. I will do it, and more.

DAUPHINE. If I quit you not presently, and for ever of this cumber, you shall have power instantly, afore all these, to revoke your act, and I will become whose slave you will give me to, for ever.

MOROSE. Where is the writing? I will seal to it, that, or to a blank, and write thine own conditions.

EPICOENE. O me, most unfortunate wretched gentlewoman!

HAUGHTY. Will Sir Dauphine do this?

EPICOENE. Good sir, have some compassion on me.

MOROSE. Oh, my nephew knows you belike: away, crocodile.

CENTAUR. He does it not, sure, without good ground.

DAUPHINE. Here, sir.

[*He gives* MOROSE *the document.*]

MOROSE. Come, nephew: give me the pen. I will

---

204 *incline*: agree.
209 *cumber*: burden, trouble.
213 *blank*: legal document with the spaces left blank to be filled in by the person to whom it is given.
219 *crocodile*: held to weep as it snapped up its prey; hence, 'one who weeps specious tears'.

subscribe to anything, and seal to what thou wilt, for my deliverance. Thou art my restorer. Here, I deliver it thee as my deed. If there be a word in it lacking, or writ with false orthography, I protest before – I will not take the advantage.

DAUPHINE. Then here is your release, sir –

He takes off EPICOENE*'s peruke.*

you have married a boy: a gentleman's son, that I have brought up this half year, at my great charges, and for this composition, which I have now made with you. What say you, master doctor? This is *iustum impedimentum*, I hope, *error personae*?

OTTER. Yes sir, *in primo gradu.*

CUTBEARD. *In primo gradu.*

DAUPHINE. I thank you, good Doctor Cutbeard, and Parson Otter.

He pulls off their beards, and disguise.

You are beholden to 'em, sir, that have taken this pains for you: and my friend, Master Truewit, who enabled 'em for the business. Now you may go in and rest, be as private as you will, sir. I'll not trouble you, till you trouble me with your funeral, which I care not how soon it come.

[*Exit* MOROSE.]

Cutbeard, I'll make your lease good. Thank me not, but with your leg, Cutbeard. And Tom Otter, your princess shall be reconciled to you. How now, gentlemen! do you look at me?

CLERIMONT. A boy.

DAUPHINE. Yes, Mistress Epicoene.

TRUEWIT. Well, Dauphine, you have lurched your friends of the better half of the garland, by concealing this part of the plot! but much good do it thee, thou deserv'st it, lad. And Clerimont, for thy unexpected bringing in these two to confession, wear my part of it freely. Nay, Sir Daw, and Sir La Foole, you see the gentlewoman that has done you

---

228 *before* –: see Textual Note, p. 434 below.
232 *composition*: settlement.
234 *iustum impedimentum*: just impediment.
235 *in primo gradu*: in the first degree.
241 *enabled*: made proficient.
251 *lurched*: cheated, robbed.
252 *garland*: wreath crowning a triumph; hence, 'glory'. See Additional Note, p. 444 below.

the favours! We are all thankful to you, and so should the womankind here, specially for lying on her, though not with her! You meant so, I am sure? But that we have stuck it upon you today, in your own imagined persons, and so lately, this Amazon, the champion of the sex, should beat you now thriftily for the common slanders which ladies receive from such cuckoos as you are. You are they, that when no merit or fortune can make you hope to enjoy their bodies, will yet lie with their reputations, and make their fame suffer. Away, you common moths of these, and all ladies' honours. Go, travail to make legs and faces, and come home with some new matter to be laughed at: you deserve to live in an air as corrupted as that wherewith you feed rumour.

[*Exeunt* DAW, LA FOOLE.]

Madams, you are mute upon this new metamorphosis! but here stands she that has vindicated your fames. Take heed of such *insectae* hereafter. And let it not trouble you that you have discovered any mysteries to this young gentleman. He is (a'most) of years, and will make a good visitant within this twelvemonth. In the meantime, we'll all undertake for his secrecy, that can speak so well of his silence.

[*He comes forward.*]

Spectators, if you like this comedy, rise cheerfully, and now Morose is gone in, clap your hands. It may be that noise will cure him, at least please him.

[*Exeunt.*]

THE END

259 *on*: about.
261 *stuck it upon*: cheated, played a trick on.
262–3 *this Amazon*: Mistress Otter.
264 *thriftily*: soundly.
270 *travail*: travel (spelt 'travail'); also, 'labour'.
make legs and faces: bow and smirk.
274–5 *metamorphosis*: transformation.
276 *insectae*: insects (the incorrect feminine plural, instead of the correct neuter *insecta*, draws attention to the knights' effeminacy).
279 *of years*: adult, mature.

This comedy was first
acted in the year
1609
by the Children of Her Majesty's
Revels.
The principal comedians were

Nathan Field	William Barksted
Giles Carie	William Penn
Hugh Attwell	Richard Allen
John Smith	John Blaney

With the allowance of the Master of the Revels.

TEXTUAL NOTES

KEY

corr. corrected
F 1616 folio
F2 1640–1 folio
F3 1692 folio
Q quarto
s.d. stage direction
s.h. speech heading
uncorr. uncorrected

Sejanus

1605 quarto: the text and its presentation seem designed to assert Jonson's artistic integrity and political innocence. He rewrote the parts by his collaborator, not out of dissatisfaction, as 'To the Readers', 48 ff., makes clear; he is demonstrating his readiness to take full responsibility for the play and its moral lessons. The presentation of the volume indicates Jonson's sensitivity to the political interpretation which saw his Roman play as a comment on the regime of James I and had led to his being summoned before the Privy Council: (1) 'To the Readers' stresses Jonson's scholarly approach to his subject, as do (2) his extensive marginal annotations to the play, referring to his authorities; (3) the many commendatory poems further support Jonson's integrity as an artist; and (4) the final paragraph of 'The Argument' proclaims a use of historical drama acceptable to the establishment. The 1616 folio text omits all these features, suggesting that Jonson no longer felt the need to vindicate himself; but the political sensitivity of his subject is shown by the alteration to Q's text in III.[i].303. It is possible that Q's revisions of the first version of *Sejanus* had included such muting of contentious passages.

TO THE READERS in Q only.

TO THE READERS 1 *following . . . labours*: commendatory verses, in Q only.

TO THE READERS 27 *quotations*: in the marginal notes of Q only.

TO THE READERS 42–5 *Tacitus . . . 1592*: Jonson's abbreviations are here expanded and modernised, as in Bolton's edition.

THE ARGUMENT 42–3 *and with a long doubtful letter, in one day*: corr. F; Q, F uncorr.: *with one letter, and in one day*.

THE ARGUMENT 46–52 *This do we . . . miraculously working*: in Q only.

I.[i].235 *hard*: Q, F; Gifford: *heard* – a possible reading.

I.[i].383 s.h. CORDUS: Q, F; Barish (following Briggs's and H&S's conjecture): COTTA. The reassignment is unnecessary; Cordus is being sarcastic.

II.[ii].188 *Ay*: H&S point out that the rhyme would be preserved by emending to 'Sir'.

II.[ii].259 *both*: Q; F: *doth*.

II.[ii].267 *them*: Q; omitted in F.

II.[ii].400 *lets*: Q; F: *bets*.

II.[iii].417 s.d. AFER *passeth by*: H&S, modelled on I.[i].104 s.d.

II.[iii].434 *virtue's*: Q; F: *virtuous*.

II.[iii].449 s.h. AGRIPPINA: F2; Q, F: ARR[UNTIUS].

III.[i].11 *take him*: Q; F: *him take*.

III.[i].30 s.h. SEJANUS: Q; omitted in F.

III.[i].216 *to*: Bolton; Q, F: *too*.

III.[i].303 *With doubtful princes, turn deep*: F; Q: *With princes, do convert to*.

III.[ii].532 *Those, bounties*: Q's punctuation. 'Tiberius hesitates as if trying to find a simpler word' (H&S).
III.[ii].551 *first*: corr. F; Q, F uncorr.: *who was*.
III.[ii].552 *my*: corr. F; Q, F uncorr.: *to*.
III.[ii].663 *our*: Q, corr. F; F uncorr.: *your*.
III.[ii].690 *too fit matter*: corr. F; Q, F uncorr., Whalley, Gifford: *too much humour*.
III.[ii].707 *saviour*: Q; F, Briggs: *savier*; H&S, Wilkes: *saver*.
IV.[iii].154 *ready*: corr. F; Q, F uncorr.: *facile*.
IV.[iv].414 s.h. MINUTIUS: corr. F; Q, F uncorr.: MAR[CUS]. Here and in 498, the ascription suggests either a cancelled character or, if MAR = Marcus Terentius, a rearrangement.
IV.[iv].435 *That . . . Arruntius*: corr. F; omitted in Q, F uncorr.
IV.[iv].438 *Pollux . . . Hercules*: corr. F; Q, F uncorr.: *Castor . . . Pollux* i.e. the Gemini. Jonson made the correction because he learned that only women swore by Castor.
IV.[iv].445 s.d. *They* . . . TERENTIUS: corr. F; omitted in Q, F uncorr.
IV.[iv].449 *Mingling*: corr. F; Q, F uncorr.: *Mixing*.
IV.[iv].498 s.h. MINUTIUS: Briggs; Q, F: MAR[CUS]. See Textual Note to IV.[iv].414 above.
IV.[iv].514 s.h. LACO: F2; Q, F: MAC.
V.[iii].175 s.h.s [FIRST], [SECOND], [THIRD]: Gifford; F: MIN[ISTER] in each instance.
V.[v].428 s.h., 429 s.h. [FIRST], [SECOND]: Briggs; F: TRI[BUNE] for both; Whalley attributes both questions to Trio.
V.[vii].486 s.h. [FIRST]: Gifford; F: SEN[ATOR].
V.[vii].502 s.h.s [FIRST], [SECOND], [THIRD]: Gifford; F: SEN[ATOR] in each instance.
V.[vii].542 s.h.s [FIRST], [SECOND]: Gifford; F: SEN[ATOR] in both instances.
V.[vii].633 s.h.s [FIRST], [SECOND]: Gifford; F: SEN[ATOR] in both instances.
V.[vii].839 *mounting*: a suspected textual corruption: 'an impossible word' (H&S). Whalley suggested the unattractive *minting* = aiming (Middle English).
Endnote *This tragedy . . . Revels*: F; not in Q.

Volpone

Dedication TO . . . HIMSELF: laid out as in Q.
Epistle heading *There follows . . . on the length*: in Q only.
Subscription *From my house . . . 1607*: in Q only.
PROLOGUE 1 *yet*: F; Q: *God*; probably changed because of the laws governing profanity on the stage.
II.i.50 *archdukes*: F; Q: *archduke*. F's reading could be plural (favoured by most editors after H&S), or possessive singular, in which case it would refer only to Albert.
II.iii.1 *Spite o'*: F; Q, Creaser: *Blood of*. Q concludes the simile of II.ii.282, 'black' being the colour of the devil's blood; F conveys Corvino's sense of victimisation – as if there is a plot of cosmic evil to cuckold him: dramatically apt, as the fox and his craft have connections with the devil.
II.v.33 *into*: F2; Q, F: *unto*.
III.iii.5 *Being, all,*: Q's punctuation; F: *Being all*.
III.iv.18 s.h. [SECOND]: Creaser; Q, F: WOM[AN]; Gifford: [FIRST].

Creaser argues plausibly that since Lady Would-be has summoned the Second Woman, she would answer.
III.iv.90 *Montagnié*: Q; F: *Montagnie*. Q reflects contemporary pronunciation.
III.ix.50 *to*: F; Q: *would*.
IV.i.17 *speak*: Q; F: *spake*.
IV.i.57 *too*: F; Q: *two*.
IV.iii.18 *see*: F, less blatantly suggestive than Q's *use*.
IV.v.9 s.h. [FIRST]: F2; Q, F: AVOC[ATORE].
IV.v.130 *Catholic*: F; Q: *christian*.
IV.vi.7 SECOND AVOCATORE: F3; FOURTH AVOCATORE: Q, F.
V.iii.57 *your*: Q; F: *you*.
V.iv.55 *Fitted*: F; Q: *Apted*.
V.x.2 s.h. [FIRST]: F3; Q, F: AVO. It is possible that all the judges speak together.
V.x.5 s.h. VOLTORE: Gifford; Q, F: VOLP[ONE].
V.x.20 s.h. [SECOND]: H&S; Q, F: AVO[CATORE]; Gifford: FIRST.
V.xii.36 s.h. [SECOND]: Q; F: AVO[CATORE].
V.xii.134 s.h. [FIRST]: F2; Q, F: AVO[CATORE].
Endnote *This comedy . . . Revels*: F; not in Q.

Epicoene

THE PERSONS 13 CENTAUR: Beaurline; F, Partridge, Holdsworth: CENTAURE. F's final *e* may (as in French) indicate a feminine ending, but there were no female Centaurs in mythology. The monstrous assuming of the male nature and the blending of male and female is sufficiently conveyed by the titles *Madam* and *Lady*.
Second Prologue heading *Occasioned . . . exception*: Jonson's marginal note in F reset; omitted in F uncorr.
I.i.201 *marching*: F reset; F uncorr.: *going*.
I.ii.40 *one Cutbeard*: F reset; omitted in F uncorr.
I.iii.46 *for*: F reset; omitted in F uncorr.
I.iii.52 *below*: F reset; omitted in F uncorr.
I.iii.61–2 *and, . . . and,*: F's punctuation probably reflects La Foole's manner of speech. F's pointing is also retained in I.iv.41–75.
I.iv.19 *but*: F reset; omitted in F uncorr.
I.iv.46 *for*: F reset; omitted in F uncorr.
I.iv.81 s.h. LA FOOLE: F reset; F uncorr.: CLE[RIMONT].
II.i.11 s.d. *breaches*: indicated in F by dashes in parentheses, to designate Mute's stage business.
II.i.55 *with*: F reset; omitted in F uncorr.
II.ii.38 *preachings*: F reset; F uncorr.: *parleys* – possibly changed to remove associations with the Hampton Court conference of 1604.
II.ii.156 *rises*: F, Q (1620); Cunningham, Beaurline: *rinses*. The emendation is suggested by Jonson's source, Juvenal's *Satires*, VI.469–70: 'She bathes herself in that milk for which she takes with her asses as her companions.' The exotic beauty treatment is equally implicit in the more dramatic *rises*, which also suggests the (artificial) heightening of beauty (compare Pope's *Rape of the Lock*, I.140), and contrasts with 'lies in' of the previous clause.
II.iii.130 s.h. DAW: F2; F: DAV[PHINE].
II.iv.139 *to blame*: F3; F, Holdsworth: *too blame* – i.e. adverb plus adjective: 'much to blame'.
II.v.3 s.d. The s.d.s given here and throughout the scene in square brackets are indicated in F by dashes in parentheses.

II.v.145 *how*: F: *How*; a reference to Edmund Howe, public chronicler and professional informer.
II.vi.34 *bride-ale*: F; also at III.vi.81. Possibly a deliberate archaism by Truewit to heighten the incongruity of imposing La Foole's would-be fashionable celebration on the unfashionable Morose, who does not intend to give even a hearty ale-drinking party (bride-ale) to celebrate his marriage.
III.iii.21 s.h. DAW: Whalley; F: DAVP[HINE].
III.iii.37 *man*: F, Holdsworth; Whalley: *main*.
III.v.70–105 F's enclosing Truewit's interjections in round brackets indicates his choric role, which echoes and augments Morose's vindictive fantasy – until Truewit takes over the comic maledictions.
IV.i.101–2 *all ways*: Whalley; F: *always*.
IV.v.323 *you you*: F3; F: *you*.
V.iv.228 *before –*: F; Gifford: *before heaven*; H&S: *before God*. Holdsworth departs from the general editorial view that a word is omitted in F in deference to the profanity laws, saying that the *Act against Abuses of Players* (1606) did not apply to printed plays; and reads 'protest before' = 'declare in advance'.

ADDITIONAL NOTES

Sejanus

THE PERSONS 1 TIBERIUS: 42 BC–AD 37; stepson and adopted son of Augustus, whom he succeeded as emperor in AD 14.

THE PERSONS 2 DRUSUS SENIOR: 10 BC–AD 23; son of Tiberius; cruel and violent in character; poisoned by his wife Livia and her physician Eudemus. Suetonius records Tiberius's lack of sorrow for his death.

SEJANUS: commander of the praetorian guard, and favourite of Tiberius. Jonson sketches his history in 'The Argument'. Put to death in AD 31.

THE PERSONS 3 NERO: eldest son of Germanicus and Agrippina; arrested in AD 29, and starved to death on Pontia in AD 33.

LATIARIS: senator; follower of Sejanus; betrayed his friend Sabinus to the regime. Jonson makes him Sabinus's kinsman, thus heightening his treachery.

THE PERSONS 4 DRUSUS JUNIOR: second son of Germanicus and Agrippina; arrested in AD 30 and imprisoned in the palace, where he was starved to death in AD 33.

VARRO: consul in AD 24; accuser of Silius.

THE PERSONS 5 CALIGULA: AD 12–41; youngest son of Germanicus and Agrippina. Joined Tiberius on Capri in AD 32; succeeded him as emperor in AD 37.

MACRO: praetorian prefect; he delivered to the Senate the letter which brought about Sejanus's fall, but did not take further part in it. Vicious and ruthless, he attached himself to Caligula, who destroyed him and his family in AD 37.

THE PERSONS 6 ARRUNTIUS: senator with wealth, talent and integrity; he does not appear in Tacitus's *Annals* until after the fall of Sejanus. Respected and probably feared by Tiberius, he is seen as less of a threat in the play ('he only talks'). Committed suicide in AD 37 after Macro had made an accusation against him.

COTTA: senator; follower of Sejanus; Jonson reflects Tacitus's view of him.

THE PERSONS 7 SILIUS: senator and soldier; served under Germanicus; defeated Sacrovir. Tried for treason and extortion (the latter charge was justified) in AD 24; later, committed suicide.

AFER: praised by Quintilian as an orator, he came into Tiberius's favour after his prosecution of Agrippina's cousin, Claudia Pulchra, in AD 26. He did not take part in the trial of Silius.

THE PERSONS 8 SABINUS: senator; friend of Germanicus; betrayed by Latiaris.

HATERIUS: senator; fluent orator. Died aged nearly 90 in AD 26.

THE PERSONS 9 LEPIDUS: senator; a man of integrity, respected by Tiberius. Died in AD 33.

SANQUINIUS: senator; accuser of Arruntius.

THE PERSONS 10 CORDUS: historian; accused of treason at the instigation of Sejanus; committed suicide in AD 25. His books were burnt, but his daughter Marcia preserved copies which were published during Caligula's reign.

POMPONIUS: follower of Sejanus; spoken of contemptuously by Tacitus.

THE PERSONS 11 GALLUS: senator; known for speaking freely in the Senate; sentenced to death by Tiberius, and starved three years later in AD 33.

POSTHUMUS: lover of Augusta's friend, Mutilia Prisca, through whom he influenced Tiberius on Sejanus's behalf.

THE PERSONS 12 REGULUS: protégé of Tiberius; consul in AD 31; consistently influential under succeeding emperors; died in AD 61.

TRIO: notorious informer; consul in AD 31; supporter of Sejanus, he escaped punishment, but was forced to commit suicide in AD 35.

THE PERSONS 13 TERENTIUS: friend of Sejanus; accused but acquitted of guilt in AD 32.

MINUTIUS: friend of Sejanus; condemned after Sejanus's fall.

THE PERSONS 14 LACO: provost of the watch at the time of Sejanus's fall.

SATRIUS: follower of Sejanus; accuser of Cordus; may have been among whose who denounced Sejanus to Tiberius.

THE PERSONS 15 EUDEMUS: physician to Livia, wife of Drusus, whom he helped her to poison. Tortured and executed when the crime was disclosed.

NATTA: follower of Sejanus; accuser of Cordus.

THE PERSONS 16 RUFUS, OPSIUS: spies who betrayed Sabinus.

THE PERSONS 18 LIVIA: or Livilla; niece of Tiberius, wife of Drusus Senior, whom she and Eudemus poisoned. She had died before Sejanus's fall; but Jonson follows Dio Cassius in having her accused when the crime was revealed.

THE PERSONS 19 AGRIPPINA: widow of Germanicus; granddaughter of Augustus; arrested in AD 29, and starved to death on Panditaria in AD 33.

THE PERSONS 20 SOSIA: wife of Silius; friend of Agrippina; both circumstances brought about her downfall in AD 24.

I.[i].29–30 *beg . . . livings*: the informer would gain more from his victims than the fourth part allotted as his reward by the state (see III.[i].359–60).

I.[i].36 *Observe him . . . clock*: as Gifford suggested, *watch* probably means the early-seventeenth-century forerunner of the pocket watch, which had to be frequently corrected by the more accurate public clocks; an anachronism, but giving good sense: 'watch him closely and obsequiously, to regulate their moods by his'. Alternatively, since the Romans had both sundials and water clocks, *watch* could mean 'guard': 'watch him attentively, as his guard takes regular note of his sundial/water clock' (in keeping times of duty).

I.[i].261 *Here*: it is possible that at this point the stage has been vacated for Satrius and Eudemus. Alternatively, the characters could remain on stage 'frozen'; Sabinus and the Germanicans having drawn Arruntius aside after his outburst, which would send Sejanus's clients into a conspiratorial huddle on the other side, leaving the central playing area to become 'the gallery' of 193. The continuous presence on stage of different groups with their different affiliations throughout the sequence of Act I would give a vivid presentation of the politics of Rome, with the court as the centre of intrigue. V.[iii].211–V.[v].430, set in the 'court' of Sejanus, offers the same opportunities for such staging.

I.[i].374 s.d. [*Enter*] TIBERIUS: the centre of the stage once more becomes the focus of attention for the Germanicans and Sejanus's clients.

I.[i].503 *The oracles are ceased*: referred to in Plutarch's 'On the Obsolescence of the Oracles'; but in Christian tradition the ceasing of the oracles was associated with the birth of Christ (see Milton's 'Ode on the Morning of Christ's Nativity', 173–80). Sejanus is not only embroidering his compliment of 379, but in the eyes of Jonson's Christian audience uttering a daring blasphemy.

I.[i].581 s.d. *Chorus – of Musicians*: perhaps included in the original court performance; or Jonson may have added the s.d. to the printed text. Not in the Globe performance, as in 1604 there was no inter-act music in this theatre (see Marston's *The Malcontent* (?1604), Induction 68–9, in *Jacobean Tragedies*, ed. A. H. Gomme (London: OUP, 1969).

II.[i].104 *rude*: Bolton glosses as 'early', from Latin *rudis*; a sense not found in OED, but certainly possible here as Jonson often uses words in a latinate sense. 'Abrupt' combines the sense of 'early' and the more usual meanings, 'unmannerly, unceremonious', which are also appropriate to Sejanus's swift departure.

II.[ii].172–209, 238–77: rhyming couplets to point maxims or pithy sayings are not used in the rest of the play as continuously or extensively as in this scene. Here, their crisp formality emphasises the cold brutality of tyranny, and the self-confidence of Sejanus, to whom most of the couplets fall. The hesitation and fears of Tiberius are deceptive, however: the mask slips chillingly in 270–1.

III.[i].5 *his*: i.e. 'him': Silius superseded Varro's father in the campaign against Sacrovir. Varro's personal hostility to Silius would be a sign of his sincerity in Roman eyes.

III.[i].154 *The curtain's drawing*: in the Elizabethan theatre, a curtain covered the doors at the back of the stage through which the actors made their entrances and exits. There was probably a 'discovery space' behind the curtain, from which dramatic entrances could be made as from a hiding place (as in IV.[iii].95), or before which a 'play within the play' could be acted (as, possibly, in *Volpone*, V.iii). Here, Arruntius draws attention to the carefully staged nature of the trial about to be played before the startled audience of senators.

III.[i].184–7 *dissembling long . . . polled the province*: Tacitus does not refute the accusation that Silius drew out the war in Gaul, and certainly thinks the charge of extortion was true (*Annals*, IV.xix.2, 4). Jonson presents these as trumped-up charges.

IV.[iii].95 *between the roof, and ceiling*: in Tacitus, the spies 'put their ears to the cracks'. Jonson's eavesdroppers hide behind the curtain covering one of the doors at the back of the stage (see Additional Note to III.[i].154). By drawing attention to the seventeenth-century use of 'ceiling' for 'curtain', Robert E. Knoll, *Ben Jonson's Plays: An Introduction* (Lincoln, Nebraska: University of Nebraska Press, 1964), Appendix A, pp. 196–7, makes unnecessary the often ingenious speculation of editors and critics about the original staging of this scene.

IV.[iii].175 *Rhodes*: Tiberius's self-imposed exile on Rhodes in fact took place during Augustus's reign.

IV.[iv].317 *Jesters' simplicity*: the 'licensed fool' was allowed a unique freedom of speech; the repressiveness of the regime is marked by this action taken against jesters who, in classical Rome as in the courts of mediaeval and Renaissance Europe, were commonly mentally subnormal.

Volpone

Introductory Note, n. 8: the date 1605 on F's title-page = old style 1605/6, with the new year beginning on 25 March. Peregrine's news from London in II.i refers to events from 1604 to 1606; but since the sighting of the marine life in the Thames (40, 46, 47) was recorded on 19 January 1606, and since Jonson wrote *Volpone* in five weeks (Prologue 16), the time of composition would appear to be February–March 1606.

DEDICATION 9 PRESENTATION: the King's Men played in Oxford in 1606 and 1607, and probably visited Cambridge on the same tours. *Volpone* was not acted in the universities themselves; Esmé Stuart's commendatory poem in Q speaks of the play being performed 'In both Minerva's cities' ('To my worthily-esteemed Mr Ben Jonson', 5).

EPISTLE: written for 1607 Q, it is characteristically both traditional in thought and very personal; combining a noble defence of poetry and a vindication of himself as poet, playwright and moralist.

The high moral and literary standards for poets and poetry derive from classical and Renaissance literary theory; those qualities of classical comedy which Jonson claims to bring to the English stage in *Volpone*, and the didactic interpretation of the plays of Plautus and Terence, by which he justifies the harsh ending of his comedy, reflect Renaissance criticism, such as J. C. Scaliger's *Poetics*. His defence of himself against attacks on his satire (59 ff.) draws on the *Epistle to Martin Dorp*, in which Erasmus defended his *Praise of Folly*, and on his own 'Apologetical Dialogue' to *Poetaster*, performed once in 1601, but not published with the play until 1616 F: as in the rebuttal of the imputation of sharpness, and the defence of attacks upon individuals. Jonson's tone of lofty contempt for his enemies is in keeping with the tone of the 'Apologetical Dialogue', though the fate reserved for them has less apparent detachment in 'The Epistle' than in the 'Dialogue'. Use of this document of the 'war of the theatres' (1599–1601) in which Jonson attacked and was counter-attacked by Marston and Dekker probably partly reflects the renewal of the quarrel between Jonson and Marston in 1606. Marston is clearly attacked in 'The Prologue'.

EPISTLE 58 *youngest infant*: perhaps *Sejanus* (1603), after which Jonson had been called before the Privy Council (see stage history to *Sejanus*, p. 5 above; Jonson had rewritten the parts by his collaborator and had published the play as his own in 1605); or perhaps *Eastward Ho!* (1605) for which Jonson and his collaborators Chapman and his erstwhile opponent Marston were imprisoned because the anti-Scottish satire had offended King James.

EPISTLE 60–1 *what nation . . . I have provoked*: the court (*Cynthia's Revels*, 1600), the lawyers, soldiers and players (*Poetaster*, 1601), and the Scots (*Eastward Ho!*, 1605).

EPISTLE 137 *lines of example*: not readily apparent to the modern reader. In Roman comedy, the attempts to outwit the 'bawds' (suppliers of girls) or rivals has little to do with morality; servants are forgiven and praised for their ingenuity (although a slave is sent to the mines for a while during Plautus's *Captives*); and the punishment of one master, the vainglorious Pyrgopolynices in Plautus's *The Braggart Soldier*, is a beating to deflate his ego.

PROLOGUE 8 *To mix profit, with your pleasure*: a tenet of Renaissance criticism from Horace: 'Poets would either profit or delight, / Or mixing sweet and fit, teach life the right' (Jonson, *Horace, Of the Art of Poetry*, 477–8).

PROLOGUE 9 *some*: in the Prologue to *The Dutch Courtesan* (1605), Marston tilts at Jonson's moral indignation: 'Yet think not, but like others, we could rail' (5); and at his didacticism: 'We strive not to instruct but to delight' (8).

PROLOGUE 17–18 Jonson's terms indicate the hierarchy of collaborative skills and talent required to satisfy the Elizabethan audience's demand by writing new plays quickly or adapting old ones.

PROLOGUE 21 *quaking custards*: based on the phrase 'Let custards quake' in Marston's *Scourge of Villainy* (1598), Satire II.4, which Jonson had mocked in *Poetaster*, V.iii.525.

PROLOGUE 31 *The laws of time, place, persons*: derived from the observations of Aristotle's *Poetics* and the advice of Horace's *Art of Poetry* which became formalised into rules by the sixteenth-century Italian critics. The law of time was that the action of a play should take place within one day, or, more strictly, should coincide with the length of the play in performance; that of place was that the scene should be restricted to one place and its immediate surroundings; of persons, that only changes or development of character which could credibly take place within the time scheme of the play should be allowed. Unity of action, that a play should have a single plot, clearly is not a 'needful rule' to Jonson, for he breaks it in Elizabethan fashion by introducing the Politic Would-be plot.

I.i.2 *Open the shrine*: by drawing the curtain covering one of the doors at the rear of the stage to display the treasure in the 'discovery space', an area between the curtain and the door into the tiring-house.

I.i.34–40 Volpone has made a witty parody of the Golden Age for himself: he avoids activities (commerce, agriculture, industry) which mark the deterioration of man from his first state, and accepts the gifts offered by men's debased natures.

I.i.64–5 *your dwarf . . . hermaphrodite . . . eunuch*: although it was not unusual in the Renaissance to find such unfortunates in the courts and houses of great men, their presence points to Volpone's pleasure in perversions of nature.

II.ii.109 *humours*: from classical times, medical theory had held that man's physical and psychological health depended on the correct balance in the body of the four 'humours' or fluids: blood, phlegm, choler or yellow bile, and melancholy or black bile. In the microcosm or little world of man, the four humours corresponded to the four elements of the macrocosm or universe, and shared their qualities; so air and blood were held to be hot and moist; water and phlegm, cold and moist; fire and choler, hot and dry; earth and melancholy, cold and dry. In psychological theory, the predominance of one humour over the others accounted for the main types of human temperaments – that is, the sanguine, phlegmatic, choleric, and melancholic; whilst an excessive predominance resulted in the extreme traits of an imperfectly balanced temperament, examples of which Jonson had portrayed in his 'Humours' comedies, *Every Man in his Humour* (1598), *Every Man out of his Humour* (1599), and *Cynthia's Revels* (1600). Volpone refers to the physical aspect of the imbalance of humours, when the flow of humour ('humid flux') from one part of the body to another results in physical distemper and therefore sickness.

II.iii.3 *Signior Flaminio*: the identification of Scoto/Volpone with Flaminio Scala is more apt than Corvino is aware: (i) both are outstanding leading actors, and in this scene Volpone is embarking on the role of lover, Flaminio's own part; (ii) both are devisers of plots and directors of other actors. *Commedia* troupes worked from *scenarii*, outlines of plots designed for the stock characters or 'masks' of *commedia*, in which actors performed their roles true to type but with the freedom of improvisation within the bounds of character and plot. Flaminio was the author of *scenarii* (including one on which Jonson based his mountebank scene); Volpone is his counterpart, devising *scenarii* tricking the legacy hunters, with himself and Mosca playing the leading roles, until Mosca, improviser *par excellence*, becomes an increasing threat to Volpone's control of the plot.

II.iii.8 *Pantalone di Besogniosi*: Corvino, 'our spruce merchant', is a younger, more dashing man than 'the lean and slippered Pantaloon', but has much in common with the *commedia* figure: both fear cuckoldry; are merchants, avaricious, cunning yet rash, given to explosions of curses and invectives; able to pose as benevolent to gain their own ends.

III.iv.89: the particular target here is probably Samuel Daniel, a rival of Jonson's as writer of court masques, whose tragicomedy *Arcadia Reformed* (1605; published as *The Queen's Arcadia*, 1606) draws on Guarini's play. See also *Epicoene*, II.ii.134 and n.

III.iv.90 *Montagnié*: Jonson's view on essayists is given in *Discoveries*: 'These, in all they write, confess still what books they have read last; and therein their own folly, so much, that they bring it to the stake, raw and undigested: not that the place did need it neither, but that they thought themselves furnished, and would vent it' (H&S, VIII, p. 586). Lady Would-be clearly has much in common with the essayists.

III.vii.39 *There's no such thing, in nature*: a commonplace: 'honour' in sexual relationships did not exist in the classical Golden Age; but indirectly an ironical comment on the Golden Age Volpone seeks to create.

III.vii.193 *eyes of our St Mark*: Ian Donaldson, '*Volpone*, III.vii.193–4 and *Il Marescalco*', N&Q, 227 (1982), pp. 139–40, suggests that Volpone's carbuncle may derive from one in Aretino's comedy, described as brother to the treasure of San Marco, so brilliant that it blinded the sight. 'Put out both the eyes of our St Mark' means it would put to shame any of the riches of the cathedral treasury; or it would foil, deceive or blind St Mark, patron saint of Venice and therefore concerned about the city's morals. Other suggestions for the 'eyes' include the jewelled eyes of an unknown, lost image of the saint; the two richest jewels in the treasure; the two small chambers in the cathedral where the city's and the church's riches were kept (Creaser).

IV.i.51 *red herrings*: the English red herring was a popular delicacy in Italy, so Sir Pol's scheme is only innovatory in his unpatriotic support of the Flemish fishing industry; and Venice was supplied with fish all the year round. The modern sense of 'red herring' did not come into use until the nineteenth century.

IV.ii.43 *solecism*: OED's first recorded use with the meaning 'impropriety' is in the *Letters* (1599) of Hugh Broughton, one of Jonson's favourite distorters of language (see II.ii.135 and *The Alchemist*, II.iii.238, IV.v.1–32).

IV.v.79 *Mischief doth ever end, where it begins*: adapted from a maxim of the rhetorician and historian, Valerius Maximus; more accurately rendered as 'Mischief doth never end where it begins.' The play proves both versions of the saying.

V.iii.8 s.d. *traverse*: either the curtain covering the 'discovery space' before one of the doors leading into the tiring-house, or a screen brought on for this scene.

V.iv.60 *device*: the popular emblematic qualities of the tortoise in the Renaissance are discussed in John Creaser's article, 'The popularity of Jonson's tortoise', *Review of English Studies*, n.s. 27 (1976), pp. 38–46. The creature's shell, a house exactly and unpretentiously fitted to its owner's requirements, represents the domestic virtues and the humility which accompanies self-knowledge; its strength, serving as a defence against attack and as a secure station from which to survey action, represents impregnability, self-reliance and prudence. The slow, steady plod of the tortoise, well known from the Aesopian fable of the hare and the tortoise, teaches pertinacity and application.

Sir Pol conspicuously lacks all these virtues; but after the unkind trick played upon him by Peregrine, Sir Pol takes to himself the lesson of his tortoise, abandons his pretence to 'intelligence', withdraws 'into his shell', and sets sail with his lady for home.

V.v.18 *Fox-trap*: Mosca's knowledge of Erasmus seems not to include his adages: '*Annosa vulpes haud capitur laqueo*. An old fox is not taken in a snare. Long experience and practice of wily and subtle fellows maketh that though in deed they be great jugglers [cheats], dissemblers, & privy workers of falsehood yet they cannot easily be taken in a trap' (trans. R. Tavener, 1539, Diiiv).

V.vii.21 *Mistaking*: the convention that minor law officials use the wrong word (compare Dogberry in *Much Ado About Nothing*) is referred to in *Bartholomew Fair*, Induction 51–3. Here Volpone uses the convention to express his true wishes.

V.viii.15 *privilege of the place*: John Creaser's suggestion that this refers to the situation of the Scrutineo within the ducal palace, and the strong penalties incurred for brawling within the 'privilege' or limits of the court, is supported by line 16, where Volpone's sergeant's uniform is a further 'privilege': '*And* your red saucy cap . . . ' Other editors gloss *place* as the office of commendatore.

V.xii.125 *mortifying*: as John Creaser points out, a number of meanings are appropriate to Volpone's situation: 'killing', 'bruising the flesh', and 'making gangrenous' relate to Volpone's physical punishment; the religious sense of 'mortifying the flesh', subduing the body by discipline and abstinence, applies ironically to Volpone's 'spiritual' condition; 'making tender by hanging', applicable to game, would not improve the uneatable fox-meat of Volpone's animal *alter ego*. Creaser also sees a possible reference to the Scots legal term meaning 'disposing of property for charitable purposes', as the court assigns Volpone's wealth to the hospital. Volpone's mordant wit proclaims his triumph: he has regained the direction of his play, even if it brings about his own catastrophe.

Epicoene

THE PERSONS: E. B. Partridge, *The Broken Compass*, ch. 7, draws attention to the epicene nature of nearly all the characters which disturbs the decorum and naturalness of society and sexual relations in the play: the effeminate men (Daw, La Foole); the mannish women (the Collegiates) with their aping of the fraternities of learning, their sexual licence and their reversal of roles in marital relationships; the Amazonian wives (Centaur, Mistress Otter and later Epicoene) subduing their wild males into hen-pecked husbands. Ambivalence touches even the gallants of the play: Dauphine's first name, which underlines his claims to be his uncle's heir, is feminine in form; Clerimont is accused by Truewit of keeping an 'ingle' at home (I.i.28) – just one of Truewit's jokes? The wit and sophistication associated with things French is balanced by French perversions – the 'French hermaphrodite' of IV.vi.33–4 – and palely reflected in the Frenchified English form of La Foole. Whilst the gallants have the wit to see through the adulteries of art, learning and social grace of the Collegiates and their foolish followers, they make little constructive use of their own more intelligent understanding of art and nature. The gallants display the fire of 'spirit' and wit (*génie*); characters from the animal kingdom belong to the other three elements: the Otters are interchangeably creatures of earth and water (Tom changing from the submissive to the railing husband when his wife is not at hand; she changing from the domineering wife to the ingratiating 'pretender' to the College); whilst Daw and Mavis are birds of the air, both given to repetition, Daw prattling about what he does not understand, and Mavis who as a thrush 'sings each song twice over' repeating the actions and attitudes of Haughty and Centaur (the latter a mythical land creature). The characters not affected by the ambivalence of gender, nature or behaviour are Truewit (whose English name distinguishes him from his friends) and the 'humours' character Morose; the fate of both is to be outwitted by Dauphine.

I.i.24 *to seek your voice in my lady's rushes*: rushes were strewn as a floor covering amongst which it would be difficult to find something small that had been lost or discarded: compare 'to look for a needle in a haystack': 'amity may now be known or found . . . by them that seek for her as diligently as a maiden would seek for a small silver pin in a great chamber strawed with white rushes' (Sir T. Elyot, *The Governor*, 1531, Everyman edn, London: Dent, 1962, p. 132). Here there is also an implication of amorous play (compare *Henry IV*, Part 1, III.i.213–14). Clerimont foresees the amorous attentions of the Collegiates hastening the boy's puberty, when his treble voice would descend into a lower register and, like his (hetero-)sexual innocence, be lost beyond retrieval.

II.ii.134 *t'other youth*: H&S favour Daniel ('suggested by the context'), mocked in *Volpone* III.iv.89, a rival poet of court masques, with whom Jonson was 'at jealousies' (*Conversations with Drummond of Hawthornden*, H&S, I, p. 136). But the tone here is of good-natured banter (in 1609, Jonson was hardly a 'youth' – 36 or 37), and the reference is probably to Shakespeare (suggested by Malone, and favoured by Holdsworth) who was about six years older than Jonson. Beaurline inclines to Dekker or Marston (suggested by Upton and Gifford respectively), the first being about two years older and the second three years younger than the poet.

II.iii.26 ff. Daw's madrigal draws on Pierre Charon, *Of Wisdom*, trans. S. Lennard (1612), 'Fair and good are near neighbours', and on *England's Parnassus* (1600), 'The single virtue may consist alone, / But better are two virtues joined in one' (noted by H&S).

II.iii.62–5 The word-games which Partridge points out in his edn (pp. 181–2) ironically make Daw speak more truly of the great men he denigrates than his ignorance of them and his limited understanding would allow.

II.iii.73–6 Daw's 'sack full of names': *Pindarus*: *c*. 522–*c*. 440 BC; greatest Greek lyric poet; *Lycophron*: *c*. 285–247 BC; Greek poet and grammarian, 'too dark and dangerous a dish' (*Poetaster*, V.iii.548); *Anacreon*: Greek lyric poet of the late sixth century BC; *Catullus*: *c*. 84–54 BC; greatest Latin lyric poet; *Seneca*: *c*. 5 BC–AD 65; Stoic, moralist and tragedian; *Lucan*: AD 39–65, author of *Pharsalia* (not in the first flight); *Propertius*: *c*. 48 BC–*c*. AD 15; Roman elegiac poet, powerful but obscure; *Tibullus*: *c*. 54–19 BC; Roman love poet, highly esteemed by Quintilian; *Martial*: *c*. AD 40–104; Latin poet and epigrammatist; *Juvenal*: *c*. AD 55–140; Roman satirist; *Ausonius*: *c*. AD 309–392; foremost Latin poet of the fourth century, graceful but not a great poet; *Statius*: *c*. AD 45–96; author of *Thebaid*, largely tedious, but with some good parts to it.

II.iii.121–2 *live by*: it was considered improper for a gentleman to authorise publication of his own work; not in keeping with his rank. As a professional poet, Jonson himself qualifies for Daw's contempt.

II.iv.120 *quarter-feast*: feast given every quarter-day when La Foole's rents have been paid in; or feast given every quarter sessions, during the town's social season; perhaps with a weak pun on *quarter* = 'part of an army or assembly', to pick up Truewit's military comparison: i.e. however many people La Foole assembled at his feast, they would only be a section of those he numbered as his friends.

II.v.22–3 *composition* . . . *harmony* . . . *temper*: the analogy with music (continued in 23, 'height', and 31, 'just length', where Morose uses it of himself) is ironic, since for the Renaissance music carried connotations of harmonious relations between man and woman, man and society, and man and nature – all areas which Morose is violating.

II.v.82 *heifer*: the term comes from Judges 14.18, where it is applied to Samson's treacherous wife, who disclosed the answer to the riddle of the lion and the honey.

III.i.26–7 *Poetarum Pegasus*: here the association is less with the winged horse of classical myth symbolising poetic inspiration than with the contents of the cup: 'Wine is . . . the poets' horse accounted' ('Verses over the Door of the Apollo', H&S, VIII, p. 657).

III.ii.10–12 *toasts and butter*: were served with woodcock: but also = 'milksops, weaklings' (compare *Henry IV*, Part 1, IV.ii.22–4), and self-indulgent, pampered citizens (compare Beaumont and Fletcher, *Wit without Money*, V.ii.81); *woodcocks*: the birds; but also, 'fools' (because woodcocks were easily snared they are the type of gullibility). Mistress Otter is therefore designating three possible 'fit provinces' for Otter: (1) supervising cooking-arrangements, or (2) running errands to the kitchen (both impugning his manhood and status as husband); (3) consorting with fools, ninnies and self-indulgent citizens (indicating his Bear Garden acquaintances, and a social station below that of the courtly gallants).

III.iii.31 *given you the dor*: referring to the elaborate, trivial, and foolish court game in which one rival attempted to score off another by making him appear ridiculous in front of his mistress (see *Cynthia's Revels*, V.ii).

IV.iv.181 *set me i'the nick*: perhaps 'put me to a reckoning' (*nick*, OED 2a), with the implication of cheating (*nicker* = 'one who cheats at dice or cards' (1666) is recorded by A. C. Partridge, *A Dictionary of the Underworld*). Holdsworth sees this as La Foole's muddled way of implying 'cleaned me out', with *set* = bet against, and *nick* = winning throw of the dice in the game of hazard.

IV.v.34 *studies*: supposed to lie beyond the two doors at either side of the back of the stage; also, theatrical term for an enclosed space, appropriate for the play-within-the-play which Truewit is going to direct. The Whitefriars had three doors into the tiring-house (see V.iii.6–7); Truewit's friends are to hide behind the 'arras' (39) covering the middle door.

IV.vii.57–60: Since Jonson had offended several professions, including the legal profession, earlier in his career (see Additional Note to *Volpone*, 'The Epistle', 60–1, p. 438 above), Truewit's disclaimed was a wise precaution.

V.i.26–7 *Prince of Moldavia* . . . *his mistress*: Stephano Janiculo, an adventurer who pretended to the hand of Lady Arabella Stuart, the king's cousin; she took exception to the possible reference here to herself as 'his' (= the prince's) mistress, although the ostensible meaning is 'Daw's'. La Foole's typically loose syntax allows Jonson to protest innocence in the 'Second Prologue'. See also stage history, p. 297 above.

V.iii.238 *prorsus . . . thorum*: Otter's mistake of *thorum* for *torum* (Latin *torus* = bed) gives a pun on *thoros* (Greek θορός = semen).
V.iv.252 *garland*: Jonson may be referring to *Coriolanus*, II.ii.99: 'He lurch'd all swords of the garland.'